MONETARY PROBLEMS
of the INTERNATIONAL ECONOMY

MONETARY PROBLEMS
of the INTERNATIONAL ECONOMY

Edited by **ROBERT A. MUNDELL**
and **ALEXANDER K. SWOBODA**

The University of Chicago Press, *Chicago and London*

International Standard Book Number: 0-226-55065-6

Library of Congress Catalog Card Number: 68–16710

The University of Chicago Press, Chicago 60637
The University of Chicago Press, Ltd., London

CONTENTS

FOREWORD

From October, 1960 (when the price of gold in London rose temporarily above $40 an ounce), to March, 1968 (when the gold pool was abandoned), the monetary leaders of the world were engaged in a struggle to preserve the gold exchange standard, buying time until the experts could produce a plan for reforming the system. Unfortunately, the plan for a new reserve asset blossomed too late to preserve the system in its old form; it was incapable of coping with the major defects of the system anyway. But the story of that plan, and the educational process that was instrumental in its creation, represents a most fascinating episode in the history of international money.

This book is part of that educational process. In September, 1966, a group of international monetary theorists gathered in Chicago to try to probe more deeply into the perplexing theoretical issues that had come up time and again in the debate over the direction monetary reform should take. Conceived of the preceding winter by H. G. Johnson and R. A. Mundell, the idea was to isolate problems for discussion and solution by the younger theorists in the field. Following an opening address by the Honorable Giscard d'Estaing (in which he presented his views on French gold policy and the outline of a path to reform), papers were presented and debated in sessions chaired by Gottfried Haberler, Sir Roy Harrod, Harry Johnson, Fritz Machlup, and Walter Salant. The issues taken up included the appropriate mix of monetary, fiscal, and exchange rate policies, the optimal speed of adjustment, the distribution of seigniorage gains from monetary expansion, the optimum currency areas, the price of gold, institutional arrangements, and international crises. The order of presentation of the papers and the discussions in the book conform as closely as possible.

Since the conference we have witnessed the creation of the SDR's and also the devaluation of sterling in November, 1967, the introduction of the two-tier system in March, 1968, and the franc-mark crisis. It would be naive to expect that disturbances of this latter kind are events of the past. Their increased frequency is itself a call for a reconsideration of the present international monetary arrangements, and it is hoped that this volume will contribute to a greater understanding of the issues involved.

The work of transcribing the tapes and summarizing the discussicn for the book was undertaken by Alexander Swoboda. Judith Kidd provided valuable secretarial assistance, both during the conference and in preparing the manuscript for publication. Elaine Goldstein contributed important help in its final stages.

We are grateful to Professor Bert Hoselitz for help and advice in arranging the conference and to the grant that made it possible.

R. A. MUNDELL
A. K. SWOBODA

December, 1968

PARTICIPANTS

Robert Z. Aliber
The University of Chicago

Bela Balassa
Johns Hopkins University

Eugene A. Birnbaum
Standard Oil Company
(New Jersey)

Marcello de Cecco
University of East Anglia

Richard N. Cooper
Yale University

W. M. Corden
Oxford University

Phillip Cortney
Geneva

Gerard Curzon
Graduate Institute of International
Studies, Geneva

A. C. L. Day
London School of Economics

Hon. Valéry Giscard d'Estaing
Chamber of Deputies, France

M. June Flanders
Purdue University

Herbert G. Grubel
University of Pennsylvania

Gottfried Haberler
Session Chairman
Harvard University

Sir Roy Harrod
Session Chairman
Oxford University

James C. Ingram
University of North Carolina

Harry G. Johnson
Session Chairman
The University of Chicago and
London School of Economics

Ronald W. Jones
University of Rochester

Alexandre Kafka
International Monetary Fund

Peter B. Kenen
Columbia University

Anne O. Krueger
University of Minnesota

Fritz Machlup
Session Chairman
Princeton University

Ronald I. McKinnon
Stanford University

Donald B. Marsh
Royal Bank of Canada

Robert A. Mundell
Conference Chairman
The University of Chicago

Jürg Niehans
Johns Hopkins University

Walter Salant
Session Chairman
The Brookings Institution

Pascal Salin
University of Poitiers and
University of Nantes

ix

Wilson E. Schmidt
Virginia Polytechnic Institute

Larry A. Sjaastad
The University of Chicago

Egon Sohmen
University of the Saar

Alexander K. Swoboda
Graduate Institute of International
   Studies, Geneva

Ruth Troeller
University of Surrey

Marina v. N. Whitman
University of Pittsburgh

Leland B. Yeager
University of Virginia

PART 1

INTRODUCTION

OPENING REMARKS

Robert A. Mundell

Welcome to the University of Chicago and to the Conference on International Monetary Problems.

The purpose of the conference is to mobilize our intellectual resources to make a frontal assault on scientific problems that have thus far resisted solution.

One problem is how to distribute fairly and efficiently the resources made available by the fact that not all international money has to be dug out of the ground. We might pose this "seigniorage problem" either as the problem of distributing the gains from the goldsmith's technological innovation or as the problem of putting a few more tears, as Professor Rueff might say, in the United States' balance-of-payments deficit.

A related question is whether the economic functions of the system should be decentralized in separate institutions. Should international institutions have limited functions and separate administrations, with GATT specializing in trade, the IMF in currencies, the IBRD in lending, or should the functional needs of the system be combined in a more centralized institution? The papers of Herbert Grubel, Robert Aliber, and Max Corden all have a bearing on this subject.

Another problem concerns international adjustment. One aspect of it concerns the appropriate sizes of currency areas and the relations between currency areas, subjects on which Peter Kenen and Leland Yeager will have something to contribute. A separate but equally hard part concerns the efficiency or different speeds of adjustment corresponding to the assignment of policy instruments to policy targets. Peter Kenen is fond of telling a story from Bellagio of how one morning at breakfast I centered my pipe in a honey dish that I mistook for an ashtray; only last week, at the American Bankers Convention at Princeton, a very distinguished central banker put cream and sugar in a cup of turtle soup; so I am in good company. But the principal point is that both strategies represent an improper pairing of instruments and targets. Thus Egon Sohmen and Ronald McKinnon will expand the theory of pairing, in a dynamic context, instruments like pipes, cream, and sugar to ashtrays, soup, coffee, and honey dishes in the more

3

pedestrian context of balance of payments, growth, and employment targets.

Another class of problem concerns the international measure or standard of value. Do we have one? Do we need one? Should the rest of the world have to adjust its prices to the United States price level or ought the United States monetary policy take account of the interests of the rest of the world? How can more of the burden of adjustment be thrown on surplus countries when the world is depressed, and how can more be thrown on deficit countries when the world is in a state of inflation? Some of these problems will be treated by Alan Day and myself.

Alexandre Kafka, on the other hand, has invented a device for shifting the burden of adjustment onto discussants. He has just been nominated as executive director to the International Monetary Fund for Brazil and is currently negotiating for more votes in Caracas at the Latin American caucus (which meets just before, as we are doing, the IMF governor's conference). Whether he will make it back or not, neither he nor I know, but Marcello de Cecco has volunteered to present his interpretation of the Italian crisis for us in case he does not.

In the next three days we will be deliberately disorganizing conventional wisdom in order to apply our scientific knowledge to deepen it. We carve the system into analytical fragments—problems—putting a microscope on each until, hopefully, a new clarity has been realized.

But we have to put Humpty Dumpty together again. Our subject is in need of sterner discipline not more chaos, and we should not leave it in a more confused state than we found it. In that sense a great burden is placed on the last speaker at our conference, Harry Johnson, who has the messy job of putting Humpty Dumpty together again.

Nor should we leave the impression to the outside world that the different opinions and positions we take as economists imply fundamental disagreement among ourselves about basic laws of economics. The fact is that our function is to choose problems that are as yet unresolved. There is no point in having a conference on issues on which we are already in agreement.

Yet there is one issue on which public and private agreement is necessary. That issue is the problem of crisis, and to its solution we all have to contribute as best we can. For our conference takes place at a critical time. An impasse seems to have been reached in the arena of international monetary reform and we are even now in the midst of a tense cyclical position in the world economy, a conjunctural phase that bears some of the disturbing signs of fundamental financial disequilibrium. How can one not be disturbed by the behavior of the stock markets, interest rates higher than we have experienced in decades, and a steady deterioration of the external position of the reserve currencies? The threat of political breakdown among the monetary authorities of the major centers is one we can ill afford.

Two dangers are particularly apparent. One is that if monetary cooperation breaks down the system could not resist a disturbance such as an uncoordinated devaluation of the pound sterling. One possible upshot of this is that we would get a chaotic, sequential increase in the price of gold. While some economists favor a change in the price of gold, we can all agree that there are better ways of bringing it about than having a pistol pointed at the heads of the monetary institutions.

Another danger comes from an entirely different direction. The normative branch of our science presupposes a framework of mores, laws, and institutions that have evolved as part of our social system. Yet temporary controls subverting that framework too often strike the bureaucrat as an easy panacea because he sees only the advantages of intervention to solve a very narrow problem in his limited sphere but not the deeper destruction of the legal and moral values that economists, in their professional capacity, hold constant but which yet make the system worthwhile. This is, of course, an issue that is entirely outside the frame of reference we have chosen for our discussions in the next three days. I mention it now, in passing, just for that reason: I promise that it is the last commercial from Chicago!

It is appropriate now to turn to our distinguished guest. M. Giscard d'Estaing has done us the great favor of coming across the Atlantic to speak to us. He is currently the leader of the Independent Republican Party in France. He has been one of the most articulate spokesmen advocating reform of the system that is often called the gold-exchange standard. Indeed, as the former French minister of finance and an author of France's gold policy, he has already contributed to our meeting here. It is therefore a great honor and privilege for us to have the Honorable M. Giscard d'Estaing speak to us.

THE INTERNATIONAL MONETARY ORDER

Hon. Valéry Giscard d'Estaing

I am perhaps one of the few persons in the world who delight in speaking about international monetary problems, and so it was with great pleasure that I accepted your invitation, Mr. Chairman, to speak, first, *before* you and then *with* you, about these problems tonight.

I will try to present my remarks in two parts: first, some reflections, perhaps familiar to many of you, but nevertheless necessary to put in perspective the basic structure of the international monetary system; second, in answer to the chairman's personal suggestions, some comments about the present state of international monetary discussions. In my comments, I will try to bring to bear my former governmental experience concerning the practical aspects of solutions.

In speaking about international monetary matters, two pitfalls should always be avoided. One is to dwell on *technicalities* which usually, and quite uselessly, obscure the debate even if they make the people who use them feel that they are more knowledgeable than others. The other pitfall is to resort to *generalities* which push practical solutions into the background. The question of reform of the international monetary system is primarily a practical problem. It is first and foremost a problem for action and so it must be studied in the particular frame of mind that seeks positive solutions. International monetary reform, after all, could have a profound effect on the world economy and on national economies; its impact on these countries, including the United States, could be more important than that of all the domestic measures currently being studied or discussed.

I will begin with some reflections about the whole of the problem. International monetary problems have two very characteristic sides. First, they are quite new and, if I dare to say so here, poorly known. In the nineteenth century, there were, strictly speaking, no international monetary problems. The great monetary controversies of the era, concerning for instance bimetalism or some aspects of the gold standard system, were characteristic more of the national than of the international order. The international order was only an outgrowth or generalization of practices followed in the national order. Even the critical monetary difficulties encountered at the international level between the world wars stemmed, by and large, from prevailing national economic factors and not international monetary factors. It is striking to note, for instance, that from the time the British abandoned gold in 1931 until the outbreak of World War II there was no more talk of a crisis as such in the international monetary system. And only in recent years has it been considered that a problem exists, even though one has in fact been taking shape for the past ten or fifteen years.

In addition to being new, international monetary problems are very *specific*. They are, first of all, usually of concern to only a very limited number of central banks. In contrast to arrangements on the national level, the same persons or institutions are both managers and users. More important, international monetary problems, as we see them, result from a very special situation. It is a historically paradoxical situation: a relatively integrated world economy (for instance, in the realm of trade) and independent national monetary systems operate jointly. The way in which this contradiction between monetary polycentrism and economic unity is resolved at any given time determines the prevailing international monetary order.

Goals, Functions, and Problems of an International Monetary Order

I will say a few words now about the need for an international monetary order. First, what are the *goals* an international monetary order should set out to achieve?

The goals are to insure the interaction of economics separated today essentially by monetary frontiers. This is almost exactly the opposite of the situation we have been accustomed to think of: economies separated by trade barriers or quotas and linked by a common monetary atmosphere. The method for insuring this interaction must be uniform, a prerequisite for its multilateral acceptance. A new international monetary order should offer every possible assurance of security and of its ability to last.

These points in effect suggest that the international economy needs a monetary unit. Since there is no such monetary unit at present, this can be studied or thought of for a later stage.

Second, we must look at the *functions* of the international monetary system. These functions are very much like those of a national currency in appearance, but they are quite different in substance. The first function of the international monetary system, to permit the accumulation of reserves, resembles one of the functions of a national monetary system. The reasons why governments set aside foreign exchange reserves, however, are not at all the same as the motives of national economic agents for holding cash. I do not know of any theory that can now explain, or put limits on, or even analyze *de facto* what the major nations (for instance ours) judge to be a normal level of foreign exchange reserve holdings. Every time we reach a new billion dollar level we feel happy, but there is no precise quantity of reserve holdings which maximizes our utility—except perhaps in comparison with our neighbors! Basically, however, there is no real method of any kind of determining in the world of today a "normal size" of international reserve holdings.

A second function of the international monetary system is to provide a standard of value; on the international level there must be an instrument whereby different national currencies can be measured in the same terms. And as a third function of the international monetary system, there must be an instrument that fulfils the classical function of means of settlement. International settlements within the international monetary order take place between central banks and between central banks only. They are therefore marginal or of a residual nature and, by the same token, fundamental. In the working of the international system reserves play almost the role that money issued by central banks (primary liquidity) plays in the national system.

In the international monetary order, there are *two main problems:* a problem of quantity, and a problem of balance.

The problem of quantity is that of determining the total amount of reserves. On the international level, the adequate amount cannot be set with the purpose of determining the amount of aggregate demand, as can be done by national monetary policy. Rather, it should be set with the vague aim of insuring sufficient cash resources. I say the vague aim because reserves represent only primary liquidities. These are supplemented by secondary liquidities and the adequacy of cash resources depends on the total of both. National views of what constitutes sufficient cash reserves are quite different and vary in time for one and the same country.

The second problem is that of balance. Lasting imbalances are unacceptable, especially when they concern deficit countries, for very practical and objective reasons. First, a deficit implies a tax on the real resources of others and represents an increase in wealth, albeit small. Second, if it lasts too long, a deficit leads to stringent corrective measures detrimental to all; this represents the crucial difference between deficits and surpluses. Although the correction of a surplus affects other countries, it does not require the same stringent and harmful measures. Third, a lasting deficit feeds inflation which undermines the stability of the modern economy.

There is, of course, a close two-way connection between the volume of reserves and the magnitude of imbalance; but this two-way connection is not sufficient in itself to determine the right solution. Two other considerations must also be taken into account: the goals of domestic policy and the degree of freedom desired in international transactions.

Past Solutions

Ever since paper money came into use on the national level, there have been international monetary problems relating to the coexistence of several independent monetary units in an international economy. Solutions to these problems have been achieved in two ways: international monetary integration under gold and integration under a national currency. Let us cast a glance at the past solutions and evaluate their success.

I think it is useful to distinguish six periods since international monetary issues were first discussed in the nineteenth century: (1) until the 1870's, gold; (2) between 1870 and 1914, a mixed system based on gold and sterling; (3) between 1915 and 1931, chaos; (4) between 1931 and 1939, as before 1870, gold; (5) between 1947 and 1960, the dollar; and (6) between 1960 and today, a mixed system based on the dollar and gold. When you consider these periods (which you all know very well), you observe that there was no steady evolution, not even a trend. For instance, the period between 1931 and 1939 was more classical than the period between 1870 and 1914; even now we are in a mixed system. Broadly speaking, only two global solutions to the problem of achieving an integrated international monetary order have been practiced thus far, and these systems have two common features that condemn them as sensible and lasting solutions.

First, both the gold integration system and the sterling or dollar integration system came into being by chance. Gold integration arose from a kind of *de facto* situation: the national circulation of gold, which automatically integrated the international monetary system. The problems were not problems of exchange, but of physical transfer. There was no express desire for this system; the theory followed the fact. There is more explanation and more justification for the gold system today than there was in the period during which the system was used. Prior to 1914, gold played less of a role precisely because monetary integration had been largely achieved by the use of sterling.

The second integration system was integration by a national currency, first sterling and then chiefly the dollar. As with sterling before 1914, there was no express desire for integration via the dollar. At Bretton Woods, provision was made for a gold system with credit facilities and revisable exchange rates (which have remained, as you know, firmly fixed). The dollar exchange standard was not asked for nor advocated by the United States—nor (obviously) by other nations. So in fact, these systems came into existence by chance; they were not devised by the will or by the human mind.

The second shortcoming of these two systems of integration is that they are delicate in their functioning, as experience has proved. The gold system, which seems to certain minds so easy to manage, is in fact expensive; extraction, storage, and transport are some of its costs. There is no reason—or at least I see no reason—for extraction to meet monetary needs. The only rationale for extraction is to supply private uses. The system implies periods of adjustment, meaning deflation or inflation. It is not a stable system because its shortcomings make it conducive to the adoption of the gold exchange standard. It is, in fact, a transitional system. It risks instability, distortion, and even collapse as proved by the past.

The other system, integration under a national currency, is also senseless. There is no relation between the reserve needs of the world and the foreign deficits of the reserve currency countries. This is quite obvious, and nowadays everybody knows it. Yet I am always impressed by the fact that, as obvious as this is, there are still some theories to back this system which has no corrective mechanism for the reserve currency countries or, at least, only a very weak one. For instance, compare the United States and Italy in 1963 and 1964. The deficits of the United States started much before the Italian deficits. Italy had to adopt a very hard and very exacting internal economic policy which made its employment, its growth, and its foreign trade suffer, all because it had to return to equilibrium within strict time limits. And Italy did return to equilibrium. Yet, in the same time period, the corrective mechanism for the reserve currency countries did not work as hard, if at all. It is a one-sided system: the non-reserve currency countries acquire the currencies of others, but not vice versa. And it is an unstable system; past a certain limit, there is a feeling of uncertainty concerning its development in the future.

The Quest for a Solution

When looking to the past, we see only two main solutions, and both have very serious shortcomings. So we go, as everyone goes, on the quest for a solution.

First, there is the possibility of returning purely and simply to gold. When we review the past we see the objections against the gold system. These objections must not be forgotten, simply because such a system is historically far from us. Moreover, in the present situation, a return to gold would have to be accompanied by revaluation of the price of gold. This would have three disadvantages. First, inflationary effects would result from such a revaluation. We are not at all in the same world trend as we were in the 1930's. Then the trend was toward world deflation, and chains of devaluations were expected; today, the situation is exactly the opposite, and an increase in the price of gold would have inflationary effects.

Second, the main question today—the root of uncertainty in the world—is the problem of equilibrium in the balance of payments of the major nations. A change in the price of gold does not contribute to payments equilibrium at all. On the contrary, such a change would tend to postpone a solution to this problem.

Third, the gold system is really a transitional standard leading to a gold exchange standard. A revaluation of gold would thus enlarge rather than diminish the gold exchange standard by reducing the proportion of currency balances in reserves and thus making the gold exchange standard easier to manage, at least for a while.

The other commonly advocated solution to international monetary problems is to create a currency-issuing world bank. This is, of course, the IMF's natural vocation. But a world bank is, at the present time, absolutely incompatible with national sovereignties. The desire for national sovereignty exists in *every* nation, not just in some, and there has been no indication up to now of an explicit will to give up any national sovereignty in the field of money. Perhaps, in a still remote future, there could be some change in this attitude, with all its consequences for fiscal policies and for the internal use of monetary policy. For the moment, this cannot be considered a practical and near solution.

Therefore, elements of a realistic solution must be sought in another direction. First, there are some improvements that could be added to the present system in order to achieve a better balance. We certainly could, without many difficulties, refine the means by which we usually try to achieve better balance either externally or internally. Externally, I think that exchange rates are fixed much too firmly. Bretton Woods made provision for changes in par values, but there have been very few such changes. A fetish of sorts about the fixity of par values has been introduced into international practice and must be combatted. To begin with, currently accepted margins of fluctuations could be slightly widened. A second way to achieve better balance would be to refine the control of domestic demand. For instance, the budgetary policy of modern economies subject to very strong, sudden booms should be made more flexible. One could introduce, for example, the possibility of changing by several percentage points the yield from certain taxes—either on individuals or on business—without legislative authorization, so as to insure more flexible and quicker control of domestic demand. In the field of short-term monetary policy, too, some progress could, I think, easily be made. Its effect on international short-term capital movements should be reduced, since such movements quite often annihilate or counteract the impact of the domestic measures as soon as they are taken.

But, even if these instruments were refined, we must improve the real, technical international monetary structure. Since neither a reserve system based on gold only, nor a system based on gold and national currencies is particularly desirable, we must take another approach. We should not use the principal currencies as an instrument, but we should keep gold and add an adjustable element. At this stage, I should like to say a few words about the present stage of discussion and negotiation on this point. It is interesting to note that this is undoubtedly the first time in a period of peace that men have been aware of the need to define a new monetary order. The first time. Bretton Woods was the only other attempt to define a new order, and its purpose was to straighten things out after a war, quite a different problem.

The present situation is more within the realm of my direct experience. When the chairman wrote me, he suggested—very tactfully, of course—that I should comment on the attitude and the position of various parties in the present action for international monetary reform. (Before such an audience as this one, however, I thought I had to make some general remarks to show that I am able to think, if not always to express myself perfectly clearly, in a foreign language.)

The reform of the international monetary system today is a race that is being run on three tracks at once. One track is the concept of a new system; the second track is the realization or the implementation of the reforms; and the third track leads to conditions necessary for successful reform—the restoration of an equilibrium in the balance of payments of the reserve currency countries. So, we have three horses, on three tracks. As far as the concept of the reforms is concerned, and contrary to what is sometimes expressed, I think that a large part of the ground has been covered, perhaps two-thirds. On the second track, the implementation of reform, progress has been slower; one-third of the track, let us say, has been covered. And on the restoration of an equilibrium in the balance of payments, we are not very far from the starting line. We shall examine these three points in succession.

First, the concepts. It was in the fall of 1963 that the problem of monetary reform was first raised and considered in its entirety. Some important progress has been made since. At that time, the official doctrine of the leading countries was to ignore the problem and to place full official confidence in the gold exchange standard. I remember very well that when we spoke (and I use the plural here out of modesty because "we" were the only one!), we created something of a scandal. First, the people who worked with me were very sad to see me take such a stand because they were members of the friendly international group of people who met month after month to discuss monetary matters with a common agreement not to raise too complicated or too violent questions. Since I was quite new in that field I wanted to express—and this is very daring of course—what I thought. I drafted my speech myself and remember very well the kind of silence that accompanied its first reading to my staff members. But today the whole world and the best minds recognize the importance of the problem and even its urgency. In the meantime, some results have been achieved. These are mainly set out in the reports of the Ten of the summer of 1964 and of last summer.

Today, four main results have been achieved with respect to our conception of the international monetary system. The first is that the international monetary system's present difficulties are attributable, not, as used to be said, to the likelihood of a shortage of reserves in the near future, but to the persistent deficit in the balance of payments of the reserve currency countries. And on this very sensitive point, I do not express a personal view only, but quote directly from the report of the Ten; this view, therefore, has been endorsed by the representatives of the United States and of Great Britain. The second result is the belief that the amount of additional liquidity to be created should not be linked to the size of the deficits of the reserve currency countries. Third, this liquidity should be created in the light of the world economy's global and permanent needs. This point is detailed, as you know, in the report of the Ten. It means that international liquidity must not be created in response to short-term conjunctural policy, but only as a function of global reserve needs. And fourth, the form which the creation of this new liquidity can take is the issuance of a new unit to supplement gold. And so, this idea, which seemed amusing but not very convincing when it was first expressed, is now described in the report of the Ten as being the most probable solution. However, two main questions remain to be settled: there is open disagreement about, first, the new unit's link to gold, and second, the decision-making process and the rules for allocating additional liquidity between the participants. But when you look at the whole of the conceptual problem, I think it is fair to say that two-thirds of the ground has been covered.

We next come to the question of implementation of reform. In this area the results are more limited. First, "multilateral surveillance"—a horrible but necessary phrase—of credit facilities which was decided on in 1964 is now working correctly. Second, the way to improve the adjustment mechanism was the subject of a detailed and very interesting report by the OECD published this year. Third—and this is a matter of satisfaction for the United States—in 1965, for the first time, the balance-of-payments deficit of the United States was below its gold outflow. So much so, that in that year financing the deficit did not result in the creation of a significant amount of additional liquidity. Of course, this event can be presented in quite a different way, but the fact is that no blame can be put upon the United States in 1965 for adding, on the whole, to the liquidity of the world. So there have been some gains and about one-third of the track has been covered.

On the third track, in contrast, the methods whereby international liquidity is now created remain subject to criticism. From the time when the ten countries emphasized concern about the correct amount of liquidity in the world and the need for breaking the link between the deficits of the reserve currency countries and the creation of liquidity, those deficits have not been eliminated although they have been reduced. For instance, from the end of 1962 to 1964, dollar holdings abroad have risen by nearly four billion dollars. I refer to this period because in 1962, for the first time, there was a formal announcement by the United States of its intention to stop the process. Furthermore, the recent decision to increase reciprocal credit facilities between central banks by some two billion dollars constitutes, in fact, a means of creating additional liquidity that is in no way related to the global needs for liquidity. Rather, it is connected to the risks facing the world payment system because of the persistence of certain countries' deficits. Therefore, this is a measure, which, in its technique and its motives, belongs to the past. We must hope that it is the last of its kind and that the breathing space it provides will be used for a rapid reduction of the deficits; this is its only possible justification.

In sum: there has been important progress in the concept of reform, more limited results in actual reform, and no change in the conditions, since the deficits of the reserve currency countries have persisted. These are the results as of today of the race started three years ago. What efforts, then, still have to be made?

The first is a strenuous effort to eliminate the deficits. They, and they alone, breed the feeling of monetary insecurity in the world. There are in the world today other feelings of insecurity concerning the economic situation, but these have no direct impact on the feeling of monetary insecurity which is due to the persistence of deficits. Monetary tools and appropriate fiscal policy, if properly combined, make it possible for the deficits to be reduced. The experience of several countries stands witness to this point. The change of attitude of the United States in this respect, for the past few months, even if dictated more by domestic than by external considerations, gives us reason for the first time to hope for a recovery—if the action taken is pursued and if no major outside factor contravenes it. In any event, monetary anxiety can be allayed more by the determination shown in this regard than by any technical device.

Because of the different rates at which the ideas on reform have advanced and the work on eliminating the deficits has proceeded—the first going faster—certain observers are led today to suggest stopping temporarily and not going beyond a study of the problem. The prospect of seeing new monetary liquidity created, they fear, might soon weaken the determination of the countries that have to take prompt and forceful steps to eliminate their deficits. I personally believe that there are means of solving this difficulty without being compelled to come to an intellectual standstill on the study of a problem vital to the whole world.

What are these means? It is known that, in this respect, there are two stages to reform: an agreement between the Ten, and then a formal decision within the International Monetary Fund, according to an appropriate procedure which has not been completely defined. So, the following decisions could be taken. First, before resuming their work, the Ten could decide not to pass to the second stage, namely, formal decision within the Fund, until there is unanimous agreement, either that the deficits have been eliminated or that they are being eliminated. This condition is necessary to lift the doubt or the fear that otherwise these deficits will never be corrected. Second, until a decision on the creation of new reserve units is taken, it is necessary to avoid the opposite and less-talked-about risk of a contraction of world liquidity, should the balance-of-payments deficits be substantially reduced and at the same time conversion of reserve currencies into gold be continued. Fear of such a situation is not totally groundless in view of the immediate economic trend in the world which is certainly not toward acceleration of growth. It would be paradoxical if the pursuit of international monetary reform should have a restrictive effect and impair the trend of economic expansion. To avoid this risk, the Ten could jointly determine the measures to be adopted or the rules to be followed in order to maintain adequate liquidity. The third decision which could be taken is that, in the meanwhile, the Ten could continue their studies in order to reach agreement on the two basic points left pending: the new unit's link to gold and the procedure for voting the creation of new liquidity. A report on these points could be drawn up, for example, by the end of 1967.

On each of these points, I would make one suggestion. A link must necessarily be established between gold—the center of the system and the unit of reference for all currencies—and the new monetary unit, so as to prevent gold from accumulating in some countries (I do not name any) and the new unit in others. For, if such unbalanced accumulations took place, the new system would be, like the gold exchange standard, a transitional system. After five or ten years, if there is an accumulation of gold in one place and of new units in another, the value of the units will be discussed in exactly the same way as the value of national currencies is now. To prevent such an outcome, provision could be made, for example, for a fixed ratio between the quantities of gold and the amount of new units used in settling deficits between central banks. It would also be possible to regulate the terms under which new units could be exchanged for gold at the central banks—even at the central banks which are not now converting their own national currency into gold.

On the second point, as regards the voting procedure, preference has been shown, as you know, for a two-stage voting procedure: first a decision between the Ten and then a decision within the Fund. In determining the amount of liquidity to be created, the vote could be weighted; each of the Ten could have a certain number of votes, depending on both its quota in the Fund and its balance of payments situation during the preceding period. But it is very difficult to be brief on such a subject without sounding superficial.

At this stage I will add another suggestion which, I personally think, is fundamental. At the same time that problems connected with the new units are being studied, the six Common Market countries should begin preliminary work on a monetary union. Apart from the fact that these countries may have their own reasons for achieving this—reasons which are linked to the good functioning of the Common Market itself—the present structure of world payments and reserves makes the absence of a single monetary instrument appear an anomaly. The figures speak for themselves: as of June 13, 1966, out of a total volume of world liquidity estimated at 70 billion dollars, the United States held 14.9 billion, the United Kingdom 3.2 billion, and the Common Market countries 23.7 billion. To deal with the problem of international settlements on the basis of only two currencies would be to ignore the contemporary facts. We can see that the debate would be made clearer by the emergence of a third monetary unit which would be the common medium for the external monetary action of the Six.

Such monetary union would both clarify things and limit the need for international liquidity. Some of the transactions now carried through international liquidities would then be carried through internal western European settlements. I am always impressed by the fact that, when one speaks today about the problem of payments, or international monetary problems, Americans speak of the dollar, the British speak of the pound, and Europeans, all Europeans, speak of gold. The reason is not that we have gold mines; of all nations, we have been said to have the fewest gold mines. Rather, it is because we desire to have an objective monetary representation of our own. Since we do not find it in either the dollar or the pound, we Europeans compensate by looking for it in gold. This is not a realistic view, however, because the reason for which Europeans are looking to gold is the same that could lead them to try to find a common monetary expression. Obviously, the initiative and the terms of such a union fall within the competence of the Six. It is, however, desirable that the international community consider this union as an important means of improving the monetary system.

Conclusion

In dealing with monetary problems one must resist the intellectual temptation to think that money is something by itself, that it has an autonomous existence, as if it were an entity, per se. Money is a reflection of economic facts. It can be, of course, an anticipation; but an anticipation is a reflection. To reform the monetary system is both to insure a more accurate representation of economic reality and to exert corrective action on it. The action to be undertaken should be conducted with the following goals in mind: (1) eliminating lasting balance-of-payments deficits because they are in themselves an economic anomaly; (2) making the creation of additional liquidity depend on a credit mechanism that would be based on global needs and not, as is now the case, on reciprocal credit facilities between debtor countries; and (3) insuring a genuine representation of European monetary reality through the establishment of a monetary union.

When you think of these goals, the responsibility shifts from the theoreticians to the statesmen. When solutions appear that are conceivable and feasible, it is incumbent upon the statesmen to demonstrate the determination necessary to carry them through. The international monetary problem, which seems unclear to many, may then appear, almost at once, to have been simplified. The present concern, which is quite deep and broad in the world, would be dispelled. World opinion would learn that in this field, so vital to its prosperity and its security, if the necessary steps are taken in time, to quote a Spanish proverb, "the worst is not always inevitable."

PROBLEMS OF THE INTERNATIONAL
MONETARY SYSTEM

Robert A. Mundell

A problem is a question proposed for solution. A valid problem, for purposes of a scientific conference, implies four attributes of the solution: (a) it is not known, (b) it is worth knowing, (c) it can be known, and (d) it cannot be known easily. The solution of a valid problem implies an increase in relevant information and accelerates the production and transmission of knowledge.

It is seldom possible to guarantee in advance that all the conditions are satisfied; search is necessary before it can be ascertained whether a problem posed is a valid problem. A solution may already exist, it may not be worth knowing, or, for practical or conceptual reasons, it may not be knowable. The act of formulating a problem may itself direct thinking toward a solution, while the act of presenting one may direct information toward a source where the solution exists, but where the existence of the problem is not known.

Recognition of the existence of problems has as important a place in economics as in the other sciences. Had Adam Smith explicitly recognized that he was confronted with a theoretical problem when he made the distinction between value in use and value in exchange, the science might not have had to wait a century for the marginalist revolution. Had Cournot recognized the usefulness of a dimensionless measure of the flexibility of demand and supply, the discipline would not have had to wait for Marshall to invent the concept of elasticity. Today economists may not recognize whether there is a problem in, say, capital theory either because they have a solution that evades other economists, or because they fail to see subtleties that others see or imagine. The existence of a problem often becomes apparent only after it has been solved and no longer exists.

The problems posed for solution at the Chicago Conference on International Monetary Problems were all taken from practical issues arising in the context of the debate on international monetary reform. Difficulties had come up in one form or another again and again at conferences, international meetings, and in public statements. It became apparent long before this conference was organized that the practical difficulties economists and officials were experiencing in reaching consensus on important economic and political matters did not reflect logical errors or different value judgments but basic theoretical gaps in the models used by theorists, experts, and negotiators. Concurrently, a great deal of effort had been expended by younger theorists in the United States and abroad working on many of the theoretical issues that needed solution. The purpose of the Chicago conference, as it was jointly conceived by Harry Johnson and myself in the winter of 1966, was to exploit the work on theory to solve problems impeding decisions on policy.

The organizing principle we adopted was to seek out and identify the major problems in the area in the hope that that method would provide the greatest economies of thought and discussion. In February, 1966, therefore, I prepared a list of problems and presented them to the workshops in international economics at The University of Chicago and at Columbia University. From my original presentation as modified by these seminar discussions, we settled on twelve problems for potential discussion at the conference, reprinted as an appendix to this chapter. The purpose of this introduction is to relate the problems to one another in a more systematic fashion.

Liquidity, Adjustment, and Confidence

Some of the theoretical gaps had already been formulated in the oral tradition that had been developed in the subject. Thus, at the meetings of thirty-two economists held at Bellagio, Italy, in 1964, organized by Professor Machlup to explore bases of disagreement on the issue of international monetary reform, the group agreed to organize discussion around three major issues concerning the present international monetary system. They were:

> 1) The problem of payments adjustment, deriving from the need for correcting persistent imbalances in the payments positions of individual countries.
> 2) The problem of international liquidity, connected with the need for long-term adaptation of the total volume of world reserves to the full potentialities of non-inflationary economic growth.
> 3) The problem of confidence in reserve media, implied in the need for avoiding sudden switches between different reserve media.

This classification of problems turned out to be a very effective first step in disciplining discussion of the different plans for reform, and an important contribution to the debate on monetary reform was made by that analytical separation. The questions of liquidity, adjustment, and confidence fall easily into the framework of demand–supply analysis if a distinction is made between the "micro" aspects of the problems at the national level and the "macro" aspects of the problems at the global level.

From a national point of view the liquidity problem is the problem of meeting any gap between the supply and demand for international reserves at given exchange rates, that is, the problem of financing a balance-of-payments deficit. The adjustment problem is the problem of eliminating a gap between the supply and demand for gold or foreign exchange, that is, the problem of correcting a deficit. And the confidence problem is the problem of preventing changes in the status of reserve assets from causing speculative shifts in the composition of stocks of gold or foreign exchange assets held as reserves by the national central banks.

At the global level, the liquidity problem is to insure the ability of the system as a whole to meet gaps between the world supply and demand for reserves at given exchange rates on the part of private holders. The adjustment problem is that of correcting disequilibrium by bringing about equality between the world demand and supply of international assets. And the confidence problem is the problem of preventing speculative world-wide shifts between the stocks of different international reserve assets from forcing an undesired change in their relative prices.

These problems are broadly defined syndromes and their generality, which was an important advantage in the early stages of theoretical discussion, soon became a defect for more refined debate. That was the purpose of breaking away from the earlier earth-air-fire-water classification of major problem areas.

The Use of Reserves

Countries need reserves because they do not have, or do not want to use, quick methods of correcting balance-of-payments deficits. The monetary authorities recognize the probability of future deficits which they cannot correct instantly and so they prepare the financing of these deficits in advance by holding reserves. The more reserves they own, and the greater access to borrowing they have, the more freedom they have in choosing among different methods of adjustment in the future. A country that is "liquid" has considerable choice over the *type, pace*, and *timing* of adjustment, whereas a country that is "illiquid" has little choice.

The advantage of holding reserves stems from the convenience that a wide choice of adjustment techniques offers. But reserves can be held only at a cost, so countries do not want to hold reserves in unlimited quantities. Taking into account the interest that can be earned on certain types of reserve assets, the cost of holding reserves is the loss of the use of real resources given up by accumulating reserves, and can be measured, as an annual flow of income, by the return that could be earned by investing the reserves in earning assets. The marginal gain from holding reserves declines as the quantity of reserves increases, while the marginal cost of holding reserves, expressed in terms of the marginal utility of foregone resources, increases with the quantity of reserves. The balancing of the gains and costs at the margin determines the optimum quantity of reserves.

Any country's *actual* level of reserves depends on *past* balance-of-payments net *surpluses*; and its *desired* level of reserves depends on (expected) future balance-of-payments *deficits*. When a country's reserves are considered excessive, the authorities try to get rid of reserves by stimulating their investment, usually indirectly (through easier monetary or trade policies) in other assets; and when a country's reserves are considered deficient, it tries to acquire more. In all these respects, the management of the reserve holdings of a country is analogous to the management of the cash reserves of an individual household; the main difference lies in the fact that individual cash holdings are spent directly, while national reserve holdings are adjusted through changes in economic policy.

If world reserves are constant, the sum of the balances of payments of all individual countries is zero, so that if all countries want to accumulate reserves by running balance-of-payments surpluses, some countries' aims are necessarily frustrated; the surplus one country has must be offset by the deficits of other countries. Similarly, if all countries try to lose reserves, they must fail if world reserves are constant, because the attempt to realize a collective deficit for the world as a whole is in nominal terms impossible. The *attempt* to realize a collective deficit can, however, encourage economic expansion in the individual countries, and, if resources are fully employed, reduce the real value of world reserves through inflation.

A collective "world" surplus or deficit is not impossible, of course, if world reserves are changing; central banks can, collectively, buy reserve assets from the private sectors and they can also create synthetic credit reserves among themselves. When world reserves are rising the sum of all measured balance-of-payments surpluses exceeds the sum of all deficits, and when world reserves are falling the sum of all measured deficits exceeds the sum of all surpluses.

This raises a question that has become known as the SEIGNIORAGE PROBLEM. Countries give up real resources in order to acquire international reserves. If international reserves consist entirely of gold the acquisition of gold involves a payment from the central banks to gold producers, which is divided between costs of production, rents, and profits. But if international reserves can be created at low cost, because they are composed partly of paper money or other forms of credit, there is a transfer of resources from the countries whose central banks acquire and hold the "paper money" to the agency or bank or government issuing it. The right to issue paper that can be used as international money therefore confers on the issuer a "seigniorage gain," and raises the problem of finding a method to determine how the gains should be distributed among the using countries.

Under a system in which a national currency is used as an international reserve asset, for example, a seigniorage gain goes to the inhabitants of the reserve currency country. Let us suppose that, because of economic growth, other countries want to acquire every year additional purchasing power in the form of, say, dollars. They earn these dollars by spending less than their income and generating balance-of-payments surpluses. The counterpart to their surpluses is the balance-of-payments deficit of the reserve country, the inhabitants of which will have acquired real resources (or claims to real resources) in exchange for non-interest-bearing liabilities. Competition among the commercial banks in the reserve currency country of course will generally lead to interest payments on reserve balances and this is one means by which the seigniorage profit can be redistributed to other countries.

The seigniorage problem arises also in connection with the creation of a world monetary authority. A world bank can issue international reserves by purchasing interest-bearing assets in the member countries—open-market operations—but it then faces the seigniorage problem of disposing of its earned income in excess of operating expenses. Alternatively, it can directly solve the problem by issuing international money as grants, or by the purchase of non-interest-bearing "dead" assets of the national countries.

We can turn now to the implications of excess and deficient liquidity. A liquidity shortage arises when countries want more liquidity than is being created, and a liquidity surplus arises when countries want less liquidity than is being created. When all countries want liquidity that they cannot collectively get—there is a liquidity shortage—all countries *act like deficit countries* and a world contraction of trade and employment, or general competitive depreciation, is threatened. The contraction can relieve the liquidity situation only insofar as it reduces the desire for liquidity; world deflation would, in principle, reduce the desire for nominal reserves and increase the commodity value of existing reserves. But adjusting the world price level to increase the real value of reserves is hardly practical in the modern world; it is almost universally considered to be preferable to adapt the supply of liquidity to the existing price level than to do the opposite. A liquidity shortage can be beneficial, however, if the world is in such a state of inflation that it is desirable to induce countries to follow more disciplined monetary or fiscal policies.

When all countries have liquidity they do not want, and there is a liquidity surplus, all countries tend *to act like surplus countries* and are more willing to allow an expansion of trade and employment. This is generally regarded as beneficial if there is general depression throughout the world, but harmful if the world is already fully employed. If the world is in a state of depression, an excess of liquidity promotes desirable world expansion; if it is already fully employed, it merely causes an undesirable inflation of prices. Since surpluses tend to promote more expansive trade and monetary policies, while deficits promote more restrictive policies, increases in liquidity are beneficial or harmful depending on whether more expansive, or more restrictive, policies are needed in the world as a whole. Although actual changes in world reserves do not necessarily measure the changes in the desire of nations to hold them, actual reserves are more likely to exceed the quantities that are desired when reserves are increasing than when they are declining.

Balance-of-Payments Disequilibria

Only rarely, however, is the world in such a state of balance that all countries want to accumulate reserves at the same rate. Normally, some countries will be in deficit while others are in surplus. A normally distributed increase in liquidity makes surplus countries act *more* like surplus countries by increasing their discomfort with respect to continued balance-of-payments surpluses, stimulating more expansive policies; whereas it makes deficit countries act *less* like deficit countries by decreasing the discomfort they experience as a result of a continuation of their deficits. The *ability* of a deficit country to sustain a continued deficit is increased by a world-wide increase in reserves in which it participates, while the *willingness* of a surplus country to delay adjustment is decreased. It is for this reason that surplus countries are apt to resist additions to world liquidity, while deficit countries are inclined to welcome additions.

Both deficit and surplus countries may also recognize that the other group can be encouraged to adapt more or less rapidly, and hence they may delay or accelerate their own adjustment on that account. For example, the United States, as a deficit country, may delay monetary contraction if it believes Europe, as a surplus area, will expand; or Europe may delay expansion if it believes the United States will contract. This possibility introduces the SPEED OF ADJUSTMENT PROBLEM. How rapidly should a country adjust its policies to correct a given balance-of-payments deficit? The adequacy of liquidity has to be judged by the appropriateness of the division of the adjustment and the relative speeds at which it is brought about between deficit and surplus countries. Other things being equal, an "equitable" sharing of the burden and timing of adjustment would indicate that liquidity is just about right; a situation in which the burden fell excessively on deficit countries would indicate a dearth of liquidity, and an excess of the burden on surplus countries would indicate a surplus of liquidity.

Countries lose reserves (or reduce their rate of increase over time) by running deficits (or reducing surpluses) in their balance of payments. Deliberate policies to reduce reserves, or "adjust" to surpluses, include appreciation of the exchange rate, wage and price inflation, more liberal import policies, and reduced exchange controls. A country may adopt any combination of these measures when its stock of reserves is thought to be too large or when its reserves are increasing at too rapid a rate.

Countries acquire reserves, or prevent their decrease over time, by running balance-of-payments surpluses or eliminating deficits. To establish surpluses or "adjust" to deficits, they can devalue, lower wages and prices, tighten money-market conditions, impose tariffs or quotas, introduce or tighten exchange controls, or any combination of these policies. A country typically will use one or another of these instruments when its reserves are deficient or falling at too rapid a rate. The use of an instrument to correct the balance of payments, however, means that its use for alternative targets of policy is correspondingly restricted.

For a deficit country experiencing inflationary pressure, monetary contraction is conducive to achieving both external and internal balance; conversely, for a surplus country experiencing deflationary pressure, monetary expansion is desirable. But in other cases, monetary policy can be used effectively only when employed in concert with other policy instruments.

Thus, in a deficit country with unemployment, tight money might improve the balance of payments, but at the expense of employment; for a surplus country with inflationary pressure, easy money might have the desired effect on the balance of payments, but at the risk of greater inflation. These situations are thought to represent the disequilibrium situations most suitable for exchange-rate changes.

Under fixed exchange rates, however, additional policy tools must be developed. One possibility is to split financial policy into its components of monetary and fiscal policy and use them separately for external and internal balance. In this case, looked at as a short-run policy, monetary policy must be aimed at achieving equilibrium in the balance of payments, while fiscal policy must be aimed at internal balance. In past writings I have referred to the general problem of determining the appropriate mix of policies as the "problem of effective market classification"; in the context of its application at the Chicago conference, Richard Cooper's term, ASSIGNMENT PROBLEM, is more appropriate.

In economic systems instruments of policy typically affect all targets. Thus a change in the money supply or tariffs will typically change the equilibrium values of all variables in a system. But this does not mean that an "assignment problem" can be disposed of by the empty statement that all targets and instruments must be taken into account. There are two questions that need to be kept analytically separate.

One is the existence and location of an equilibrium solution. If a solution exists, and its location is known, instruments need merely be put at their equilibrium values for the targets to be reached, after due account is paid to time lags. If the location of the equilibrium is known there is no assignment problem at all.

The assignment problem arises in the context of dynamics and limited information. Disequilibria symptoms (unemployment, inflation, or a balance-of-payments surplus or deficit) are observed. There is, presumably, a set of instruments available to correct the disequilibrium. The assignment problem is the problem of establishing rules or guidelines indicating the direction in which particular instruments should be adjusted in order to lead to equilibrium. It is, in other words, the problem of devising a dynamic *system* that has a convergent solution. One of the most relevant international monetary problems is that of devising a practical mechanism of insuring internal balance, external balance, and the desired rate of economic growth in the context of a fixed exchange-rate system.

Another problem connected with the use of monetary and fiscal policy as the sole instruments of achieving internal and external balance is that it does not leave enough scope for specific targets within the concept of the balance of payments. There is an assignment problem within the balance of payments itself, that we can call the COMPOSITION PROBLEM, that of finding instruments to determine the desirable mix between the capital account and the current account in the balance of payments. One reason the monetary-fiscal policy mix was referred to earlier as a short-run solution is that internal and external balance might be achieved with an undesirable amount of foreign borrowing. Expressed in another way, this problem could be regarded as the problem of determining the appropriate rate of foreign lending.

The choice among adjustment policies that a single nation makes has obvious international ramifications. Because as one country's surplus is another country's deficit (except for the continuing growth of reserves) adjustment could be achieved by deflation or devaluation in the deficit country, by inflation or revaluation in the surplus country, or by some division of changes in the instruments between the two countries. This problem can be referred to as a DISTRIBUTION OF THE BURDEN OF ADJUSTMENT PROBLEM. It is at this point that we see the intimate connection between the desired level of reserves in the world as a whole and the adjustment policies of national economies. In an n-country world, $n - 1$ adjustment instruments are sufficient to achieve world equilibrium because of the mutual interdependence of the balances of payments, giving rise to a possibility of an over-determinacy. Only $n - 1$ countries in an n-country world need have balance-of-payments policies in the sense that if $n - 1$ countries achieve balance-of-payments equilibrium the nth country must also be in equilibrium. There is, therefore, a REDUNDANCY PROBLEM, an extra instrument of policy. The extra instrument can be allocated to fixing the price of a metal such as gold, or fixing the level of world prices, whatever the international standard is.

If surplus countries inflate while deficit countries maintain stability of their own price levels, there will result an upward trend to the world price level; the system is said to have an inflationary bias. If on the other hand, deficit countries deflate while surplus countries maintain stability of their domestic price levels, there will result a downward trend to world prices or, if wages and prices are rigid downward, unemployment; the system is then said to have a deflationary bias. The system will only result in a stable world price level if the burden of adjustment is shared between deficit and surplus countries.

The extent to which the adjustment burden "should" be shared between deficit and surplus countries depends on the world price index it is desired to stabilize. If the world price index is a weighted average of national prices of home-produced goods, the burden of adjustment should be shared roughly in inverse proportion to the sizes of the countries. For example, if a very large country is in surplus, inflationary policies to correct that surplus would promote inflation in the world as a whole, whereas the same percentage price changes in smaller countries would have a smaller effect on world prices because the weight of small countries in the world price index is low. A 1 per cent increase in the price level of a large country may be much more "inflationary," from the point of view of the world as a whole, than a several percentage increase in the price level of a small country.

An analogous problem would exist in the context of exchange-rate adjustment. If there are n currencies there are only $n - 1$ exchange rates and whether there is a choice of adjustment policies is a question of whether surplus countries appreciate or deficit countries depreciate. If there is no outside money reserve unit such as gold, it makes no substantive difference what happens to the weighted index of "par values," since a uniform change in par values would have only an accounting significance. But if currencies are directly or indirectly tied to gold or domestic money supplies, appreciation of the currencies of surplus countries will lower the currency value of gold reserves and thus exert a deflationary force in the world as a whole, whereas devaluation of the currencies of deficit countries, through an increase in the price of gold expressed in those currencies can exert an inflationary influence.

These considerations illustrate the intimate connection between the world supply of international money and the adjustment policies of national countries. The final link in the connection is supplied by the influence of changes in liquidity on adjustment policies.

Increases in liquidity, distributed in a given way over the world as a whole, allow deficit countries to postpone, and surplus countries to accelerate adjustment, imparting a more inflationary, or less deflationary, bias to a given world price index; whereas decreases in liquidity have an opposite effect. Excess liquidity, world inflation, and an undue adjustment burden on surplus countries go hand in hand, just as do a liquidity scarcity, world deflation, and an undue adjustment burden on deficit countries.

The realities of economic life may, however, make it impossible to adhere to a strictly automatic rule for determining the appropriate division of the burden of adjustment. One consideration of importance will be the state of internal demand in the surplus and deficit countries. If there is inflationary pressure in the deficit country, it is clear that the deficit country should contract to prevent inflation; or if there is unemployment in the surplus country, it is obvious that the surplus country should expand; and if there is both unemployment in the surplus country and inflation in the deficit country, the surplus country should expand and the deficit country contract concurrently. The solutions in these cases are obvious and easy because the monetary action necessary to bring about international adjustment is consistent with the monetary actions required for the restoration of internal balance (full employment and a stable price level) in the two countries.

The actions needed in these cases may not, however, suffice to bring about internal balance and international equilibrium at the same time. The expansion necessary to achieve full employment in a surplus country may be insufficient to restore external balance even when combined with the actions needed to stop inflation in the deficit country.

If the monetary policies needed to bring about internal balances are insufficient to restore international equilibrium, should the surplus country continue expanding, in the interests of international balance, at the expense of inflation at home, while the deficit country continues contracting and forsakes its internal goal of full employment? Should the distribution of the burden of adjustment be divided so that the deficit country suffers some unemployment and the surplus country some inflation?

Apart from the question of relative size, economists would be inclined to say that it depends on the relative cost of inflation in the surplus countries compared to the cost of excess unemployment in the deficit countries. If, for example, the cost of a given level of unemployment were greater (according to a specified system of measurement) than the cost of a given level of inflation, maximum income would be preserved, at constant exchange rates, by the burden of adjustment falling mainly on the surplus countries; if inflation were more costly, the reverse would be true.

Variable Exchange Rates

A number of problems arise when we depart from the context of a fixed exchange rate system. One problem raised by a system of flexible exchange rates concerns the domain over which exchange rates are supposed to be fixed. This raises the OPTIMUM CURRENCY AREA PROBLEM, the problem of ascertaining the appropriate domain of a fixed exchange rate area. Should each national currency fluctuate with respect to one another? Should large blocs be formed? What is the criterion by which an optimum currency area is to be defined and what are the criteria by which the conditions of optimality are to be met?

This is only one approach to the question of flexible exchange rates, although it is both theoretically interesting and practically important. Alternative approaches to the problem of flexible exchange rates are to ask which exchange rates (spot or forward) should be allowed to float, or how widely should exchange rates be allowed to fluctuate? A system of "fixed" exchange rates means, as used by the major countries today, spot exchange rates that fluctuate within narrow exchange margins of less than 1 per cent on either side of parity. The EXCHANGE MARGINS PROBLEM is the problem of finding criteria to determine how wide spot or forward exchange rates *should* fluctuate, given the goals implicit in the idea of a fixed exchange rate system. Should forward rates be fixed as well as spot rates? Should forward rates be subject to exchange margins?

Yet a third question that is involved, and is as yet unsolved, is the nature of the exchange-pegging arrangements that are desirable. Should each currency be pegged to an ultimate reserve asset like gold, such as under the gold standard as it operated in the nineteenth century, or should a major currency like the dollar be pegged to gold while other currencies are pegged directly, or through other currencies, to the dollar? The last possibility closely resembles the present system. Or should gold be demonetized? This was called, for the purposes of the conference, the GOLD-PEGGING PROBLEM, although we had no opportunity to discuss it.

Closely related to the gold-pegging problem is a CURRENCY-CHAIN PROBLEM. When dollars are attached to gold, pounds and francs are attached to the dollar, and other currencies are attached to pounds and francs, all within specified exchange margins, what mechanisms, if any, should be used to restrict the variation of exchange rates between the "satellite" currencies? If currency A is pegged to the pound sterling, and currency B to the French franc, each within 1 per cent exchange margins, the exchange rate between A's and B's currencies will be substantially wider than 1 per cent. Current International Monetary Fund rules allow a 2 per cent margin on either side of parity to avoid this problem, sanctioning this arrangement, under the articles of agreement of the IMF, as a "multiple-currency" practice. But what theoretical justification exists for this kind of exchange-pegging arrangement? These subjects need far deeper intellectual probes.

International Assets

Under a pure gold standard, central banks (if they exist at all) hold only gold. Under a bimetallic standard central banks may hold both gold and silver. Under the gold standard as it developed in the 1920's, and as it exists today, countries hold gold and foreign exchange. The choice between gold and foreign exchange, and between different types of reserve assets, depends on the yield they offer and on the relative safety of the assets, as well as on tradition and banking law.

When countries or individuals lose faith in the convertibility, at a given price, of one reserve asset into another asset, they are inclined to change the composition of their reserves. For example, when after the 1934 increase in the price of gold in the United States, hot money flowed to the United States, there was speculation that the United States authorities might lower the price of gold, and many countries and individuals shifted from gold assets to dollars. In the early postwar period, during the era of the dollar shortage, European countries built up large dollar-holdings.

In the late 1920's, there were mass conversions of foreign exchange into gold. These shifts in demand can be accounted for in part by lack of confidence in the reserve currencies, in part by a belief in the political leverage of gold (including its strategic value as a war chest), in part by a desire to force discipline on the reserve countries, and in part by a desire on the part of some countries to change the system based on the use of national currencies as international reserves. Since 1958, European countries have again been raising the proportion of gold-holdings in total reserve assets for somewhat similar motives.

The confidence problem concerns the exchangeability of one reserve asset for another at a fixed price. It can only arise if there is more than one international reserve asset, and if the mechanism for insuring convertibility of the two assets at a fixed price is not adequate. The problem arising from bimetallism in the nineteenth century is the classic example of confidence problems. The demonetization of silver in the United States, for example, had a big impact on those countries that had adopted silver as their standard of value. Under the present system the confidence problem is largely a problem of the relation between gold and the reserve currencies.

If there are two international reserve assets, say gold and a reserve currency, and if there is complete confidence that the reserve currency country can buy and sell gold freely at a fixed price, countries would be indifferent about holding either gold or the reserve currency—unless there are extra incentives for holding currency or gold. For example, if currency deposits yielded a rate of interest, or gold bore a storage cost, currency deposits would be preferred. Foreign countries may still wish to hold gold, however, for traditional reasons, or because they do not want to provide the reserve country with the benefits of a low interest loan.

Confidence is not, however, a matter of complete certainty, so that when international reserves are composed of both a reserve currency and a gold component, peripheral countries have an incentive to diversify their assets. Thus it was that, during the gold standard period, countries that were not on a strict gold standard typically held both currency reserves (especially sterling) and gold. Similarly, in the post-war period countries have held dollars, sterling, and gold, while some sterling area countries hold both sterling and dollars.

Whenever the exchange ratio between gold and a reserve currency is not believed to be permanent, speculation—both private and public—goes in one direction or another. When there is a substantial probability of a fall in the gold price, countries shift more of their balances toward currencies, as during the period following the increased United States gold price in 1934. And when the probability of a rise in the gold price, in terms of the reserve currency, is believed to be high, the demand for gold by public and private institutions goes up. These speculative demands are self-reinforcing, since sufficient gold sales during a time of bearishness about the gold price (bullishness about the currency price) may embarrass the reserve currency country sufficiently to force the price change; and similarly, speculation about a rise in the gold price, with consequent gold purchases, may embarrass the reserve country (by drawing down gold stocks) to bring about revalorization. Weakening of confidence can thus easily turn into a CRISIS PROBLEM, the problem of determining the appropriate policies in the event of a run on one or another of the reserve assets.

It has long been recognized, of course, that one possible solution to the present confidence problem, the weakness of the dollar, has been an increase in the price of gold. If gold is undervalued its price can be raised as provided for in the Articles of Agreement of the International Monetary Fund, which allow for a uniform reduction in the par values of all currencies. This solution is not attractive to economists or to U.S. authorities, for a number of well-known reasons, but it does raise an intriguing theoretical question: If practical difficulties associated with increasing the price of gold were overcome what theoretical considerations would determine a new appropriate price? This is the GOLD PRICE PROBLEM.

The international exchange-rate system is one which has n par values where n is the number of member countries in the system. The par values are expressed in terms of units of gold (or 1944 gold dollars). As we noted in discussing the redundancy problem, if gold were merely a fictitious unit of account the balance-of-payments equations of the system would be homogeneous of degree zero in the par values; if *all* par values were changed no *exchange rates* would be altered. But because gold is a commodity used as an asset in the system, the balance-of-payments equations are not homogeneous of the zero-th degree. Doubling the price of gold in terms of all currencies would affect the currency value of gold reserves. More exactly, when gold is an asset in the system, the equations are homogeneous in the first degree in three sets of variables: the par values, the domestic currency prices of commodities, and the national money supplies. In this sense there is a practical meaning to the theoretical question, how high should the price of gold be? Adjustment of stocks may allow a disequilibrium to prevail for a long time, as can the use of gold substitutes such as the dollar or a new reserve unit. But if the price of gold is a disequilibrium price the question arises—a question often brought up in practical discussions— whether an increase in the price of gold would generate new inflation in the world or simply prevent a deflation that would otherwise occur. Because gold is the only "outside money" in the system as a whole its price has definite economic significance, and cannot be assumed to be an entirely arbitrary factor.

An Institutional Problem

One final question that was considered to be in need of clarification and appropriate for discussion at the conference relates to the role of the institutions in the system. The International Monetary Fund is a participant in the international monetary system, and it is also the senior forum in which discussions for reform are centered. But time and again suggestions had been made for reforming the system along lines that would contribute to the provision of aid to less developed countries. Proposals of this type would involve linking the problem of monetary reform with the question of development aid—linking the IMF and, say, the IBRD. This possibility raises the more general institutional, theoretic problem of deciding whether functional problems in the international system—the provision of liquidity, balance of payments adjustment, freer trade, supervision of exchange rates, development planning, and so on—ought to be matched by separate institutions or whether these institutions would be more efficiently united under a more centralized control system. Since each of the functions overlaps—

tariffs, capital flows, exchange rates, exchange controls, rules of balance-of-payments adjustment, and provision of liquidity have to be looked at as instruments in a general arsenal of policy weapons—what relations ought to be developed between the institutions—GATT, IBRD, IMF, BIS—which have responsibility for one or more of the functions? For purposes of the conference this problem was referred to as the INSTITU-TIONAL MIX PROBLEM.

In the selection of papers for the conference an outline of the problems was circulated. But it was not possible for obvious reasons to match papers with problems in any precise fashion on such short notice; there is much overlapping and numerous omissions. Nevertheless, most of the participants did attempt to make an explicit contribution to one or more of the problems outlined. The reader can judge the relevance of the problems and the success achieved by the participants at resolving them. Most of us were agreed, however, that the purposes of the conference would have been served if it helped to direct attention to gaps in the state of current knowledge and promote further theoretical research in areas where new ideas in theory have immediate practical interest.

Appendix

This appendix outlines the problems formulated for discussion at the conference, as they were circulated to participants in the spring of 1966.

The Assignment Problem

How should (monetary, fiscal, wage, tariff, exchange-rate) instruments of policy be assigned to (employment, price level, indebtedness, growth) targets of policy? Should instruments and targets be used in the same way in each country?

The major stumbling block is the assignment problem in the case of fixed exchange rates when the targets include internal balance, external balance, and economic growth.

The Speed-of-Adjustment Problem

How rapidly should adjustment to balance-of-payments disequilibria be effected? Is slow adjustment preferable to fast adjustment? What are the costs of deficits (surpluses) and how do they compare with the costs of correcting them? What precise relationships exist between the amount of available international finance and the speed of adjustment?

The Redundancy Problem

Only $n - 1$ countries in an n-country world need achieve balance-of-payments equilibrium (because of Cournot's Law). Which country, if any, should be the nth country that is spared a balance-of-payments constraint? And if all countries are required to share in the adjustment, what institutional means can be explored to exploit the extra degree of freedom for world employment or price stability? The problem is closely related to the problem of determining the distribution of the burden of adjustment between countries.

The Seigniorage Problem

Seigniorage is the difference between the value of produced money and the cost of producing it. Historically it meant the mint charge for turning gold or silver into money (often reflecting, besides cost, the degree of debasement of the currency), but in the modern context of paper money, the term can be used to refer to the command over resources (created at negligible printing cost) acquired by the authority with monopoly over the note issue. In unitary national states the seigniorage "goes to the government," and thus creates few important political problems; but in the international context the seigniorage must be "disposed of" in alternative ways.

The seigniorage problem needs much more study. How much does it amount to and who gets it? Precisely how would the seigniorage be distributed under alternative schemes to improve the international monetary system, and how should it be distributed in an ideal monetary system? If a world central bank were created what formula could be found for distributing the seigniorage gains equitably, efficiently, and in a politically acceptable way?

The Optimum Currency Area Problem

Which exchange rates (if any) should be allowed to fluctuate? How is the optimum currency domain related to the optimum political domain? What criterion of optimum currency area is most relevant?

The Currency-Chain Problem

When dollars are attached to gold, pounds and francs are pegged to the dollar, and satellite currencies are pegged to the pound and franc, all within exchange margins, what mechanisms should be used to restrict the variation of exchange rates between satellite currencies?

The Gold-Pegging Problem

Some economists have proposed that European countries should peg their currencies to gold rather than the dollar. What criteria should be used to determine optimal pegging attachments? Should gold-pegging countries hold only gold reserves; should gold-holding countries peg to the dollar? Who should perform the arbitrage operation if two areas peg to gold when private gold-arbitrage is illegal?

The Exchange-Margin Problem

How wide should exchange margins (or gold margins) be and should the central parity be fixed or allowed to "slide"? Should forward rates be pegged within the same margins as spot rates? Should forward rates be pegged and spot rates be allowed to fluctuate (freely or within wider margins)?

The Gold Price Problem

Gold has several unique qualities as an international money; *inter alia*, nobody owes it and nobody can print it. Should its role be strengthened or weakened in designing a world money? Should its price be allowed to go up, down, or remain constant?

The Composition Problem

The composition of the balance of payments matters to most countries. If the balance-of-payments statement is divided into a current account, a capital account, and a reserve account, and if adjustment is defined as correction of the reserve account, should adjustment be achieved by improving the capital account or the current account? What criteria should determine the appropriate composition of adjustment?

The Institutional Mix Problem

At present, GATT looks after tariffs, the IBRD looks after long-term lending and IMF looks after balance-of-payments problems and exchange rates. Yet each institution invades the jurisdiction of another especially in the areas of multiple exchange rates, capital flows, import substitution, and exchange control; economic problems cannot realistically be so neatly separated. This raises the question of the appropriate division of labor between institutions and, in relation to the international monetary system, the merits or disadvantages of a joint attack on lending and debt problems, commodity problems, and liquidity problems. A related problem concerns the merits of regional solutions.

The Crisis Problem

Most current proposals for international monetary reform that appear to have much chance of success are directed at making marginal changes in a fair-weather system. The most neglected problem of all is the appropriate action to take in the event of a sudden crisis, when individual central banks will be tempted to act unilaterally. What contingency plans for action in a crisis are available?

PART 2

THE CURRENCY AREA PROBLEM

THE THEORY OF OPTIMUM CURRENCY
AREAS: AN ECLECTIC VIEW

Peter B. Kenen

Introduction

When should exchange rates be fixed and when should they fluctuate? What criteria define the optimum currency area, within which the exchange rates should be pegged immutably, but whose rates should fluctuate, or at least be varied, vis-à-vis the outside world? We owe the first explicit formulation of this question to our conference chairman, Robert Mundell, and I shall preface my reply by summarizing his.[1]

In his very terse treatment of the subject, Mundell does not pause to give us many definitions, but two of them emerge inside his argument— a definition of optimality and a definition of an economic region. Optimality relates to the state of the labor market. If the prevailing exchange-rate regime, fixed or flexible, can maintain external balance without causing unemployment (or, on the other side, demand-induced wage inflation), that regime is optimal. If the currency regime within a given area causes unemployment somewhere in that area (or compels some other portion of that same area to accept inflation as the antidote to unemployment), it is not optimal. In Mundell's own words:

> In a currency area comprising different countries with national currencies the pace of employment in deficit countries is set by the willingness of surplus countries to inflate. But in a currency area comprising many regions and a single currency, the pace of inflation is set by the willingness of central authorities to allow unemployment in deficit regions.
>
> . . . But a currency area of either type cannot prevent both unemployment and inflation among its members. The fault lies not with the type of currency area, but with the domain of the currency area. The optimum currency area is not the world.[2]

1. Robert A. Mundell, "A Theory of Optimum Currency Areas," *American Economic Review*, 60, no. 4 (September 1961): 657–65.
2. *ibid.*, p. 659. Mundell's definition of optimality is quite similar to Meade's; see James E. Meade, *The Balance of Payments* (London: Oxford University Press, 1951), pp. 104–7 and 114–24.

One could readily adopt many other points of view. Thus, McKinnon has employed a different definition of optimality

> ... To describe a single currency area within which monetary-fiscal policy and flexible external exchange rates can be used to give the best resolution of three (sometimes conflicting) objectives: (1) the maintenance of full employment; (2) the maintenance of balanced international payments; (3) the maintenance of a stable internal average price level. Objective (3) assumes that any capitalist economy requires a stable-valued liquid currency to insure efficient resource allocation. ... The inclusion of objective (3) makes the problem as much a part of monetary theory as of international trade theory. The idea of optimality, then, is complex and difficult to quantify precisely. ... .[3]

I shall have something more to say about McKinnon's third objective, especially his reasons for calling it to our attention. But most of my analysis will make use of the simpler labor-market criterion.

Mundell's other definition, likewise implicit rather than explicit, relates to the delineation of an economic region. It is, again, quite simple and leads his analysis to powerful results. But those same results may not be too helpful from the standpoint of policy and will cause the two of us to part company at an early stage. Mundell's notion of a region is functional not literal. You will not find his regions on an ordinary map but must instead use an input-output table. As I understand the substance of his argument, a region is defined as a homogeneous collection of producers that use the same technology, face the same demand curve, and suffer or prosper together as circumstances change. Thus:

> ... Suppose that the world consists of two countries, Canada and the United States, each of which has separate currencies. Also assume that the continent is divided into two regions which do not correspond to national boundaries —the East, which produces goods like cars, and the West, which produces goods like lumber products.[4]

Here, Mundell has used the geographer's language, but solely for expositional convenience. It is, in fact, the difference in the product mix that distinguishes East from West.

Combining his labor-market view of optimality and his rather special

3. Ronald I. McKinnon, "Optimum Currency Areas," *American Economic Review*, 53, no. 4 (September 1963): 717. In McKinnon's model, flexible exchange rates can generate a conflict between (1) and (3) because depreciation will augment the demand for "tradable" output, draw labor away from "non-tradable" output, and cause a general increase in wages and prices.
4. Mundell, "Theory of Optimum Currency Areas," p. 659.

definition of a region, Mundell proceeds to furnish an elegant answer to the question of currency areas. He asks us to suppose that consumers shift their spending from cars to lumber products—from eastern goods to western goods. The East, of course, develops a current-account deficit in its balance of payments and an excess supply of labor. The West develops a current-account surplus and an excess demand for labor.

If workers cannot move from East to West, some way must be found to augment the demand for cars (eastern goods) and diminish the demand for lumber products (western goods). The East has to accept worse terms of trade—a decrease in the price of cars relative to lumber products sufficient to reallocate aggregate demand and thereby to eliminate the disequilibria in both regions' labor markets. And if money wage rates are sticky in both regions, eastern currency must be made cheaper in terms of western currency, whether by depreciation (a free-market change) or devaluation (a calculated alteration in a pegged exchange rate). East and West should not be joined in a monetary union, nor be made to peg their currencies once and for all; they do not comprise an optimum currency area.

What happens, however, if workers can move freely between East and West? The westward migration of unemployed eastern workers will serve to ameliorate the labor-market problems of both regions and, at the same time, will help to solve their payments problem. As workers move from East to West, their purchases of cars will be transformed from home demand into extra eastern exports; their purchases of lumber products will be transformed from western exports into extra home demand. In brief, Mundell contends that interregional factor mobility can substitute for changes in regional exchange rates, and that the entire zone through which labor can move freely delineates the right domain for a monetary union or for fixed exchange rates; with labor mobility, East and West do comprise an optimum currency area.

Peripheral Objections

Aspects of this argument call for further work. What should be done, for instance, when there is a major difference in the labor intensities of eastern and western production? Migration might then leave a residual imbalance in one region's labor market—an enduring excess supply in the East or excess demand in the West. And are we really sure that factor movements can restore a perfect balance in the regions' trade even when it does resolve both of their employment problems? Rather special patterns of consumer demand and methods of production may be needed in each region if a simple labor movement and the corresponding change in the locus of demand are to end an imbalance in two regions' labor markets and also to equilibrate the trade flow between them. Notice, finally, that the increase of demand for lumber products could stimulate additional investment in the West, leading to an increase in its income and imports large enough to open up a current-account deficit in its balance of payments.[5]

But the main lines of the argument are not at issue. Nor can one accuse Mundell of failing to perceive the ultimate, unhappy implication ✓ of his argument. When regions are defined by their activities, not geographically or politically, perfect interregional labor mobility requires perfect occupational mobility. And this can only come about when labor is homogeneous (or the several regions belonging to a single currency area display very similar skill requirements). In consequence, Mundell's approach leads to the sad certainty that the optimum currency area has always to be small. It must, indeed, be coextensive with the single-product region. In Mundell's own words:

> ...If, then, the goals of internal stability are to be rigidly pursued, it follows that the greater is the number of separate currency areas in the world, the more successfully will these goals be attained...But this seems to imply that regions ought to be defined so narrowly as to count every minor pocket of unemployment arising from labor immobility as a separate region, each of which should apparently have a separate currency![6]

Mundell and I agree that "such an arrangement hardly appeals to common sense," and we likewise agree on some of the reasons.[7] If every community, however small, could issue its own currency, money would no longer serve to lead us out of barter; and if each region's central bank could run its own printing press with complete autonomy, we would soon have to face the difficult problem that McKinnon posed.

5. See Marina v. N. Whitman, *International and Interregional Payments Adjustment: A Synthetic View. Princeton Studies in International Finance*, No. 19 (Princeton: Princeton Univ. Press, 1967). Mrs. Whitman suggests that this variety of current-account deficit may even be needed to maintain overall balance in interregional payments, for some of the additional investment in the West may be financed by capital imports from the East.

6. Mundell, "Theory of Optimum Currency Areas," p. 662.

7. One of them, in fact, anticipates McKinnon's view, and can best be summarized by quoting Mundell again: "The thesis of those who favor flexible exchange rates is that the community in question is not willing to accept variations in its real income through adjustments in its money wage rate or price level, but that it is willing to accept virtually the same changes...through variations in the rate of exchange.... Now as the currency area grows smaller and the proportion of imports in total consumption grows, this assumption becomes increasingly unlikely." (*Ibid.*, p. 663.)

Investors would be deprived of a "stable-valued liquid currency" to hold as a store of value or use as a standard of value when allocating capital among single-product regions.[8]

It has, of course, been argued that changes in exchange rates, actual or possible, do not much deter international investment and, *in extenso*, might not be barriers to a satisfactory allocation of capital among single-product regions.[9] This argument, however, draws heavily on the very special experience of Canada; it assumes that exchange rates will not wobble much; and, most importantly, it forecasts that forward markets will come into being so that traders and investors can translate uncertainty into calculable costs. Given a multitude of microregions, each with its own currency, the foreign exchange markets might be quite thin; few banks and brokers would be able or willing to deal in the host of currencies that would then abound and might not be capable of taking on net positions, long and short, large enough to guarantee stabilizing speculation. To make matters worse, single-product regions may suffer significant disturbances in their foreign trade and payments, so that exchange rates may fluctuate quite widely. More on this point soon.

I come now to another collection of arguments that Mundell and McKinnon have not explored sufficiently. Economic sovereignty has several dimensions, two of them particularly relevant to the problem of managing aggregate demand and maintaining full employment. Fiscal and monetary policies must go hand in hand, and if there is to be an "optimum policy mix," they should have the same domains.[10] There

8. If there were a single region larger than the rest, or more prudent in managing its money, that region's currency might well come into use as an interregional standard of value. In such a case, however, many debts and claims internal to smaller regions would come to be denominated in that "key currency," driving other currencies out of common use. One wonders if the courts of the other microregions would be willing to enforce contracts of this type. Doing so, after all, they would help to undermine their own regions' currencies, much as the Supreme Court of the United States would have undermined the legal status of the dollar if it had upheld the gold-clause contracts in the 1930's.

9. See, e.g., Egon Sohmen, *Flexible Exchange Rates* (Chicago: University of Chicago Press, 1961), p. 19.

10. This term, another of our chairman's contributions to our jargon, is usually employed to denote the combination of monetary and budgetary policies needed to maintain external and internal balance. If, of course, exchange rates are left free to fluctuate, furnishing external balance, the two internal instruments need not be aligned precisely. Yet an "optimum policy mix" is not unimportant to domestic demand management, taken by itself. Too much reliance on one of the two instruments, monetary or budgetary, can have severe and deplorable consequences for particular sectors of the domestic economy. When, as this is written, interest rates are driven high to make good deficiencies in fiscal policy, construction is hit hard, as is investment in public facilities that have to be financed by bond issues subject to approval by the electorate.

should be a treasury, empowered to tax and spend, opposite each central bank, whether to cooperate with monetary policy or merely to quarrel with it. From other viewpoints, too, the domain of fiscal policy ought to coincide with the currency area or, at least, be no larger than the monetary zone. Otherwise, the treasury will face a host of problems.[11]

How would taxes be collected if a single fiscal system were to span a number of currency areas, each of them entitled to alter its exchange rate? How would a treasury maintain the desired distribution of total tax collections? Suppose that the treasury levied an income tax to be paid in each resident's regional currency and that the West was printing money faster than the East, causing a more rapid rise in prices and incomes. Unless the West's currency were to depreciate *pari passu* with the faster rise in money incomes, the West would come to pay a larger fraction of the tax (and if the tax were graduated, might also have to furnish a larger share of the goods and services absorbed by the government, as its tax payments would rise faster than its prices). The same problem would arise even more dramatically if the treasury relied on property taxation. Property values and property assessments might not keep pace with money incomes, and even if the difference in rates of inflation were exactly matched by the change in the exchange rate, there could be a significant redistribution of the tax burden.[12]

In which currency, moreover, would the central government pay for goods and services? Which one would it use to pay its civil servants?[13] And what may be the thorniest practical problem, in which currency should the central government issue its own debt instruments? None of these difficulties would be insurmountable, but ulcer rates in govern-

11. At one point, Meade appears to take a different point of view, arguing for flexible exchange rates within a common market (see James E. Meade, "The Balance-of-Payments Problems of a European Free-Trade Area," *Economic Journal*, 67, no. 3 (September 1957): 379–96. But Meade is not talking of an economic union with a common fiscal system.

12. Analogous problems would arise in respect to transfer payments—and are not hypothetical. Many close observers of the European scene argue that exchange rates can no longer change within the European Economic Community, for any change would undermine the precarious agreement that will govern contributions to the fund financing EEC farm price supports.

13. Notice, in this connection, that a major difference between the currency composition of government receipts and the currency composition of government spending would force the treasury into the exchange market where, willfully or otherwise, it might well become the single speculator capable of altering regional exchange rates. In this case, "the speculative argument against flexible exchange rates would assume weighty dimensions" (Mundell, "Theory of Optimum Currency Areas," p. 663).

ment are already far too high, and ought not to be increased unnecessarily. In our day, too, government activities may well be subject to important economies of scale. This is surely true in matters of defense and may be true of civil functions. If, then, an optimum currency area should be no smaller than the rather large domain of a least-cost government, it may have to span a great number of single-product regions. If, further, a fiscal system does encompass many such regions, it may actually contribute to internal balance, offsetting the advantage claimed for fragmentation. It is a chief function of fiscal policy, using both sides of the budget, to offset or compensate for regional differences, whether in earned income or in unemployment rates. The large-scale transfer payments built into fiscal systems are interregional, not just interpersonal, and the rules which regulate many of those transfer payments relate to the labor market, just like the criterion Mundell has employed to mark off the optimum currency area. When one looks at fiscal policy in macroeconomic terms, one comes to the unhappy view espoused by Mundell; budgetary policies cannot help but cause inflation in already-prosperous parts of an economy if they are designed to stimulate demand and thereby to eliminate local unemployment. Yet this is not the only way to look at fiscal policy. Given the big numbers, total taxation, and total expenditure, the budget can still combat localized recessions. When a region or community suffers a decline in its external sales, a trade-balance deficit, and internal unemployment,

> ...its federal tax payments diminish at once, slowing the decline in its purchasing power and compressing the cash outflow on its balance of payments. There is also an inflow of federal money—of unemployment benefits. Furthermore, a region can borrow (or sell off securities) in the national capital market more easily than countries can borrow abroad. Finally, regions can...obtain discretionary aid from the central government; special programs of financial and technical assistance to depressed areas have been enacted by a number of countries, including the United States.[14]

On balance, then, a region may come out ahead by foregoing the right to issue its own currency and alter its exchange rate, in order to participate in a major fiscal system.

To sum up, an efficient fiscal system must be made to span many single-product regions and should be coextensive with (or no larger

14. Peter B. Kenen, "Toward a Supranational Monetary System," mimeographed (International Economics Workshop: Columbia University, 1966), pp. 13–14.

than) a single, if non-optimal, currency area. The logic of Mundell's approach, however impeccable, should not cause us to convene another San Francisco conference, there to carve the world up, rather than unite it, so that single-product regions can have their own currencies and can let them fluctuate.

And here, perhaps, Mundell and I are not far apart. The purpose of his argument, he tells us at the end, is not to recommend that there be more currencies, but merely to determine when one ought to recommend that existing currencies be fixed or flexible. He asks us to agree that "the validity of the argument for flexible exchange rates...hinges on the closeness with which nations correspond to regions. The argument works best if each nation (and currency) has internal factor mobility and external factor immobility,"[15] On first reading this last passage, incidentally, I was certain that "regions" had been redefined. Here, it would appear that a region is delineated by factor mobility, not by its principal activity and, therefore, the degree to which its industries suffer the same changes in product demand. Yet when one reads these sentences a little bit differently, the seeming inconsistency vanishes at once. For "regions" let me substitute "optimum currency areas," then paraphrase the argument.[16] Exchange rates should be fixed between single-product regions when labor moves freely between them, for then there is no need to change the terms of trade when a region encounters an external disturbance; and when there is mobility across all the regions making up a nation, that whole nation is an optimum currency area. When, further, workers can move freely between any pair of countries, those two countries jointly form an optimum currency area and can peg their currencies, one to the other. When, contrarily, there is no mobility between the single-product regions of a single nation, it may be very difficult to maintain full employment and price stability throughout its territory; the nation must rely on rather sophisticated internal policies to reallocate demand rather than augment or curb it. When, finally, labor does not move between a pair of countries, their currencies should fluctuate, one against the other, so as to accomplish changes in their terms of trade. Regions, to repeat, are still to be defined by their activities; optimum currency areas are to be defined by the interregional mobility of labor.

15. Mundell, "Theory of Optimum Currency Areas," p. 664.
16. I dwell on this small point in order to be spared another dozen papers by students who believe that they have discovered a fatal flaw in Mundell's analysis and that the whole argument must therefore be wrong.

A Competing Principle

But now it is my task to show that Mundell's approach is not wholly adequate—that marking off zones of perfect labor mobility may not be the best way to delineate optimum currency areas, for perfect mobility rarely prevails. Other criteria will have to be employed when, at the millennium, central bankers come to us and ask if an exchange rate should be fixed or flexible. In my view, diversity in a nation's product mix, the number of single-product regions contained in a single country, may be more relevant than labor mobility. I hope, indeed, to make three points:

> 1) That a well-diversified national economy will not have to undergo changes in its terms of trade as often as a single-product national economy.
> 2) That when, in fact, it does confront a drop in the demand for its principal exports, unemployment will not rise as sharply as it would in a less-diversified national economy.
> 3) That the links between external and domestic demand, especially the link between exports and investment, will be weaker in diversified national economies, so that variations in domestic employment "imported" from abroad will not be greatly aggravated by corresponding variations in capital formation.

The first of these three points can be made most easily. A country that engages in a number of activities is also apt to export a wide range of products. Each individual export may be subject to disturbances, whether due to changes in external demand or in technology. But if those disturbances are independent, consequent on variations in the composition of expenditure or output, rather than massive macro-economic swings affecting the entire export array, the law of large numbers will come into play. At any point in time, a country can expect to suffer significant reversals in export performance, but also to enjoy significant successes. Its aggregate exports, then, are sure to be more stable than those of an economy less thoroughly diversified. From the standpoint of external balance, taken by itself, economic diversification, reflected in export diversification, serves, ex ante, to forestall the need for frequent changes in the terms of trade and, therefore, for frequent changes in national exchange rates.[17]

17. Anyone familiar with random processes knows, of course, that they may not average out quickly or perfectly. That is why the gambler has to have a bankroll and why central banks have to have reserves. If, in fact, one views the balance of payments as a simple sum of stochastic processes, the deficit or surplus, measured by the change in central bank reserves, should obey the central limit

One has at once to qualify this simple proposition. A diversification of output and exports cannot guarantee domestic stability, even when external shocks tend to average out. There must be sufficient occupa-tional mobility to reabsorb the labor and capital idled by adverse disturbances. Here, two possibilities arise. If, on the one hand, external disturbances are truly independent because each export product is quite different from the rest, export earnings will be stable but factor mobility may be very low. Products that differ when classified by final use may differ in their modes of manufacture, so that the factors of production used in making one of them may not be adaptable to making any other. If, on the other hand, the several separate exports of a single country are, in fact, close substitutes when classified by final use, disturbances afflicting external demand will not be fully independent—the law of large numbers will not apply—but there may be more mobility between export industries. Products that are similar in final use are apt to have similar factor requirements, and workers who are idled by an export disturbance may be more readily absorbed in other activities.

My second point is closely related to the first but deals with the consequence of export fluctuations after they appear. A diversification of output will mitigate the damage done by external shocks, not merely diminish the likelihood of major shocks. To make this point, I shall contrast four distinct economies, asking what they have to do to maintain external balances when they are afflicted by exogenous disturbances. These four economies are perfectly competitive and make use of a single variable input, standardized labor, but they differ in two ways.[18] Output is diversified in the first and second countries; each of them produces an export good and an import-competing good. The third and fourth economies, by contrast, are not diversified; they specialize completely in export production. Furthermore, the first and third are small economies, with no influence at all on world prices,[19] while the second

theorem, exhibiting a normal or nearly normal distribution, and a central bank's reserves ought to be an increasing function of the variance or standard deviation of that normal distribution. Surprisingly enough, these things are true; see Peter B. Kenen and Elinor B. Yudin, "The Demand for International Reserves," *Review of Economics and Statistics*, 97, no. 3 (August 1965): 242–50. For a further look at the balance of payments as a somewhat fancier stochastic process, see my *Computer Simulation of the United States Balance of Payments*, mimeographed (International Economics Workshop: Columbia University, 1965).

18. For a more formal representation of these economies, and proofs of the theorems that follow, examine the Appendix.

19. Hence, the first and third resemble the model economies considered in McKinnon's note on optimum currency areas, except that they do not produce "non-tradable" commodities and cannot shift labor (or domestic demand) to and from their local sectors when domestic prices change.

and fourth are large economies, facing a determinate demand for their exports.

Consider, first, a simple exogenous disturbance, an increase in wage rates more rapid than in import prices. Here, all four economies must make the same exchange-rate change to stabilize employment; the requisite devaluation or depreciation must equal the difference between the rates of change of wages and of import prices. Yet the four economies behave rather differently when their central banks opt for fixed exchange rates. In each case, employment is certain to decline, but the changes in employment will not be identical. In the small-country case, the two-product economy will suffer a smaller decline in employment if its export industry has the larger elasticity of demand for labor with respect to real wage rates.[20] In the large-country case, this same condition has to hold, but does not suffice; there is, indeed, a strong presumption that the two-product national economy will suffer the larger change in employment.[21] Facing this type of exogenous disturbance, then, diversified economies may be at a handicap.[22]

Consider, next, a different class of exogenous disturbances, more like the one that figures in Mundell's analysis. Seen by the small countries, this type of shock will appear as an exogenous change in the terms of trade; seen by the large countries, it will appear as an exogenous change in export demand at given terms of trade. Here, there are perceptible differences in the size of the exchange-rate change needed for internal balance, not just in the size of the change in employment occurring when the central banks opt for fixed exchange rates. Whether small or large, the two-product economy is bound to experience the smaller change in its exchange rate.[23] Furthermore, product diversification always serves to shield the labor force from this class of shock. The two-product economy suffers the smaller change in employment under fixed exchange rates, and the larger the fraction of the labor force engaged in import-competing production, the smaller the change in employment occasioned by a change in the terms of trade or demand for exports.[24]

20. See equation (4.5) of the Appendix.
21. See equation (4.6) of the Appendix.
22. Notice, moreover, that this strange result derives from the mere fact of diversification, not from mobility inside an economy. Both parts of the labor force, in export- and import-competing production, are affected the same way by changes in the money wage relative to import prices.
23. See equations (4.7) and (4.8) of the Appendix.
24. See equations (4.9) and (4.10) of the Appendix, and notice once again that the extra stability afforded a diversified economy derives from the mere fact that it has more industries, not from any labor flow inside the country. The two disturbances considered here do not affect employment in the import-competing

I come now to my third point concerning diversification. Here, I shall combine the first of those three points, concerning the advantages conferred ex ante by export diversity, with my earlier remark, concerning the connection between export demand and the stability of capital formation.

Suppose that an economy is operating at full steam, with no idle capacity in any of its sectors. An increase of demand for that country's exports will introduce damaging inflationary pressures. And those pressures will be amplified in two separate ways—by the familiar Keynesian multiplier and by an increase in capital formation as exporters undertake to satisfy their customers. Exports and investment will increase together, giving a double thrust to aggregate demand. From the standpoint of external balance, this may not be bad. Imports will rise faster and are more apt to offset the initial rise in exports, narrowing the gap in the current-account balance. But from the standpoint of internal balance, the increase of investment induced by the rise in exports will put a larger strain on domestic policy.[25]

Clearly, a country will be least exposed to this compound instability if its exports are thoroughly diversified and the disturbances afflicting

---

industry. For labor mobility to play a part in stabilizing overall employment, there must be a change in the exchange rate or a decrease of the money wage relative to import prices; these would stimulate production in the import-competing industry and transfer idle workers from the export industry.

25. In the paper cited earlier, Mrs. Whitman has supplied an elegant analysis of these phenomena and, what may be most important, of the complications introduced when some of the investment is financed by foreigners. Here, some simple algebra can illustrate my point. Using the familiar Keynesian relationships:

$$dY = dC + dI + dX - dM,$$
$$dC = (1 - s) dY,$$
$$dM = m \cdot dY,$$
$$dB = dX - dM.$$

Introduce a simple link between exports and investment:

$$dI = r \cdot dX.$$

Then:

$$dY = (1 + r) dX/(s + m) \quad \text{and} \quad dB = (s - rm) dX/(s + m).$$

The change in income is an increasing function of the link between exports and investment, while the change in the trade balance is a decreasing function of that same connection, r. Note, in passing, that a diversified economy may have a rather small marginal propensity to import (see Whitman, *International and Interregional Payments*, p. 8), so that dY and dB may be increasing functions of diversification; external disturbances will not spill back out. This may be the chief counterargument to my own contention that diversified economies are the least vulnerable to external shocks and have the least need for flexible rates to maintain internal balance.

those exports are, in consequence, fairly well randomized. The corresponding fluctuations in domestic investment may not average out as well, since an increase of demand for any single export may increase investment in that export industry, while an equal decrease of demand for some other export may not cause a corresponding decrease in investment. Here, much will depend on the capital-intensities of the nation's industries and on investors' judgments regarding the duration of the export disturbance. Yet the asymmetries, if they exist, cannot be large enough to vitiate my basic point. Diversity in exports, protecting the economy from external shocks, will surely help to stabilize capital formation, easing the burden that has to be borne by internal policies.

Again, a major caveat: My argument does not apply when changes in export demand arise from business-cycle swings. When those occur, the whole range of exports will be hit, and export diversification cannot forestall "imported" instability.

This point has been made before and has, indeed, been offered as the principal criterion for choosing a particular exchange-rate regime. Fixed rates, it is said, are much to be preferred if one's own authorities, especially the central bank, are less adept or more prone to err than those of other countries. With fixed rates, the outside world can be made to bear some part of the consequences of one's own mistakes.[26] If, conversely, foreigners are less adept at economic management, flexible exchange rates are much to be preferred, to insulate a stable domestic economy from another country's errors.

These are potent arguments and may even be decisive. They did, in fact, dominate the Canadian debate a few years ago. But surely they do not belong to the theory of optimum currency areas. Optimality has always to be judged from a global point of view,[27] and these defensive arguments are far from cosmopolitan. Countries which adopt fixed

26. This point is the counterpart of another by Mundell: That fiscal policy is more potent under flexible exchange rates "because leakages through foreign trade are closed by changes in the exchange rate," and that the potency of monetary policy is increased even more because of its effects on capital movements; an increase of interest rates, attracting foreign capital, forces an appreciation of the home currency and a concomitant deflationary change in the current-account balance. See Robert Mundell, "Flexible Exchange Rates and Employment Policy," *Canadian Journal of Economics and Political Science*, 27, no. 4 (November 1961): 516; also Sohmen, *Flexible Exchange Rates*, p. 84.

27. If not in other areas of economic thought, certainly in matters pertaining to exchange rates. How many times have we to remind our students—and ourselves as well—that an exchange rate is common to two countries, not the exclusive national property of one or the other? How many times have we heard and ridiculed the remarkable recommendation that "all currencies should fluctuate except the U.S. dollar"?

exchange rates to diffuse their own mistakes inflict those same mistakes on their trading partners; countries which adopt flexible exchange rates compound the consequences of their neighbors' errors.

Conclusion

Where, then, do I wind up? Fixed rates, I believe are most appropriate —or least inappropriate—to well-diversified national economies. *Ex ante,* diversification serves to average out external shocks and, incidentally, to stabilize domestic capital formation. *Ex post,* it serves to minimize the damage done when averaging is incomplete. It is also a prerequisite to the internal factor mobility that Mundell has emphasized, because a continuum of national activities will maximize the number of employment opportunities for each specialized variety of labor.

One more desideratum emerges from my argument. Countries with fixed rates have also to be armed with potent and sophisticated internal policies. Remember that diversified national economies may be particularly vulnerable to the "monetary" shocks represented by a change in money wages relative to import prices. Hence, they must maintain rather close control over money-wage rates, or at least be able to align the rate of change of the money wage with rates of change prevailing abroad. Furthermore, fixed-rate countries must be armed with a wide array of budgetary policies to deal with the stubborn "pockets of unemployment" that are certain to arise from export fluctuations combined with an imperfect mobility of labor.

In brief, I come quite close to endorsing the status quo. The principal developed countries should perhaps adhere to the Bretton Woods regime, rarely resorting to changes in exchange rates.[28] The less-developed countries, being less diversified and less well-equipped with policy instruments, should make more frequent changes or perhaps resort to full flexibility.

Appendix

To sort out the effects of diversification, consider the economies described in the text.

The Small Two-Product Economy

As labor is the only variable input, the two outputs, X_1 and X_2, can be

---

[28] If so, however, they must have large reserves. For a longer argument along these same lines, see my "Toward a Supranational Monetary System," cited above.

written as functions of employment, N_1 and N_2, and those functions will display diminishing returns:

$$X_1 = g_1(N_1), \qquad g_1' > 0, g_1'' < 0 \qquad (1.1)$$
$$X_2 = g_2(N_2), \qquad g_2' > 0, g_2'' < 0 \qquad (1.2)$$

Next, define total employment, N, and real income, Y, using the price of the export product as numeraire:

$$N = N_1 + N_2 \qquad (1.3)$$

$$Y = X_1 + \frac{1}{p} \cdot X_2 \qquad (1.4)$$

$$p = P_1/P_2 \qquad (1.5)$$

Furthermore, labor will be paid a money wage, W, equal to the value of its marginal product, so that:

$$W = P_1 \cdot g_1' \qquad (1.6)$$
$$W = P_2 \cdot g_2' \qquad (1.7)$$

Now define the domestic consumption of X_1 and X_2 on the supposition that there is no net saving, so that expenditure will always equal income:

$$X_1^c = C(Y, p) \qquad (1.8)$$
$$X_2^c = (Y - X_1^c)p \qquad (1.9)$$

Note that (1.8) and (1.9) imply a continuous equality between exports and imports.[29] Finally, define the foreign-currency prices of the two products, P_1^f and P_2^f, and write the exchange rate, R, in units of foreign currency per unit of home currency. Then:

$$RP_1 = P_1^f \qquad (1.10)$$
$$RP_2 = P_2^f \qquad (1.11)$$

If W, R, P_1^f and P_2^f are treated as exogenous, the eleven equations given above uniquely determine X_1, X_2, N_1, N_2, Y, p, P_1, P_2, X_1^c, and X_2^c.

The Large Two-Product Economy

Use (1.1) through (1.9) and (1.11) above, but replace (1.10) with a demand function for exports, X_1^e:

$$X_1^e = X_1 - X_1^c = E(RP_1/P_2^f, t) \qquad (1.10')$$

where t is an exogenous disturbance.

29. Exports will be $(X_1 - X_1^c)$ and imports will be valued at $(X_2^c - X_2)/p$. Invoking (1.9) and (1.4), above, imports can be written as $(Y - X_1^c - X_2/p)$, which is $(X_1 - X_1^c)$.

The Small One-Product Economy

Use (1.1), (1.5), (1.6), and (1.8) through (1.11), but replace (1.3) and (1.4) with:

$$N = N_1 \tag{1.3'}$$
$$Y = X_1 \tag{1.4'}$$

This economy has nine equations and an equal number of endogenous variables; equations (1.2) and (1.7) have dropped out, but so too have X_2 and N_2.

The Large One-Product Economy

Use (1.1), (1.3'), (1.4'), (1.5), (1.6), (1.8), (1.9), (1.10'), and (1.11). This economy, like the one before has nine equations and nine endogenous variables.

To simplify subsequent analysis, rewrite the essential part of each economic model. For the small two-product case:

$$N = N_1 + N_2 \tag{2.1}$$

$$Y = g_1(N_1) + \frac{1}{p} \cdot g_2(N_2) \tag{2.2}$$

$$p = P_1^f/P_2^f \tag{2.3}$$

$$RW = P_1^f \cdot g_1' \tag{2.4}$$

$$RW = P_2^f \cdot g_2'. \tag{2.5}$$

For the large two-product case, use (2.1), (2.2), and (2.5), above, but replace (2.3) and (2.4) with

$$p = P_1/P_2^f \tag{2.3'}$$

$$W = P_1 \cdot g_1' \tag{2.4'}$$

and combine (1.8) and (1.10') into

$$g_1(N_1) = C(Y, p) + E(p, t). \tag{2.6}$$

For the small one-product case, use (2.3) and (2.4) above, but replace (2.1) and (2.2) with

$$N = N_1 \tag{2.1'}$$

$$Y = g_1(N_1), \tag{2.2'}$$

and for the large one-product case, use (2.1'), (2.2'), (2.3'), (2.4'), and (2.6).

Differentiate (2.1) through (2.5) to furnish four equations for the small two-product country:

$$dN_1 + dN_2 - dN = 0 \tag{3.1}$$

$$g'_1\, dN_1 + g'_1\, dN_2 - dY - (X_2/p)\overset{*}{p} = 0 \tag{3.2}$$

$$\frac{1}{e_1 \cdot N_1}\, dN_1 - \overset{*}{p} = (\overset{*}{P'_2} - \overset{*}{W} - \overset{*}{R}) \tag{3.3}$$

$$\frac{1}{e_1 \cdot N_1}\, dN_1 - \frac{1}{e_2 \cdot N_2}\, dN_2 - \overset{*}{p} = 0 \tag{3.4}$$

where $\overset{*}{p}$, $\overset{*}{P'_2}$, $\overset{*}{W}$, and $\overset{*}{R}$ are the percentage rates of change in p, P'_2, W, and R, and where $e_1 = -(g'_1/g''_1)/N_1$ and $e_2 = -(g'_2/g''_2)/N_2$, the elasticities of N_1 and N_2 with respect to real wage rates. Here, the percentage change in relative prices, $\overset{*}{p}$, is exogenous; the four equations (3.1) through (3.4) suffice merely to solve for dN_1, dN_2, dN, and dY.

Differentiate (2.1), (2.2), (2.3'), (2.4'), (2.5), and (2.6) to obtain five equations for the large two-product country: equations (3.1) through (3.4) and

$$g'_1\, dN_1 - c_1 \cdot dY + (n^c \cdot X_1^c + n^e \cdot X_1^e)\overset{*}{p} = dX_1^{ea} \tag{3.5}$$

where $c_1 = (\partial C/\partial Y)$, the marginal propensity to spend on X_1; where $n^c = -(\partial C/\partial p)(p/X_1^c)$, the price elasticity of home demand for X_1; where $n^e = -(\partial E/\partial p)(p/X_1^e)$, the price elasticity of foreign demand for X_1, and where dX_1^{ea} is the autonomous change in export demand, $(\partial E/\partial t)\,dt$. Here, the percentage change in relative prices, $\overset{*}{p}$, is endogenous; the five equations (3.1) through (3.5) suffice to solve for dN_1, dN_2, dN, dY, and $\overset{*}{p}$.

Differentiate (2.1'), (2.2'), (2.3), and (2.4) to obtain two equations for the small one-product country:

$$g'_1\, dN - dY = 0 \tag{3.6}$$

$$\frac{1}{e_1 \cdot N}\, dN - \overset{*}{p} = (\overset{*}{P'_2} - \overset{*}{W} - \overset{*}{R}). \tag{3.7}$$

Here, again, $\overset{*}{p}$ is exogenous; equations (3.6) and (3.7) suffice merely to solve for dN and dY.

Finally, differentiate (2.1'), (2.2'), (2.3'), (2.4'), and (2.6) to obtain three equations for the large one-product country: Equations (3.6), (3.7), and (3.5), but with total N replacing N_2 in (3.5). These three equations suffice to solve for dN, dY, and $\overset{*}{p}$.

—

Now write out the changes in employment, dN, attaching a superscript to each result so as to identify the case from which it comes. In the small one-product country:

$$dN^{1s} = Ne_1(\overset{*}{P_2^f} - \overset{*}{W} - \overset{*}{R} + \overset{*}{p}). \tag{4.1}$$

In the small two-product country

$$dN_1 = N_1 \cdot e_1(\overset{*}{P_2^f} - \overset{*}{W} - \overset{*}{R} + \overset{*}{p}),$$

$$dN_2 = N_2 \cdot e_2(\overset{*}{P_2^f} - \overset{*}{W} - \overset{*}{R}),$$

$$dN^{2s} = [Ne_1 + N_2(e_2 - e_1)](\overset{*}{P_2^f} - \overset{*}{W} - \overset{*}{R}) + (N_1 \cdot e_1)\overset{*}{p}. \tag{4.2}$$

In the large one-product country

$$dN^{1l} = \frac{1}{D_1} [n^\alpha(\overset{*}{P_2^f} - \overset{*}{W} - \overset{*}{R}) + dX_1^{ea}] \tag{4.3}$$

where $n^\alpha = (n^c \cdot X_1^c + n^e \cdot X_1^e)$ and $D_1 = g_1'(1 - c_1) + n^\alpha/Ne_1$ (with $D_1 > 0$ because $c_1 < 1$ when X_2 is not an inferior good). Finally, in the large two-product country

$$dN_1 = \frac{1}{D_2} \{[(n^\alpha + c_1 \cdot X_2/p) + c_1(N_2 \cdot e_2)g_1'](\overset{*}{P_2^f} - \overset{*}{W} - \overset{*}{R}) + dX_1^{ea}\},$$

$$dN_2 = (N_2 \cdot e_2)(\overset{*}{P_2^f} - \overset{*}{W} - \overset{*}{R}),$$

$$dN^{2l} = \frac{1}{D_2} \left\{ \left[\frac{Ne_1 + N_2(e_2 - e_1)}{N_1 \cdot e_1} (n^\alpha + c_1 \cdot X_2/p) + (N_2 \cdot e_2)g_1' \right] \right.$$
$$\left. \times (\overset{*}{P_2^f} - \overset{*}{W} - \overset{*}{R}) + dX_1^{ea} \right\} \tag{4.4}$$

where $D_2 = D_1 + [n^\alpha(N_2/N) + c_1 \cdot X_2/p]/(N_1 \cdot e_1)$. The new arguments figuring in D_2 represent the two effects of product diversification. The term $n^\alpha(N_2/N)$ is the direct effect of splitting the labor force into N_1 and N_2. The term $c_1 \cdot X_2/p$ is an indirect terms-of-trade effect, measuring the change in home spending on X_1 resulting from a change in relative prices that alters the X_1 value of X_2 output and, to that extent, alters the national income. It takes this form because the X_1 value of national income, Y, is used as an argument in the demand function for X_1, equation (1.8), above.

Now let $\overset{*}{p} = 0$ in (4.1) and (4.2), let $dX_1^{ea} = 0$ in (4.3) and (4.4), and let $\overset{*}{R} = 0$ for fixed exchange rates. Pairing off the countries according to size:

$$dN^{1s} - dN^{2s} = N_2(e_1 - e_2)(\overset{*}{P_2^f} - \overset{*}{W}) \tag{4.5}$$

$$dN^{1l} - dN^{2l} = \frac{1}{D_2} \left\{ N_2(e_1 - e_2)(n^\alpha + c_1 \cdot X_2/p)/(N_1 \cdot e_1) \right.$$
$$\left. - g_1' \left[N_2 \cdot e_2 + (1 - c_1)Ne_1 \left(\frac{D_2 - D_1}{D_1} \right) \right] \right\}$$
$$\times (\overset{*}{P_2^f} - \overset{*}{W}) \tag{4.6}$$

In the small-country case, the condition $e_1 > e_2$ is sufficient to diminish variations in employment arising from disparities between $\overset{*}{P_2^f}$ and $\overset{*}{W}$. In the large-country case, $e_1 > e_2$ is needed but does not suffice; the other argument of (4.6) is unambiguously positive. When $\overset{*}{P_2^f} \neq \overset{*}{W}$, then, the diversified economy may suffer larger changes in employment.[30]

Next, let $\overset{*}{P_2^f} = \overset{*}{W}$ to study the external shocks $\overset{*}{p}$ and dX_1^{ea}. Whereas, before, all four economies had to make the very same changes in exchange rates for internal balance ($dN = 0$), here, each economy must make a different change. Using (4.1) through (4.4), compute the requisite changes in exchange rates and the pairwise differences. As:

$$\overset{*}{R}^{1s} = \overset{*}{p},$$
$$\overset{*}{R}^{2s} = (1 - \overset{*}{V})\overset{*}{p},$$
$$\overset{*}{R}^{1l} = \frac{dX_1^{ea}}{n^\alpha},$$
$$\overset{*}{R}^{2l} = \frac{(1 - V)\,dX_1^{ea}}{n^\alpha + c_1 \cdot X_2/p + N_2 \cdot e_2(1 - V)g_1'},$$

where $V = (N_1 \cdot e_1)/[(N_1 \cdot e_1) + (N_2 \cdot e_2)]$, then:

$$\overset{*}{R}^{1s} - \overset{*}{R}^{2s} = (1 - V)\overset{*}{p} \tag{4.7}$$

$$\overset{*}{R}^{1l} - \overset{*}{R}^{2l} = \frac{Vn^\alpha + c_1 \cdot X_2/p + N_2 \cdot e_2(1 - V)g_1'}{n^\alpha[n^\alpha + c_1 \cdot X_2/p + N_2 \cdot e_2(1 - V)g_1']}\,dX_1^{ea}. \tag{4.8}$$

The one-product economy is bound to experience the larger change in its exchange rate.

30. Mere size, however, is advantageous. In the one-product case, for example: $dN^{1s} - dN^{1l} = \frac{1}{D_1} Ne_1(1 - c_1)g_1'(\overset{*}{P_2^f} - \overset{*}{W})$. The small country will experience the larger change in aggregate employment.

If, now, $\overset{*}{R} = 0$, $\overset{*}{p}$ and dX_1^{ea} lead to different changes in aggregate employment:

$$dN^{1s} - dN^{2s} = (N_2 \cdot e_2)\overset{*}{p} \tag{4.9}$$

$$dN^{1l} - dN^{2l} = \left(\frac{D_2 - D_1}{D_1 \cdot D_2}\right) dX_1^{ea}$$

$$= \left[\frac{n^\alpha(N_2/N) + c_1 \cdot X_2/p}{(N_1 \cdot e_1)D_1 \cdot D_2}\right] dX^{ea} \tag{4.10}$$

In each case, the diversified national economy suffers the smaller change in employment.

FLUCTUATING EXCHANGE RATES IN THE NINETEENTH CENTURY: THE EXPERIENCES OF AUSTRIA AND RUSSIA

Leland B. Yeager

Historical experience is relevant to present-day discussions of alternative monetary and exchange-rate systems. This paper bears on the question whether a fluctuating rate is likely to fluctuate *wildly*, and what circumstances increase or reduce the danger of its doing so. The paper mainly emphasizes the degree of fluctuation in the short run, within and between days, weeks, and months; the evidence comes largely from specific episodes.

Similar Backgrounds

Austria-Hungary and Russia in the late nineteenth century were both semideveloped countries, at best, with foreign trade heavily dependent on agricultural exports, with long histories of government budget difficulties, and with haphazardly regulated money supplies. Both countries supposedly provided standard illustrations of the arguments against irredeemable currency and fluctuating exchange rates (the same arguments still so usual nowadays), though few writers discussed the two experiences in detail. This paper focuses mainly on the thirteen years 1879–91, since that period counts as a qualitatively distinct episode in Austro-Hungarian monetary history and is the period I have looked into most closely. By coincidence, the same period forms a rather distinct episode for Russia, also, since 1879 was its first year of peace after another bout of wartime inflation and 1892 saw Sergei Witte become finance minister and begin his operations to put Russia onto the gold standard.

After the Napoleonic Wars, both Austria and Russia eventually restored the redeemability of their currencies in silver at new (devalued) parities. Around mid-century, the expenses of wars and revolutions inflated both currencies off their silver standards again. Partly because of further wars, efforts to re-establish their parities met little success. The irredeemable gulden continued to fluctuate with no effective parity until

I am indebted to Mr. Earl W. Good for computations and to the Relm Foundation and persons too numerous to list here for help with a larger project on which the Austrian part of this paper is based.

1892. By 1879, meanwhile, the world-market price of silver had fallen far enough to make a paper gulden again worth fully as much as its legal equivalent in bullion. The Austrian and Hungarian governments, in a legally informal and precarious way, then discontinued the free coinage of silver on private account. The officially stated reason was that a huge spurt in the volume of private orders had completely swamped the capacity of the coinage machinery for the foreseeable future, but unofficial observers were more frank in pointing out the danger of silver inflation if the step had not been taken. For the next thirteen years (but most markedly from mid-1885 on) the gulden was worth *more* than the quantity of metal that legally defined it. This phenomenon was almost unprecedented in monetary history and caused difficulties for metallist theories of the value of money. Not until 1893 did the world-market depreciation of silver carry far enough to put the more severely inflated ruble into the same peculiar position (except briefly in 1876, just before the war with Turkey brought further inflation).

The Gulden

The Austrian gulden was quite free of any stabilizing official intervention along the lines of an exchange equalization account. (The nearest thing to an exception—and not very near—is the gold-buying program begun by the Hungarian government in 1889 or 1890 in preparation for adopting the gold standard.) This fact seems clear from my finding no mention of any such intervention in contemporary writings and debates, from statements by the Austro-Hungarian Bank that it did not intervene and from its balance sheets, from the reluctance of the Bank to begin intervening even after passage of the gold-standard legislation of 1892, from comment on these post-1892 operations as a novelty, and from the more recent judgments of several monetary historians.[1] The contrasting Russian policy will be noted below.

In the thirteen years that mainly concern us, the price of a ten pound bill on London on the Vienna Bourse moved between an intra-day high of 129.40 guldens on February 3, 1887 and an intra-day low of 111.00 guldens on September 3, 1890; the rate on London thus fell by 14.2 per cent in 3 years and 7 months. But no single figure adequately describes the degree of stability or instability; we must consider the extent of

1. Including Dr. Siegfried Pressburger, economist and historian at the Austrian National Bank, and Georg Friedrich Knapp, *Staatliche Theorie des Geldes*, 2d ed. (Leipzig: Duncker & Humblot, 1918), pp. 375–76.

fluctuation in all parts of the period, as well as what was happening at times of unusually large and unusually small fluctuation.

However, it is worth noting first that the major swings of the rate seem to have been associated with changes in economic conditions at home and abroad. Figure 1 shows annual averages of the rate and of a

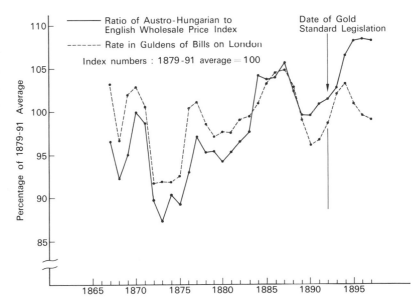

FIG. 1—Austro-Hungarian and English prices and exchange rate, 1867–97. SOURCE—Jankovich's price index for Austria-Hungary, Sauerbeck's for England, and the annual-average exchange rate from Jankovich (1899), pp. 492, 568.

purchasing-power-parity index computed with admittedly imperfect price indexes.[2] (The coefficient of correlation between the annual-average exchange rate and the ratio of the two price indexes, both for the whole period 1867–91 and for 1879–91 only, is 0.79. If significance levels are meaningful for correlations of time-series data, both these co-efficients of 0.79 are significant at 1 per cent. Correlating the *percentage changes* from one year to the next in the two series yields coefficients of 0.74, significant at 1 per cent, and of 0.52, significant at 10 per cent, for the longer and the shorter of the periods mentioned.) Prices trended

2. The fluctuations of purchasing-power parity were on the whole wider than those of the actual exchange rate and were due more to movements in the English than in the Austro-Hungarian index; this may be some slight clue to the direction of causation and perhaps even to the nature of speculation.

definitely downward after about 1873 in the gold-standard world. The trend was downward after about 1871 in Austria-Hungary also,[3] a fact no doubt connected with the rather slow and occasionally interrupted growth of the money supply (of which by far the largest part was paper money; see Table 1). The downward trend of prices was less steep in Austria-Hungary than in England, however, particularly after about 1880. Interest rates at home and abroad, prospective and actual harvests at home and abroad, political events, and conjectures about official monetary policies also influenced the exchange rate, at least in the short

TABLE 1

TOTAL PAPER-MONEY CIRCULATION OF AUSTRIA-HUNGARY, 1867–91

Year	Yearly Average End-of-Year Amount (millions of guldens)		Percentage Change during the Year
1867	511.2	548.2	. . .
1868	549.5 −	574.5	4.80
1869	602.4	598.8	4.23
1870	616.4	649.0	8.38
1871	658.2	690.9	6.46
1872	684.6	694.4	0.51
1873	700.5	703.0	1.24
1874	650.5 −	639.0	− 9.09
1875	628.8	632.7	− 0.99
1876	621.2	651.4	2.96
1877	630.8	628.2	− 3.56
1878	628.1	652.8	3.92
1879	628.6	629.8	− 3.52
1880	634.3	656.4	4.22
1881	650.3	674.6	2.77
1882	673.6	720.1	6.74
1883	702.9	731.4	1.57
1884	701.9	730.0	− 0.20
1885	682.7	701.9	− 3.85
1886	690.1	715.9	1.99
1887	700.9	728.5	1.76
1888	713.6	762.5	4.67
1889	735.0	791.9	4.86
1890	765.8	816.3	3.08
1891	788.1	834.1	2.18

SOURCE—Austria, Finance Ministry, *Statistische Tabellen zur Währungs-Frage der Österreichisch-ungarischen Monarchie* (Vienna: Hof- und Staatsdruckerei, 1892), pp. 124–27, 154–55, 160. The yearly averages were obtained by adding the averages of the *state* note circulation at the beginning, middle, and end of each year to the figures given for each year's average *bank* note circulation. Because of lack of the necessary figures for most of the years, state notes in possession of the Austro-Hungarian Bank are not subtracted from the totals of the two kinds of paper money outstanding: fortunately, the Bank held relatively small amounts of state notes.

3. Fragmentary data available on wages and on costs of army rations are compatible with the picture given by the index mentioned in the note to Figure 1.

run, as was apparent on many occasions, some of which will be mentioned below. Tables 2 and 3 employ a measure of exchange-rate fluctuation that, while open to some challenge, has the advantage of being intuitively

TABLE 2

RANGE BETWEEN THE LOWEST AND HIGHEST VIENNA RATES ON LONDON WITHIN EACH MONTH AND EACH YEAR EXPRESSED AS A PERCENTAGE OF THE MONTHLY OR YEARLY AVERAGE RATE

Year	NUMBER OF MONTHS IN WHICH THE RANGE WAS—					Average Range within Months (%)	Range within the Year (%)
	between 0 & ½%	between ½ & 1%	between 1 & 1½%	between 1½ & 2%	over 2%		
1866							21.84
1867							8.07
1868							7.33
1869							6.99
1870							8.65
1871							7.57
1872							6.92
1873							4.33
1874							3.97
1875							3.18
1876							10.84
1877							9.66
1878							6.78
1879	4	5	2	1		0.71	1.96
1880	3	7	2	...		0.69	2.12
1881	7	4	1	...		0.53	1.91
1882	6	4	1	1		0.66	2.04
1883	10	2	...	...		0.34	1.37
1884	8	3	1	...		0.49	2.17
1885	3	6	1	2		0.83	2.48
1886	5	7	...	...		0.59	1.82
1887	3	6	3	...		0.74	3.23
1888	3	6	2	1		0.79	5.56
1889	1	5	5	1		0.93	3.88
1890	2	3	3	2	2*	1.40	7.41
1891	1	7	3	1		0.91	4.36
Entire Period, 1879–91	56	65	24	9	2	0.74	3.10
Percentage of the 156 Months	35.90	41.67	15.39	5.77	1.28		

SOURCE—Computed from Austria, Finance Ministry (1892), pp. 215–17. The figures given there are the official asked quotations (Warencurse nach den amtlichen Notierungen) on the Vienna Bourse. Up to 1873, the pound sterling was reckoned as 10.21 *silver* gulden. (A typographical error in the range of fluctuation in 1883 has been corrected here.)
* August 1890, 3.75%; October 1890, 2.79%.

meaningful and of permitting comparison with corresponding figures available for Russia.[4] The rate was more unstable before than after 1879. Part of the explanation seems obvious: 1866 saw war and paper-money inflation, and 1876 saw not only a sharp decline of capital inflow into Austria-Hungary[5] but also international tension that finally led to the Russo-Turkish War the following year. The contrast may also reflect the gulden's different status in the two periods. Before 1879 it traded at

TABLE 3

RANGE BETWEEN THE LOWEST AND HIGHEST VIENNA RATES ON LONDON WITHIN EACH MONTH AND EACH YEAR EXPRESSED AS A PERCENTAGE OF THE MONTHLY OR YEARLY AVERAGE RATE

Year	NUMBER OF MONTHS IN WHICH THE RANGE WAS—					Average Range within Months (%)	Range within the Year (%)
	between 0 & ½%	between ½ & 1%	between 1 & 1½%	between 1½ & 2%	over 2%		
1879	...	8	3	...	1*	1.00	2.27
1880	...	9	2	1		0.90	2.37
1881	...	10	2	...		0.79	2.16
1882	...	9	1	2		0.90	2.25
1883	8	3	1	...		0.52	1.71
1884	5	5	1	1		0.66	2.42
1885	1	6	2	2	1†	1.09	2.80
1886	1	9	2	...		0.87	2.14
1887	...	5	5	2		1.06	3.47
1888	...	5	6	1		1.09	5.93
1889	...	5	5	2		1.17	4.22
1890	...	3	3	4	2‡	1.68	7.72
1891	...	6	3	3		1.14	4.83
Entire Period, 1879–91	15	83	36	18	4	0.99	3.41
Percentage of the 156 Months	9.62	53.21	23.08	11.54	2.56		

NOTE—This table shows slightly wider fluctuations than Table 2 because it is derived directly from the rate of actual transactions recorded in the daily *Coursblatt* of the Vienna Bourse, whereas Table 2 is based on compilation of maximum, minimum, and average *asked* rates. Until the end of 1880, the quotations underlying this table were for three-month bills on London; thereafter, for sight drafts. The *Coursblatt* reported the rates o transactions during each day's main trading session only; it is likely that transactions in small volume sometime took place outside the main session at rates slightly higher or lower than those reported.
* August 1879, 2.06%.
† April 1885, 2.11%.
‡ August 1890, 4.10%; October 1890, 3.10%.

4. Two tables are presented in order to show intra-year fluctuations before 1879, for which only the data of Table 2 are available, and the slightly more precise measurements of Table 3 for 1879 on. See the notes to the tables.
5. Béla Jankovich, "Agio és Áralakulás az Osztrák-Magyar Monarchiában 1867–1897-ig, vonatkozással a világpiacz viszonyaira," *Közgazdasági Szemle*, 23 (1899): 643 n.

a fluctuating discount from its silver parity amidst volatile expectations —which changed according to movements on the silver market and political events—about when and whether redeemability would be resumed. But when the suspension of free coinage left the gulden with neither upper nor lower limit, these psychological influences weakened— until expectations about gold policy and again about silver policy became important from 1889 on. Over the entire period 1879–91, the range of exchange-rate fluctuation within months averaged slightly less according to Table 2 and slightly more according to Table 3 than the corresponding figure of 0.87 per cent for the fluctuating Canadian rate on the United States dollar from October 1950 through May 1961. Both tables show a smaller average range of fluctuation within years than Canada's 4.17 per cent in its ten full calendar years of a free rate.

TABLE 4

THE TEN MONTHS OF WIDEST RANGE OF FLUCTUATION IN
THE VIENNA RATE ON LONDON, 1879–91

Month	Range between Month's Highest and Lowest Quotations Expressed as a Percentage of the Monthly Average
August 1890	4.103
October 1890	3.099
April 1885	2.109
August 1879	2.057
April 1891	1.934
January 1887	1.928
September 1885	1.836
September 1888	1.803
January 1891	1.793
September 1890	1.783

SOURCE—Daily issues of the *Coursblatt* of the Vienna Bourse.

Table 4 ranks the ten months of widest exchange-rate fluctuation by the measure employed in Table 3. Was anything unusual happening in those months?[6] Three of them came in 1890, a year when the gulden strengthened partly under the influence of excellent harvest and export prospects. Furthermore, a weak psychological connection that the exchange rate had still kept with the world price of silver (partly because of uncertainties about official silver policy) turned much stronger. In

6. The facts that follow were drawn from several sources, including each year's *Bericht* of the Handels- und Gewerbekammer in Vienna (*Bericht über die Industrie, den Handel und die Verkehrsverhältnisse in Nieder-Oesterreich während des Jahres 18—* [Vienna: Verlag der nied. -österr. Handels- und Gewerbekammer, annually]), and the *Neue Freie Presse*. (The *Neue Freie Presse* was Vienna's leading daily newspaper and contained a large section, called "Der Economist," of business and financial news. Its financial writers were well versed in the economic orthodoxy of the day and strongly favored the gold standard.)

July the United States enacted the Sherman Silver Purchase Act, as had been expected for some time. Bullish speculation in silver grew intense in New York and London. The price of foreign exchange in Vienna dropped far more sharply in August 1890 than in any other month of the period. Particularly on August 17, 19, and 20, the *Neue Freie Presse* bewailed the "convulsions" occurring daily on the market. Bankers seemed to have lost the courage, temporarily, to hold foreign exchange sold to them, since they were intimidated by the prolonged decline in its price; the market was said to be functioning in a "not quite orderly way." Brief interruptions to the trend were attributed to speculators' responses to reported dips in the London silver price.

Just how could the rising silver price have strengthened the gulden on the exchanges? No direct connection had yet developed. Only if the bullion content of the gulden had reached face value, if the price of silver still kept rising, and if the Austro-Hungarian Bank had made banknotes *de facto* redeemable in silver could silver have pulled up the exchange value of the gulden in any mechanical way. Even the third of these conditions seemed possible, since the Bank was known to be inconvenienced and annoyed by the gravitation of silver coin into its vaults. (This had been going on for years as the Austrian and Hungarian governments continued coinage on their own account and as the public persistently got rid of the coins, finding them less convenient than paper money.) The *Neue Freie Presse* repeatedly stressed the key question: What would the Bank do with its silver at the critical point?

Any distinction between a "direct" and "indirect" influence may be hair-splitting. The critical relation between the silver price and the exchange rate that would make silver exports profitable never was quite reached (though at one point it was only $\frac{1}{2}$ of 1 per cent away); part of the reason was precisely that, through speculation, the silver price was chasing up the foreign-exchange value of the gulden. The speculative "indirect" influence was forestalling the mechanical "direct" one. Under the circumstances, people could consider a gulden worth more than the silver in it because it represented that bullion value, at least, and also its own monetary value, which would not collapse even if the price of silver should. As experience since 1879 had demonstrated, the price of silver could not put a ceiling on the value of the gulden but might conceivably put a floor under it. Of course, this speculative attitude presupposed the possibility that silver coins would remain available (from circulation or from the Bank) at their face value. This possibility never came to the test because speculation kept creating afresh the premium of the gulden over its silver content. By reckoning with the possibility of silver exports and their effects, speculation kept deferring their actual profitability.[7]

Perhaps not just by coincidence, the London price of silver and the foreign-exchange value of the gulden both reached their peaks on September 3. Both then underwent a reaction. (Then as all along, however, the exchange rate moved much less violently than the silver price.) Throughout the whole episode of 1890, the *Neue Freie Presse* repeatedly fulminated against "the American silver-kings": "A gulden of Austrian currency has now become a gambling counter whose value is determined by the foolhardy speculators in New York.... [If] one stitch rips there, the price of silver could crash overnight and the price of foreign exchange hurry sharply upwards."[8]

In subsequent debates, in and out of Parliament, about going onto the gold standard, people keenly remembered the relatively wild fluctuations of 1890. Finance Minister Steinbach warned the Austrian Chamber of Deputies on May 14, 1892 that the danger was still very real:

> *If you follow the discussions on the questions of free coinage of silver in the United States of North America* and if you see how small the differences between majority and minority continually are there, then you can draw a conclusion from them about *what influences on our currency conditions can possibly be exercised from that direction—without their being intended. The rate fluctuations of the year 1890*, which you all remember, gentlemen, have brought us a *small foretaste* of what would happen if silver coinage were made free today in the United States of North America.[9]

Few people at the time even conceived of a currency deliberately and permanently severed from any link with precious metal. Under the circumstances, the gold standard could seem the best way out of the danger from silver.

In October 1890, uncertainties about silver were joined by fresh rumors about an impending currency reform. By then the expectation had gained ground that if the gold standard were adopted the gulden would be given a gold content *lower* than corresponded to its current unusual strength; hence, reform prospects tended to raise the prices of foreign exchange. In January and April 1891—also listed in Table 4—rumors and uncertainties about gold-standard legislation had similar

7. *Neue Freie Presse*, August 31, 1890, p. 8, explains this last point in particular.
8. *Neue Freie Presse*, September 21, 1890, pp. 8–9.
9. Austria, Chamber of Deputies, *Stenographisches Protokoll*, 11th sess. (Vienna: Hof- und Staatsdruckerei, 1892), p. 5930. (The words italicized here are "gesperrt" in the original.)

effects. On various occasions, actual or rumored trips of the Austrian finance minister to Budapest or of the Hungarian finance minister to Vienna were the apparent cause of ripples in the exchange rate.[10] From about 1889 on, the influence of rumors both about gold and about silver illustrated, by contrast, Subercaseaux's observation that exchange rates tended to be most stable when notions of a metallic parity of the gulden were most nearly absent.[11] Fluctuations were most violent—relatively— when notions of a silver or a gold parity and of a supposedly imminent *pegging* had acquired an important influence and so had made the gulden no longer a completely free fiat currency.

April 1885 stands third on the list of most unstable months; the alternately waxing and waning danger of war between England and Russia was exciting securities and foreign-exchange markets in Vienna and abroad. The day-by-day account in the *Neue Freie Presse* is dramatic. A review of the week ending Saturday the 18th, for example, was enthusiastic about Gladstone's having saved the peace: "The Bourse is like an old woman at the brink of death who was suddenly transformed into a blooming maiden." By Monday, the danger had returned, and reimports of government bonds were contributing to the gulden's renewed weakness.

The episodes of April 1885, as well as others reported in the *Neue Freie Presse*, illustrate the influences of international securities arbitrage and of war fears. If war threatened Austria-Hungary itself, memories of earlier wartime inflations would prompt some flight into gold currencies. When the Monarchy was expected to remain neutral, securities arbitrage could affect the exchange rate of the gulden. Anticipations that the belligerent governments would spend more money, float more bonds, and bid up interest rates would drive the prices of their outstanding bonds down in advance. Because investors could substitute some securities for others, the decline would spread to corporation bonds and

10. On some occasions before 1890, reform rumors tended to affect the exchange rate in the opposite direction, since an older opinion still prevailed that a reform would *raise* the value of the gulden. This opinion rested on a mistaken conception of the gulden's "gold parity." Legally, the gulden had had only a silver parity; the mistake hinged on the nearly fixed gold value of the silver gulden in the days when French bimetallism was still maintaining a nearly fixed relation between the two metals. A quirk of Hungarian and Austrian coinage laws of 1869 and 1870 kept memories of this earlier relation alive: some gold coins were still minted bearing denominations in francs and guldens *both*. They had no fixed value in ordinary guldens and enjoyed only limited use, as "trade pieces," outside the regular monetary system. See, for example, *Neue Freie Presse*, December 15, 1889, p. 9.

11. Guillermo Subercaseaux, *El Pabel Moneda* (Santiago de Chile: Cervantes, 1912), pp. 188–90.

stocks. Until the decline had spread from the prospective warring countries to the Vienna Bourse, arbitrageurs could profitably buy securities abroad for resale in Vienna. In particular, arbitrageurs would reimport local securities previously held abroad, and outward remittances to pay for them would weaken the gulden on the exchanges.[12]

Returning to the list in Table 4, we find January 1887 (as well as early February) influenced by expectations of war between Germany and France. September 1885, near the depths of an international business depression, saw a sharp decline in the price of silver and disturbances in the Balkans that caused apprehension of something bigger than the war between Serbia and Bulgaria that did in fact break out a few weeks later; in addition, the long-standing Anglo-Russian dispute was not settled until that month. In September 1888 the gulden strengthened markedly under the combined influence of domestic and foreign conditions favorable to exports of grain and securities and a temporary recovery in the price of silver. In August 1879, the only remaining month listed, disappointment of earlier optimism about harvest and export prospects was apparently at work.[13]

Looking for months of *least* instability, we find that the range of fluctuation expressed as a percentage of the average rate was smallest— and to two decimal points the same, 0.29 per cent—in September, March, and April 1884 and June and July 1883. The sixth through tenth most stable months were September and August 1883, August 1884, June 1885, and March 1883, the last with a range of 0.42 per cent. Five of the ten months occur in 1883, the most stable year of the period. Contemporary comment was scanty; only instability but not stability seemed to require explanation. Over the year 1883 as a whole, the gulden was depreciating mildly under the apparent influences of a decline of foreign relative to domestic prices, greater prosperity at home than abroad, poor harvests of exportable grains, and continued repurchases

12. If the Monarchy itself was a potential belligerent and securities fell in Vienna first, arbitrageurs, according to this reasoning, would export securities, tending to strengthen the gulden. The apparent clash with actual experience means simply that the arbitrage influence was outweighed by expectations of inflation.

13. Other criteria tried for singling out particularly unstable months were the variance of daily exchange rates, the steepness of straight-line trends fitted to daily rates, and the percentage change in the rate between the ends of the preceding and current months. The resulting lists do not fully coincide, but August and October 1890 and April 1885 remain high on all of them. One of the most interesting months turned up by alternative criteria was December 1887, when a possible war threatened to involve Austria-Hungary; this episode will be mentioned later in another connection. Another month of interesting instability is April 1889, when currency reform was under active discussion and was still understood to mean an *upward* pegging of the gulden to gold.

of domestic securities from foreign holders. Despite threats to peace in the Balkans in November, the depreciation remained mild. Four of the most stable months came in 1884. During that year Austria-Hungary began sharing in the depression ranging abroad and the paper-money circulation began shrinking, panic seized securities markets in New York and elsewhere, repatriation of securities continued, foreign agricultural protectionism and good harvests in competing supplier countries hampered Austro-Hungarian exports, and the decline of foreign relative to domestic prices sharpened. During that year (August 31, p. 8) the *Neue Freie Presse* bewailed "The revolution of prices! We live in a time of economic revolution!" One would hardly have guessed any of this from the orderly movement of the exchange rate. June 1885, finally, was the ninth most stable month, although April 1885 had been the third most *un*stable. June saw enactment of the German bourse tax, which was expected to hamper international arbitrage in securities. It came in the midst of a year plagued by depression at home and worse depression abroad, shrinkage in the domestic paper-money supply during the first half of the year, and unfavorable changes in German and French tariff policy.

The foregoing survey suggests that obvious economic or political disturbances were a necessary but not sufficient condition (in a historical, not logical, sense) for relatively great exchange-rate fluctuations.

So far we have considered ranges of fluctuation only within calendar years and months. What happened between and within single days? Sometimes there were strings of days on which the newspaper laconically recorded no change or a change of only $\frac{1}{10}$ of 1 per cent in the exchange rate. In October 1890, the second most unstable month in thirteen years, the newspaper did once mention a fluctuation of more than 1 per cent within a single day: on Wednesday the 8th, amidst conflicting rumors about currency-reform plans, the price of mark notes dropped more than 1 per cent from its intra-day high.[14] In March 1891, a month of about average range of fluctuation, again amidst conflicting rumors about monetary reform, the prices of sterling bills and mark notes reached peaks on the 16th and then declined by 0.52 and 0.31 per cent respectively before the close of trading.[15] In the three most unstable

14. *Neue Freie Presse*, October 9, 1890, p. 10. No such wide range appears, however, in the *Coursblatt* (Vienna Bourse, *Amtliches Coursblatt der Wiener Börse* [an issue for each business day]). As mentioned in the note to Table 3, the *Coursblatt* records only transactions during the main trading session of the day; transactions at other prices may sometimes have taken place outside this session.
15. Computed from *Neue Freie Presse*, March 17, 1891, p. 11. Again the *Coursblatt* shows narrower intra-day fluctuations.

consecutive months, August through October 1890, no indication turned up in either the newspaper or the *Coursblatt*, other than the single one already cited, of intra-day fluctuations in sterling or marks as large as 1 per cent. Indeed, intra-day or day-to-day fluctuations half that large would have been considered highly unusual, as suggested, for example, by the *Neue Freie Presse*'s mention of "violent convulsions" in describing a decline of "a full half per cent."[16]

A search of the *Coursblatt* turns up a few more relatively large changes in the Vienna rate on London over the course of several days. In order not to understate the fluctuation, each percentage refers to the change between the intra-day high or low on the first day and the low or high, respectively, on the later day. The rate rose 1.12 per cent from the first Monday to the first Thursday of August 1879. At the time of the Paris stock-market crash in January 1882, it rose 1.51 per cent between a Thursday and a Monday. In April and May 1885 it rose 1.93 per cent in a week, fell 1.03 per cent in two days, fell 1.46 per cent in four days, and fell 2.01 per cent in six days. In September 1885 it rose 1.32 per cent between a Saturday and a Wednesday. Early in 1887, from Wednesday, January 26, to Thursday, February 3, when the rate on sterling reached its highest level in twenty years, a peak never again approached, the rise was 1.81 per cent. In 1888 the rate fell 1.56 per cent from the last Friday in July to the first Thursday in August. In the first two business days of June 1890 the rate rose 0.86 per cent. In August 1890 a rather smooth though steep decline amounted to 2.24 per cent in a week. In October 1890 the rate rose 3.16 per cent between the first Thursday and the following Wednesday. In January 1891 it rose 1.81 per cent between the first Friday and the following Thursday. Almost all these episodes occurred at times already noted as especially unstable.

Contemporary writers parroted each other in bewailing the supposedly large fluctuations, usually without citing specific figures and episodes.[17] A few, however, took a calmer view. Jankovich, for example, after surveying various determinants of the exchange rate, including

16. August 17, 1890, p. 11. Cf. the issue of August 12, 1890, pp. 8–9, which expressed alarm at a decline of $\frac{1}{2}$ of 1 per cent (0.44 per cent, actually) in mark notes between August 1 and 11 and of 0.94 per cent in sterling and 1.44 per cent in marks since July 1.

17. An abundant pamphlet literature flourished in and around 1892, the year of the gold-standard legislation. In articles published that year, even the judicious Carl Menger, *Schriften über Geldtheorie und Währungspolitik*, Collected Works, vol. 4 (London: London School of Economics, 1936), pp. 138, 201, worried about "the great fluctuations that the rate of our currency, expressed in gold, has undergone in the last 10 years" and about the "aleatory character" that these fluctuations gave to business.

capital movements and their role in equilibrating the balance of payments (as distinguished from the balance of trade), noted that some people might suppose the fluctuations had no limit. With evident satisfaction he added: "If despite this we find, regarding our Monarchy's currency, that in the lapse of 30 years it fluctuates relatively little in value and that its fluctuation in yearly average is no larger than eight per cent upwards or downwards, we can also explain that with the factors mentioned, which there too call forth the necessary counter-influence."[18]

It would be interesting to conduct a survey among economists who had no details freshly in mind of historical experiences with fluctuating exchange rates. How much instability would they consider mild? How widely would fluctuations have to range to count as extreme? My guess is that in comparison with typical answers, the fluctuations of the gulden would count as mild. This is not to say that smallness of fluctuation is by itself a criterion of good performance. Unless somehow magnified or exaggerated, functional fluctuations should be less a reason for dismay than the sharp changes in economic fundamentals that might have caused them. Nevertheless, smallness of fluctuation does suggest that the usual horror stories about disruptive speculation had proved inapplicable. This, in the absence of data on short-term capital movements, is perhaps our best clue.

What explains the apparent orderliness of the Austrian exchange rate? I am not going to argue a priori that speculation "must have been" stabilizing.[19] We simply face a phenomenon that invites hypotheses.

18. "Agio és Áralakulás," p. 645. Jankovich's analysis of the gulden's exchange rate was remarkably thorough and sophisticated for its time—more so, in fact, than any other work known to me of that time or since. Jankovich published his studies in his three-part article of 1899 and in others of 1894 and 1895; see "Az Aranyagio és Áralakulás," *Közgazdasági Szemle*, 19 (1895): 855–72; and "Külkeresked elem és Váltóárfolyam," *Közgadasági Szemle*, 18 (1894): 747–83.

19. At least one contemporary writer, however, came close to explicitly stating that it ordinarily was. Referring particularly but not solely to the mark-gulden rate, Walter Lotz, *Die Währungsfrage in Österreich-Ungarn und ihre wirtschaftliche und politische Bedeutung* (Leipzig: Duncker & Humblot, 1889), pp. 21–24, mentioned the operations of professional speculators, some of whom sought profit from the small day-to-day fluctuations. They would accumulate mark notes and mark balances in times of abundance for resale when demand would be stronger. International trade in securities weighed at least as heavily in the judgments of speculators, Lotz thought, as did trade in commodities. Sometimes they correctly foresaw the influence on exchange rates of such things as political developments, good foreign participation in new Austrian securities issues, and harvest conditions abroad.

Similarly, Jankovich mentioned the palliative available "for remedying a temporary disturbance in the balance of payments in the form of finance bills [*üres váltók*] and transactions in securities. As long as this is at our disposal, a favorable

One hypothesis would center on the role of forward transactions in foreign bills, banknotes, and gold coins, just as in securities, together with nearly equivalent transactions in the form of "report" and "deport" or "prolongation" business and even in the form of puts and calls in foreign exchange. To judge from incidental but numerous references to them in the daily newspaper, in the rules of the Bourse, and in some economic writings, facilities for such transactions were remarkably well organized in late-nineteenth-century Vienna.[20] This literature gives the impression that forward transactions and their equivalents tended to soften the impact on existing prices of any very-short-run mismatching of spot supply and spot demand for any item traded on the Bourse—whether Nordbahn stock, mark or ruble notes, bills on London, or what not. In a sense, arbitrage among the spot, forward, and "prolongation" markets had an effect analogous to that of multilateral currency arbitrage which kept random, fleeting supply-and-demand imbalances from sharply changing the price of spot twenty-franc-pieces specifically or spot London bills specifically, out of line with the general movement of exchange rates. Just as multilateral currency arbitrage spread the impact of a change in supply or demand for a specific foreign currency over foreign currencies generally, so the system of time transactions in securities and currencies apparently smeared the impact of a change in spot supply or demand for an item out over the whole range of the market's time-sectors.

---

or unfavorable movement in our balance of trade does not exercise an influence on our balance of payments and on the agio." (The "agio" was one form of exchange-rate quotation.) Furthermore: "Ordinarily the large banks hold in stock a certain reserve in gold bills in which they easily invest funds at short term. If, therefore, their price rises, they probably put part of them at the disposal of the money market at a suitable profit; and then the unexpected payment obligation can be met out of the accumulated reserves." Jankovich, "Agio és Áralakulás," pp. 627, 632; see also p. 625.

20. Forward exchange rates stayed close to spot rates, incidentally, as the interest-arbitrage theory suggests for truly free rates. Rates in Vienna did not exhibit the big forward premiums and discounts so familiar in our time when a pegged spot rate comes strongly under suspicion. The premium or discount on one-month-forward mark notes at around the end of each month in and after 1885 can be computed from the *Coursblatt*. The largest forward-spot discrepancy was a premium of 3.43 per cent per annum, and in only 6 months of the whole period 1885–91 was the discrepancy (premium) as large as 3 per cent. The average discrepancy, ignoring direction, was only 1.27 per cent. The usual closeness of spot and forward rates is reflected in the *Neue Freie Presse*'s description of the forward premium as "enormous" when it was wavering around 2 to 3 per cent (July 4, 1886, p. 8).

Being expressed on a per annum basis, the percentages mentioned are comparable with interest rates. The premium on forward marks usually prevailing is compatible with the excess usually prevailing of Vienna over Berlin interest rates.

Another hypothesis would center on the market-broadening role of a different but related kind of arbitrage: international trade in securities. Often, of course, a disturbance originating on the securities market in Vienna or abroad tended to *cause* a movement of exchange rates. No one argues that securities arbitrage was always exchange-stabilizing. Rather, the foreign-exchange market was in effect broadened by its linkage with securities markets at home and abroad; any given temporary disturbance to the exchange rate was smaller in relation to the volume of actual and potential foreign-exchange transactions than it would otherwise have been. In linking various markets together—those in different countries, those for different stocks and bonds and currencies, those for gold and silver, those for loans, those for spot and futures and "prolongation" transactions and perhaps even for puts and calls—arbitrage gave each of them more "breadth, depth, and resiliency" than it would have had in isolation. This cohesion of markets cushioned the impact on the price in a particular market of a temporary disturbance or random imbalance that would otherwise have fallen with full weight on that market alone; it did so by diffusing the impact over all the markets.

Consider, for example, some disturbance tending to raise the price of foreign exchange—perhaps something favoring imports or hampering exports, or a random mismatching of supply and demand at the old exchange rate, or outright bearish speculation against the gulden. With price comparisons now made at a weakened exchange value of the gulden, securities temporarily seem cheaper than before in Vienna relative to the same securities quoted on foreign markets. Arbitrageurs therefore buy securities in Vienna for profitable resale abroad. These exports of securities—imports of capital—tend to restrain the gulden's depreciation. Consider, conversely, some disturbance tending to lower the price of foreign exchange. With the gulden worth more than before, securities temporarily command higher prices in Vienna than abroad. The response of arbitrageurs—import of securities, export of capital—tends to restrain the appreciation of the gulden. The analogy is obvious with the commodity arbitrage that would restrain a major departure of a free exchange rate from its purchasing-power parity.[21]

21. Only after newspaper articles such as those quoted below had persuaded me of the role of arbitrage did I really understand the rather cryptic passages in Montz Rubrom, *Neues Wiener Börsebuch* (Vienna: Perles, 1872), pp. 62–63, 179–80 (and, for Rubrom's use of the word "manipulation" as a synonym for "arbitrage," see p. 67), and Gerhart v. Schulze-Gävernitz, *Volkswirtschaftliche Studien aus Russland* (Leipzig: Duncker & Humblot, 1899), pp. 513, 521. In effect these writers were concisely stating as a fact what I am calling a hypothesis. Compare Jankovich's mention of securities trade, quoted in n. 19.

The *Neue Freie Presse* seldom described actual episodes of exchange-stabilizing arbitrage, perhaps because stability does not cry out for explanation, because good news is no news. But it did describe several. An interesting episode occurred in December 1887. Fears that Balkan problems would ignite a war between Russia and Austria-Hungary sharpened, while discussions continued among the Monarchy, Germany, and Italy about cooperation in a possible war with France. "...when the danger of war seemed to have been pushed so close, one could observe the anxious purchases of the public in every little foreign-exchange shop, the rush for gold."[22] The rise from the lowest *Coursblatt* quotation in that month on Thursday, the 1st, to the highest on Saturday, the 31st, amounted to 1.63 per cent for sterling and 1.25 per cent for mark notes. Friday, the 16th, was called the worst day on the Bourse since the international tension had flared up.

> In foreign exchange the movement was a stormy one, although the rise here was far from keeping pace with the fall in securities prices. Significant purchases of gold currencies and bills were carried out for the public; only the great securities purchases from abroad created such an afflux of foreign currency that the prices closed with relatively small increases compared with yesterday. Mark notes rose briefly to 62.10 and closed at 62.02, 10 kr. higher than yesterday.[23]

The newspaper's Sunday issue told more about the stabilizing influence of continuing arbitrage during Friday's "panic," when orders to sell securities and buy sterling were flooding onto the Vienna Bourse:

> So the panic broke out, and the Bourse has indeed experienced more terrible but scarcely ever any more interesting hours. There stood a director who had to buy three millions of mark notes, there another who sought two hundred thousand pounds; the leader of one of the largest firms needed millions in foreign exchange, and all thought with secret horror about the effect of the operations imposed upon them. Now came one of the most remarkable surprises. The stock of foreign bills was downright inexhaustible; he who demanded three millions could have ten millions, the reservoir was not to be emptied, the gold for which countless hands greedily grasped was almost put on clearance sale; and seldom yet has Austria been, at least for a few moments, a creditor of foreign markets to such an extent as in this fearful moment. The turn of events was amazing; and it will still be reported about in later times as about a saving financial miracle. The *turnovers* in foreign currencies that were made

22. *Neue Freie Presse*, September 8, 1888, p. 8—a retrospective article.
23. December 17, 1887, p. 8.

in these few days are estimated at sixty million marks, and the enormous demand was able to be satisfied without any shock to the currency, without fundamental worsening of the balance of payments and of the price of foreign exchange. What explanation can be offered for this phenomenon, which still causes a sensation? Last week Frankfurt and Berlin bought at least thirty million marks worth of Austrian securities.... [Other orders to buy securities poured in from abroad.]...the force of the panic is broken, at least for the moment. There was no arbitrageur who did not have big operations to carry out; one of the most powerful Vienna institutes alone had to acquire four millions of securities for the account of foreign customers; every purchase of securities brought gold into the country, and so a sum of foreign exchange was piled up that was able to satisfy even a demand boosted by the political anxiety. Germany threw itself with its whole huge strength against the jolt that proceeded from the Vienna Bourse. Berlin bankers fought like courageous lions against Austrian pessimism, they made fun of all war fear, they mocked our pusillanimity and supported the structure that was cracking in all its joints.²⁴

An unambiguous example occurred during the period of transition from a free exchange rate to a fixed gold parity. By mid-April 1892 the public knew that the transition really was imminent at last. The exact parity that the Austrian government would propose in Parliament became public knowledge on Thursday, April 14 (or possibly the day before). The announced figure implied a somewhat higher price of foreign exchange than had been expected—1.01 per cent above the average rate on London so far that month. Rate fluctuations were sizable on the 14th as speculators bought gold currencies heavily. After rising, "the rates moved downwards again and closed easy after arbitrageurs had made remittances for bank stocks and government bonds they had bought."²⁵ Evidently the initial weakening of the gulden promoted arbitrage exports of securities, bringing foreign exchange onto the market and checking the initial movement of the rate.

The influence of the announced "relation" was still noticeable on the Bourse of Saturday, April 16 (after a holiday). The rise of foreign-exchange rates was continuing. But "such sharp price changes are not accomplished without agitation. On Monday mark notes were quoted at 58.20, and today they closed above 58.50, while the relation rate is

24. *Neue Freie Presse*, December 18, 1887, p. 8. (The word italicized here was "gesperrt" in the original.)
25. *Ibid.*, April 15, 1892, p. 11. A later issue (May 15, 1892, p. 10) speaks of "the great storm that arose from publication of the conversion figure...."

58.78." Twenty-franc pieces and sterling likewise failed to reach their new parities. The adjustment of the market rate to the relation rate was being impeded.

> To be regarded as a counteracting factor, furthermore, is the circumstance that just now large purchases of Austrian securities took place in arbitrage trading. Bound up therewith as a counter-operation is the sale of foreign exchange, which weakens the upward tendency. Thus it is explained that the leaping rise of exchange rates is ever again accompanied by a falling-back, so that the peculiar phenomenon appears that the Vienna Bourse is not in a position to achieve the relation rate that nevertheless designates the value of foreign bills and currencies at present rather precisely. In today's trading the following rate fluctuations occurred for mark notes: 58.35, 58.40, 58.50, 58.47, 58.52, and 58.50. These figures best show the irregular price movement that has taken place. The process of equalization will probably take a few days yet; and then, we hope, the foreign-exchange market will offer the picture, in peaceful times, of trifling fluctuations moving in small deviations around the relation.[26]

The market did adjust, of course; but the delay in adjustment, and in particular the role of securities arbitrage in blocking immediate adjustment, is further evidence of an almost automatic stabilizing mechanism operating earlier, at the time of the free rate. The close linking of the Berlin and Vienna bourses by abitrage may be relevant, incidentally, to present-day suppositions that fluctuating exchange rates mean financial isolation and that financial and economic integration requires fixed rates.

The Ruble

The Russian ruble fluctuated more widely than the Austrian gulden, as Table 5 shows. Although economic fundamentals presumably governed the major movements of the rate, evidence so far located is skimpy; in particular, there seems to be no nineteenth-century Russian price index. In default of that, various casual observations warrant attention as a kind of negative evidence:[27] except during and following periods of

26. *Ibid.*, April 17, 1892, p. 9. "Today" meant the 16th.
27. Alfred Marshall believed that the purchasing-power-parity doctrine applied to the sterling-ruble exchange rate; see his memorandum in Great Britain, Gold and Silver Commission, *Reports*, with minutes of evidence and appendixes (London: Eyre and Spottiswoode for Her Majesty's Stationery Office, 1887–88), 4: 48. Wilhelm Launhardt, *Mark, Rubel und Rupie* (Berlin: Ernst, 1894), pp. 30–31, expressed a similar judgment. On the absence of price inflation in Russia (since that caused by the war of 1877–78, anyway), see the testimony of William Fowler,

wartime paper-money inflation, Russia seems to have experienced no conspicuous price-level inflation. This supposition finds some slight support in the slow, though unsteady, growth of the Russian money supply, as shown in Table 6. A warning is in order, however: the unreliability of Russian statistics antedates the Bolshevik Revolution.

Jankovich reasoned that world-market conditions, and not just local conditions, influenced the exchange rates of paper currencies. He called attention to the movements of Sauerbeck's English price index and to a correspondence between the movements of the ruble and gulden.[28] Figure 2 shows that correspondence.[29]

Tables 5 and 7 and Figures 2 and 3 invite attention to 1888, the year of greatest instability, by far, for the ruble, and the second most unstable year for the gulden during the period 1879–91.[30] What explains that year's extreme instability? Although nineteenth-century market commentaries probably overstressed newsworthy events at the expense of economic fundamentals, the bits of explanation they offer are still worth

---

p. 106, and Hermann Schmidt, pp. 169–70, in Great Britain, Gold and Silver Commission *Reports*, vol. 2, and I. I. Kaufman, *Kreditnye Bilety, ikh Upadoki Vozstanovlenie* (St. Petersburg: Balashev, 1888), pp. 22–23, 42, 55–61, 80, 83–85, 88–90. (Despite his German name, Kaufman was a pro-gold-standard Russian economist.)

28. He also compared the fluctuations of some other paper currencies during 1893. He thought some lapses in correspondence between foreign prices and the ruble rate could be explained by spurts and slumps in the Russian money supply. See Béla Jankovich, "Az Aranyagio és Áralakulás," esp. pp. 862–68, and Jankovich, "Agio és Áralakulás," esp. pp. 577, 579.

29. The coefficients of correlation between the annual-average sterling exchange rates of the gulden and the ruble (rates given in Jankovich, "Az Aranyagio és Áralakulás," pp. 860–61) are 0.50 for 1867–91 and 0.81 for 1879–91, significant at the 2 and 1 per cent levels, respectively. The year-to-year *percentage changes* in the two exchange rates show correlation coefficients of 0.41 for 1868–91 and 0.68 for 1879–91, significant at about 5 and at 2 per cent, respectively. On Figure 2, some of the deviations from parallelism between the two series simply reflect the larger size of fluctuations in the ruble than in the gulden; others are attributable to specific events, such as the monetary and other consequences of the Russo-Turkish War of 1877–78 and of the Russian famine of 1891.

Another suggestion of world-market influences affecting the gulden and ruble rates alike is that both rates tended to fluctuate unusually much or unusually little in the same years. Their ranges of intra-year fluctuation (shown in Tables 2 and 5) correlate with coefficients of 0.42 for 1866–91 and 0.72 for 1879–91, significant at 5 and 1 per cent. Their average ranges of intra-month fluctuation in the thirteen years 1879–91 (Tables 2 and 5) give a correlation coefficient of 0.57, significant at 5 per cent.

30. The correlation coefficient of the two series shown in Figure 3 is 0.97. (If so close a correlation is not apparent from the chart, the reason is the much wider fluctuations in the ruble rate than in the gulden rate; a scatter diagram, however, does show the close correlation.) The coefficient of correlation between the two series of week-to-week *percentage change* is 0.50, also significant at 1 per cent.

TABLE 5

RANGE BETWEEN THE LOWEST AND HIGHEST ST. PETERSBURG RATES ON LONDON WITHIN EACH MONTH AND EACH YEAR EXPRESSED AS A PERCENTAGE OF THE MONTHLY OR YEARLY AVERAGE RATE

Year (Julian Calendar)	Number of Months in Which the Percentage Range Was—								Average Range within Months	Range within Year
	0 to 1	1 to 2	2 to 3	3 to 4	4 to 5	5 to 6	6 to 7	over 7		
1866										23.17
1867										10.95−
1868										3.04
1869										12.47
1870										11.55
1871										7.80
1872										2.96
1873										2.60
1874										3.00
1875										7.06
1876										10.94
1877										29.21
1878										18.88
1879	2	2	4	1	1	1	1		2.80	13.40
1880	3	5	1	2	1	...	...		2.10	9.47
1881	1	7	2	2					1.86	7.94
1882	1	7	3	1	...				1.77	8.01
1883	4	8							1.30	4.22
1884	2	5	4	...	...		1		1.95−	8.72
1885		6	4	...	...	...	1	1*	2.50−	10.47
1886	2	5	4	1	...	...			1.76	8.56
1887		4	5	1	1	1			2.58	8.77
1888		1	2	1	4	...	2	2†	4.96	31.19
1889	2	6	1	3					2.04	9.73
1890		3	2	4	1	1	1		3.23	17.32
1891	1	3	3		1	1	1	2‡	3.67	24.47
Entire Period, 1879–91	18	62	35	16	9	5	6	5	2.50	12.48
Percentage of the 156 Months	11.54	39.74	22.44	10.26	5.77	3.21	3.85	3.21		

SOURCE—Average, maximum, and minimum rates for three-months bills on London on the St. Petersburg Bourse, in Kashkarov (1898), I, 169–70, and II, appendix to chap. 5, pp. 40–41.
* March 1885, 7.48%.
† June 1888, 9.01%; August 1888, 8.42%.
‡ June 1891, 7.59%; August 1891, 7.64%.

TABLE 6
PAPER MONEY IN CIRCULATION IN RUSSIA
OUTSIDE THE STATE BANK

Year (Julian Calendar)	Yearly Average (millions of rubles)	Percentage Change from Previous Year's Average
1866	652.7	...
1867	678.2	3.91
1868	693.8	2.30
1869	678.3	−2.23
1870	692.2	2.05 −
1871	694.4	0.32
1872	724.2	4.29
1873	743.4	2.65
1874	755.4	1.61
1875	745.2	−1.35
1876	718.9	−3.53
1877	837.4	16.48
1878	1102.8	31.69
1879	1107.4	0.42
1880	1082.0	−2.29
1881	1037.0	−4.16
1882	1001.9	−3.38
1883	966.5	−3.53
1884	914.8	−5.35
1885	892.8	−2.40
1886	900.7	0.88
1887	950.0	5.47
1888	982.4	3.41
1889	940.3	−4.29
1890	902.2	−4.05
1891	977.1	8.30
1892	1069.7	9.48
1893	1062.0	−0.72
1894	1061.5	−1.93

SOURCE—Kashkarov (1898), II, appendix to chap. 3, pp. 7, 9.

considering.[31] A number of conditions unfavorable to the ruble happened to coincide early in the year, giving way to an equally unusual

31. The following draws mainly on Finance Minister Vyshnegradsky's report on the budget for 1889, translated in Arthur Raffalovich, *Les Finances de la Russie, 1887–1889* (Paris: Guillaumin, 1889), pp. 21–22; Mikhail Kashkarov, *Denezhnoe Obrashchenie v Rossii* (St. Petersburg: Gosudarstvennaïa Tipografiîa, 1898), 1:176; Georg von Falck, *Russische Wirthschafts- und Finanzfragen* (Reval: Kluge, 1889), pp. 88, 92–99; Konstantin Apollonovich Skalkovsky, *Les Ministres des Finances de la Russie*, trans. P. de Nevsky (Paris: Guillaumin, 1891), p. 280; David Ratner, *Rubel- und- Wechselkurse, 1885–1895* (Munich: Kastner & Lossen, 1898), pp. 51–53; E. Struck, "Der internationale Geldmarkt im Jahre 1888," *Schmoller's Jahrbuch*, 13 (1889): 1175–78; William L. Langer, *European Alliances and Alignments, 1871–1890*, Vintage ed. (New York: Random House, 1964), chaps. 12 and 13.

combination of favorable conditions later on. Early in the year, Russian securities dumped by nervous German investors were still coming home in heavy volume; this was a continuing response to Bismarck's campaign to weaken Russian government credit, a campaign waged in semiofficial newspaper articles and by the discontinuance (in November 1887) of the eligibility of Russian government bonds for use as collateral

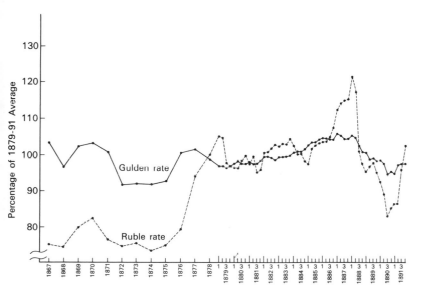

FIG. 2—Indexes of gulden and ruble prices of sterling (1879–91 average = 100; annual through 1878 and quarterly thereafter). SOURCE—For gulden rates through 1878, Jankovich (1899), p. 492; for gulden rates from 1879 on, daily Vienna *Coursblatt*; for ruble rates, Kashkarov (1898), II, appendix to chap. 5, pp. 38–41 (the average pence-per-ruble rate for each year or quarter was divided into the average pence-per-ruble rate for 1879–91).

for loans from the Reichsbank. The Russian government's initial failure in trying to float still another bond issue abroad raised apprehensions that the government might resort to the printing press and that it might sell ruble notes abroad to get the gold needed for interest on its outstanding foreign debts. Rumors of a poorly understood plan for introducing an optional metallic currency in Russia touched off worries abroad that foreign creditors might somehow be victimized. Mistrust among foreign investors was intensified by the news, toward the end of February, that a jury in Moscow had freed two postal employees and an accomplice who had stolen securities addressed to a firm in Berlin; the jury accepted the defendants' argument that they had acted patriotically to impede bearish manipulations of the market for Russian securities. War fears had ample material to feed on: the usual troubles in the Balkans; a heightening of Franco-Italian tensions in January and February; jingoistic agitation centering around General Boulanger in France; publication in February of the Austro-German alliance of 1879, followed by a speech by Bismarck widely misinterpreted as bellicose; and still other events. Uncertainty about the peaceful or the warlike intentions of Crown Prince William contributed to the sensitivity of securities and foreign-exchange markets, since his father, Frederick III, was correctly guessed to be near death when he inherited the German throne early in March.

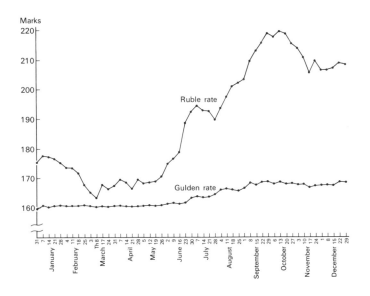

FIG. 3—Gulden and ruble rates in Berlin, Saturdays in 1888 (marks per 100 guldens or rubles in banknotes). SOURCE—Struck (1889), pp. 1192–93.

Real and psychological influences turned favorable to the ruble with increasing clarity during the spring and summer of 1888. The German dumping of Russian securities had pretty much run its course. At the beginning of April, preliminary figures on the outcome of the 1887 budget helped calm apprehensions about Russian government finances. Shortly after becoming Kaiser in June, William II paid a visit to St. Petersburg that drew much attention and quieted fears of war. More important, perhaps, were the increasingly definite signs that the harvest would be excellent in Russia but bad in the rest of the world except Hungary; grain prices were falling in Russia and rising in importing

TABLE 7

RATES FOR THREE-MONTH BILLS ON LONDON ON THE ST. PETERSBURG BOURSE
(Annual Averages through 1878; Quarterly Averages Thereafter;
Julian Calendar; Pence Per Ruble)

1866 29.67	1881 25.01	1886 23.60	1891 28.31
1867 32.55−	24.54	23.59	28.25
1868 32.84	25.73	23.30	25.45−
1869 30.58	25.55	22.73	23.85
1870 29.75	1882 24.39	1887 21.79	1892 24.00
1871 32.03	24.31	21.44	24.76
1872 32.72	24.10	21.30	24.28
1873 32.44	23.86	21.22	23.91
1874 33.31			
	1883 23.91	1888 20.09	1893 25.14
1875 32.77	23.74	20.81	25.27
1876 30.84	23.75	24.21	25.03
1877 26.00	23.46	25.03	25.39
1878 24.50			
1879 23.28	1884 23.86	1889 25.67	1894 25.73
23.31	24.42	25.24	25.73
25.08	24.39	24.96	25.83
25.27	24.93	25.69	25.92
1880 25.40	1885 25.09	1890 26.39	1895 25.82
25.44	24.06	27.41	25.80
24.93	23.86	29.47	25.83
24.48	23.70	28.71	25.74

SOURCE—Same as for Table 5.

countries. Amidst moderate prosperity, prices in general were rising—
for a change—in England, France, and Germany. Toward the end of the
year, the Russian government established new financial connections in
Paris and successfully floated a new loan there.

The Contrast

Unusual though the coincidences of 1888 may have been, they illustrate
a condition that was *chronic*—the ruble's greater sensitivity than the
gulden's to the psychological magnification of real influences.[32] What

32. The size of the ruble's *short-run* fluctuations in that year, when the range
between the lowest and highest daily rates on London reached an unusually huge
31 per cent of the yearly average, may deserve mention. The largest Saturday-to-
Saturday rise in the mark price of rubles came in the week ending June 23, and
amounted to 5.6 per cent; the largest declines came in the weeks ending February
25, and November 17, both and amounted to 2.4 per cent; the average size of the
fifty-two weekly changes, ignoring direction, amounted to 1.2 per cent. Perhaps
the reader is surprised at how large, perhaps at how small, these changes were in a
year of relatively extreme instability. Instead of making such judgments, this paper
merely offers some basis for comparison, some basis for knowing what to be
surprised or not surprised at in other historical episodes.

accounts for the contrast? Some possible bits of explanation, mostly inferred from contemporary writings, follow.

Imports and exports of securities were a much-mentioned influence on exchange rates, and changing quotations of domestic securities on foreign markets had more influence in the Russian than the Austro-Hungarian case.[33] The Russian government was more dependent on covering its budget deficit (as well as financing railroad construction) by repeated borrowing abroad. Opinions about the government's "needs" to borrow—about the condition of the budget—accordingly had more scope to influence bond quotations. Russia was more involved than Austria-Hungary in wars (including the campaigns in Central Asia), war scares, and domestic uprisings.

Russian bonds tended to be rather speculative, which gave corresponding scope to fluctuating opinions not only about the creditworthiness of the Russian government in particular but about the economic and general soundness of the country as a whole. In this way, trade in securities could reinforce the influence of developments affecting commodity trade. For example, favorable export prospects tended to reassure foreign investors about the country's "ability to pay," increasing the demand for Russian securities and further strengthening the ruble. And a stronger ruble was in turn taken as a sign of a sounder country.

A certain suspiciousness prevailed abroad about the Russian autocracy and its decency and trustworthiness. (Episodes of deviousness concerning paper-money issues and announced programs to shrink the money supply, for example, provided material for suspicions to feed on.) Official statistics and published financial news tended to be suspect, especially in view of the occasional suppression of private financial publications. Even non-economic domestic policies had an influence on the opinions of foreign investors; for example, intensified discriminations against Jews might affect the cooperativeness of foreign investment bankers in floating Russian securities.

One further piece of evidence on the importance of foreign public opinion was the prevalence of efforts to manipulate it through press-agentry—favorably by Russian agents and sometimes unfavorably by foreigners, as by Bismarck in 1887.

As the foregoing points suggest, the instability of the ruble does not

33. The influence of trade in securities was particularly stressed in Ratner, *Rubel- und- Wechselkurse.* (Ratner, a Russian graduate student in Germany, wrote that book as a doctoral dissertation.) Similar observations appear in Kaufman, *Kreditnye Bilety*, pp. 17–19, and Vlasiĭ Sudeĭkin, *Birzha i Birzhevyĭa Operatsii* (St. Petersburg: Tipografiĭa Severnago Telegrafnago Agentstva, 1892), pp. 52–53.

necessarily show that destabilizing speculation ordinarily prevailed specifically in the foreign-exchange market. The instability may well have hinged on "fundamentals," if the condition of foreign securities markets can count among these. True, the Russian press and of course Russian finance ministers routinely blamed dips and slides of the ruble on the speculators in Berlin, where the main market for trading rubles against other currencies was located. Some critics of speculation even imagined a conspiracy deliberately trying to depress the ruble. Some other observers disagreed. Schulze-Gävernitz judged that professional speculators exerted a stabilizing influence and that the well-organized forward-trading facilities in Berlin facilitated their beneficial operations.[34]

Still another possible reason remains why speculation specifically in foreign exchange may have been more destabilizing or less stabilizing in the Russian than in the Austro-Hungarian case: changing hopes and expectations of a return to redeemability at gold par (a mistaken but widely used concept in both cases) presumably affected the ruble more than the gulden. The more changeable credit standing and general prestige of the Russian government could have a bigger influence on expectations of redeemability. Besides, redeemability at the (misconceived) par would bring bigger gains to bulls on the ruble than to bulls on the gulden, since the ruble was fluctuating further below par. Mistaken hopes of redeemabilty at the supposed par were noticeable in the ruble market as late as the summer of 1890.[35]

A final hypothesis hinges on the fact that Russian history contained more examples of official market intervention and authoritarian controls—and so presumably bred more active suspicions and expectations of new ones—than did Austro-Hungarian history. Overt attempts to peg or even raise the ruble's foreign-exchange value had failed conspicuously, with heavy losses for the government, after the Crimean War, again in 1863, and again in 1876. One-way-option speculation on the pegged or manipulated rate worked on those occasions just as it does in our own time. Between those occasions and after 1876, official

---

34. Schulze-Gävernitz, *Volkswirtschaftliche Studien*, esp. pp. 504–7, 510–17, 524–27, 534–36. Schulze-Gävernitz distinguished between professional and amateur speculation and said (p. 514) he had been told that some speculators in rubles "scarcely knew where Russia is located." Another generally favorable judgment about speculation and forward trading appears in Alfred Ruetz, *Zur Geschichte der russischen Valutareform. Die Währungspolitik Russlands in den Jahren, 1881–1895* (Stettin: Hessenland, 1899), pp. 58–59.

35. Ratner, *Rubel- und- Wechselkurse*, pp. 56–57; Schulze-Gävernitz, *Volkswirtschaftliche Studien*, pp. 476, 517n.

intervention was less overt and ambitious. Between 1867 and 1875, the State Bank's gold-acquisition policy generally had the effect of putting a vague ceiling on the exchange value of the ruble. In 1877 and 1878 the government sold paper rubles for foreign exchange to finance its armies in the Balkans and the Caucasus. Nikolai Bunge, who was finance minister from 1882 through 1886, had previously expressed himself in print on the folly of official intervention in the foreign-exchange market; his official reports stated that his administration was refraining from such intervention, and his word may presumably be trusted.[36] His successor Ivan Vyshnegradsky, however, was more than once accused of having intervened on government account during 1888 and at other times, sometimes to raise and sometimes to depress the ruble and sometimes with the aid of *ad hoc* paper-money issues, and even of having speculated profitably as a bear against the ruble on his own personal account.[37] Whether or not those charges were in fact justified, they epitomize the atmosphere of suspicions and conjectures in which private speculators decided on their own operations. The Russian press campaign against operations on the Berlin market must also have affected the thinking of speculators. The continual efforts of financial agents and press agents of the Russian government to manipulate foreign markets for Russian securities abroad amounted to indirect attempts at manipulation of the ruble rate. Sergei Witte, who became finance minister in 1892, carried out some well-known interventions, including his rather dishonorably conducted bear squeeze on the Berlin ruble market in October 1894, while preparing Russia's transition to the gold standard.

A final contrast between the Austro-Hungarian and Russian experiences that cries out for an explanation (which I cannot offer) concerns the different climates of opinion about policy. In both countries, it is true, the general public was apparently unenthusiastic and even wary about the gold standard. Among recognized experts and the

36. An article of 1880 and a report of 1885 by Bunge are quoted in Aleksandr Gur'ev, *Reforma Denezhnago Obrashcheniĩa*. (St. Petersburg: Kirshbaum, 1896), pt. 2, suppl. 1, pp. 181–83. Also relevant is the quotation (pp. 179–80n.) from a book translated by Bunge in 1865.

37. Theodore H. Von Laue, *Sergei Witte and the Industrialization of Russia* (New York: Columbia University Press, 1963), pp. 24–25, 30; Maxime Kovalewsky, *Le Régime Économique de la Russie* (Paris: Giard & Brière, 1898), pp. 24–29, 30; Ludwik Zieliński, "Der Rubel jetzt und vor 100 Jahren," *Jahrbücher für Nationalökonomie und Statistik*, 71, no. 4 (1898): 482, no. 5 (1898): 628–29; Élie de Cyon, *M. Witte et les Finances Russes*, 4th ed. (Paris: Chamerot et Renouard, 1895), pp. xxix–xxx, 51, 203–4. Cyon had been Vyshnegradsky's agent in Paris but later became an outspoken enemy of both Vyshnegradsky and Witte; his trustworthiness is open to question.

majority of legislators in Austria-Hungary, however, being in favor of the gold standard was part of the conventional wisdom; yet in Russia, dissent was conspicuous even among economists. Following the initiative of his finance minister, the Tsar had to bypass the usual legislative procedure and establish the gold standard by autocratic decree.

Conclusion

Instead of stressing the rather obvious present-day relevance of the history just reviewed, I shall make two brief points. First, we must beware of excessive generalization about the lessons of historical experience with fluctuating exchanges. Superficially similar experiences may be fundamentally different, even though in ways usually unappreciated and requiring detailed, episodic study. When tempted to draw lessons from experience, we should make sure we understand just *what* the experience was *of*. Second, policy-makers who want to impose controls on or intervene in domestic or international financial transactions should be quite sure they understand, first, what they are going to do. They should understand in detail how different transactions and trading practices interrelate with one another, how restrictions on some could impair the performance of others, and how restrictions or interventions too casually decided upon could thus defeat their own purposes.

COMMENT: THE CURRENCY AREA PROBLEM

Donald B. Marsh

I believe that all here will agree with me that we have before us two excellent papers by Professors Kenen and Yeager. I do not propose to deal in any detail with Kenen's paper; I shall leave that to the giants in the "Optimum Currency Area" debate, some of whom are present and have been mentioned in the course of his discussion.

Kenen's main conclusion regarding fixed *versus* flexible exchange rates is that "fixed rates...are most appropriate—or least inappropriate—to well-diversified national economies" (i.e., the developed countries); and that, conversely, flexible rates are better suited, even perhaps essential, to the peculiar problems of the less-developed countries.

I am not contradicting this statement; and yet it seems to me that the success, or at least the stability, of Canada's floating rate in the decade of the 1950's was due in large measure to the sophisticated exchange trading of the Canadian banking system, and here I include the smoothing operations of the Bank of Canada through the Exchange Fund Account. We had a good, smoothly-operating exchange market. Many of us were sorry to see it go.

Moreover, to shift to Kenen's "global point of view" as opposed to "defensive arguments," does it really matter what exchange-rate system the less developed countries adopt? What does matter, surely, is that the large, developed countries should not waste their substance in a self-defeating scramble for reserves. Nevertheless, such a scramble is inevitable under a fixed-rate system; and the big destabilizing shifts in reserves occur among the highly industrialized, developed countries of the West. Shifts in reserves to, from, or among the less developed countries are matters of supreme indifference to the stability of the international monetary system. This would suggest that a flexible-rate system, because it leaves everyone in external balance, should satisfy Kenen's "global"—as opposed to his "defensive"—criterion for the countries that really face instability under fixed rates, namely, the highly developed countries of Europe and North America.

I now return to the "defensive." In contrast to the smooth and sophisticated mechanics of the exchange market, to which I have referred, Canadian monetary policy over the period of the floating rate was anything but smooth or sophisticated. During the investment boom of 1955–57, the central bank's built-in bias against inflation corresponded with the policy dictated by the course of economic events, and the floating rate worked very well indeed. But during the period 1957–61, when a slack economy with over-capacity and under-employment cried out for expansionist measures, monetary restraint continued; and, in this tragicomedy of policy errors, the flexible exchange rate was blamed for the consequences of policy. So much so that when, with a change in monetary management, some degree of economic lucidity was restored, a reversal of the tight-money policy (too long delayed) was accompanied by a deliberate policy of "talking down" the Canadian dollar and thus manipulating the exchange rate to a "significant [but undisclosed] discount."[1]

The immediate and, in the end, overwhelming speculation against the manipulated rate and later against the IMF pegged rate is blamed, not upon the obvious recklessness of first completely undermining confidence in the currency and then attempting to arrest its consequent decline at some desired level; it is blamed instead upon certain allegedly innate weaknesses of flexible exchange rates. Oddly enough, these weaknesses appeared only after the flexible-rate system had, with much public fanfare, been completely abandoned by the monetary and fiscal authorities! It was manipulation of the rate not the flexible rate itself, that led, first, to the massive loss in reserves and, second, to the Canadian austerity program announced on June 24, 1962, which, with the devaluation then existing, was at length sufficient to turn the speculative tide.

It is, I think, essential to get the Canadian story straight, if we are to use that story as part of the evidence for or against flexible exchange rates. I do not for a moment suggest that anyone at this conference needs any guidance from me on the subject, but I do suggest that, in this as in many other cases, we should combat those distortions of current history which, however naïve and innocent the distorters themselves may be, can do incalculable harm in the future.

This brings me to Professor Yeager's paper, which is an excellent example of how to get the story straight. I must confess that before reading Yeager's paper, I knew nothing of the fascinating range of problems faced by the Austrian and Russian authorities under their flexible exchange-rate systems in the nineteenth century. Even the purveyors of conventional ignorance, the distorters of current history, were

1. Canada, *Parliamentary Debates* (Commons), June 20, 1961, p. 6649.

at work! As Yeager points out: "Contemporary writers parroted each other in bewailing the supposedly large fluctuations, usually without citing specific episodes." We must, of course, make exception here for the wholly admirable Jankovich!

If stability is not the sole criterion of success for a floating-rate system, real or alleged instability does seem to be the major (or only?) argument of those who oppose that system. In this light, Yeager's results are especially interesting. It would seem that, in spite of "chronic government budget difficulties" and "haphazardly regulated money supplies" in both Austria and Russia, the floating gulden, but not the manipulated ruble, performed remarkably well in the period 1879–91. Yeager's comparison with Canada indicates that, at least in intra-year fluctuation, the gulden out-performed the Canadian dollar. In intra-month fluctuation the gulden averaged slightly more or slightly less than the Canadian dollar, depending on which of Yeager's Tables 2 and 3 one chooses for comparison.

However, the performance of the Canadian rate might look better if the correction period, October, 1950 to January, 1952, were left out of the calculation. During this period the United States dollar in Montreal fell from a premium of 10 per cent or $10\frac{1}{2}$ per cent (when the parity value of the Canadian dollar was 90.9¢ U.S.) to a premium of zero. The subsequent discount on United States funds after January, 1952, never went beyond $5\frac{25}{32}$ per cent (in 1957) and United States funds went to a small premium of $\frac{1}{16}$ per cent at one point in 1955.[2] Allowing for this, the overall variation was confined within the range of $5\frac{27}{32}$ points, or approximately plus or minus 3 per cent over the whole eight-year period. Intra-year and intra-month variations, as measured by Yeager, would be smaller.

Yeager is forced by the shortage of data to entertain certain hypotheses to explain the stability of the floating gulden. One of these is the possible stabilizing effect of arbitrage in securities. In the Canadian experience, one of the most important stabilizing influences was the United States exchange overhanging the market following the flotation of large issues of new securities in New York. The client's bank would buy Canadian (sell United States) in the market in such a way as to avoid having the market move against the bank and its client. That is, any softening of the Canadian dollar would lead the bank to buy Canadian (sell United States), thus bringing the Canadian dollar back up again. But, as the Canadian dollar approached or exceeded its

2. Bank of Canada. *Statistical Summary: Supplement, 1965* (Ottawa: Bank of Canada, 1966), p. 143.

former position, the bank would stop buying Canadian (selling United States), thereby reducing support for the Canadian dollar until its value dropped back again. Thus the Canadian dollar tended to remain very close to a "notional equilibrium" determined by those banks seeking to place large holdings of United States exchange.

Finally, one source of short-run stability for the floating Canadian dollar was apparently denied to the gulden and applied only in a perverse, and presumably destabilizing, form to the ruble. I refer to the Bank of Canada's smoothing operations in the exchange market. The gulden, according to Yeager "was quite free of any official intervention along the lines of an exchange equalization account"; and the ruble was apparently manipulated (sometimes allegedly for private gain) after 1886 by Finance Minister Ivan Vyshnegradsky. Except for the suspicion of dishonesty in the Russian case, this parallels to some extent the Canadian system of manipulation after December, 1960, and especially from June, 1961, to May 2, 1962, when an official parity of 92.5¢ U.S. was filed with the IMF.

Unlike the gulden in October, 1890, when it rose more than 1 per cent against mark notes in one day, the Canadian dollar would have been checked by Bank of Canada action before it rose (or fell) by more than, say, $\frac{1}{4}$ of 1 per cent in any day's trading. The exact point of intervention was not fixed because traders could then make money at the Bank's expense; but the amount of daily fluctuation was held within narrow limits. However, if the trend continued on the next day, the Bank would intervene only moderately until, again, the permissible limit was reached. Thus the Bank of Canada smoothed out purely temporary, and possibly disrupting, fluctuations without bucking a trend in either direction based on longer-run market factors.

One interesting parallel between the two nineteenth-century examples of floating-rate systems described by Yeager and the Canadian floating-rate system in the twentieth century is the spate of groundless fears and faulty analysis that preceded their demise. In this context, Hegel's pessimistic appraisal of the influence of history on policy seems especially apt: ". . . what experience and history teach is this—that peoples and governments never have learned anything from history, or acted on principles deduced from it."[3]

3. G. W. F. Hegel, *The Philosophy of History* (New York: Willey Book Co., 1944), p. 6. In fairness to Hegel, it must be added that he did not think history *could* teach peoples and governments; but he was clearly thinking of comparisons made over long periods of time.

COMMENT: THE CURRENCY AREA PROBLEM

James C. Ingram

First I will make a brief comment about Professor Yeager's paper. With so few episodes of genuinely fluctuating exchange rates, it is good to have a study of these little-known cases in the nineteenth century. Professor Yeager's prediction, that economists would be surprised to know that the Austrian exchange rate was so stable during the period he studied, was entirely correct in my case. I was also puzzled because such stability contradicts contemporary newspaper accounts of great instability and even chaos in the foreign exchange markets. Another puzzle is that these rates remained stable in the face of chronic budget difficulties and what Yeager calls "haphazard regulation of the supply of money."

The interesting question is why such stability existed and what explanations we can find for it. I first thought that the sterling exchange rate might be the wrong one to use. For example, if one examined the behavior of the Belgian and French francs in the early 1920's, he would find that these two currencies were stable in terms of each other, but they were quite unstable in terms of dollars. However, I can see no reason to think that the sterling rate is the wrong one for Yeager to use in his calculations. During his main period, 1879–91, the dollar had already settled down and was itself stable in terms of sterling.

Yeager suggests that one explanation is that the forward exchange market was highly organized, large, and stabilizing in its influence during this period. No doubt the Austrian market was better developed than the Russian one, which may account for some of the difference in the two.

Yeager also suggests that international trade in securities may have been stabilizing, though he is properly cautious about this point. Part of his account puzzles me. If some disturbance—say an increase in demand for imports—caused the gulden to fall in value, I should think that securities quoted on foreign markets would automatically and immediately be marked up in price in terms of gulden on the Vienna Bourse. Yeager says such securities would be temporarily cheaper in Vienna and that arbitrageurs would buy securities in Vienna for resale

95

abroad, thus adding to the demand for gulden and restraining its fall. I think that very little (perhaps zero) such arbitrage would be needed to equate Viennese and foreign security prices at a new exchange rate. If the securities were traded only in Vienna—for example, if they were common stocks of Austrian firms—it seems difficult to say what the effect would be. Presumably much would depend on the expectations of the future held by domestic and foreign asset-holders.

The episode in 1887 described by Yeager seems to involve such differences in expectations. The war scare evidently alarmed Austrians, who sought to unload gulden and also to sell securities to get funds for transfer into foreign currencies. But foreign investors appear to have taken a more optimistic view and backed that view by heavy purchases of securities on the Viennese Bourse, so the increase in supply of gulden was matched by an increase in demand. As Yeager's vivid quote concludes, "German bankers fought like courageous lions against Austrian pessimism,...they mocked our pusillanimity." This account does not make clear the nature of the securities traded, but I assume they were Austrian securities not traded on foreign markets. (If they were listed on foreign markets, the owners could have sold them there. Then their sale would produce the desired foreign exchange without the necessity to go through the foreign exchange market at all.)

The Russian case in 1888 seems rather different, and trade in securities not so stabilizing. German investors dumped Russian securities and thereby weakened the ruble, and this apparently was a cause of the instability of the ruble in that year.

Turning to Professor Kenen's paper, I confess that I do not think the question of an optimum currency area is any longer a very interesting one. Mundell's 1961 paper is now pretty badly dated, largely because of his own subsequent writings. His later work allows for mobility of capital and provides much fuller treatment of alternative combinations of policy. It seems to me that Kenen's paper is closer to the 1961 paper in content and is handicapped by its omission of capital movements and its emphasis on a single factor, labor. However, as always in Kenen's work, there are many useful comments and insights, especially before and after the core of his paper. First I will make a few points directly on Professor Kenen's paper, and then I will comment on the broader issues involved.

His analysis of optimum currency areas implies that, when one region has unemployment, other regions will have to accept inflation in order to relieve the unemployment. Thus, we expect differing degrees of inflation in the regions. This implication does not seem to be borne out by the facts in a multiregion area, such as the United States. Whether this is due to the openness of the economy or to other factors is not yet clear.

Second, Professor Kenen's analysis implies that the terms of trade will vary more for regions with few products than for those with many products. He says the terms of trade will change more often, but I think he means to say that the amplitude of fluctuation will be greater. This point is similar to one made about the degree of export concentration, but recent studies have not confirmed the a priori expectation that concentration will be correlated with instability. Personally, I have never understood the empirical results that have been reported on this point; and I wish to say only that the evidence, such as it is, appears to run counter to Kenen's analysis. On this point, I also have some doubts about whether comparison of one-product and two-product economies is a sufficient basis for determining the influence of diversification.

Third, Professor Kenen says that the domains of the currency area and the fiscal authority must coincide. However, most of his argument on this point is directed toward showing that the fiscal domain should not span two or more currency areas. He does not say much about the reasons why the currency area should not include two or more fiscal domains. I think, in fact, that it is feasible to have many regional fiscal authorities within a single-currency area just as we have in the states of the United States. Even within the constraints of a currency area, some scope could remain for fiscal policy in regions or nations within a currency area.

Turning now to broader comments, it seems to me that the geographic extent of a currency area—including in that term national currencies rigidly linked by fixed rates and full convertibility—can be whatever we want it to be, large or small, although I do agree that when the currency area becomes very small we lose the advantages of the use of money. I do not think the optimum size of a currency area can be discovered by looking for real economic determinants of it, such as degree of labor mobility or homogeneity of output, although these factors may certainly affect the speed and ease of adjustment. I think the efficacy of a currency area depends on policy positions taken by governments and on the firmness of their commitment to them, on attitudes of the population toward the adjustment processes involved, on the nature of financial and other institutions, and on some economic considerations that are largely omitted from much present analysis. At a high enough level of abstraction, we can achieve internal and external balance under either fixed or flexible exchange rates as Meade, Mundell, and others have shown; but at that level of abstraction, there is not much basis for a choice between the two, not much guidance to policy-makers who need, above all, an operational solution.

When we attempt to analyze payments-relationships among advanced industrial countries which are connected through fixed exchange rates, but proceed by assuming that no capital movements occur (or, indeed, that capital does not even exist), that net investment is zero, that we have one factor (labor) and one, or perhaps two, products, and that we can ignore the accumulation of wealth and the forms in which it is held, I think we have little hope of saying anything useful. Such analysis seems to leave little room for money at all. It is virtually equivalent to barter, with prices expressed in real terms of trade and full adjustment occurring on current account. The other functions of money and most of the interesting issues seem to have been excluded altogether.

Even though formal models complex enough to handle all these elements may still lie beyond us, I think we must deal with them by cruder, less elegant, and more intuitive analysis. I think a meaningful analysis of the adjustment process among advanced industrial countries should take account of net investment, the accumulation of wealth, a variegated structure of financial claims to that wealth, and the increases in productive capacity associated with any investment. McKinnon has made a promising start with his emphasis on portfolio balance; but he still has net investment equal to zero, except for the last few pages of his most recent paper; and he does not really incorporate much of a wealth effect into his analysis.

I hope that these remarks will not be interpreted as expressing any hostility to pure theory. All I am really suggesting is the need for a little more relevance and greater willingness to use cruder analysis. The loss in elegance will be more than offset by the gain in relevance, in my opinion.

If a group of nations whose currencies are linked together at fixed exchange rates can simultaneously achieve internal and external balance, we should presumably be content. However, if internal and external balance could also be achieved through separate currency areas and flexible exchange rates, how are we to say which system is optimal? Mundell's work has now made it clear that, with rigid exchange rates and perfect mobility of capital, external balance could be achieved, at least for some short or intermediate period. The major questions remaining seem to be:

> 1) Can a sufficiently high degree of capital mobility be achieved in practice if nations were committed to this end?

Does the institutional structure permit it, or can it be made to do so?

2) For how long a run can this system be expected to work?

3) Is it possible for a nation to achieve internal balance given the constraints it must accept in order to achieve external balance?

The hardest case is that in which a nation has an adverse movement in its balance of payments—an incipient deficit—along with unemployment. In a fixed rate currency area, perfect capital mobility takes care of external balance, and D (the deficit country) draws down or sells off financial assets, while S (the surplus country) accumulates assets. The first impact of these shifts in financial assets probably falls on short-term, liquid-asset holdings. (One shred of empirical evidence on this point is that in recent years European surplus countries show a rise in the ratio of quasi-money to GNP, while the United States shows a decline. Similar data for the United Kingdom are not available.)

It seems plausible to suppose that such changes in liquid-asset holdings would upset the portfolio balance of wealth-holders and tend to cause a shift from longer-term to shorter-term assets in D and the opposite in S. With perfect capital mobility, these shifts would result in what we would observe as long-term capital movements from S to D. (Unfortunately, available statistics on wealth are so scarce and fragmentary that no empirical evidence can be brought in. In any case, existing barriers to capital movements probably block this aspect of the adjustment process.)

It may be that the changes in the stock of wealth in D and S would have some effect on current expenditures for goods and services. If so, some adjustment in current account would take place. However, even if this effect does not occur, it would seem that capital movements could continue to equilibrate the balance of payments for as long a run as it seems reasonable to be concerned about. For one thing, the aggregate value of financial assets is very large in comparison to the annual loss to foreigners. More important, however, is the fact that asset formation is continuing in D (net investment positive), and the *proportion* of national wealth owned by foreigners need not be rising much, if at all. Thus there is no reason why a current account imbalance could not be financed almost indefinitely by capital transactions. If D is suffering from unemployment, expansionary fiscal policies would be pursued, with budget deficits financed in world capital markets at going interest rates. At this point, someone usually says this is a very short-run expedient. But why? Fiscal policy should not be viewed simply as demand-creating, so that the government's credit grows steadily weaker. For the long run, emphasis must be placed upon productive public expenditures, or on governmental encouragements of private investment, in order to increase capacity to produce. Fiscal policy must be imaginative, and this may be a severe practical objection. The objective is to achieve real growth which, when converted into larger output, will be likely to reduce the import balance on current account.

It is easy to say that nations will not have such a system, will not accept it. But if that is so, does it follow that the nations concerned do not form a currency area? Or that they are unwilling to do so? We have often heard it said that nations are unwilling to abridge monetary sovereignty, but we can also see some signs that the Six are moving toward monetary union. I do not believe any analysis of real economic factors will discover a basis for a currency area in the Six, but not in the Seven, Thirteen, or even Twenty-one.

COMMENT: THE CURRENCY AREA PROBLEM

M. June Flanders

The two papers under discussion ask the following questions: (1) Kenen—What considerations should be applied in deciding (from the point of view of any country) whether to have fixed or flexible rates? (2) Yeager—How well did the foreign exchange market work during an experience of flexible rates in the case of one country (Austria), and how does this experience compare with that of another country (Russia) during its period of flexible exchange rates? We have, then, two aspects of the same larger problem: the workings of the international equilibrating mechanism under fixed and under flexible exchange rates.

The differences between the papers are striking. First, one paper is historical and relates to a particular set of events, while the other is a general, analytic exercise; one is descriptive, the other, if not prescriptive, seeks at least to establish criteria for prescription. But the most striking difference, nay, contrast, between the papers is what they reveal about the level of sophistication of the "general attitude" toward the goals of the international adjustment mechanism "then"—the last quarter of the nineteenth century—and "now." One gathers from Professor Yeager's paper that the main (if not the sole) criterion in the late nineteenth century (at least as far as the economic journalists of the *Neue Freie Presse* were concerned) for judging whether flexible exchange rates were working successfully was how little they flexed. "Orderliness" and stability in the exchange markets appeared to be the major criteria. We get occasional glimpses of underlying economic variables, such as the levels of domestic and foreign prosperity, the abundance of the harvest (which tended to affect export prospects), and the like, but (a) these are brought to our attention by Professor Yeager, not by the *Neue Freie Presse et al.*, and (b) they are always discussed in terms of their probable effect upon the exchange rates, rather than the reverse relationship. Compare on the one hand frequent comments about the recent Canadian experience, the fear that appreciation of the exchange rate would lead to a rise in unemployment, via the balance of trade, with, on the other hand, the *Neue Freie Presse*'s alarm over the high world price of the gulden on the grounds that it could not continue and must necessarily be succeeded by undesirably high prices for foreign exchange.

Professor Yeager's story is an exciting one. The contrast between the Russian and the Austro-Hungarian experiences is instructive. It is always pleasant to have one's prejudices confirmed, and in this case we can take comfort from the evidence that, indeed, a truly flexible exchange rate will tend to fluctuate less than one which is interfered with by monetary authorities in a sporadic and ill-defined way. Also of interest is the difference in the roles played by the securities markets. In the Russian case, government borrowing—capital imports—seemed to have caused movements in the exchange rates; whereas in the Austrian case, the existence of a broad and well-organized international market in securities appears to have had a stabilizing influence. However, Professor Yeager's interpretation of this as compensating short-term capital movements is open to question. It is clear that the existence of another type of asset, in addition to foreign exchange, broadened the market and lessened the impact of political and other speculation on the price of foreign exchange. But that changes in the exchange rate led to arbitrage in securities I find more difficult to understand. If the securities in question were issued by non-Austro-Hungarian governments, banks, or firms, I should think that their price in terms of gulden would rise instantly when the price of the gulden fell, without waiting to be bid up by actual transactions or increased foreign demand for them. Stated differently, it seems to me that any opportunity for arbitrage would be so quickly eliminated by a rise in the supply price of foreign securities in Vienna, that there would be few actual transactions taking place, hence the exchange rate stabilizing short-term capital inflows would not, in fact, occur. If there is any market where it seems to me unreasonable to assume that the participants are stupid, slow to react, or oblivious, it is the market for foreign securities in a major money and capital market. As to Austrian securities denominated in gulden, I fail to see why foreigners would want to buy or hold them in greater quantities at a time when attitudes toward the gulden were bearish. Only speculators who thought the decline in the price of the gulden would be temporary would be tempted to make this purchase. There may have been some interest arbitrage involved, but that, I think, is another story. Professor Yeager's first example supports my point. According to the *Neue Freie Presse* account, it was not arbitrage in securities which saved the gulden, but a different assessment of political prospects and the likelihood of war. "Berlin bankers fought like courageous lions against Austrian pessimism, they made fun of all war fear, they mocked our pusillanimity and supported the structure that was cracking in all its joints."

The last example which Professor Yeager gives is, on the other hand, what I would call a genuine case of securities arbitrage. As the price of the gulden fell, it was buoyed up by the purchase of Austrian securities. But this took place in the context of a return to the gold standard and fixed exchange rates, so that the purchasers of the securities were almost certain in advance what the price of the gulden would be when the securities matured.

Turning to Kenen's paper, if one dare summarize an eclectic view, the Mundell-McKinnon-Kenen consensus seems to be that an optimum currency area as heretofore defined, i.e., an area within which exchange rates are fixed, should include only regions between which there is (presumably perfect) mobility of labor. Many political nations are obviously, by this criterion, not optimum currency areas, but are rather superoptimal. If an over-sized currency area happens to be a political nation, however, the "highly sophisticated budgetary policies" which are required to reallocate demand may be socially and politically feasible, despite the redistributions of wealth and income which they will, in general, involve. We do not seem as yet to be prepared to make similar alterations in the international distribution of income.

The next step is to note that the world as a whole is not an optimum currency area; in fact, the implication of the subsequent discussion is that there are no optimum currency areas which include more than one country (and, we noted, many nations are obviously not optimum currency areas) or, if they are, we are not discussing them here. The problem Kenen has turned to next, and it is an interesting one indeed, is the following: If a nation wants to maintain fixed exchange rates (and, as Kenen has aptly reminded us, it can do so only if at least one other country is willing to maintain fixed exchange rates), it puts itself, by definition, into a currency area, and this currency area is very probably not an optimal one. This means that external shocks cannot be adjusted to by depreciation or devaluation (or appreciation) of the exchange rate, and they cannot be adjusted to by international labor movements. They will have to be adjusted to by domestic fiscal and/or monetary policies directed at restoring employment (or compensating the unemployed) in the affected sectors while minimizing the changes in the terms of trade. An economy will be more resilient to external shocks (hence better able to afford the luxury of entering into currency areas with other nations, i.e., to have fixed exchange rates) if it has many single-product regions, regardless of how great, or small, the mobility of labor between these regions is; that is, if it is itself a currency area. There are three reasons for this.

1) The insurance principle. If shocks are random, the more different commodities a country exports, the smaller will be the percentage of exports likely to be affected by any particular shock. Kenen's digression on the need for some mobility is to the point and need not be repeated. However, I should like to append a footnote to strengthen Kenen's case: It may very well be that products which have similar factor requirements are not at all similar in final use, so the mobility of these factors between industries may be quite high and yet the demand changes for the finished goods may be quite independent of one another.[1]

2) "That when, in fact, it does confront a drop in the demand for its principal exports, unemployment will not rise as sharply as it would in a less-diversified national economy." The model demonstrating this is elegant, but it does not really demonstrate the proposition as stated. Perhaps I am quibbling about the use of the word "diversified." What Kenen's results show is that if a country is subjected to external shocks involving "decreased world demand for its exports" (deteriorating terms of trade, or a downward shift in the foreign demand curve, depending on whether we are thinking of a small or a large country respectively), and if the exchange rate is not free to fluctuate in response, then the effect on domestic employment will be smaller, the larger the fraction of the domestic labor force not engaged in the production of exports. The less you trade, the less you are likely to be made to suffer from changes in the conditions of trade. What is not clear to me, from his model, is what happens if there are two export goods, rather than one. This would involve him, of course, in a three-commodity model, and life would be complicated. But whether there is a difference, apart from the insurance principle of point 1, between more and fewer export goods or even between more and fewer goods in total, is not clear.

3) Kenen's third point is that the greater the number of export goods, the smaller the changes in investment which will be induced by changes in the demand for exports. This is the "insurance" principle of risk-spreading again. In a world in which disturbances consist of random shifts in demand for a country's export goods, the more goods a country is exporting, the smaller the decline in demand for exports—as a percentage of total exports—that will result from any given world shift in tastes, hence the smaller the effect on induced investment and the smaller the multiplier effect on employment or on the price level.

1. Edward Ames and Nathan Rosenberg, "The Progressive Division and Specialization of Industries," *Journal of Development Studies*, Vol. 1 (July, 1965).

In conclusion, I should like to interject a caveat of my own, in response both to Kenen's paper and to comments one hears frequently in the great debate over fixed versus flexible rates. By omission, Kenen (and others) seem to imply that there is no interregional, or intersectoral, adjustment problem when there are flexible exchange rates. Except in the case of the country which literally is completely specialized in production, however, it is not clear to me why this should be so. Consider the large, two-commodity country, with flexible exchange rates. A decline in the foreign demand for its export good will result in a depreciation of its exchange rate, *ceteris paribus*, sufficient to maintain external equilibrium. What happens to the earnings in terms of domestic currency of its producers of the export good, is indeterminate (until we know the relevant domestic and foreign elasticities of demand and supply). In a national economy where factors are relatively immobile, we may yet find ourselves with "localized" unemployment or declines in income, and the need for "a wide array of budgetary policies" to reduce or remove these inequalities. What I am saying is that flexible exchange rates clear the foreign exchange market; they do not necessarily clear the domestic goods and factor markets. In sum, flexible exchange rates release the monetary and fiscal authorities from the constraint of having to fix money prices and wage rates at particular levels. They do not remove the need for intersectoral adjustments, and if such adjustments are difficult (and whether they are difficult or not, is, of course, an empirical question), the authorities will still be faced with the problem of depressed areas and pockets of unemployment.

SUMMARY OF DISCUSSION

The summary of the discussion is divided into three parts: rejoinders, discussion of Professor Kenen's paper, and discussion of Professor Yeager's paper.

I

Professor Kenen began by replying briefly to a point made by Marsh. Kenen agreed with Marsh that the developed countries would be able to maintain more stable flexible exchange rates than the less developed ones. Flexible rates, however, are desirable because of their ability to fluctuate: the less developed countries have a stronger claim on flexibility because of a greater need for changes in their terms of trade.

Turning to Ingram's comments, Kenen pointed out, first, that his neglect of capital mobility and his choice of a two-factor model were deliberate. Hence his choice of the word eclectic rather than encyclopedic as descriptive of his view. However, perfect capital mobility would tend to reinforce his, Kenen's, conclusions. Since capital is more likely to be highly mobile among developed than less developed countries, it is again easier to argue for fixed rates among developed countries and flexible rates for less developed countries.

Second, the empirical evidence on instability and concentration refers to macroswings in foreign trade and not to the kind of microeconomic instability that Kenen considers in his paper. Nevertheless, this evidence does raise the possibility that instability in the composition of trade is not as important as the paper makes it out to be.

Finally, it is true that it is not necessary that fiscal and monetary zones coincide. In general, however, fiscal zones should not be larger than monetary zones. On the other hand, a fiscal zone can be smaller than a monetary zone; in fact, this is what is implied by a system of fixed exchange rates between two countries with different monetary policies.

As for the points raised by June Flanders, Kenen agreed that products which are similar in factor use may be quite dissimilar in final demand, though the various and relevant cases suggested by June Flanders may strengthen his conclusions rather than weaken them. It is also quite true

107

that his two-product economy is not so much a more diversified as a less open economy. Finally, the question of intersectoral adjustment and flexible rates, which Kenen had only alluded to in a footnote, is indeed a very important one.

Kenen concluded by stating that he was a little unhappy with arguments about practical policy that rely on statements about *perfect* labor mobility or *perfect* capital mobility. His own results are a little less precise than those obtained by Ingram or Mundell in their work because he attempts to deal with imperfections in mobility. One of the reasons why economists are sometimes ignored, when they think they should be heard, is that they deal with the limiting cases which policy-makers simply do not recognize as relevant to the real world. Important and complicated policy issues have to be decided in terms of more or less, of this *and* that, rather than in terms of the extremes that are so often found in economists' formal models.

Professor Yeager's first comment was addressed to Ingram's surprise at the small degree of fluctuation, not only of the gulden, but also of the ruble. Yeager's own, and June Flanders', emphasis would rather be on the contrast between the two. The contrast is partly—but only partly—explained by the fact that international trade in securities and forward exchange were more restricted on the Petersburg than on the Vienna Bourse. In fact, the main forward market for rubles was located in Berlin and not in Russia itself.

Yeager then commented on the role of securities arbitrage in April, 1892. The Austrian government announced that it intended to enact new gold parity which would represent a depreciation of the gulden of approximately 1 per cent from the level at which it had been fluctuating. The point of that episode is not that arbitrage jumped in to establish the new legal rate. On the contrary, for a few days after the announcement, whenever the gulden started depreciating toward its new legal parity, that depreciation was checked and reversed for a few hours by international trade in securities.

Turning to a point raised by June Flanders, the difference in people's attitudes in the nineteenth century and today is indeed quite striking, especially with respect to the criteria applied to the assessment of the performance of a monetary system. Yeager stated that, from newspaper articles, the abundant pamphlet literature of the time, and from parliamentary debates, he had formed the impression that the chief argument against the existing floating-rate system was: "Such a system is just plain humiliating; why, it is the lot of a backward country not to be on the gold standard, which, as everybody knows, is the modern form of monetary system...." This attitude also colors the parliamentary speeches of one prominent deputy who, at various stages of the 1892 debate, was called on to sum up the case for the gold standard. This deputy said in substance, "I know that the opponents of the gold standard say that paper is not the only unstable money and that even gold can be unstable in value. If these people would only take the trouble to look at the statistical tables, they would see that the price of gold on the London market has stayed practically rigid, fluctuating only a minor fraction of 1 per cent year after year. So you see how wrong they are about gold not being stable in value." As Yeager pointed out, this deputy suffered not only from money illusion but from a sterling illusion specifically. For this deputy, the pound was the only and absolute measure of value against which the value of even gold and silver had to be tested.

Finally, Yeager expressed agreement with June Flanders' concluding comments, stressing that flexible exchange rates are not a cure-all. It does not help the case for flexible exchange rates when people argue as if they thought flexible rates were a panacea for all economic ills. The only thing flexible rates do is to simplify the task of monetary authorities by giving them a better chance to achieve other goals besides external equilibrium.

II

The discussion of the problems raised by Professor Kenen's paper focused on four main issues: the relevance of the optimum currency area analysis; the validity of Professor Kenen's diversification argument; the proper definition of a region; and the proper definition of the currency area problem.

Professor Sohmen's intervention dealt with the first and, to some extent, the last of these issues. Sohmen's main objection to Kenen's paper is that the latter does so little to dispel the notion that the analysis of optimum currency areas has something to do with the issue of fixed versus flexible exchange rates, if fixed is meant to apply to the system incorporated in the I.M.F.'s *Articles of Agreement*. The trouble with that type of analysis is that the fixity of exchange rates is only one attribute of a common currency area; perfect convertibility between the different regions of a common currency area is at least equally important. The evidence of recent years clearly indicates that, in many cases, it is possible to buy more exchange-rate stability only at the expense of less convertibility.

Toward the end of his paper, Kenen concludes that "the principal developed countries should perhaps adhere to the Bretton Woods system"; at the same time Kenen added orally that he would like to see more frequent exchange-rate adjustments even between these countries. These two arguments, according to Sohmen, are difficult to reconcile with each other; any possibility of parity adjustments between different countries linked by fixed exchange rates will certainly disrupt the possible unity such an area might have.

One further problem should be considered in evaluating the relevance of the optimum currency area analysis to the fixed versus flexible exchange rates issue. When people speak of optimum currency areas, they consider the issue only in terms of the spot exchange rate. The implied constancy of all "forward" rates of exchange is at least equally important in a unified currency area. If forward rates can differ from spot rates, perceptible interest-rate differentials between regions of a multiple currency area can arise even if spot rates are fixed and even if convertibility is perfect. This is obviously impossible in a single currency area. Therefore, Sohmen argued, the logical conclusion from the analysis of currency areas would be to propose not only that spot rates should be kept constant for ever and without any margin of fluctuation, not only that perfect convertibility should be maintained for the indefinite future, but also that governments should assume the solemn responsibility to insure the constancy of all forward rates for the indefinite future. Only then is it possible to make a case for the fixing of exchange rates on the grounds that the advantages of a common currency area are realized.

Professor Kenen agreed that Sohmen was right in saying that the theory of optimum currency areas fails to establish the case for flexible exchange rates. The question posed by the optimum currency area analysis is a different one. It is: Over what range should exchange rates be free to fluctuate? Sohmen would not want each individual to have our own currency and our own exchange rate. There must be a zone in which a money is used and Kenen was trying to ask what kind of criteria one would use to delineate that zone. By way of application Kenen suggested that the best candidates would be the developed countries; that does not imply that he endorses all their policies, however silly. Of course, it is correct to state that there are substantial differences between a fixed exchange rate regime and a common currency area except on the most extreme assumptions regarding capital mobility.

Professor Mundell stated that he did not completely agree with Ingram on the lack of importance or relevance of the currency area issue. The analysis of currency areas does have some practical significance. For instance, Europe today has a choice as to what kind of currency area it is going to have: whether it is more important to develop a gold bloc in Europe, or to keep Europe's currencies pegged to the dollar and to remain part of an Atlantic currency area. It is also quite important to know whether West Africa will remain on the C.F.A. franc, and whether different parts of that area will remain in the sterling area. Whether the sterling area is a logical creation *today* depends, at least in part, on whether it meets the conditions of an optimum currency area. We disagree about what these conditions are, Mundell added, and that is what Kenen's paper is about.

Professor Curzon, pursuing Mundell's point, argued that the relevance of the optimum currency area analysis to policy problems would become increasingly apparent, especially in connection with customs-union theory. For instance, some of the problems of integrating countries on the economic periphery of a customs union, for instance Portugal in EFTA, probably arise from those countries not being part of the optimum currency area constituted by the union's present members. Customs-union theory has largely ignored monetary issues; for instance, it is almost always assumed that fixed exchange rates or monetary union will come with a customs union. It might in fact be very relevant to regard the conditions which delimit an optimum currency area as preconditions for any regional trade arrangement. Seen in this light optimum currency area analysis is a subject which is far from closed and irrelevant.

Turning to another topic, *Professor Mundell* raised some questions about the conclusions which Kenen draws from his diversification argument. The most highly diversified economy is the world economy. Then, in terms of an insurance principle and from the point of view of hedging against risks of fluctuation, a world currency is the best solution. Moreover, with respect to the less developed countries, Kenen's argument could be turned around: those countries that are highly diversified can afford to have flexible exchange rates while other countries cannot. As an example, Mundell proposed the following extreme case: suppose a country produces only coffee. If that country follows a policy of maintaining a constant index of prices, this means simply that the exchange rate moves with the price of coffee. The exchange rate in the extreme case of a completely specialized economy becomes simply another name for the price of the major export of that economy. It is not at all clear that Brazilians are subject to such a great degree of money illusion that they would not recognize fluctuations in their real wages due to fluctuations in the exchange rate. In terms of the insurance principle, taken in isolation and apart from other considerations, less developed countries might gain little by having flexible rates; they would perhaps gain more by becoming part of a larger currency area. Mundell argued that in such a larger area the insurance principle might have a better chance to work. Thus, if the Latin American or the West African countries could form a currency area, they may become large enough and diversified enough to make the external fluctuation of their currency small.

Professor McKinnon shared some of Mundell's doubts about the adequacy of the diversification criterion. He realized that summarizing Kenen's results in one sentence is unfair, yet Kenen's main conclusion could be put as follows: the more diversified an economy the stronger the case for fixed exchange rates. However, the more diversified an economy, the larger it is, and, because it is diversified, the smaller the foreign trade sector. Therefore, Kenen's conclusions imply that a large diversified economy with a small foreign sector should have fixed exchange rates whereas small open economies should adhere to floating rates. This means that, in a large economy, monetary and fiscal policy might have to be used to maintain external balance even though the foreign trade sector represents a very small proportion of total GNP. This seems distinctly non-optimal to McKinnon.

Professor Kenen replied to these two points in turn. He considered that Mundell was attempting to reduce his argument to the absurd by suggesting that one could always increase diversification by increasing the size of the region and by simply merging countries into larger regions. Such a procedure would indeed increase the diversification of the output of the larger region; it would not, however, affect the diversification of the output of the given region. Kenen's question pertains to a given region. That question is "should that region attach itself to others or not?" Kenen's answer is: "Ask what that region, taken by itself, produces and ask, then, whether it should become part of a larger monetary zone or not. Adding it to, or merging it with, other countries does not affect *its* product mix and *its* vulnerability as an entity."

In answer to McKinnon, Kenen stated that he explicitly recognizes that the smallness of the foreign trade sector of a highly diversified economy is the chief counterargument to his conclusions. Such smallness does imply greater instability when monetary and fiscal policy are used for internal balance and essentially does involve more of the tail wagging the dog. This point is, therefore, a valid counterargument though its strength is doubtful.

The proper definition of "region" was the next issue raised by *Professor Mundell*. Mundell indicated that in his original discussion of the optimum currency area problem he had been careful to define "region" in the classical sense, namely, internal factor mobility and external immobility of factors. His examples were purely illustrative and should not be taken to imply that regions in this sense can be identified with particular geographical entities, or with single-product regions. Under such a definition, if one takes a world of complete mobility of factors, then the optimum currency area is the world. In that case it is possible to obtain all the benefits of a single currency (in terms of the functions of money such as unit of account, etc.). It is true that money illusion may exist and present problems. However, money illusion is essentially a short-run phenomenon subject to a learning process since income is redistributed from those with to those without money illusion. Mundell asked Kenen whether he would agree that a single currency would be enough in a world of perfect capital mobility.

Professor Kenen agreed that if there were perfect factor mobility over the world as a whole the world would be a single-currency area. The burden of Kenen's argument, however, is that we do not have *perfect* mobility because perfect interregional mobility implies perfect occupational mobility and the latter does not prevail. The labor force is not so homogeneous that it is possible to talk about perfect mobility, or even hope to delineate a region over which there is perfect mobility, unless that region is a single-product region, the kind of region described in Kenen's paper. Therefore, the paper's point of departure was to ask: If we don't have perfect mobility over any region, what other criteria may be used besides the degree of perfection of labor mobility? This is why Kenen would think of the criteria he proposes as a useful supplement or alternative to that proposed by Mundell.

Professor Niehans addressed himself to the more general question of the definition of the currency area problem. Niehans stated that the currency area analysis offers two opposite and extreme solutions to the problem of taking care of disturbances, depending on the circumstances: an inventory (i.e., exchange reserves) policy with fixed prices (i.e., exchange rates), and a price policy with zero or constant inventories. It is possible that with perfect certainty and knowledge one could determine an optimum mix of inventory policy (i.e., exchange reserve movements) and price variations (i.e., exchange-rate fluctuations). From this point of view, it is very likely that neither of the pure strategies under discussion would be optimal except under extreme assumptions. The choice between fixed and flexible rates, then, is really a problem in the theory of the second best and it is necessary to determine which of the two pure strategies comes closer to the ideal policy mix.

Moreover, in defining the optimum currency area problem it is necessary to distinguish between two separate questions which are sometimes intermingled. One is the problem of the optimal policy of one country as against the rest of the world; the other is to find a suitable policy for a group of countries among themselves. The answers to these two problems might be entirely different. Kenen seems to have addressed himself more to the first problem, one country as against the rest of the world, whereas, according to Niehans, the more relevant problem might be that of the appropriate policy to be followed by a group of countries among themselves.

Professor Machlup pointed to another aspect of the problem of defining an optimum currency area. He noted that Ingram in his comments had stated, approximately, that if a group of countries could simultaneously achieve internal and external balance with fixed exchange rates, then Ingram would be quite satisfied and would consider it irrelevant whether or not these countries were an optimum currency area. In this particular case, it is not irrelevant whether they form such an area or not; on the contrary, if these countries can simultaneously achieve internal and external equilibrium, it probably proves that they constitute an optimum currency area. It is necessary to distinguish a definition from the description of instances which fall under that definition. Machlup argued that one might base a definition of an optimum currency area on the fact that both external and internal balance can be maintained simultaneously in that area with fixed exchange rates and, as Sohmen proposes, with perfect convertibility. But then one must ask: "What is it that makes this possible?"

III

Three main points were raised in the discussion of Professor Yeager's paper. Sir Roy Harrod compared the problems of the gulden and the ruble to those of the Indian rupee; Professor Mundell indicated the relevance of the historical record for the international monetary system today; and Professor Aliber raised some questions about the role of silver arbitrage.

Sir Roy Harrod pointed out that, at the very time the gulden and the ruble were being discussed, the Indian rupee, which had also been a silver currency, became the center of a great deal of controversy in England. In fact, some of Alfred Marshall's greatest contributions to economics are those that he made to the rupee exchange-rate discussion of that time—greater in Sir Roy's opinion than any contributions to economics in his *Principles*.[1]

The rupee started floating against sterling when the bimetallic standard was disrupted in 1873, the rupee staying on silver while sterling was on gold. The rupee remained on silver until 1893, when the Indian government closed the mints to the free coinage of silver. This, of course, is quite similar to the Austro-Hungarian case described by Yeager. After 1893 the rupee was, in a sense, a freely floating paper currency. It was, however, subject to some management, which aimed at the eventual attachment of the rupee to gold, a step which occurred around 1900.

The pattern of events was quite similar, and a few points are worth making. First, when the silver parity was broken in 1893, the rupee's behavior was similar to that of the gulden. The rupee started rising above its previous silver value. Second, by staying on silver after 1873, the rupee depreciated against gold and India escaped the period of gold deflation which affected all gold standard countries during the last quarter of the nineteenth century. Prices in India remained stable, and India returned to gold only after the gold situation had started to ease, in part because of South African production.

Sir Roy noted that at the time (after 1873), rightly or wrongly, it was thought that the fluctuation of the rupee was a great evil. It was thought that a floating rupee impaired trade, and, more important, that it impeded British investment in the Indian infrastructure. This attitude contributed to the severance of the rupee's link with silver, and the adoption of a paper rupee floating rate with a view to an eventual attachment to gold.

One of the apparently surprising features of the latter part of the nineteenth century is that silver was more volatile, had a larger range of fluctuation, than those currencies which became detached from silver and were floating. The main reason was that political considerations were creating a great deal of uncertainty about silver. The question of silver was debated in national legislatures and at three international conferences. Some people thought that silver's demonetization would be permanent while others thought that the silver-gold parity would be re-established.

Sir Roy then stated that one point must be kept in mind when considering the stability of a detached currency like the gulden. Though the gulden was not on the gold standard, forces very similar to those at work under that standard were present. Suppose, for instance, a change in the trade structure of a country. As exports fell and imports increased,

1. See *Official Papers of Alfred Marshall*, I, II, and IV.

this country, with a given stock of money, would experience deflation—unemployment would increase, profits decrease, and prices fall. Since there was no policy mechanism to correct that kind of effect, the return to equilibrium was effected in quasi–gold standard style.

This does not mean that the lessons of that period can be applied directly to modern countries, which have monetary and fiscal policies designed to secure full employment. To illustrate this point, suppose that, when some adverse turn in the balance of trade occurred, the Austro-Hungarian government had gone in for public works, expansionary monetary policy, and so on. The exchange rate would have fluctuated more than it actually did. Had monetary and fiscal policy been used to maintain full employment, the exchange rate would not have been as stable.

Therefore, though Sir Roy felt a great deal of sympathy for flexible exchange rates, problems might arise if they were instituted today. This would be especially true in the case of a system in which all, or most, exchange rates floated. In a two-country world, when there is a change in trade structure, the exchange rate appreciates in terms of one currency and depreciates in terms of the other. In a world of many countries with flexible rates, however, there could be in fact a great deal of stability of exchange rates if all countries were committed to a full employment policy. There are two reasons for this. First, suppose every country fights the reduction in employment due to a worsening in its trade balance by inflationary policies. Then, exchange rates might remain relatively stable while all currencies depreciated in terms of goods. The cost of this would be a world price inflation. Secondly, for institutional and political reasons, central banks might start intervening, if rate fluctuations became excessive, and the system would return to some sort of fixed-rates arrangement.

Professor Mundell emphasized the contemporary relevance of Yeager's discussion of a nineteenth-century problem. Until 1870 the world was on a triple-asset standard of gold, silver, and pounds. The retreat from bimetalism in France and the demonetization of silver led to a crisis in the silver market and a great fragmentation of the international monetary system since some countries were on the silver standard and others on the gold standard. In one sense, it did not make much difference to which of these standards particular countries were adhering; what was important was that they were on different standards. This made for the possibility of fluctuations of the price of silver in terms of gold and led to significant exchange margin variations and repercussions on economic activity.

The relevance of these events today, according to Mundell, is this: As Giscard d'Estaing pointed out in his opening speech, the world was on a dollar standard from approximately 1945 to 1955; it then moved into a mixed dollar-gold system; today, with the rising importance of the currency bloc in Europe which holds its reserves fundamentally or primarily in gold, considerable harm could be done to the international monetary system if either of two things, reminiscent of the nineteenth century, occurred. The first is a demonetization of the dollar by the European continental countries; the second a demonetization of gold by the United States.

Take, first, the demonetization of gold. Mundell argued that, though tactics such as the recently suggested formula of selling gold but not buying it might prevent speculation and a flight into gold, the world would automatically be forced into a kind of currency system very analogous to that prevailing in the latter part of the nineteenth century. In such a system the European countries would have to decide to stabilize their currency either in terms of the dollar or in terms of gold. On the other hand, the European countries could bring great damage to the system by demonetizing the dollar and taking the gold. This would not only damage the status of the dollar, in Mundell's view, but also other currencies by creating exchange fluctuations that countries did not plan and could not afford. The monetary history of the second half of the nineteenth century is relevant as a picture of what could occur today in the event of an international monetary crisis.

Professor Aliber asked whether the stability of the gulden exchange rate could be explained by silver arbitrage. If silver had been redeemable "both ways" in Austria and silver prices had been fixed and quoted in London, the exchange rate could not have fluctuated by more than transport costs in the presence of arbitrage. This leads to two questions. First, relaxing the assumption of a fixed price of silver in London, how much of the fluctuation of the gulden–sterling rate can be explained by movements of the price of silver in London? Second, even if guldens were not perfectly convertible into silver, what was the role of silver in the fluctuations of the Austrian money supply? And, what was the importance of silver imports and the proportion of silver in the money supply? An answer to these questions would help to determine whether there was a band set by the costs of silver arbitrage within which the exchange rate remained.

Professor Yeager replied that there are no very precise estimates of the volume of silver coins in active circulation in Austria for that period. However, all existing estimates agree that the coins in active circulation were well below 10 per cent of the money supply. The coinage of silver by the Austro-Hungarian government up and into 1892, it is true, was important. However, these coins were systematically returned to the central bank in exchange for notes thus putting great strain on the bank's storage space. In fact there was widespread conjecture in 1890 that, if the price of silver should be bid up far enough by American legislation and speculation on that legislation, the Austro-Hungarian Bank would make its notes *de facto* redeemable; this would give the bank an opportunity to get rid of its unwanted stocks of silver coin.

Yeager stated that he had investigated the possibility that silver movements had accounted for the stability of exchange rates. As far as he could tell, they did not. In this context, one must bear in mind the special nature of the events of 1890. The price of silver and the exchange value of the gulden were nearly back in contact again, and there was great uncertainty about future silver policy. Thus, if silver had any influence at the time it was probably more destabilizing than stabilizing.

As to what would have happened if the gulden had remained pegged to silver while silver was not pegged to gold, Yeager agreed with Sir Roy that the experience of the Indian rupee is the best example of that type of situation. It tempted Yeager to quote a passage from Oscar Wilde's *The Importance of Being Earnest*. The governess, Miss Prism, says to her ward: "Cecily, you will read your *Political Economy* in my absence; the chapter on the 'Fall of the Rupee,' you may omit. It is somewhat too exciting for a young girl."

At this point *Dr. Salant* adjourned the morning's session.

PART 3

INSTITUTIONAL ARRANGEMENTS

IMPROVING THE BRETTON WOODS SYSTEM

Robert Z. Aliber

In the design of economic institutions, economists too often resemble those generals who believe that the next war will be like the last one. Because those selected by their national governments to negotiate changes in international financial arrangements are unlikely to share the same view about an uncertain future, they may find it easier to agree on arrangements that have served an observed past well rather than on those likely to serve the future. To compensate for the lack of foresight about an uncertain future, it might be thought that any new financial institution should be granted the powers necessary to cope with alternative developments; however, national governments are reluctant to grant extensive powers and financial capabilities to new, untried, international organizations without staff. This is not to suggest that an institution with a broad range of powers is undesirable—but rather that sovereign nations are more likely to delegate substantial independent authority to institutions, the narrower the range of their powers.

The Articles of Agreement of the International Monetary Fund and of the International Bank for Reconstruction and Development and the General Agreement on Tariffs and Trade indicate that economists are also short on foresight. The Fund Agreement was aimed at avoiding a repetition of the disastrous experiences of exchange-rate instability in the interwar period, both during the era of flexible exchange rates between 1919 and 1926 and that of adjustable pegs between 1931 and 1936. The Bank Agreement was aimed at moving the financing of postwar reconstruction from the private sector, which had been used in the 1920's, to the public sector; the promotion of development, now its sole activity, was not an important concern of its founders. GATT was originally intended to be an interim arrangement before the International Trade Organization became operational; GATT would prevent any increase in preferential tariff areas and provide a forum for negotiating tariff reductions on a multilateral basis.

This paper was written in September, 1966, and was not revised to take recent developments, such as Special Drawing Rights, new capital controls by the United States, the British devaluation, and so on, into account.

121

During the mid-1940's, the problem was to fill an institutional gap—to devise new multilateral institutions in trade and finance. The institutions established then have had to adapt to a world very different from the one for which they were designed. They may be poorly designed to cope with the future; but since it seems unrealistic to assume they can be easily replaced, the immediate problem is to discover what changes will enable these institutions to cope with the problems of the next ten to fifteen years and not to design these institutions for an unlimited life.

These changes involve the division of responsibility among the institutions—the institutional mix—which is most likely to realize international order in trade and finance. Order suggests regularity in the sense of meaningful and acceptable "rules of the game" entailing commitments, obligations, and privileges in various circumstances. Some of the relevant policy questions are: Are the contractual relationships among Fund, Bank, and GATT optimal? Are the powers of these institutions sufficiently extensive? Are the GATT and Fund positions on measures for adjustment consistent and comprehensive? Are the Fund and Bank roles in generating reserves adequately adjusted to each other?

Currently the international financial system is underdetermined in the sense that the supply of reserves for financing imbalances is not compatible with the accepted means for adjustment to reduce imbalance. A substantial gap exists between what countries say about adjustment and how they act about adjustment. There is no consensus on how the burden of adjustment should be divided among deficit countries and surplus countries, and on which measures of adjustment are best-suited for particular circumstances. Moreover, existing arrangements are potentially unstable, in the sense that an increase in the demand for gold could cause the existing structure of exchange rates to collapse and reserve levels to decline sharply.[1] Gaps in existing contractual arrangements have been filled by *ad hoc* measures. The need is to select from among politically feasible arrangements those that can lead to improved performance and also reduce or eliminate the threat of instability.

But can the uncertainty and potential instability implicit in the system

1. The single most pressing reason for establishing a Fund agreement was to reduce the likelihood of unnecessary and competitive devaluations. The shortcomings of the IMF system are revealed by concern over the impact of a devaluation of sterling. There is concern that if the British were to devalue, they would prefer to err on the side of too large a devaluation rather than on the side of too small a devaluation. A sizeable group of Europeans believe that if sterling devalued, most continental currencies would follow. The IMF is too weak to prevent an excessive devaluation by the British, and too weak to prevent countering devaluations by other countries even if sterling were not devalued excessively.

be reduced by new contractual arrangements? A political will is necessary if countries are to agree to the necessary new arrangements and to abide by their commitment. Even though countries may agree on the diagnosis of the problem, some may prove unwilling to enter into new contractual arrangements that might limit their future freedom of action.

A View of the Future

Prospective developments in the movement of national price levels suggest that pressure on the structure of exchange rates is likely to increase. The revolution of rising expectations also affects the industrial countries. Their increasing concern with material values suggests high time rates of discount and reduced resistance to inflationary pressures. Since there is little reason to believe that rates-of-price increases among the industrial countries are likely to be approximately the same, the uneven pace of inflationary pressures may lead to extended payments imbalances. More extended imbalances may intensify the need for reserves for financing deficits, while higher price levels may reduce the real value of the existing stock of reserves. Moreover higher prices may both dampen the incentives to produce gold and increase the non-monetary demand for gold.

Prospective developments in the political relationships among the larger, more industrial countries suggest that it may prove increasingly difficult to negotiate new international arrangements as well as changes in existing arrangements. In this period of increasing nationalism, political power tends to become decentralized. Within the EEC, powers have gravitated from the Commission to the Council. De Gaulle has drained the United States gold stock, vetoed the British membership bid in the EEC, and removed NATO from France—and France from NATO.

These national conflicts on defense issues and on financial issues would have arisen without the General—although they would then have been less dramatic. The German gold stock has increased nearly as rapidly as that of the French, and the Dutch have backed the reserve policy of the General. De Gaulle has provided such a focus for policies not immediately sympathetic with the United States that other Europeans have not needed to demonstrate their opposition to United States policy proposals; in a real sense, the General has given them a free ride.

In a world where power is more decentralized, relatively small groups can limit the extent of changes in the system. France has less than 5 per cent of the votes in the IMF—and yet, because of the French, Fund quotas were increased by 25 per cent rather than by the 50 per cent favored by nearly all Fund members. Successful negotiations are likely to entail agreement of nearly all major countries; formal voting majorities are not sufficient.

International cooperation continues, but within a less formal framework. Increasing reliance must be placed on *ad hoc* measures because of the shortcomings in more formal, contractual arrangements. The Fund's strength has been weakened by the Group of Ten, Working Party Three, and the monthly meetings of central bankers of the industrial countries at Basle. The Group of Ten becomes attached to the IMF and begins to assume the role of upper house; the central bankers meet at Basle to consider, among other things, the support of weak currencies.

Consequently the probability of generating substantial new reserves under multilateral agreement seems low. Thus the adequacy of the supply of reserves for financing imbalances will diminish, for the likelihood of generating reserves without explicit agreement, as under the reserve currency arrangements, seems small. The combination of greater divergence in the patterns of price-level increases and the difficulties in adding to reserves suggest that the developed countries will find it increasingly difficult to attain satisfactory payments balance and to finance imbalances. The willingness of countries to reduce imbalances by use of deflationary measures may decline because of the greater emphasis given to domestic objectives. The alternatives to deflation are more frequent changes in parities or additional direct controls on foreign payments. The prospect of more frequent changes in exchange parities does not seem high, largely because explicit changes in parities are not readily operational. Almost by default, present arrangements compel growing reliance on direct controls as a balance-of-payments adjustment measure.

If this prognosis is correct, it suggests two needs. The first is to make the most effective use of the available mechanisms for generating reserves. The second is to insure that the measures to be taken for adjustment have a minimal adverse impact on the welfare of countries adopting the measures and on the welfare of their trading and financial partners.

Changes in the Institutional Mix

The Fund and the Bank.   Much of the discussion of the last few years on the problem of reserve adequacy has focused on mechanisms for generating new reserve assets. In part the deliberate pace of the negotiations about enlarging reserves reflects a lack of agreement on such issues as the distribution of seigniorage, the control of the new reserve institution, and the interconvertibility of new reserve assets and gold. Frustration over these negotiations has led to proposals for an increase in the gold price, for flexible exchange rates, and for greater reliance on private capital flows to finance imbalances.

One alternative is to modify existing financial assets so that they qualify as reserves. This alternative is illustrated by several techniques used by the United States. Debt due the United States has been paid in advance and military expenditures in the United States by foreigners have been prepaid. These transactions are reported as if they reduce the United States payments deficit, even though their major impact is to finance the deficit. The question is whether other financial assets exist which are not now included in the stock of reserve assets and which might be transferred to finance imbalances.

Currently the stock of intergovernmental financial claims not counted among reserve assets exceeds $40 billion. External public debt of the developing countries is nearly $30 billion, paid-in subscriptions to the World Bank's capital exceed $2 billion, and the funded debt of the Bank is about $3 billion. Some of these financial assets could be transferred to settle imbalances. For example, the United States government has a claim on the IBRD of $600 million; Germany has a claim on the Bank of $100 million.[2] When the United States is in surplus and Germany is in deficit, the United States might acquire German-held claims on the Bank; when Germany is in surplus and the United States in deficit, Germany might acquire United States–held claims on the Bank. Similarly both the United States and Germany have claims on a number of developing countries which might be transferred to settle imbalances.

Transferring claims on the World Bank to settle imbalances raises questions about the distinction between the financial roles of the Bank and of the Fund. Historically these institutions were separated to eliminate the possibility that the institution in charge of short-term balance-of-payments support might become overly loaded with long-term reconstruction credits. Even if this view was valid in the mid-1940's, it has ceased to be relevant. A substantial part of the current stalemate about generating new reserve assets within the Fund mechanism reflects a lack of agreement on the assets the Fund might buy. The apparent paradox is that the Bank has many assets that it might buy and lacks money, while the Fund has substantial monies and appears to be faced by a shortage of assets that it might acquire.

2. Legally, these claims are subscriptions to the Bank's capital rather than Bank liabilities.

Several of the plans for monetary reform try to resolve the Bank-Fund dilemma through the back door by having the Fund buy claims on the IBRD. But it may be feasible to monetize for international reserves some of the financial assets generated in the aid-transfer process rather than to distribute some of the seigniorage associated with the creation of new reserve assets to the developing countries.

There are numerous ways in which some of the assets generated in the aid-transfer process can be monetized for reserves. Since the problem is not mechanical, the relevant question is whether countries are likely to prove more ready to accept this scheme than to accept changes in the Fund designed to increase the supply of reserves. In the former case the liquidity of existing assets is increased; in the latter case, new assets must be generated.[3] Because financial claims generated in the aid-transfer process could be transferred to settle deficits, the "real burden" of aid would decline somewhat.

An arrangement of this type raises several questions about the relationship between the Bank and the Fund—their respective roles in generating reserve assets, in evaluating country performance, and in managing the rules of the monetary system. Since the historical reasons for having two separate institutions are no longer valid, efficiency-minded management experts could undoubtedly cite some savings from a merger. But the costs of overlapping are small and would appear to be overwhelmed by some political considerations.

Changes in claims of industrial countries on the Bank would supplement changes in their claims on the Fund as a means to finance imbalances. Fund quotas would still be increased from time to time. The claims of industrial countries on the Bank could be construed as a secondary reserve asset; this component of reserves would increase by $1 billion or more annually.

Under this arrangement, the Fund would retain its primary role in managing the rules of the international monetary system. The Bank would be concerned with the adjustment to imbalances by members to whom it has extended credits, but this concern is very different from being concerned with the pattern of adjustment among industrial

3. Such a scheme raises many problems, including the need to insure that such claims do not become inferior reserve assets. This set of problems is similar to that associated with most reserve-generating schemes. Perhaps the unique aspect of this scheme is to limit the volume of claims generated in the aid-transfer process which might be transferred in the settlement of imbalances. Countries participating in the scheme would be subject to a limit on the amount of claims on the Bank or developing countries that they could transfer automatically to settle payment imbalances.

countries. The Fund would still retain the primary role in assessing the adequacy of reserves and the pattern of adjustment to imbalances.

The Fund and GATT. The current approach toward balance-of-payments adjustment consists largely of a series of *ad hoc* measures, mostly in the form of direct controls on foreign payments. There is a lack of systematic order in the selection of controls on capital movements, in the mix of controls on capital movements and on current-account transactions, in the mix of controls on government payments and on private payments, and even in the form of control on private payments on current account.

The Fund's Articles of Agreement do not provide a systematic approach to adjustment. The Articles of Agreement are focused almost exclusively on procedures for altering exchange parities and for applying restrictions on current-account payments; the Articles neglect most of the measures that countries actually take for adjustment.[4] The "rules of the game" implicit in the Articles include limitations on the use of restrictions on current-account payments by private parties and a prohibition against changes in exchange parities except when a fundamental disequilibrium arises, and then only by an approved amount.

The activities of GATT have complicated the adjustment problem in two ways. The first is that, since it does not want previously negotiated tariff bargains to become unstuck, GATT condones the use of quantitative restrictions as a temporary balance-of-payments device and prohibits the use of tariff surcharges. But quantitative restrictions are impractical for countries which have long since abandoned most such controls and the mechanisms for administering them. Inevitably the inability to use quantitative restrictions and the prohibition against tariff surcharges force adoption of other measures for adjustment. The second complication is that GATT prohibits direct export subsidies, a position which is a legacy from a depression period when beggar-thy-neighbor policies were used for employment-creating purposes.[5] Largely as a consequence, most of the measures for adjustment are designed to restrict foreign payments.

4. Fund members come of age when they move from article 14 status to article 8. Article 14 permits restrictions on current-account transactions during a postwar transitional period. Article 8 countries have indicated to the Fund that they will not apply exchange licensing arrangements to current-account payments. Less than thirty Fund members of a total of more than a hundred have moved to article 8.

5. The logic behind GATT's willingness to accept rebate of indirect taxes on export sales and to reject rebates on direct taxes rests on certain presumptions about shiftability which appear to lack empirical validity.

The concept of the IMF system of adjustable pegs is for fixed, unitary exchange rates and for free convertibility at least on current account with adjustment accomplished by reliance on general measures rather than selective measures. The IMF system works differently in practice and puts great emphasis on selective measures, as is evident from analyzing the effective exchange rates for several major currencies.[6] There are four market quotations for sterling—external-account sterling, security sterling, investment sterling (and the effective rate for buyers of investment sterling differs from the effective rate for sellers), and real estate sterling. In addition, a variety of transactions are subject to exchange controls by the Bank of England; these controls cover tourist spending abroad, the foreign currency position of British banks, and the investments abroad of British firms. In effect, there are numerous effective exchange rates for sterling, which vary with the purpose of the transaction and where the money will be spent.[7]

Similarly there are numerous effective exchange rates for the dollar, depending on the purpose of the transaction and where the money will be spent. Nearly all foreign aid expenditures of the United States government are tied to domestic procurement. The Buy America policy stipulates that foreign prices must be anywhere from 12 to 50 per cent below United States prices before government agencies can buy foreign products. Purchases of foreign securities issued by borrowers in developed countries are subject to the Interest Equalization Tax. Direct investments abroad in other industrial countries are limited by a voluntary program. Bank credits abroad are limited on a worldwide basis.

6. This evaluation of the operation of the Fund system does not agree with the Fund's own evaluation. "With the exception of one large-scale and widespread devaluation in 1949, which was a part of the postwar readjustment process, there have been relatively few changes in agreed par values. Similarly, the instrument of quantitative restriction on imports which was provided for in the GATT as a facility for meeting balance of payments difficulties, has in fact been practically abandoned by countries once they have succeeded in dismantling controls. Payments restrictions have similarly lost importance as a means of balance of payments adjustment, particularly since the widespread acceptance of Article VIII in 1961. Finally, restrictions on capital payments, which were not placed under the requirement of Fund approval as were restrictions on current payments, have been subject to a substantial dismantling, although this trend has recently been checked. On the other hand, the instrument of monetary policy—or, more generally, internal financial policy—has been applied for balance of payments purposes far more generally than might have been anticipated at the time of the Bretton Woods Conference." International Monetary Fund, *Annual Report* (Washington, 1965), p. 12. The effective exchange rate represents the rate which would clear the market of a particular class of transactions in the absence of quantitative restrictions and exchange licensing arrangements.

7. Sterling-dollar transactions probably occur at twenty or thirty effective exchange rates, ranging from $2.00 to $5.00.

Even countries with payments surpluses maintain a variety of controls and taxes on their international transactions, with the result that the effective price for their currency differs, depending on the purpose of the transaction. Exports are subsidized through a variety of credit arrangements and promotion schemes. Most economic aid to developing countries is tied to domestic procurement. Domestic tourist industries and domestic airlines are subsidized to increase foreign exchange earnings. The result of these taxes, subsidies, exchange controls, and exchange premiums is much like a multiple exchange-rate system, in that there are numerous effective rates for different classes of transactions between the same two countries.

The distinction between the concept of the IMF system and the implicit rules suggested by the behavior of IMF members is sharp. The emphasis in the Articles of Agreement is to prevent unnecessary or excessive devaluations. In practice the problem has been that countries have proved extremely reluctant to devalue to more realistic parities. The IMF agreement, with its system of penalties and rewards, appears insufficiently strong to have a major impact on the exchange-rate practices of its members.

The critical issue in adjustment is to devise measures that would facilitate more frequent use of the exchange rate as an instrument of adjustment or would provide a more orderly approach toward the use of direct controls if the exchange-rate structure remains frozen or sticky. The reluctance of countries to change their parities involves several issues. Political explanations focus on the costs of devaluation to national prestige. Economic explanations focus on the possible loss in real income and on the impact of devaluation on capital values. Operationally, there rarely appears to be an appropriate time for a devaluation, in the sense that the imbalance at the existing level of restrictions might be corrected by a change in parity of five or ten per cent. At the margin, it almost always appears preferable to tighten restrictions further to attain a satisfactory balance. An adjustable peg system may not be a viable system in that it might prove necessary to alter exchange parities relatively frequently in order to adjust to changes either in the relationship between national price levels or in structural relationships.[8]

8. Assume prices in country A rise by 5 per cent and then stabilize. Formerly A was in payments balance, now it has a sizable deficit. The imbalance may be too small to demand a change in the parity and too large to be easily rectified by other measures. It might be noted that the devaluations of the 1930's were by relatively large amounts. Sterling depreciated by more than one-third during the last four months of 1931. The dollar had depreciated by nearly three-fourths in late 1933. The gold bloc currencies depreciated by nearly 50 per cent in late 1936.

Frequent changes in parities may not prove feasible, since they would generate destabilizing expectations. A 5 per cent increase in United States prices relative to those in other industrial countries might worsen the United States trade balance by $2 billion. But a 5 per cent devaluation may not be operational. Ultimately, if there are sharp changes in price level relationships a change in parities is necessary.[9] What the IMF system lacks is continuity between the types of measures necessary to adjust to small changes in price level relationships and to large changes in these relationships.

Alternative Approaches to Adjustment

There are several basic approaches toward devising rules for adjustment under systems of fixed exchange rates; these include delegating powers to an international institution to prescribe the measures that countries in deficit and countries in surplus should and should not take in various situations. This approach, however, begs the intellectual issue of the criteria to be used by the institution in formulating its prescription. Moreover, in a period of decentralization of power, this approach does not seem feasible. A second approach is to negotiate an explicit set of rules for the adjustment measures that countries would follow in different situations; the content of the rules would depend on the negotiations. The third approach is to allow countries to follow the measures they wish; then the division of burden between deficit and surplus countries would be determined in response to bargaining on an explicit or implicit basis. Recent practices conform to the third approach.

The operational question is whether the industrial countries would agree to a set of comprehensive rules which would lead to improved economic performance. The desirable characteristics of the set of rules include neutrality among classes of international transactions—between payments and receipts, between current-account transactions and capital-account transactions, and between government transactions and private transactions. The measures adopted to implement these rules should be reversible and designed so that they can be easily tightened or relaxed. The rules should be equally applicable to large countries and to small countries, to countries with large foreign trade sectors and to those with small foreign trade sectors. Finally, the measures should

9. In August, 1966, Working Party No. 3 of the Economic Policy Committee of the Organization for Economic Cooperation and Development issued a report on *The Balance of Payments Adjustment Problem.* Their study assumed the continuation of the IMF system. The Committee's discussion of changes in parities occupied no more than four or five lines in a thirty-page report.

create neither perverse incentives nor permanent havens for protective interests.

One set of rules which satisfies most of these characteristics is that countries adopt uniform tariff surcharges on all commodity imports together with uniform subsidies on all commodity exports. A variant is that the uniform tax-subsidy be applied to all foreign payments and receipts. The tax-subsidy arrangement could cover government transactions as well as private transactions; it could be applied to capital-account transactions as well as to current-account transactions.

The tax-subsidy could be administered by the customs authorities, or by authorized foreign exchange banks.[10] The tax-subsidy rates could be varied quarterly, monthly, or as needed. On occasion the tax-subsidy rates and the exchange parity could be changed in an offsetting way, so as to have a neutral impact on the payments balance.[11] Under the tax-subsidy arrangement, each country would be free to vary the relative emphasis given to the tax-subsidy rate and to aggregate financial policies in the achievement of balance-of-payments equilibrium.[12] Drawings on some of the IMF's branches could be related to, or even conditional on, altering the level of the tax-subsidy rate.

The advantage of the tax-subsidy approach is that it provides effective exchange rate flexibility on an orderly basis. The tax-subsidy approach would prove unnecessary if the adjustable peg system were operational or if countries were willing to adopt floating rates. In this sense the tax-subsidy approach is a second-best solution, less desirable than explicit changes in parities, but preferable to a variety of *ad hoc* direct controls.[13]

10. The experience with various border taxes suggests the tax-subsidy scheme is administratively feasible, at least when applied to commodity transactions. Whether it would be administratively feasible to apply the tax-subsidy to service and capital-account transactions is less clear.

11. Assume that Great Britain decided to eliminate all exchange controls and to unify the exchange markets for various types of sterling at a new fixed rate. Whether this new rate would be nearer $2.60 or $2.40 cannot be determined under existing arrangements; it would be much more easily determined under the tax-subsidy approach. A country altering its parity might be obliged to adopt a new parity consistent with a tax-subsidy of 5 or 10 per cent; this would provide an easy way to compensate for excessive devaluations. Thus if the country achieved a surplus after the parity change, it could reduce the tax-subsidy level.

12. The tax-subsidy approach is feasible, even if some countries focus on the basic balance, others on a liquidity balance and still others on an official settlements balance, in setting targets for an appropriate payments balance.

13. It would be heroic to assert that countries would give up all their special rates because they could adopt the tax-subsidy scheme. The basis of Professor Haberler's criticism that tax-subsidy rates would be discriminatory is that the rates would not be uniform on all international transactions. The issue is whether the extent of discrimination is likely to be greater with a tax-subsidy approach than

While the tax-subsidy approach would require substantial changes in the Fund and GATT structures, most of these changes would involve lessening the commitments laid on members. The Articles and GATT would have to be amended to permit taxes and subsidies on the purchase and sale of foreign exchange. The only additional major commitment is that a member might be required to satisfy the Fund that the tax and subsidy would be uniform in amount and that a substantial proportion of international transactions would be subject to the tax-subsidy. The Fund might ask that members use the tax-subsidy before changing their established parities.

The major problem for GATT under the tax-subsidy arrangement is whether variations in tax-subsidy rates would make it more difficult to negotiate new trade bargains and to keep previously made bargains from becoming unstuck. The increased ease of adjusting to balance-of-payments problems might reduce the reluctance of countries with payments deficits to participate meaningfully in tariff negotiations. If the height of the tax-subsidy were related to the purchase or sale of foreign exchange rather than to commodity imports or exports, no difficulty should arise. The need to maintain uniformity in levels of the tax and of the subsidy would prevent countries from using these devices to protect certain industries or to subsidize exports excessively. Because temporary balance-of-payment adjustment would occur through changes in the tax-subsidy level, GATT would no longer need to be concerned with quantitative restrictions.

Conclusion

The proposals in this paper for monetizing existing assets for reserve purposes and for using a uniform tax-subsidy to improve payments balances are only a few of the possible ways to increase reserves and to facilitate adjustment. Reserves can be increased in many ways, as the extended debate of recent years shows; the problem is selecting which of the possible mechanisms is politically acceptable. Similarly there are several and varied approaches toward adjustment; the problem is whether any possible approaches which might improve economic performance could be negotiated in an international treaty.

Increased nationalism and the concomitant tendency toward the decentralization of power suggest that it is highly unlikely that contractual arrangements that might greatly reduce the risks of instability

---

with the existing system of direct controls and its probable growth. See Gottfried Haberler, "Taxes on Imports and Subsidies on Exports as a Tool of Adjustment," below.

in current arrangements could be negotiated. These same political tendencies make it unlikely that the supply of new reserve assets will increase as fast as the demand. The pressure on the adjustment mechanism will increase, and the question is whether the response to these pressures can be more orderly and consistent with improved economic performance. The relaxation of certain aspects of the Fund and of GATT would permit countries to adopt a uniform tax-subsidy even in the absence of an international agreement. An international agreement on the tax-subsidy would lead to improved economic performance by reducing the multiplicity of effective rates and diminish the threat of instability by providing an orderly approach to changes in parities.

REGIONAL MONETARY INTEGRATION
OF THE DEVELOPING COUNTRIES

Alexandre Kafka

This paper tries to show that limited monetary integration may offer some direct and indirect benefits to the developing countries and to the world; however, complete monetary integration of these countries is not a practical proposition. The ideal areas of limited monetary integration differ according to the purposes one has in mind, and the determining factors will be as much political as economic.

Meaning of Monetary Integration

I shall adopt a rather wide definition of the concept "monetary integration," including not only the replacement of several currencies by a single one—complete monetary integration—but any arrangements under which the effects of the existence of separate currencies merely approach, more or less, the effects of the existence of a single one. Limited monetary integration may comprise no more than a common international reserve or mutual credit arrangements. Some kinds of limited monetary integration are conceivable without even pegging the exchange rates of the participating countries to each other. I hope this terminology will not be disturbing, but when I use the term "monetary integration" in connection with developing countries, I am referring exclusively to this limited kind.

It is obvious that if a group of currencies is convertible at an absolutely fixed rate, excluding even fluctuation between gold points, then no further integration is feasible except in name, provided that there is also implicit belief in the maintenance of the exchange rates. This may seem surprising, but the belief mentioned cannot exist without conditions which must be very like those in a single currency area: that is to say, similar rates of inflation within the area, area-wide acceptability of securities held by monetary authorities and banks, etc., in fact, co-ordinated monetary policies. It is, in the last analysis, the divergence of monetary policies that defines separate currencies. Convertibility plus belief in the maintenance of fixed rates is a more stringent economic condition than the single currency. Transferability, similar to that in

Europe in the middle fifties, plus a belief in its persistence at fixed rates, would constitute the equivalent of a single currency.

There is obviously a strong feeling today in favor of limited (though not complete) regional monetary integration and there have even been suggestions for some forms of monetary integration comprising all developing countries. The popularity of limited regional monetary integration is, perhaps, a reflection of the success of the European Payments Union, although conditions today in developing countries are largely different, as we shall soon see.

Purposes of Monetary Integration

What are the specific purposes which regional monetary integration is supposed to serve; or, more exactly, what is the specific way in which it is supposed to promote the "general welfare"? I have found three purposes mentioned. In chronological order, though not in order of importance, they are: (1) the promotion of economic integration; (2) economizing on international reserves; and (3) strengthening multilateral surveillance. It is obvious that in terms of strict economics none of these purposes requires a regional basis. In fact, however, there is a degree of "intimacy" required for their realization which exists to some extent on a regional basis, but rarely otherwise. It is possible that it will emerge among the so-called seventy-seven of UNCTAD, but that is not yet the case.

To what extent can various degrees of monetary integration promote the several purposes indicated? I shall not discuss the question whether all or any of them will promote "the general welfare." It is quite obvious that by the usual criterion—labor mobility—groupings of developing countries are rarely likely to constitute optimum currency areas.[1] But the usual point of view is, as it were, "static" and partial; above all, it focuses on complete integration, i.e., the single currency. Nevertheless, even taking into consideration those "dynamic" aspects or "static" advantages of monetary integration which the usual discussion neglects, one would rarely recommend the adoption of a single currency by a group of developing countries which is beginning its integration. It is true that one of the main factors which makes monetary integration of a lower degree so difficult is divergent rates of inflation, which the single currency would obviate; yet, there remains the basic economic factor of

1. See especially R. A. Mundell, "A Theory of Optimum Currency Areas," *American Economic Review*, 51, no. 4 (September, 1961); Ronald J. McKinnon, "Optimum Currency Areas," *American Economic Review*, 53, no. 4 (September, 1963).

labor immobility, not to mention politics. After all, even the monetary unity of existing large, developing countries is sometimes something of a problem. On the other hand, the three purposes mentioned above may well justify what one may call limited forms of monetary integration. In all three cases a degree of reserve pooling is indicated. Moreover, in the first case—the promotion of economic integration—relative rate stability seems to be justified among the integrating countries. It would undoubtedly cause some temporary sacrifice of current "welfare" in return for larger future benefits, just as economic integration itself causes such sacrifices.

Regional Monetary and Regional Economic Integration

A single currency area is obviously not necessary in order to promote even fairly comprehensive degrees of economic integration. The European example here is illuminating. Trade barriers can fall effectively without a single currency, though it is not as clear whether investment barriers, at least for portfolio and short-term private investment, can do so fully. But it may be no disaster to inhibit these types of investments, which so easily lead to disturbing capital movements.

It is necessary that there should be no exchange controls between integrating countries, unless one wishes to replace one type of barrier to trade or capital movement (tariffs or taxes) by another one (exchange controls). (Multiple rates, except those which are jointly applied by a group of countries against third countries only, are payments restrictions and pose the same obstacles to economic integration as other types of restrictions on trade or payments.) Exchange controls vis-à-vis third countries are not excluded, however. But such controls superimpose an additional system of restrictions vis-à-vis the outside world over and above the restrictions made effective through tariffs. This additional system alters the impact of economic integration.

Must rates be stable between economically integrated countries? And, if not, to what extent should they be pegged, that is, in the face of what kinds of disequilibria and within how narrow a range? Or should they be free to float? The first thing is to ask whether rates which are free to float would actually fluctuate or whether speculators would step in and prevent them from doing so. The defenders of freely floating rates generally assume that speculators would not prevent rate adjustments in the face of "fundamental disequilibrium." Although the concept is elusive, speculators are alleged not to prevent what a sensible man, such as a sensible central bank governor, would diagnose as "fundamental disequilibrium," i.e., a disequilibrium which looked like being rather substantial and irreversible in the medium run. But speculators are supposed by the defenders of freely floating rates to step in to even out everything else except fundamental disequilibrium. Whatever one may think of the applicability of these assumptions to the developed countries, I doubt very much if speculators would be forthcoming quickly to stabilize the currencies of many less developed countries, which have a somewhat exaggerated but nonetheless firmly believed reputation for being inflation prone. Thus, even if one concludes that speculation need not be destabilizing, even in the less developed countries, I doubt whether it would be stabilizing. At best, in developing countries, it would be neutral, and rates free to fluctuate *would* fluctuate, not only in fundamental but also in temporary disequilibrium.

What will floating rates do to economic integration? (We are *not* concerned with the general advantages or disadvantages of floating versus fixed rates for developed countries or for underdeveloped countries or generally, but simply with the question of what they will do to economic integration.) In other words, what will they do to price relations between an integrating country's products and the products of its partner countries? Goods which have a world-wide market subject to pure competition may not be much affected by the exchange system adopted by a group of integrating countries. But goods with sticky prices, presumably the manufactured goods which play or are expected to play such an important role in the economic integration of developing countries, will be affected. While fixed rates would keep the sticky prices stable among the integrating countries, floating rates would alter their relationships with respect to substitutes from partner countries and from third countries. This would not matter where rate changes occur because of fundamental disequilibrium; for there is no acceptable alternative in this case. But it *would* matter in temporary disequilibrium, where there is an acceptable alternative (i.e., fluctuation in reserves). Frequent fluctuations of relative prices due to temporary disequilibrium will not be conducive to the growth of intratrade in less than perfect markets, where good will has to be built up over the years. There is no question that riding out even a temporary disequilibrium by means of reserve fluctuations has its social costs; but they may be outweighed by the benefits of more rapid economic integration. One must conclude that floating rates are not particularly conducive to economic integration even as far as trade is concerned. Thus fixed rates —in the face of temporary disequilibrium—would be preferable and the narrower the range within which they may fluctuate, the better. But fluctuating rates will be by no means fatal to the purpose of economic integration. After all, there has already been some economic integration, for instance in the Latin-American free trade area, without any kind of monetary integration whatsoever, and there could be a good deal more. Moreover, as long as integrating countries maintain effective tariffs of as much as 300 per cent, why should one worry about rate fluctuations even of 100 per cent? They could be offset by changes in effective tariffs.

That regional stability of exchange rates appears advisable among integrating countries in the face of temporary disequilibria is hardly a sensational conclusion. This, after all, is the system prescribed by the Articles of Agreement of the International Monetary Fund. The import of the conclusion is that "temporary disequilibria" should be widely rather than narrowly defined, i.e., when in doubt a disequilibrium should be qualified as temporary and treated accordingly. This has some important consequences (see below). Limited, regional stability of exchange rates may mean either general pegging, or joint pegging, or joint fluctuations of the integrating countries' currencies vis-à-vis those of the rest of the world (since broken cross-rates won't work). In other words, the choice is between pegging the currencies of the integrating countries to each other and letting them fluctuate vis-à-vis third currencies; pegging them as before and adjusting them jointly by deliberate action vis-à-vis third currencies in the face of fundamental disequilibrium between the group and the rest of the world; and pegging each currency vis-à-vis all others but readjusting it in the face of fundamental disequilibrium between the particular country and other countries whether inside or outside the integrating group.

The fact that changes in economic conditions do not necessarily affect all members of the integrating group in the same way with respect to fundamental disequilibrium rules out anything but the third possibility. In any case, it will take some sort of an agreement among integrating countries on how to distinguish fundamental from temporary disequilibrium. The only way to do this might be to have some sort of a regional joint reserve arrangement; the size of the joint reserve and its permissible losses would define the difference between temporary and fundamental disequilibrium. Such an agreement may in any case be necessary unless each integrating country's reserves are very large, as is the case in the EEC. For if reserves are not large, those members of an integrating group which are at any moment earning reserves may be called upon to help out those that are losing them. Yet, it would not be practicable to have negotiations in each particular case and even a series of bilateral or multilateral stand-by arrangements might be too uncertain. Insofar as the reserves of the integrating group are to be bolstered from the outside in consideration of the advantages which integration may confer upon the world as a whole, it may be easier to obtain it through a common regional fund than through loans to each separate integrating country and easier to use it through such a regional fund than if it were available through a world-wide agency.

If economic integration is to mean less fluctuation of exchange rates than otherwise, it should increase the net reserve needs of the integrating group. If net reserves cannot become negative to the same extent as they can become positive, riding out larger or longer temporary disequilibria by reserve fluctuation as a result of a desire to promote economic integration obviously implies higher average reserve needs than would otherwise be the case. But there is a second consideration. If an integrating group includes countries which would otherwise ride out disequilibrium by fluctuation of rates, the group's net reserve needs may in theory either increase or decrease. But it is more likely that they will increase, because, in the absence of integration, countries are somewhat more inclined to ride out deficits than surpluses through rate changes. Hence, we can have, as a result of integration, possible additional net reserve needs, quite apart from whether integration otherwise increases these needs for the group (which it may do).

These arguments, which show that integration may lead to an increase in the net reserve needs of the integrating group, are quite distinct arguments from the usual ones. These run in terms of each individual integrating country's reserve needs due to the additional temporary disequilibria which the process of integration itself may lead to, either among the integrating countries, or between some of them and third countries. (This is distinct from the desire to promote integration by rate stability in the face of larger temporary disequilibrium than one would otherwise wish to ride out.) It has been suggested that reserve needs might be met by mutual credits granted each other by the integrating countries. It has also been suggested that, by making these credits inconvertible, integrating creditors will be encouraged to speed up regional liberalization; and making them automatic would be particularly effective in relieving the fears of potential intragroup debtors which would also encourage liberalization.

Here the European example—the European Payments Union—seems to have confused the issue. In postwar Europe, liberalization threw up mainly intra-European disequilibria; for, except for the trade barriers created in the thirties and in the postwar period, the already existing degree of integration of Europe was very high and each country's trade was mostly with the other European countries. Today, the less developed countries which are integrating have, in general, very limited economic relations with each other. Hence, any structural change affecting them, such as regional integration, is more likely to throw up disequilibria with the outside world than with the integrating group. Consequently, inconvertible credits will not work. The availability of convertible credits will still encourage potential debtors but cannot be used directly to encourage potential creditors to speed up liberalization. Credits could hardly be other than conditional. However, if the past performance of a country as creditor is taken into consideration in determining its entitlement to credit, the idea of using the credit mechanism to speed up the integration of potential creditors as well as debtors may be partly salvaged.

What is the upshot of this? *First*, that to promote economic integration, rate stability between integrating countries is not necessary, but is definitely desirable, though only in the face of temporary disequilibria. In other words, a limited degree of monetary integration is desirable at best. *Second*, to promote this intragroup stability, additional reserves in gold or in convertible currencies may be needed. *Third*, part of the reserves of the integrating countries may have to be pooled and drawings on the pool should preferably be conditional rather than automatic.

Economizing on International Reserves

Limited monetary integration designed to promote economic integration in the form of maintaining stability between the exchange rates of integrating countries, except in the face of limited disequilibrium, is likely to increase the integrating group's reserve needs. On the other hand, limited monetary integration in the form of a joint reserve has been proposed as a means of economizing reserves.

Economizing on international reserves seems to have two aspects. In the first place, two countries trading with each other can economize on reserve needs, insofar as these needs arise among themselves, by granting each other appropriate credits. Short-term or—in the parlance of the European Monetary Agreement—"interim" credits seem to be the only kind of economizing which has so far found a practical expression in agreements between developing countries. Secondly, however, a group of countries can economize on their reserve needs vis-à-vis third countries if these are mutually offsetting and they pool their reserves, which is again a very limited degree of monetary integration. Offsetting reserve needs can be the result of mutually offsetting terms of trade movements (or, less likely, of offsetting monetary movements).

But the scope for limited monetary integration of this kind is limited among developing countries. First, as already mentioned, their mutual trade is limited. Second, offsetting terms of trade are less likely among them than between developing and developed countries. The sterling area is—or was—a good example of the latter type of grouping. It should be noted, however, that offsetting terms-of-trade movements between members of the two categories of countries would become less likely if these movements were dominated more by supply than by demand factors.

These considerations may suggest that one can expect few reserve economies from efforts at integration which are limited to developing countries. But there is no harm in attempting to gain the maximum benefit that can be achieved through such experiments. This is true as long as the degree of monetary integration is limited to the minimum need for this purpose, that is mutual lines of credit and a common reserve fund respectively. (Any clearing arrangement among integrating countries as a vehicle for mutual lines of credit should, of course, be voluntary rather than compulsory because a compulsory clearing would simply establish a new system of restrictions vis-à-vis the outside world.)

Furthermore, reserve needs may be reduced by channeling payments between developing countries directly rather than via the great financial centers. Such a practice will reduce the need for working balances in reserve currencies. It may even make it easier to replace working balances altogether through arranging swaps. It will also relieve the developing countries of service charges, if these are made where working balances are held. It is, however, not clear whether the actual cost of such payments is higher than the costs of setting up payment channels for limited volumes of transactions between the developing countries.

Multilateral Surveillance on a Regional Basis

A third argument, purely political in nature, for regional monetary integration is based on the possibly greater ease of establishing multilateral surveillance; I shall not ask whether the latter is a good thing. It is widely believed that there are certain things to which each developing country will more easily listen from its colleagues than from a developed country. Even if this were granted, the question might be not whether the developing countries will listen, but whether they will speak, from fear that they may in turn have to listen. The establishment of a common regional fund, in which each country's drawings dramatically reduce the amount available for the rest, making it dramatically obvious that using the pool is a zero-sum game, might induce members to speak.

This purpose requires, of course, discretionary rather than automatic drawings.

Conclusion

The scope of monetary integration among developing countries can only be quite limited as long as their economies are not considerably more integrated with each other than they are likely to be for many years to come. Yet, there is no question that even this limited kind of monetary integration can perform a useful service. It is clear that monetary integration, in its various forms, will serve the "general welfare" (to the extent that the meaning of this term can be agreed upon) according to the precise way in which the underlying purposes of integration are tackled.

COMMENT: "IMPROVING THE
BRETTON WOODS SYSTEM"

Gerard Curzon

Asked to examine the present "institutional mix" problem in the context of international economic relations, one cannot but agree with Mr.
Aliber's definition of his terms of reference—to see how far existing
economic institutions, given the political constraints within which they
work, can be modified to improve economic performance.

But Mr. Aliber leaves aside what is perhaps at the root of many of the
shortcomings of the present system—the administration by two separate
international organizations of the real and monetary sides of international economic relations—and concentrates too exclusively on the
monetary organizations of the Bank and the Fund. The final question
to be asked when examining the "institutional mix" is whether there is
any sense in having one organisation (the IMF) attacking the adjustment problem by price variations (i.e., devaluation), and another
(GATT) proposing to do so with quantitative restrictions. Should one
not examine whether permission to use one or the other of these tools of
adjustment could be better administered by a single body? Or at least,
should one not discuss to what extent co-operation between the two
separate bodies is essential, so as to establish on what occasions one or
the other of these tools of adjustment should be used?

Though we are discussing modifications within the given political
framework and though one cannot but agree with Mr. Aliber that
governments are increasingly reluctant to relinquish further sovereignty
to international organizations, there might be a considerable gain in the
efficiency with which international economic affairs are at present
administered if the IMF-IBRD could in practice be integrated more
closely with GATT.

Mr. Aliber proposes two separate means of attenuating present in-
adequacies: the one relating to the liquidity problem, the other relating
to the adjustment issue. Though criticism of the three international
institutions occupying themselves with economic matters is at present
fashionable and often justified, it is going too far to say that they were
more designed to deal with the problems of the interwar period than
with those of our own times. There is, after all, much evidence to suggest

that some of the interwar disasters have been avoided because of the existence of these organizations, which in itself testifies to the willingness of sovereign states to treat international problems internationally, as opposed to the beggar-my-neighbor spirit prevalent in the interwar period. The IMF system, after all, resembles the gold exchange standard, and a repetition of the 1931 catastrophe has probably been avoided by the international co-operation which found concrete expression in the Fund. Similarly, there is considerable evidence suggesting that important trading countries were dissuaded from using the more selfish types of trade restriction in their adjustment policies because of the restraints they had imposed upon themselves by signing GATT.

Since international organizations have no life of their own, but simply reflect the common will and purpose of their members, the relevant criticism today is surely not one of the inadequacy of the institutions themselves, but of the willingness (or rather unwillingness) of their members to prepare for the problems of the future.

My main criticism of Mr. Aliber's paper is that it proposes some fairly fundamental changes in the present system which have no more chance, in my opinion, of being accepted in practice than the more thorough-going reforms currently discussed in academic circles. I also believe that the present system is not quite as rickety as Mr. Aliber would have us think.

Mr. Aliber feels that one of the shortcomings of the IMF system is that it does not provide a means of increasing world liquidity, and he goes on to propose a scheme by which he believes this could be done within the present institutional framework. In doing so, he enters a heated debate. He bases his thesis of the need for increasing world liquidity on the hypothesis (by no means universally accepted) that countries need additional reserves because of their unwillingness to reduce imbalance through domestic measures. This may, in fact, be true of the United States, and the view is certainly fashionable among American (and British) economists. But it is not true of other developed countries, and finds little sympathy among Continental European economists.

Their view is that it is not so much the level of reserves that is the problem (this is generally considered to be perfectly adequate) but their composition: they feel that the dollar, as an international store of value, presents certain disadvantages, or rather that the present system does not spread the advantages (and disadvantages) in an equitable fashion. It is felt that the issue is more one of equity than of liquidity.

Mr. Aliber's second premise—that countries are increasingly unwilling to reduce imbalance through domestic measures—is again a rather sweeping generalization of a situation peculiar to the United States and certain underdeveloped countries. Since 1958 at least, most European countries (including even the United Kingdom of late) have either corrected their deficits or prevented them from developing by adopting often stringent measures of a deflationary nature. Now this is not the place to discuss the desirability of such measures, but the fact remains that they are nevertheless applied by many industrialized countries. Mr. Aliber rightly points to the ever-present danger that countries may be tempted to rely on direct controls to adjust their balance of payments; it is of course here that international institutions can and must dissuade individual countries from pursuing policies that would be detrimental to the community as a whole.

Basing his arguments on the premise that total world reserves have to be increased (and discounting the possibility that all that is needed at the present time or in the near future is a redistribution of reserves currently held by central banks), Mr. Aliber proposes a means of doing so. The device he proposes is a variation of the Stamp Plan, which suggested channeling reserve creation through the aid mechanism. Mr. Aliber proposes that aid already given (and presumably also aid yet to be given) should constitute an internationally acceptable asset for the aid donor. The idea is not new to the banking mechanism. The World Bank has occasionally replenished its funds by selling portions of loans from its portfolio, and there is theoretically no reason why governments should not do the same; the problem is to find a buyer. Intergovernmental loans without a gold or foreign exchange guaranty have no market, and governments would have to agree to take in each other's non-marketable assets in exchange for claims upon their several economies. In other words, governments would have to give a foreign exchange guaranty to the aid assets of other governments. Anything less would be mere window dressing and would not fool the foreign exchange market (non-marketable assets in themselves cannot bolster a currency weakened by successive deficits). The scheme would allow deficit countries to behave like key currency centers at the cost of the surplus countries and would to nothing to solve the "equity" problem. It would be asking surplus countries to finance other countries' deficits beyond what can reasonably be expected, and I do not believe, given existing political constraints, that the scheme would be negotiable.

I should now like to comment briefly on Mr. Aliber's proposal to add to our existing adjustment arsenal the possibility of using a uniform but adjustable tax-subsidy.

There is no theoretical difference between the effect of a uniform but variable tax-subsidy and an adjustable peg system, and Mr. Aliber prefers the former to the latter for practical reasons. I do not, however, believe that there is much to choose between them from a practical point of view, or that Mr. Aliber's case for the tax-subsidy is entirely convincing. Mr. Aliber, for instance, says that the tax-subsidy rates could be varied quarterly, monthly, or as needed, but why should this be easier than altering exchange parities? He says that "frequent changes in parities may not prove feasible" but does not explain why this would not also be the case for frequent changes in tax-subsidy rates. He maintains that the tax-subsidy approach caters to the preferences of men of affairs, in particular to their abhorrence of the uncertainty associated with varying rates of exchange. But why should businessmen prefer varying rates of taxation or subsidy? Mr. Aliber states that one of the major advantages of the tax-subsidy approach is the fact that the present system of effective multiple rates of exchange (due to existing taxes and subsidies) would be eliminated. In theory this would indeed be an advantage, but I very much agree with Mr. Aliber that it would be heroic to assert that all special rates would be abandoned in practice, and it is the practical case with which we are dealing.

If asked to choose between the adjustable peg system—and here I mean a system where the peg is more adjustable than it is today—and the tax-subsidy approach, I would prefer the former. In the first place, it would embrace the whole range of international transactions. I agree with Mr. Aliber that it is not clear how the tax-subsidy approach could be applied to service and capital-account transactions; to apply the tax-subsidy arrangement to the foreign exchange market alone would, in practice, be identical to adopting an adjustable peg, and all discussion as to the relative merits—except for administrative costs—of the one or the other would cease to have any meaning. Secondly, the adjustable peg system would accustom that inscrutable animal, the businessman, to varying rates of exchange and to the mysteries of forward markets, while waiting for the adoption of the only long-term solution to the adjustment *and* liquidity problems—flexible exchange rates. Finally, the adjustable peg system would not even involve a modification of the Fund articles, and the considerable institutional barriers to change might perhaps be very slightly diminished as compared with those attendant upon the tax-subsidy approach, which, as Mr. Aliber again rightly points out, "would require substantial changes in the Fund and GATT structures."

But in fact I would prefer not to be asked to choose between the adjustable peg system and the tax-subsidy approach. I believe that neither of these alternatives is a really practical proposition at the present time; and if the day comes when governments are prepared to recast the world's economic features, I am sure Mr. Aliber would be the first to agree that something more satisfactory than either of these alternatives could be devised.

COMMENT: "REGIONAL MONETARY INTEGRATION OF THE DEVELOPING COUNTRIES"

Bela Balassa

I am somewhat at a disadvantage in discussing Mr. Kafka's paper since it was not distributed before delivery as were the other papers. May I turn this to my advantage in prevailing upon your patience by offering a few comments on Mr. Corden's paper before I turn to Kafka.

We are indebted to Corden for having spelled out some of the assumptions that underlie the discussion of the implications of liquidity arrangements for the less developed countries. Corden first analyzes the redistribution of world income associated with changes in the terms of trade that would result from the policies followed by developed countries in the event of a lack of adequate liquidity. He gives us a nice taxonomy—a 2 × 4 case—by taking the case of a scramble for reserves, as well as that involving an adjustment on the part of the deficit country, and considering four ways of handling each of them. All this is most sensible and, given the conditions existing today, one may gain little by adding a case where the surplus country undertakes the adjustment.

Next, Corden introduces the seigniorage problem which was discussed in considerable detail in an earlier session: depending on how the increase in liquidity is distributed among countries, there will be gainers and there will be losers. According to Corden the potential losers on this count are the nations that have a surplus in their balance of payments and the gainers the deficit countries. This would indeed be the case if we assumed that increases in liquidity are distributed among countries that show a deficit. There is no reason to assume, however, that surplus countries would not get some of the increase in liquidity as they indeed do under most of the schemes under consideration. Now if the surplus countries use this increase to buy additional commodities, they will gain from seigniorage.

Corden, furthermore, considers reductions in world income due to the need for making adjustments in domestic activities in the event that there is not enough liquidity to ride out a deficit. I would like to add here another reason for losses in world income in case of insufficient

Kafka's and Corden's papers were actually read during the same session.

151

world liquidity which might be quite important and was indeed important during the 1930's. This is the departure from an efficient structure of world trade due to measures taken by individual countries in competition with each other to restore their balance-of-payments equilibrium. Lack of liquidity may then lead to a loss in world income through reductions in the amount of international trade and through distortions in relative prices of domestic and foreign goods.

Finally, let me take note of an important long-term benefit that liquidity schemes provide for the less developed countries. This is due to their being able to avoid disruptions in long-term plans that would result from the lack of liquidity. Many of these countries prepare long-term plans on the basis of forecasts of foreign exchange earnings and a shortfall in exports would compel them to retrench and to reduce investment activity below the level provided for in the plan. An international liquidity scheme, or the World Bank's supplementary finance scheme, could help the less developed countries to avoid disruptions in their long-term plans by providing for the financing of such deficits.

Let me now get to Mr. Kafka's paper. I will comment on three of the major issues raised by him: first, the arguments against exchange rate flexibility in the less developed countries; second, the possibility of joint fluctuations in the balance of payments and in the exchange rates of groups of less developed countries; and third, the question of whether these countries could economize on their foreign exchange resources through reserve pooling arrangements.

Kafka suggests that for countries that participate in regional integration schemes fixed rates are preferable to flexible rates. The arguments used against flexible rates are the traditional ones advanced in regard to developed countries: speculation will fail to stabilize the rate of exchange, and fluctuations in exchange rates will create disincentives to trade. But while these arguments have relevance for integration schemes of developed economies such as the European Common Market and EFTA, the conditions in the major countries of South America, to which Kafka refers in his paper, are rather different.

It seems to me that there are two basic international monetary problems which the countries of South America (for reasons that will become obvious, I exclude Mexico) face in their integration. One is that the degree of overvaluation varies from country to country; another that the degree of overvaluation changes over time in the individual countries. As I will indicate below, both of these factors create difficulties for integration in the area and they have to be considered in discussing the fixed versus flexible rate issue.

First, consider the existence of intercountry differences in the degree of overvaluation that is to be defined by comparison with a free trade situation. Differences are quite considerable here, inasmuch as some countries, such as Argentina, have high tariffs and a relatively over-valued exchange rate, while tariffs are lower and hence the exchange rate is less overvalued in Brazil. Now, the elimination of tariffs on intra-area trade without an adjustment in exchange rates would create an imbalance in this trade—an imbalance that is bound to become an obstacle to economic integration. In fact, according to a recent calculation, the elimination of tariffs between Argentina and Brazil would permit Brazilian producers to encroach upon the market for something like 45 per cent of the Argentine industry, whereas in the opposite direction the relevant figure is only 5 per cent.

More generally, changing one variable—tariffs—without adjusting another—exchange rates—will often create disequilibria in economic relations among countries. Kafka appears to de-emphasize this point (thereby weakening his case against flexible exchange rates) by arguing that "as long as integrating countries maintain effective tariffs of as much as 300 per cent, why should one worry about rate fluctuations even of 100 per cent?" But the existence of high tariffs should not be interpreted to mean that variations in exchange rates would be of no importance since even marginal changes will affect the profitability of individual activities. Note further that if we take an average tariff figure of 200 per cent for the countries of South America, in its effects on import prices a reduction of tariffs by one-half is equivalent to a devaluation of 50 per cent.[1]

But by emphasizing the importance of exchange rates—and changes in rates—have I inadvertently provided ammunition for Mr. Kafka's thesis that rate fluctuations are undesirable? I do not believe so. This should become clear if we consider that in an inflationary situation, as experienced in Argentina, Brazil, and Chile among the larger countries of South America, what matters is not variations in the "nominal" (parity) exchange rate but in the "real" rate of exchange, defined as the ratio of an index of the exchange rate to that of domestic prices. This rate will indicate changes in the international competitiveness of domestic products that result from disparate movements in domestic prices and exchange parities.

Under a flexible rate system, the real exchange rate would not

1. The relevant formula is $(1 + t)/(1 + t') = r'/r$ when t and r are the original tariff rates and exchange rates and t' and r' are the changes in these rates that would leave the domestic prices of imports unchanged.

fluctuate since increases in domestic prices are immediately translated into changes in exchange parities. It does fluctuate, however, under fixed exchange rates since increases in domestic prices are continuous while changes in parities occur discontinuously. What usually happens is that the domestic price level rises and the exchange rate parity catches up with it only after a time lag.

Fluctuations in the real exchange rate create uncertainty in foreign trade and—under the usual assumption that producers are risk-averters—discriminate against exporting activities. This conclusion follows because the producer can usually translate increases in costs into higher prices in domestic markets while this possibility is not available to him in foreign markets where prices are mostly set in dollars. Thus, his receipts in terms of the domestic currency will depend on the stage of the inflation-devaluation cycle in which his country finds itself at the time of the repatriation of the proceeds. This can be indicated by an example of what recently happened in South America.

Two Brazilian producers entered into a contract to deliver similar kinds of machines to Argentina. One of them delivered the machinery on time, sold his dollar earnings at the exchange rate prevailing at the time of delivery, and incurred a loss because costs increased since the time the contract had been signed but there was no change in the rate of exchange. The other producer was two months late and had to pay a penalty; nevertheless, he made a large profit on the transaction because the cruzeiro was devalued in the meantime, and thus his sales and profits in terms of the domestic currency increased considerably.

These fluctuations in the real exchange rate, then, create obstacles to integration in South America. As I have just indicated, given the uncertainty regarding the domestic currency equivalent of export proceeds, producers will prefer selling in domestic markets to exporting activities. Moreover, in making decisions on integration, governments take into account the fact that fluctuations in the real exchange rates of the individual countries will introduce distortions in trade patterns. Thus, in a favorable phase of the inflation-devaluation cycle, Argentina will undersell Brazil while Brazil will do the same as the situation changes.

But what are the implications of these conclusions for the integration of less developed countries? Kafka suggests that "there has already been some economic integration...in the Latin-American free trade area, without any kind of monetary integration whatsoever, and there could be a good deal more." However, most people are dissatisfied with the progress that has been made in LAFTA—hence the recent efforts to change its institutional structure. At the same time, in the presence of intercountry differences in the extent of overvaluation and variations in overvaluation over time, countries appear reluctant to undertake further reductions in tariffs. For one thing, if integration is confined to reductions in tariffs on intra-area trade, some countries would benefit at the expense of others; for another, fluctuations in the real exchange rate would create sudden shifts in the pattern of trade.

As regards the latter point, the arguments used by Kafka against flexibility in the nominal exchange rate should properly be applied against flexibility in the real exchange rate, i.e., the continuation of pegging in the face of changes in domestic prices. Putting it differently, we need constancy of the real exchange rate and, in an inflationary situation, this can be ensured only through flexibility in nominal rates. This lesson has apparently been learnt in Chile where parallel changes in domestic prices and nominal exchange rates are attained through monthly devaluation. If other Latin-American countries follow Chile's example, this source of instability in trade will have been removed.

This is not to say that monetary stability *cum* fixed rates would not be preferable to the suggested procedure. But it is hardly realistic to assume that the countries of South America would achieve monetary stability in the near future. This goal can be approached only gradually, as it has been in Chile. In the meantime, the maintenance of stability in the real exchange rate through appropriate flexibility in nominal rates should be the objective.

Turning now to the question of intercountry differences in the extent of overvaluation due to differences in the policies used by various countries, the solution appears to lie in adopting a common tariff for the integrated area. This conclusion is strengthened if we consider that the maintenance of existing disparities in duties is bound to create deflection in trade and in production since a country that has lower duties on the material inputs of a certain product would enjoy an artificial advantage over its competitors.

These considerations point to the need for a common tariff in integration schemes of less developed countries and for the maintenance of the constancy of the real exchange rate through flexibility in nominal rates. The distinction between temporary and fundamental disequilibrium has little meaning in an inflationary situation, and interpreting temporary disequilibrium in a wider sense as Kafka suggests (i.e. when in doubt a disequilibrium should be qualified as temporary and thus rates should remain fixed) will introduce undue rigidity in exchange parities and lead to fluctuations in the real exchange rate. At the same time, in the underdeveloped financial markets of the countries in question, speculation hardly presents a danger.

But how about introducing joint fluctuations in the exchange rates of the integrating countries vis-à-vis the rest of the world? There is little doubt that this would be a mistaken policy. The countries of South America, as well as the countries that may participate in integration schemes in other parts of the world, conduct the bulk of their trade with outsiders and have rather different export patterns. Correspondingly, changes in the export receipts of these countries are not correlated and, even apart from intercountry differences in the rate of inflation, they would require disparate changes in exchange rates.

I get now to the last point concerning possible economies in foreign exchange reserves that may be obtained through reserve pooling arrangements. Kafka asserts that "one can expect few reserve economies from efforts at integration which are limited to developing countries," in part because their mutual trade is relatively small and in part because "offsetting terms of trade are less likely among them than between developing and developed countries." But, as the example of Central America indicates, integration does lead to increases in intra-area trade. More importantly, Kafka's statement concerning terms-of-trade changes does not correspond to the actual facts of the situation.

While it has become part of contemporary folklore, even a casual empirical investigation reveals that the terms of trade of individual countries in an area such as South America fluctuate more widely than those of the group as a whole. At the same time, as I indicated above, differences in the export patterns of these countries lead to divergent changes in foreign exchange receipts. In the absence of a synchronization of fluctuations in the volume of exports and in the terms of trade, therefore, a reserve pooling arrangement would offer definite advantages to the countries of the area. It is a different question that, whether with a considerable degree of exchange flexibility, the need for reserves would diminish.

SUMMARY OF DISCUSSION

I

Several issues were raised in the discussion of Professor Aliber's paper. Two points were the subject of short interventions: What is the relation of tariff bargaining to exchange-rate changes? and, Do surplus countries really mind giving up real resources? The discussion of these two problems is summarized first. The major part of what follows, however, outlines the conference's discussion of the two main questions which were raised: How far should economic organizations be integrated? and, What are the merits and demerits of Aliber's tax-subsidy scheme?

Professor Curzon argued that tariff bargaining often assumes fixed exchange rates. When countries spend several months arguing whether tariff levels on chemicals should be 25 per cent or 28 per cent and end up agreeing to a tariff rate of 26½ per cent, they will not readily accept a devaluation of 10 or 20 per cent by their negotiating partner the next morning. If only on these grounds, and however myopic the views expressed by tariff bargainers, the interrelationship of GATT and the Fund is of some importance.

According to *Professor Johnson*, it is nonsensical from a general equilibrium point of view that tariff bargaining negotiations should depend on the exchange rate. Under a system of fixed exchange rates the purpose of tariff bargaining is to increase trade, imports as well as exports. A country usually has to devalue because something has thrown its exchange rate out of equilibrium, increasing its imports from other countries. Therefore, there is no reason to think that tariff bargaining should be conditional on the maintenance of exchange rates. The one exception to this statement is the case where a country follows a beggar-my-neighbor policy of increasing its exports by devaluation combined with some other policy.

One of the problems of international organizations, in Johnson's view, is that their representatives think in terms of their own bailiwick without paying attention to the general equilibrium problem. Hence the myopia, and the usefulness of closer contacts between GATT and the

157

Fund if only to explode ideas such as that fixed exchange rates are needed if tariff bargains are not to be invalidated.

Dr. Salant raised the issue of whether surplus countries really do mind giving up real resources. This question is relevant to Aliber's proposal for supplementary international reserves since it has been argued that such a scheme would be unacceptable to developed countries on the grounds that it would mean giving up real resources. One sometimes wonders, according to Salant, whether this is not an argument that economists have invented for surplus countries to put forward. As a matter of historical fact there seem to be very few countries which object to giving up real resources. Most countries seem to show extreme pain when their export surpluses are reduced, none whatever when they increase. Though the rationale of the argument is abundantly clear, according to Salant, it does not stand up as an explanation of economic fact.

Professor Mundell turned to the issue of the institutional mix and the problem of how far the functions of existing international organizations should be integrated. Economists in the past ten years have typically held the view that institutional affiliations should be separated according to the functions various institutions are designed to serve. The IMF looks after liquidity, short-term capital, and so on; the IBRD looks after long-term capital, GATT deals with trade, and nobody looks after world employment. Europeans, for instance, have held firmly to the view that the question of liquidity should not be pegged to that of foreign aid.

From a logical point of view, the separation of functions into their individual cubby holes is quite neat and satisfying. From another point of view, however, it may turn out that otherwise feasible solutions to the liquidity problem are ruled out unless there is some mixture of various institutions. For instance, the IBRD has been issuing large amounts of short-term securities. The Bank for International Settlements would apparently like to hold some of the IBRD's paper, but the latter is prohibited from issuing the type of liabilities which the BIS could hold. Similarly, the IMF, which needs liquid assets for earning purposes, buys national securities; instead, it might very well buy IBRD paper. These sets of possible relationships between the Fund and the World Bank have not been exploited. The separation of functions between the two neighboring institutions runs counter to the make-up of national financial institutions where short- and long-term lending are not sharply distinguished and the markets are connected.

Mundell also argued that the division of labor between the IMF and

GATT comes close to being shocking. Switching from one set of trade restrictions to another shifts a country from the jurisdiction of the IMF to that of GATT. The IMF deals with exchange controls while GATT looks after tariff restrictions. Yet these two methods of restricting trade are perfectly equivalent from an analytical point of view. This suggested to Mundell that a good deal of sorting out of the possible ways in which the three institutions (and perhaps a fourth which would deal with world stability) could or should be meshed remains to be done.

Professor Ingram added that he thought that the discussion of the institutional mix should be broadened to include the unplanned or unofficial institutions that have developed in recent years, for instance, the Euro-dollar or Euro-currency market, and more recently the international bond market. Practice may be running ahead of academic recognition of the importance of these markets. Commercial banks of surplus countries have with increasing frequency been encouraged to place funds in the Euro-dollar market; those of deficit countries have borrowed in the market. The interesting feature of this market is the resemblance it bears to a domestic money market, a federal funds market, bill market, and so on, in the interregional adjustment process. The Euro-dollar market has performed a very similar function in integrating the money markets of several countries. In Ingram's view, the international bond market may well play the same role for long-term capital in the future. These markets hold a great potential for helping to finance deficits and surpluses.

Professor Balassa addressed himself to Aliber's tax-subsidy scheme. Aliber's reliance on gadgets, according to Balassa, is disturbing. Referring to recent policies, Aliber spoke of "*ad hoc*-ery"; in regard to his proposal, one may well speak of gadgetry. At any rate, Aliber's scheme is open to objections on various grounds.

In the first place, under this scheme, governments would make decisions on their exchange rates independently of each other. Suppose that, tomorrow, the British government imposes a 20 per cent tax and subsidy; the French government may well follow the next day. In other words, a scramble of competitive devaluations may well follow the introduction of the tax-subsidy scheme. This is the more likely since the balance-of-payments objectives of many countries include the attainment of a surplus. At the same time, a scramble for reserves via competitive increases in the level of taxes and subsidies is less subject to international control than competitive devaluations.

Second, Aliber's scheme, according to Balassa, implies a form of exchange controls. Every transaction will have to pass through the central bank which will impose a tax or subsidy on the transaction. This might create arbitrage in third markets, with large profits for brokers. There are many examples of how exchange controls have been evaded and have led to large gains.

The third problem raised by Balassa concerns the uncertainty associated with foreign transactions. The tax-subsidy scheme would create a good deal of confusion in traders' minds for they would now have two types of devaluations to cope with. If a trader had only flexible rates to deal with, he could cover himself in the forward market. A scheme under which traders have to brace themselves not only against a possible devaluation but also against a change in the tax-subsidy level of taxes and subsidies applied by individual governments would increase uncertainty in foreign transactions and might prove disruptive for the forward market. These are some reasons why, according to Balassa, it is doubtful whether Aliber's proposal presents sufficient advantages to outweight its many potential defects.

Professor Mundell expressed a similar dislike for variable tariff rates on imports and rates of subsidy on exports. Such a scheme is likely to lead to a bureaucratic mess. There is a limit beyond which economists should not go in devising complicated gadgetry as a substitute for very simple mechanisms. A tax-subsidy scheme, if adopted, would open a Pandora's box of confusion.

Dr. Salant expressed agreement with these objections to the tax-subsidy proposal. In addition, Salant did not agree with Aliber on the ease with which a tax-subsidy change could be reversed. Aliber's argument, according to Salant, ignores the strength of political vested interests which would grow around a tax-subsidy type arrangement. This is a consideration which economists too often ignore when proposing particular schemes.

Professor Day, on the other hand, argued that the blame for resorting to gadgetry such as the tax-subsidy scheme should not be laid at Aliber's door. The trouble is that politicians or administrators too often tie economists up and refuse to give them any degree of freedom in the choice of policies. They reject the various sensible policies which are potentially available and economists, then, have to come forth with third- or fifth-best little schemes which attempt to circumvent the stupidity of politicians or administrators. This is why Aliber's attempt deserves a good deal of sympathy.

Professor Cooper voiced agreement with this position. He stated that, like Mundell, he did not particularly like the tax-subsidy scheme. However, the question, as Aliber pointed out, is what the alternatives are.

According to Cooper, there is at least one analytical reason why a tax-subsidy scheme presents some advantages over the kind of exchange-rate changes that occur in today's imperfect world. While both a change in the level of the tax-subsidy and a change in exchange rates would affect capital values, the tax-subsidy change would affect them far less. To the extent that prospective changes in the value of stocks engender a great deal of destabilizing speculation and to the extent that it is easier to speculate in financial assets than in commodities, a tax-subsidy scheme may reduce the prospects of destabilizing speculation.

Moreover, while the possibility of competitive use of taxes and subsidies raised by Balassa is a real risk in such a system, this must be weighed against the even greater risk of an increase in the competitive use of policies under the present system of *ad hoc*-ery. Today, many balance-of-payments policies masquerade as domestic policies and are therefore less subject to open international scrutiny and control than explicit use of taxes and subsidies for balance-of-payments purposes would be. For instance, international control over tax policies is limited to border taxes under GATT and many countries do in fact effect occasional changes in their internal tax structures for balance-of-payments reasons. Similarly, budgetary expenditures for tourism in the Atlantic community have been increasing year after year as countries have tried to improve their balances of payments, though it should be noted that these expenditures are largely mutually offsetting in terms of their balance-of-payments effects. Moreover, many of the growth policies adopted by various countries aim at balance-of-payments surpluses. At least Aliber's scheme, however unpleasant and distasteful to the purist, would be subject to much more open discussion and hence control than *ad hoc*-ery.

Professor Balassa expressed some doubts about this line of reasoning. It is important to keep in mind what systems are being compared. On the one hand, one can compare the tax-subsidy scheme with a system of floating rates, on the other, with *ad hoc*-ery.

When comparing the tax-subsidy scheme with flexible rates, it is clear that the former, even in its more ideal forms, presents some distinct disadvantages relative to the latter. Therefore, the case for the tax-subsidy scheme must rest here on its being more easily acceptable than flexible rates. According to Balassa, it is very doubtful that Aliber's scheme would be more acceptable than flexible rates to those very people who are opposed to flexible rates. Historically, the tax-subsidy scheme has not been accepted as an alternative to exchange-rate changes.

France resorted to such a scheme for a year or two but abandoned it when it proved more advantageous to devalue.

Furthermore, in the realm of arguments about the real world, it is doubtful, Balassa stated, that the choice is between *ad hoc*-ery and a "pure" tax-subsidy system. If the tax-subsidy scheme were adopted, there is a strong likelihood that one would have *ad hoc*-ery in addition. That is, countries would keep using *ad hoc* policies in addition to, or instead of, variations in tax-subsidy rates. This, Balassa stated, raises the possibility that the evils of both systems would be compounded.

Replying to these comments, *Professor Aliber* began by stating that Day's remarks correctly drew attention to an important difference between his and several other participants' approach to international monetary problems. Many economists want people to act wisely; Aliber wants them to avoid acting foolishly. Whereas many economists are concerned with the whole range of people's preferences, Aliber is concerned with their choices.

When examining the use of gadgetry, it is necessary to consider first the options before us. Given general agreements on Aliber's political diagnosis, the options are schemes similar to Aliber's on the one hand, and increasing restraints to convertibility on the other. To mention but the British case, there are currently four exchange rates for sterling. This is definitely gadgetry and is not confined to Britain; without even taking quantitative restrictions into account, there are very few currencies for which there are not several implicit or explicit exchange rates. The options, then, are either to travel the road of increasing the variety of trade and exchange restrictions or to try to simplify existing barriers by unifying them into one scheme or gadget, for instance, the tax-subsidy device. Flexible rates unfortunately do not appear to be a politically acceptable alternative.

With respect to the questions raised by Curzon as to the feasibility or desirability of increasing reserves via monetization of claims arising from aid to the less developed countries, Aliber argued that Mundell's example of the potential for monetization of IBRD liabilities showed the way of what might be achieved. Such monetization does not represent gadgetry and could be implemented with little change to existing institutional arrangements. It is true that the outstanding volume of government claims on less developed countries is extremely large. It would be possible, however, to set simple limits on the amounts which could be monetized each year and on the amount that any one country could transfer to settle its deficits in any one year. The point is simply that there exists a substantial stock of international reserves which could be, but are not, transferred in order to settle payments imbalances.

As to specific objections to the tax-subsidy scheme, Aliber stated that competitive devaluations under the scheme could be avoided by some simple rules. Similarly, multiple-currency practices could be avoided. Moreover, reversibility would not be very hard to achieve. The level of the tax-subsidy need not be changed frequently. The issue is really whether, for instance, it would reduce the protectiveness of the aid program. As to the French experience with the tax-subsidy scheme in 1958, Aliber would consider it to have been quite successful. The tax-subsidy enabled the French to make a successful transition from a situation in which their exchange rate was overvalued to the post-devaluation situation without provoking a huge flow of speculative capital.

In concluding, Aliber stated that, if the choice tomorrow was to move from a system of explicit and implicit multiple-exchange practices either to unrestrained convertibility and unitary exchange rates or to a tax-subsidy scheme, he would clearly opt for convertibility. This, unfortunately, is not the choice which confronts us. The most likely line of evolution of the system is toward increasing restraints on convertibility. The tax-subsidy scheme is one attempt at a rational approach to the adjustment problem in view of the variety of *ad hoc* devices that now prevail and limit convertibility.

II

Discussion of Professor Kafka's paper centered on five main issues. The first question to be raised concerned the relevance of the European example for integration among less developed countries. Second, the question of automatic versus discretionary credits within the integrating area was raised. Third, it was asked whether the emphasis on regional integration among developing countries was not a mistake in view of possibly more urgent objectives. Fourth, the relationship between integration and the analysis of optimum currency areas and of the policy mix was discussed. Fifth, it was asked whether monetary integration should precede economic integration and whether the gains from more efficient resource allocation through trade could be achieved without monetary integration.

The question of the relevance of European experience with integration was raised by *Professor Curzon*. According to Curzon, Kafka probably tends to underrate the importance of monetary integration for regional economic integration. There seems to be some contradiction in Kafka's argument. For he states, on the one hand, that it was possible for

European economic integration to proceed without monetary integration. On the other hand, he defines monetary integration as fixed exchange rates plus convertibility and this in fact is, with minor deviations, the situation which prevailed in Europe. In Curzon's view, it is an open question, or even doubtful, whether European economic integration could have survived major deviations from fixed exchange rates and convertibility.

Professor Kafka replied that, taking a wide view of European economic integration and considering it to have begun with the first OEEC liberalization schemes, several devaluations and revaluations had taken place since it started. Moreover, monetary integration is not complete in Europe since the belief that exchange rates are absolutely fixed is lacking. He agreed, however, that whether economic integration could have proceeded as fast as it did if monetary integration in Europe had been even more imperfect is an open question.

Professor Cooper turned to the issue of who should finance imbalances, and of how automatic credits should be, in a prospective regional monetary arrangement among less developed countries. Kafka suggested that creditors should not—or could not—be asked to finance regional imbalances and that facilities for regional financing of such imbalances should be discretionary rather than automatic.

Cooper stated that, if one regards regional economic integration as a desirable objective and some kind of monetary integration as a necessary concomitant, it is possible to argue for reasonably automatic credits provided by the creditors within the region. For many countries one of the main deterrents to entering a regional arrangement is the fear of running into balance-of-payments difficulties while at the same time, as a result of integration, losing some of the instruments for coping with balance-of-payments difficulties. This fear is quite universal even if, in fact, all countries in the group cannot simultaneously incur deficits vis-à-vis each other.

Proposing *discretionary* credit arrangements to help cushion these imbalances does little to surmount this deterrent to regional groupings since potential participants have no assurance that they would actually receive this aid, which they feel they need to protect themselves against the prospective effects of trade liberalization. This is why there is some value in setting up machinery that links as automatically as possible the availability of credits to balance-of-payments deteriorations that result from regional integration. The only area for discretion would be in deciding which part of balance-of-payments changes results from integration.

Furthermore, Cooper argued, once the financing of imbalances is linked to liberalization, creditors should provide the bulk of this financing. As a matter of fact, this is one way of distributing some of the alleged economic gains from regional integration to all members of the integrating region. Presumably those countries whose intraregional balance of payments improves, namely the creditors, are also those who enjoy to a greater extent the economies of scale and other advantages that are said to be associated with integration. Extending reasonably automatic credits to the deficit countries, then, is one way of distributing the real gains from regional integration.

Professor McKinnon raised the next (and third) issue. According to McKinnon, the current, strong emphasis on regional integration may well be a red herring in terms of what is really important for the development of many of the poor countries. The most important task which faces Latin American countries is the rationalization of their trade in the world market for goods and services where the greatest gains from trade are to be had. If, in fact, the most rational evolution of the trade structure of many of these countries is that they start specializing in the large-scale production of a few manufactured products and use the proceeds to purchase most of their direct consumption needs, little scope will be left for trading with each other. In these circumstances, attempts at regional integration behind common tariff walls would only complicate the basic and administrative problems of rationalizing foreign trade with Europe and the United States. Indeed, if any single Latin American economy developed the political will for monetary stability, currency convertibility, and removal of trade restrictions and taxes, the implementation of such a program would be made very difficult by the existence of multilateral commitments to its neighbors (who are unlikely to be similarly inclined).

Even if regional integration behind high tariff walls against the outside world succeeded, McKinnon argued, it is very unlikely that the result in terms of welfare would be desirable. For, in terms of the standard argument of trade diversion versus trade creation, trade diversion would be very substantial in Latin America. For instance, one might find Argentina specializing in the production of very high-cost automobiles which it would ship to Brazil in return for very high-cost refrigerators. Part of this high cost would arise out of continued excessive protection to real value added in both industries which remain dependent on American and European components and capital goods. This is unlikely to raise real welfare and suggests that it might be better to leave the issue of regional integration aside and to concentrate on correcting the overall trade structure.

Mr. de Cecco argued that the picture was not quite as bleak as McKinnon painted it. For instance, the climate in which the original steps toward European integration were taken is not totally unlike that which prevails in Latin America today. These steps were taken by countries with highly defensive trade policies, at the time of the dollar gap. Their problems were problems of bilateral disequilibrium between each of them and the United States. Their trade policies were often almost as inept as those pursued by Latin American countries. This suggests, de Cecco stated, that the case for regional integration should not be dismissed out of hand.

Professor McKinnon replied by emphasizing the dissimilarity between the postwar European situation and that of Latin America today. The great gains from European integration came to a large extent from trade liberalization within Europe rather than from liberalized trade with the rest of the world. In the case of Latin America, complementarity in trade relationships would call for increases in the trade of each of the Latin American countries with the United States. The largest immediate gains for these countries reside in trade with the outside world.

Turning to another issue, *Mr. Swoboda* suggested that some of the problems raised by Kafka could be put in terms of the analysis of the policy mix, on the one hand, and of optimum currency areas, on the other. For instance, whether countries which form a customs union should pursue a policy of joint fluctuations against the outside world, adopt an adjustable peg, or let all rates float depends, in part, on the policy instruments available to them. Some systems may be easier to run with a limited battery of policy instruments than others. Moreover, the optimum policy mix to be followed by individual countries in a customs union may differ from that to be followed by a country acting in strict isolation.

Furthermore, the way in which Kafka poses the question of the goals of monetary integration suggests a different approach to the analysis of the optimum currency area problem. The usual approach to that problem takes the degree of economic integration as given; if the region is sufficiently integrated, that is, if it constitutes an optimum currency area, fixed exchange rates are recommended; if it is not, flexible rates are in order. Kafka, Swoboda argued, puts the problem the other way around when he states that monetary integration, that is, fixed exchange rates and so on, is desirable because it promotes economic integration.

This poses an interesting problem for the analysis of optimum currency areas. The usual analysis of the choice of an environment or exchange-rate regime assumes certain things, for instance, the degree of capital mobility, to be given. If there is a relation between, say, the degree of capital mobility and the exchange rate regime—though which way the relation goes is not clear as Balassa's remarks about some of the evils of fixed nominal rates in Latin America suggest—the choice of an exchange-rate regime becomes a much more difficult analytical problem.

Professor v. N. Whitman addressed herself to the applicability of economic models, especially those dealing with the policy mix, to less developed countries. According to Mrs. Whitman, several points mentioned in the course of the conference's discussion suggest that, in dealing with the problems of the less developed countries, one cannot help but run up against a variety of constraints as a consequence of the presumed lack of sophistication of the instruments at their disposal. It was stated, at another session, that the less developed countries should not adopt fixed exchange rates because they do not have the sophisticated fiscal and monetary policies which would enable them to survive fixed exchange rates without sacrificing internal balance. On the other hand, Kafka argues that less developed countries cannot cope with flexible rates because they do not have the kind of institutional structure in which flexible exchange rates can be kept stable, and therefore exchange rates should be changed only in cases of fundamental disequilibrium.

The obstacles posed by what one may call institutional constraints, Mrs. Whitman argued, suggest the need to recast the whole problem of targets and instruments in terms of those instruments in which the less developed countries have a comparative advantage—since they apparently have an absolute disadvantage in the use of all of them! The problem of monetary integration, flexible rates, and so on, should then be approached in terms of those instruments in the use of which the less developed countries have the least disadvantage. Even in the case of developed countries, it is not necessarily correct that policy instruments are available which can be utilized in the sophisticated way assumed by the models of the economist.

Professor Mundell raised the last issue brought up in the discussion, by asking whether some form of monetary integration in Latin America could not prove a useful spur to the development of that region. According to Mundell, the monetary disorganization in Latin America seems to be quite similar to that of Europe after World War I. Some sort of rationalization of Latin American currencies seems in order after fifteen or twenty years of monetary chaos. Latin America has experimented with the whole gamut of exchange rate systems: flexible rates, fixed rates, adjustable pegs, high degrees of exchange controls, multiple exchange rates, trade restrictions, high tariffs of every possible kind, and what not.

In Mundell's view, it does not seem to make much sense to talk about flexible exchange rates as a means of avoiding economic controls in the Latin-American context. Controls will exist in any event, flexible rates notwithstanding. In view of this, it may be relevant to ask whether or not monetary integration in Latin America would be a force which could eventually lead to some political integration and some rationalization of, to say the least, very erratic monetary policies.

Professor Sjaastad expressed some doubts as to whether these aims, and the gains that are to be found in resource allocation, could be achieved through monetary integration of the fixed exchange-rate type. The problem with fixed exchange rates in Latin America is simply that they do not stay fixed. The attempt to preserve fixed rates while widely different rates of inflation prevail in various countries has taken a heavy toll in terms of real resource costs.

Sjaastad cited the massive Argentine devaluations of 1955, 1959, and 1962 as an illustration. After each of these devaluations, the government tried to contain the subsequent inflation. At least 30 per cent of Argentine GNP is sold at world market prices. The domestic currency prices of these goods tend to rise immediately after a devaluation and, through a chain of substitution effects, a strong upward pressure is exerted on other prices. In order to achieve the change in relative prices which is the goal of the devaluation, the government must bring heavy deflationary pressure to bear. The results, in terms of increased unemployment and reductions in the money supply, have not been very much milder than those of the great depression in the United States. The losses in real output which followed these Argentine devaluations have been extremely large. A more sensible approach to exchange rates, therefore, Sjaastad argued, would be to vary them more frequently as Chile has done in the recent past.

Professor Troeller argued that, in the present Latin-American situation, after every exchange-rate system has been tried without much success, it might be better to start with economic integration and to leave monetary integration to a later stage. After all, the Treaty of Rome does not spell out in any detail the path monetary integration is to take in the European Economic Community.

Once economic integration is well under way, it might be much easier to decide on the right exchange-rate system for the region. How can one decide whether to have flexible, fixed, or jointly fluctuating rates, before knowing how and to what extent trade restrictions will be relaxed? It might thus be premature, Mrs. Troeller stated, to decide at this stage what the most appropriate system for Latin America will be.

Professor Krueger, on the other hand, took issue with the view, implicit in several of the preceding comments, that it is possible to achieve meaningful economic integration without restoring some order in Latin American monetary and exchange-rate systems. The reason why some kind of stable monetary framework is needed can be illustrated with the example of the tire industry in Latin America. There are reputed to be three tire plants located fairly near each other, one in Argentina, one in Brazil, and one in Uruguay. At any point of time, one of these plants is operating at full capacity while the other two are shut down. The plant operating at full capacity is obviously located in the country which devalued most recently. This same type of situation, according to Miss Krueger, probably occurs in many more industries.

It is likely that any benefits from economic integration will be overwhelmed by the costs of such misallocations of resources as long as monetary chaos prevails. This is especially true since Latin American countries have engaged in large import-substitution drives. They all have their high-cost industries and, as McKinnon has pointed out, when one shifts from Argentine to Brazilian automobiles one is still shifting to a high price product and not to the cheaper European car. In any event, it is hard to see how resources can be allocated efficiently in terms of location within Latin America as long as sudden large changes in relative exchange rates occur.

Replying to these interventions, *Professor Kafka* commented, first, on two points raised by Balassa. Kafka stated, regarding fixed versus floating rates, that he did not in his paper refer specifically to South America, to LAFTA, or inflation-ridden countries but was talking of developing countries generally; these were not significantly more inflation-ridden than developed ones and any recent issue of *International Financial Statistics* would show that this is so, i.e., that over one half of developing countries and a not much larger proportion of developed countries had annual rates of inflation of less than 5 per cent. On the other hand, he had specifically endorsed floating rates for the correction of fundamental disequilibrium; perhaps he should have been more explicit in stating that he had in mind the case where such disequilibria were being constantly recreated through inflation. His objection to floating rates referred exclusively to countries where the main problem was temporary disequilibrium. He doubted if economic integration would be feasible in the future if fundamental disequilibria were to exist to any large extent. This, in a sense, was also the point underlying Miss Krueger's comments. Tariffs, today, are still high enough to allow for limited progress in the direction of integration despite the persistence of fundamental disequilibria. As tariff walls come down, however, even this limited progress will not be possible any more.

On the other hand, he should perhaps have stressed more than he did that his recommendation of a relatively wide definition of temporary disequilibrium was qualified by the suggestion that the difference between fundamental and temporary disequilibrium should be defined by the acceptable reserve loss.

Moreover, Kafka argued, the Chilean example did not constitute a counter-example to the proposition that less developed countries have neither the ability nor the courage to let rates float. Developing countries have frequently allowed their exchange rates to float when first embarking on a stabilization program. This situation, however, never seems to last; most of the time, the rate is stabilized after a few months. In Chile, there were several rates, not all of which moved on the same trend and some of which were protected by restrictions.

As to Balassa's remarks on the possibility of economizing on reserves, it is true, according to Kafka, that, as the developed part of the world learns to control its business cycle, terms of trade fluctuations will increasingly tend to be governed by supply rather than demand conditions. As a consequence, the importance of offsetting rather than parallel movements in the terms of trade of developing areas may also increase. However, it is not possible to be sure of this.

Kafka turned next to McKinnon's argument that the underdeveloped countries should not concentrate on regional economic integration since this would mean trade diversion rather than trade creation. This argument does not take into account, however, the strength of the drive toward industrialization and protectionism in the developing countries. Because of this strength, the choice is not really between a statically optimal organization of the trade of developing countries and a statically less than optimal one. It is a choice between degrees of less than optimality from the static point of view; but regional economic integration may be optimal from the dynamic point of view (e.g., the infant industry case). The choice is not between having one automobile factory in a developing country and importing cars from the United States; the choice is between having three factories in each of three developing countries, or having one in each, or perhaps three in one and none in the other two. This is the only choice likely to be available (for political reasons), and this is why regional economic integration is very important. De Cecco's example of the early days of European integration, Kafka argued, is quite relevant here.

Turning to the financing of imbalances, Kafka stated that, on the question of automaticity of credits, his differences with Cooper are rather minor and of a semantic nature. The question of who should supply the reserves to finance the deficits, on the other hand, is a very important one. The problem, according to Kafka, is that the small volume of intra-regional trade makes it unlikely that the main reserve needs will be for intra-regional balances. Rather, reserves will be needed mainly to finance the trade of the region with the outside world. This means that there may be no creditors to supply the reserves within the region. This is why Kafka argued that, since reserves have a social cost, underdeveloped countries feel—and many developed countries seem to feel—that some help should be given to the integration of developing countries by supplying reserves from outside.

Finally, Kafka agreed with Mundell that monetary integration has an important role to play in the process of economic integration. It should help to promote better policies, if only because countries would have an interest in seeing their partners follow better policies.

APPENDIX: TAXES ON IMPORTS AND SUBSIDIES ON EXPORTS AS A TOOL OF ADJUSTMENT

Gottfried Haberler

Introduction

Stubborn disequilibria in the balance of payments due largely to the inability or unwillingness of deficit countries to disinflate (which would require that wage levels rise less rapidly than productivity),[1] in conjunction with the strong aversion to any change in exchange rates and the unwillingness to experiment even with limited flexibility, have induced the search for substitutes for exchange-rate changes. In a sense, direct controls are such a substitute and they often are, or lead to, partial, more or less thinly disguised depreciation. An example is the quotation of a rate for the "investment dollar" in London which commands at present a high premium in the market, thus reflecting a substantial, if partial, depreciation of sterling.

A closer substitute for currency devaluation is a comprehensive tax on imports combined with subsidies for exports. It is an old idea but has been recently revived in numerous informal discussions and unpublished memoranda. Thus R. Z. Aliber, at the end of the paper he submitted to this conference, recommends, for serious consideration as a method for balance-of-payments adjustment, a system "of uniform tariff surcharges on all commodity imports or foreign payments together with subsidies on all commodity exports or foreign receipts."

In the present note, I discuss, first, three earlier proposals of tax-subsidy substitutes for currency depreciation as well as some current policies of that type. Secondly, I give reasons why, in my opinion, this method of dealing with balance-of-payments disequilibria is not advisable.

This note, stimulated by Robert Z. Aliber's paper, was written after the conference.

1. Have the surplus countries no responsibility, the reader may ask? They certainly do, but I do not know of any surplus country in recent years that did not allow substantial inflation to go on, while there are many countries that let inflation proceed while they were in deficit.

173

Earlier Proposals and Current Practices

It will be recalled that prior to the devaluation of sterling in 1931 Keynes had recommended a system of import tariffs and export bounties. He claimed that such a scheme would be much superior to devaluation because it would avoid the depreciation in terms of gold of British foreign obligations and assets denominated in sterling. "This proposal would avoid the injury to the national credit and to our receipts from foreign loans fixed in terms of Sterling which would ensue on devaluation." "A plan of this kind would be immeasurably preferable to devaluation."[2] Since Britain was a large net creditor, this was a rather nationalistic argument, especially in view of the fact that, because of the sharp decline in world market prices, the real burden of sterling debts to Britain's numerous debtors, many of them less developed countries, had sharply increased.

Keynes always spoke of tariffs and bounties on commodity exports and imports and not of taxes and subsidies on purchases and sales of foreign currencies. At first he recommended a uniform *ad valorem* duty on all imports and an equal uniform *ad valorem* bounty for all exports. This would be equivalent to a devaluation, except that service and capital transactions are not covered. But he later dropped the uniformity principle and recommended different percentage taxes and subsidies for different commodities. Keynes must thus be regarded as the inventor of what later became known as the "Schachtian" system of international trading. This system was admired and recommended for adoption elsewhere in different variations and guises by Keynes' more radical disciples, but Keynes himself later returned to advocating more orthodox trading methods and in his famous posthumously published article on the American balance of payments[3] sharply rejected the modern stuff, "gone silly and sour," of his radical erstwhile followers, who in the meantime had become his critics.

The idea of a uniform import duty plus export subsidy as a substitute for devaluation was later proposed by John R. Hicks.[4] Hicks's motives were not selfishly nationalistic. On the contrary, he proposed the tariff plus subsidy scheme precisely because he wanted to avoid the nationalistic terms-of-trade exploitation of other countries. He argued that

2. See Addendum I, which Keynes together with six others submitted to the Macmillan Committee report. (*Committee on Finance and Industry: Report* [London: Government Printing Office, 1931], pp. 199, 200.)

3. "The Balance of Payments of the United States," *Economic Journal*, 56 (June, 1946).

4. "Free Trade and Modern Economics." Reprinted in *Essays in World Economics* (Oxford: Clarendon Press, 1959).

import restrictions are often necessary to combat unemployment but have the undesirable and unneighborly side effect of turning the terms of trade against foreign countries. Hence import restrictions should be supplemented by export subsidies.[5] Strangely, he did not refer to Keynes, nor did he point out that the tariff plus subsidy policy is a very close substitute for devaluation.[6]

My third example is a proposal made many years ago by Robert Triffin—one of the earlier of the numerous reform plans for the international monetary mechanism that we owe to his fertile mind. Only the basic principle will be discussed here.[7]

While Keynes and Hicks proposed taxes on commodity imports and subsidies for exports, Triffin's proposal is for double or multiple exchange rates for imports, which is equivalent to differentiated taxes on the purchase of foreign exchange collected by the monetary authorities. The official rate would apply to all exports (with few exceptions) and to the imports of "necessities." Other imports would be divided into a few broad categories arranged in the order of the degree of "urgency" or "importance" accorded to them by the authorities. Foreign exchange would then be allotted to each category of import commodities to be sold to importers in free auctions in such a way that the price of foreign currency would vary inversely to the urgency of the category of imports for which it was used.

5. Hicks, *Free Trade*, p. 24. He did not discuss the possibility—some people would say the probability—that the method of import tariffs plus export subsidies (which is almost equivalent to currency devaluation) might improve the terms of trade.

6. It is true, however, that elsewhere in his paper (p. 00) he did say, in passing, that "devaluation is hardly an appropriate way out for what may well be...a very temporary trouble," namely, a cyclical depression or recession. "If we are to make it a rule to use exchange variation to deal with troubles of this sort, then...we have got to go right over to a system of flexible exchange rates." But he refrained from expressly recommending the latter system, perhaps because in 1951 the chances of getting the system of floating exchange rates adopted must have seemed more remote than in 1966.

7. One version can be found in his paper, "National Central Banking and the International Economy," in *International Monetary Policies*, Postwar Economic Studies, no. 7 (Washington, D.C.: Board of Governors of the Federal Reserve System, 1947), pp. 46–81. (See also my critical comments *ibid*. pp. 82–102.)

Triffin's proposal strongly influenced monetary legislation in at least two Latin-American countries, Paraguay and Guatemala. The *Monetary Law of Guatemala* of 1945 was drawn up according to his specifications. (See the English translation in *The Federal Reserve Bulletin*, March 1946, pp. 257–88.) As was to be expected, the actual legislation is much more complicated than the principles laid down in the article cited above. (For details see my comments in *International Monetary Policies*, p. 93.) As far as I know, the policy was never anywhere carried out according to plan.

Triffin describes his system as a kind of "nondiscriminatory exchange control." A better, more descriptive designation would be "partial depreciation."[8]

In the postwar period many countries have adopted the policy of refunding internal excise taxes on exports and collecting such taxes, in addition to tariffs, on imports. Something like a general tariff-plus-subsidy scheme is being operated, if a general turnover tax, sales tax, or value-added tax is collected on all imports and refunded on all exports. This is actually being done in several European countries. In Germany, the general import tax and tax refund on exports is something like 6 per cent *ad valorem*, and in France 20 per cent. It has been suggested by some writers that in lieu of an appreciation of their currencies these countries should stop the collection on imports and refund of taxes on exports. And the proposal has been made that Great Britain and the United States replace their corporate income tax by a general value-added or sales tax in order to be able to collect a tax on imports and pay a tax refund on exports which would be equivalent, as far as commodity trade is concerned, to currency devaluation.

Finally, let me mention a recent case reported by *The New York Times* (October 22, 1966). While the IMF recommended an open devaluation of the Egyptian pound, "Soviet economists are understood to believe that the Nasser regime should undertake an indirect devaluation of the pound through export subsidies and import taxes to cushion the political impact of the move and to ease the immediate economic strain on the poorer classes."

Naturally, the Russians wanted to differentiate their advice from that of the IMF. It should be observed that if the stated purpose is to be achieved, differentiated, not uniform, taxes and subsidies would be required.

Criticism

I have always felt that the Keynesian and Hicksian proposals were, especially at the time when they were made, utterly impractical and objectionable. They were impractical because at that time machinery for the payment of export subsidies did not exist. The adoption of the

8. Triffin did not rule out straight, general devaluation, but wished to reserve it for clear cases of "fundamental" disequilibrium, which he defined rather narrowly. His own scheme was meant to apply to non-fundamental disequilibria which he defined broadly and usually characterized as "cyclical," i.e., caused by the cyclical depressions. Just as Keynes and all Keynesians, he did not foresee that inflation and not cyclical depressions would be the predominant cause of postwar balance-of-payments difficulties.

proposal would have required adding an entirely new dimension to the existing apparatus of international trade controls, namely, export controls. The situation is somewhat different now, at least in those countries that practice general tax refunding on exports.[9] The proposals were objectionable because the proposed system was bound to be discriminatory. It would never have been, in practice, a uniform tax and subsidy on all international transactions. There would be discrimination between commodities and services. It would be impossible in practice to resist the temptation to differentiate between different categories of imports. Keynes actually proposed differentiation himself. Even if the nominal rate were the same for imports from all countries, difficulties of ascertaining unit values would lead to *de facto* discrimination. And it certainly would be used for discrimination between countries—overt or implicit—through the differential treatment of different commodities. The system cannot be more than a very imperfect substitute for an exchange-rate variation. That is why I said that Keynes was the real inventor of the Schachtian trading system.

Triffin's proposal is equivalent to a tax on the purchase of foreign currency. This is, in principle, preferable to a tax on commodities because it can apply also to services and capital transactions. But the discrimination between exports and imports—there was no export subsidy in Triffin's proposal corresponding to the import tax—stamps the proposal as protectionist and makes it objectionable on efficiency grounds. The discrimination between different categories of imports, too, is objectionable on efficiency grounds and makes it administratively arbitrary and unwieldy; it invites abuse and in an inflationary situation becomes utterly unworkable.

A uniform tax on all purchases of foreign exchange from the authorities and equal uniform premium on all sales of foreign exchange to the authorities would, of course, eliminate all difficulties, discrimination, and inefficiencies. But this would be depreciation almost without disguise and therefore would meet substantially the same resistance as an overt change in the exchange rate.

Concerning the proposal that the United States and other countries should replace the corporate income tax by a turnover or value-added tax in order to be able to follow the European example of remitting the tax on exports and levying it on imports, I would say that it is, in

9. However, in the United States and in many other countries, the administrative apparatus for generalized export control does not exist. The creation of such an apparatus would be a dangerous by-product of the tax-subsidy scheme— dangerous because once in existence it is bound to be used for other purposes.

principle, objectionable that tax policy be decisively influenced by balance-of-payments considerations. Balance-of-payments deficits and surpluses are, after all, short-run phenomena and tax reform is a long-term affair which should be governed by considerations of efficiency and equity and nothing else.

On the other hand, if a country has a turnover or value-added tax which it remits on exports and levies on imports, it is perhaps less objectionable to change this detail in the interest of balance-of-payments adjustment than to change the whole tax system. But even in this case it should not be forgotten that we have here merely a one-shot measure, lacking in flexibility.[10] Furthermore, once adopted, the policy would offer a standing temptation to differentiate taxes and refunds as between different commodities and thus use the system for other purposes than balance-of-payments adjustment.

It is true, however, that there is no objection on long-run efficiency grounds to removing a general and uniform import tax and corresponding general and uniform export subsidy which were imposed for the purpose of compensating domestic industry in their international dealings for the cost imposed by a *general* sales tax, turnover tax, or income tax. Or, to put it the other way round, the introduction of such a general tax does not require or justify, on long-run efficiency grounds, the introduction of compensating duties and subsidies. A tax on a particular commodity is, of course, a different matter. This truth was clearly seen by Ricardo:

> For the same reasons that protecting duties are not justifiable on account of the rise of wages generally, from whatever cause it may proceed, it is evident that they are not to be defended when taxation is general, and equally affects all classes of producers. An income tax is of this description. . . .
> The rise of wages, a tax on income, or a proportional tax on all commodities, all operate in the same way; they do not alter the relative value of goods, and therefore they do not subject us to any disadvantage in our commerce with foreign countries. . . .
> A tax, however, which falls exclusively on the producers of a particular commodity tends to raise the price of that commodity. . . .
> If no protecting duty is imposed on the importation of a similar commodity from other countries, injustice is done to

10. Aliber's proposal is for uniform taxes and subsidies unconnected with an existing turnover or sales tax. His system could be flexibly managed, but as I pointed out above, it would be a too thinly disguised substitute for exchange-rate changes to offer any advantage over the real thing.

the producer at home, and not only to the producer but to the country to which he belongs. It is for the interest of the public that he should not be driven from a trade which, under a system of free competition, he would have chosen, and to which he would adhere if every other commodity were taxed equally with that which he produces.... [11]

Needless to add that if it could be shown that an ostensibly general tax is in fact not general but has an unequal impact on particular branches of the economy, *ideally* a compensating duty or subsidy may be in order.

Conclusion

My general conclusion then is that it is unsound policy and tactically unwise to concentrate propaganda for reform of the international monetary system on the substitution of a system of tariffs and subsidies for exchange-rate variations. If the tax and subsidy is really comprehensive and therefore unobjectionable from the standpoint of long-run economic efficiency, the disguise is too thin: it will not deceive anybody and the resistance will be just as strong as against the real thing—overt devaluation or upvaluation. If the disguise is to be effective, the substitute must be differentiated from the real thing. For that and other reasons, taxes and subsidies will in actual practice *not* be equal and uniform. Differential taxes and subsidies imply undesirable and inefficient discrimination and open the door to full-fledged exchange control.

To think of currency depreciation as the equivalent of a uniform tax on imports plus subsidy on exports and of upvaluation as the equivalent of a uniform tax on exports and subsidy on imports is a very useful analytical device for the purpose of elucidating certain relationships (for example, the effect of devaluation on the terms of trade); but it is a dangerous policy recommendation.

11. See "On the Protection of Agriculture" (1822) in *The Works and Correspondence of David Ricardo*, edited by P. Sraffa (Cambridge University Press, 1951), 4: 216–17.

PART 4

THE ADJUSTMENT PROBLEM

THE ASSIGNMENT PROBLEM

Egon Sohmen

Means and Ends of Economic Policy

The topic I have been assigned in this conference calls for an investigation of the appropriate pairing of policy instruments and target variables in the pursuit of the major objectives of economic policy. This is indeed the basic question in any discussion of monetary reform, but its systematic treatment in pure theory has been mostly the work of Robert Mundell. Applying Tinbergen's abstract reference system for economic policy,[1] Mundell has largely concentrated his attention on the choice between fiscal, monetary, and exchange-rate (or price-level) policies in the simultaneous pursuit of full employment and balance-of-payments equilibrium.[2] Every policy instrument will in general affect several target variables. As a principle of "effective market classification," however, every instrument of policy ought to be directed primarily toward the one variable on which it has the relatively strongest effect. This agrees comfortably with common sense.

From a more general point of view, targets such as full employment and balance-of-payments equilibrium (or, for that matter, price stability and growth) cannot be regarded as ends in themselves, but only as

1. J. Tinbergen, *On the Theory of Economic Policy*, 2d ed. (Amsterdam: North-Holland Publishing Company, 1955).
2. R. A. Mundell, "Capital Mobility and Stabilization Policy under Fixed and Flexible Exchange Rates," *Canadian Journal of Economics and Political Science*, 29 (1963): 475–85; "The Appropriate Use of Monetary and Fiscal Policy for Internal and External Stability," International Monetary Fund, *Staff Papers*, 9 (1962): 70–79; "On the Selection of a Program of Economic Policy with an Application to the Current Situation in the United States," *Banca Nazionale del Lavoro Quarterly Review*, 16 (1963): 263–84. See also J. Marcus Fleming, "Domestic Financial Policies under Fixed and under Floating Exchange Rates," International Monetary Fund, *Staff Papers*, 9 (1962): 369–80; A. O. Krueger, "The Impact of Alternative Government Policies under Varying Exchange Systems," *Quarterly Journal of Economics*, 79 (1965): 195–208; P. Salin, "La Controverse des Changes Flexibles et le Problème de l'Equilibre Simultané Interne et Externe," *Economia Internazionale*, 18, nos. 3, 4 (August and November, 1965); H. G. Johnson, "Some Aspects of the Theory of Economic Policy in a World of Capital Mobility," *Essays in Honour of Marco Fanno* (Padova: Cedam, 1966), pp. 345–59.

means of realizing an optimal use of the world's resources. This is not the place to discuss the intricacies of welfare economics in any detail. Some reference system involving notions of welfare must, however, necessarily be in the back of one's mind in any discussion of the relative merits of different policy alternatives.

For allocative optimality, only real variables matter: the geographical, personal, and intertemporal distribution of quantities of commodities and factors of production. International monetary arrangements and the conduct of the domestic policies of every country are, from this wider point of view, of interest only so far as they tend to move the world economy closer or farther away from a pattern of real variables that is, for whatever reasons, considered optimal.

In several respects, we may proceed further from this excessive level of generality without entering areas of legitimate controversy. Under-utilization of scarce resources in any region of the world is clearly suboptimal. From a cosmopolitan point of view, it is also fairly well acknowledged that, as a general proposition, trade should be impaired as little as possible by artificial impediments to assure optimal resource allocation. This will generally require that economic conditions in the world at large correspond as closely as possible to the situation typically found within countries. It is probably also uncontroversial to state that, as far as such movements occur at all, any temporary or permanent transfers of real capital ought to take place from those countries that are relatively better endowed with capital to the less developed regions of the world.

The realization of optimal resource allocation would require only a minimum of discretionary policy action in a world of perfect price flexibility. I suppose it is now generally agreed that involuntary un-employment of scarce factors of production would be ruled out in that case. Even as a transitory phenomenon, unemployment is possible only when certain prices (including wages and interest rates) are relatively inflexible. With the employment problem taking care of itself in a world of perfect markets, fiscal policy could be devoted exclusively to assuring the proper division of the available resources between private and public use. Depending on whether or not a country has established a fixed par value for its currency in terms of another currency (or in terms of a commodity such as gold), monetary policy would be used either to equilibrate its over-all external balance at the prescribed exchange rates or to keep some index of domestic prices as stable as possible. The choice between a regime of fixed and one of flexible exchange rates would primarily depend on the relative weight being attached to the desirability of a stable domestic price level. There could never be any problem of balance-of-payments adjustment that would require the use of exchange controls or of trade restrictions.

In the last analysis, all important difficulties in the assignment of policy variables to different targets can thus be attributed to insufficient price flexibility in the real world. There are many possible reasons for price rigidity, most important among them wage rigidity and lack of competition in commodity markets. I am increasingly impressed by evidence that the latter factor, in particular, tends to receive far too little attention. If one does not want to deal with these major defects of most economies directly, all analysis of the proper assignment of the traditional tools of macroeconomic policy acquires a distinctly "second-best" flavor. In the sequel, let us proceed under the customary assumption that nothing is done to improve matters on the score of price rigidity—an assumption whose realism nobody will deny, much as I personally tend to question the alleged inevitability of this state of affairs.

Employment Policy and Balance-of-Payments Equilibrium

I will postpone for later discussion the issue of fixed *versus* flexible exchange rates in a world of inflexible prices and turn first to the choice of stabilization instruments under the two systems.

Mundell has pointed out that the relative effectiveness of the two traditional instruments of stabilization policy, fiscal and monetary policy, differs fundamentally under the two extreme forms of exchange-rate policy.[3] In a limiting case, he found that monetary policy is completely incapable of affecting employment when exchange rates are pegged. Fiscal policy, in turn, becomes completely impotent when exchange rates are flexible in this limiting case.[4] These conclusions hold under the assumptions that—(*a*) monetary policy in the country

3. R. A. Mundell, *ibid.*, and his earlier article, "Flexible Exchange Rates and Employment Policy," *Canadian Journal of Economics and Political Science*, 27 (1961): 509–17. The crucial difference in the effectiveness of monetary policy under fixed and flexible exchange rates was also pointed out in my *Flexible Exchange Rates* (Chicago: University of Chicago Press, 1961), esp. pp. 83–90 and 123–24.

4. Following Mundell's usage in most of the papers cited, we shall define monetary policy as a change in the money supply with unchanged government budget and fiscal policy as a change in government expenditure (or in tax-induced private expenditure), with the central bank passively allowing the credit base to change as its holdings of foreign exchange adjust in response to whatever balance-of-payments changes are induced by fiscal measures.

considered does not affect the level of interest rates in the rest of the world; (*b*) capital moves internationally without transactions costs or other sources of friction; (*c*) spot, forward, and expected future exchange rates are identical at any moment (even though they may change over time).

The varying effectiveness of fiscal and monetary policies under different monetary systems finds its explanation in the effects of stabilization policies on international capital movements and the further changes that are induced by the latter in other economic variables. Under the limiting assumptions listed above, the domestic interest rate cannot be affected by domestic policy. For any given level of national income, the amounts of money and of bonds the public is willing to hold at the given interest rate will be determinate.

Expansion of government expenditure or tax reduction at a given money supply implies that the public debt increases. In the limiting case of perfect interest elasticity of international capital flows, any addition to the public debt will be acquired by foreigners. When the central bank does not intervene on the foreign exchange market, the increased capital inflow is matched by a worsening of the trade balance by exactly the same amount. The effects of the changes in public expenditure (or tax-induced private expenditure) and in the trade balance on aggregate demand for domestic output exactly cancel each other.

When the money supply is expanded under fixed exchange rates, on the other hand, the tendency for interest rates to fall leads to a capital export which exactly cancels the increase in the domestically created credit base. All real variables will remain unchanged.

Under less austere assumptions, the conclusion remains that, in a regime of fixed exchange rates, fiscal policy ought to be directed primarily at the level of aggregate demand while changes of interest rates should be the principal tool for securing balance-of-payments equilibrium. As Mundell has shown, the opposite pairing of targets and policy variables, i.e., the use of fiscal policy for external and of interest rates for internal balance, would lead to dynamic instability.[5] This is a consequence of the "comparative advantage" of fiscal policy as a tool for employment stabilization and of monetary policy as an instrument for keeping the balance of payments in equilibrium when exchange rates are fixed.

When exchange rates are flexible, the task of keeping the balance of payments in equilibrium is left to the free exchange market. The superior

5. See his articles in *Staff Papers*, and *Banca Nazionale del Lavoro Quarterly Review* (cited in n. 2).

effectiveness of monetary policy as an employment stabilizer under flexible exchange rates makes it possible to rely exclusively on this instrument for preserving full employment. Fiscal policy is liberated for the tasks of allocating the available resources to public and private uses and of redistributing income and wealth in accordance with the community's preferences.

In the earlier models set up by Mundell and others,[6] the change of the terms of trade as a possible consequence of exchange-rate variations was not explicitly taken into account. The equilibrium level of real national product is determined by effective demand for *physical* quantities of commodities, including exports and imports. For the determination of balance-of-payments equilibrium, on the other hand, it is *values* of exports and imports that matter. Adjustments in the terms of trade will also influence the level of consumption for any given level of physical production in an economy.[7]

One interesting technical point may be noted that follows in a corrected model which explicitly recognizes the possible terms-of-trade adjustments under flexible exchange rates. The analysis of the limiting case of perfect capital mobility, as sketched above, might lead one to believe that monetary policy always has a less pronounced effect on employment under fixed as compared to flexible exchange rates, and that exactly the opposite would always hold for fiscal policy. The presumption for monetary policy can be proved correct, but it does not hold for fiscal policy. Under certain circumstances, fiscal policy may be a more effective tool of employment policy under flexible than under fixed exchange rates.[8]

This outcome is possible, in particular, when the response of international capital movements to changes of interest rates is relatively weak. It is seen most clearly in the limiting case of zero interest elasticity of capital flows. The rise of effective demand resulting from fiscal expansion always causes an increase in the demand for imports. When

6. See the articles by Mundell, Fleming, Krueger, and Johnson, cited in n. 2.

7. See my paper, "Fiscal and Monetary Policies under Alternative Exchange-Rate Systems," *Quarterly Journal of Economics*, 81 (1967): 515–23.

8. Under the assumptions of my paper, *ibid.*, p. 521, this occurs when

$$\frac{\partial K}{\partial i} \bigg/ -\frac{\partial L}{\partial i} < \frac{\partial M}{\partial Y} \bigg/ \frac{\partial L}{\partial Y},$$

where $K(i)$ is the capital inflow as a function of the interest rate (foreign interest rates being given), $\partial M/\partial Y$ is the marginal propensity to import, and $L(i, Y)$ is the demand for money as a function of the interest rate and national income (the price level being assumed constant).

the rate of exchange is constant, the balance of trade in real and in money terms worsens. Under flexible rates, domestic currency depreciates, but the domestic currency value of the trade balance remains unchanged when capital flows remain constant. Under the standard assumption of macroeconomic models that the domestic prices of each country's products rise by less than the rate of currency depreciation induced by an extension of economic activity, depreciation goes hand in hand with a deterioration of the terms of trade. Given constancy of the money value of the trade balance in terms of domestic currency, the *real* trade balance must have improved. This result would also come about if capital flows respond positively to interest-rate changes as long as their interest elasticity does not exceed a certain level.

These divergent movements of the real trade balance after fiscal expansion explain the reversal of the relative effectiveness of fiscal stimulation under the two exchange-rate systems. When full currency convertibility for capital movements is assured, the critical level for the interest elasticity of capital flows is likely to be exceeded for the major trading nations, so that we can probably be fairly certain that fiscal policy is normally a more powerful tool of employment policy under fixed than under flexible exchange rates.[9]

The increased power of monetary policy under flexible exchange rates is sometimes seen as a "beggar-my-neighbor" phenomenon since the induced changes of the trade balance obviously have an exactly opposite employment effect in the rest of the world. There is no basis for regarding this as an undesirable development, however. To speak of an "improvement" or a "deterioration" of a country's trade balance has unfortunate emotive connotations. Only the environment of the great depression could engender a mentality that sees something undesirable in the possibility of having command temporarily over more resources for domestic use. It is also frequently forgotten that a "worsening" of the *trade balance* was seen with such alarm during the depression years because, with full currency convertibility at pegged exchange rates, the resulting loss of foreign exchange reserves could force a country into monetary restriction at a time when its economy was already stagnating.

When a country experiences a rise in imports relative to exports as a result of expansionary monetary policies elsewhere, this does not pose the slightest threat of unwarranted monetary contraction in a regime of *flexible* exchange rates. The worsening of the trade balance finances itself; it can, in fact, only come about as a consequence of voluntary private capital inflows.

9. This is easily seen by considering the criterion given in n. 8.

Welfare Aspects of Stabilization Policies

On the basis of a comparison of the numbers of target variables and of policy parameters, it is often thought that, when fiscal policy is used for internal and monetary policy for external balance, there will always be a combination of both that achieves internal stability and balance-of-payments equilibrium simultaneously, even in a system of constant exchange rates. Apart from the fact that this conclusion disregards the problems possibly posed by "sellers' inflation," there are other reasons for doubt whether it is an acceptable guide for practical policy.[10] Only by accident would the resulting situation be more than a position of rest in a purely technical sense.

An infinite variety of combinations of current-account and capital-account imbalance are compatible with equilibrium in the over-all balance of autonomous payments. For allocative optimality, only the state of the *trade balance* in any given period matters. It may be perversely non-optimal even though there is technical "equilibrium" in aggregate external payments (in the sense that excess demand for foreign exchange is zero). To give an example, the United States might perhaps have achieved full employment together with balance-of payments equilibrium by a combination of fiscal expansion and monetary restriction in the late 1950's and early 1960's. Full employment would probably have entailed sizable trade deficits, but higher interest rates could have attracted enough foreign capital to finance the trade gap. It can hardly be disputed, however, that a situation in which the most highly developed economy incurs trade deficits and thus borrows resources from the rest of the world for an extended period is decidedly non-optimal.[11]

10. The question of whether fiscal policy is a sufficiently flexible instrument for employment stabilization (or whether it is possible to make it sufficiently flexible) will not be touched upon here. Serious doubts are obviously justified on that score also.

11. Opposition to this verdict would have to rest on one or more of a number of interesting theoretical propositions. For example, one might hold that factor-price equalization through trade operates to perfection, rendering international factor movements unnecessary, or one might interpret the "Leontief paradox" as having indeed shown that the United States is, after all, a country that is relatively poorly equipped with capital.

It is clearly not only the sign but also the *level* of trade balances that matter. The countries relatively best endowed with capital should not merely achieve positive, but even rather sizable export surpluses in the interest of optimal resource allocation from a cosmopolitan point of view. In the years 1952–62, the United States exported real resources amounting to 1.3 per cent of its gross national product (0.6 per cent when military aid shipments are excluded). This appears less impressive when it is compared to West Germany's record of 2.3 per

The opposite case of a country suffering from excessive demand combined with balance-of-payments surpluses is equally instructive. This was the situation in which West Germany found itself during the late 1950's and early 1960's. From a purely technical point of view, the appropriate policy mix to restrain the excessive demand associated with a process of imported inflation under constant exchange rates would have been a combination of restrictive fiscal policy and cheap money.

A regime of fixed exchange rates establishes a rather inflexible link not only between foreign and domestic interest rates, but also between prices at home and abroad. If fiscal policy is used to keep the average rate of increase of a country's domestic prices below the rate at which prices rise in the rest of the world, the balance of trade and services will progressively improve.[12] There is an obvious upper limit to this process: an economy cannot export more than its national product. Starvation and revolution, if nothing else, would effectively prevent even a remote approach to this limit. As more and more resources are being transferred to the rest of the world in the form of trade surpluses, less and less is available not only for domestic consumption, but also for domestic investment. A falling growth rate is the inevitable consequence and will presumably make it impossible already after a relatively short time to sustain the rising export surpluses required by the proposed policy mix of tightening budgetary policy and expanding credit. The efficiency of the world economy will in all probability not be well served by a development of this kind.

"International Liquidity" as a Policy Instrument

By comparison with the profuse discussion of institutional technicalities, surprisingly little attention has been paid to considerations of allocative efficiency in the debate over a possible expansion of "international liquidity."[13] There are obvious economic as well as political reasons why voluntary private capital movements may not always be forth-

---

cent (3 per cent when West Berlin is excluded) for the same period (however involuntary much of this resource transfer may have been on Germany's part).

There is a widespread "money illusion" that sees aid to developing countries only in purely financial transactions, irrespective of the real resources that may (or may not) be made available by a country to the rest of the world in any given period.

12. This global description abstracts from possible structural changes that may counteract the evolution of the macroeconomic aggregates. In the case of West Germany, structural factors even reinforced inflationary pressure from abroad.

13. Out of a voluminous literature, a number of the most important papers have been collected in Herbert G. Grubel, ed., *World Monetary Reform* (Stanford University Press and Oxford University Press, 1964).

coming readily enough to bridge temporary deficits in the balances of autonomous payments of less developed countries. Proposals for increasing international liquidity have not, however, had primarily the problems of these countries in mind. For the time being, the balance-of-payments difficulties of the United Kingdom and the United States continue to receive most of the attention in discussions of world monetary reform.

This is a somewhat incongruous state of affairs, for the world's leading financial centers ought to find it easier than most other countries to attract mobile private capital for financing temporary imbalances in their external accounts. It would seem that it must always be possible for the United States and the United Kingdom to combine internal and external balance by fiscal expansion and monetary contraction *if* this is to be possible for any country at all. Private sources of finance would, to be sure, be more expensive under normal circumstances than borrowing from the International Monetary Fund or from central banks on the basis of *ad hoc* agreements, but there is no valid reason why the rest of the world should lend to the most advanced countries at only fractions of the interest charges that confront public and private borrowers in the creditor countries themselves.

Apart from these considerations, there remain the efficiency aspects of international lending that have been dealt with in the preceding section. To the extent that easier borrowing makes it possible to avoid trade restrictions or unemployment in the wake of payments difficulties, it can have a most salutary effect. In this respect, it does not differ from exchange depreciation. But will an increase in international liquidity raise or lower the export surpluses, hence the real resource transfers of the leading industrial nations to the rest of the world? There are convincing reasons for believing that the proposed reforms would at the present moment enable the United States and the United Kingdom to get along with smaller export surpluses, in sharp contrast to the consequences that could be expected from depreciation. This would in all probability worsen the allocative efficiency of the world economy.

When all this is taken into account, most of the present schemes for world monetary reform appear in a rather peculiar light. One can hardly escape the conclusion that the root causes of the balance-of-payments problems that have been plaguing England and the United States, in particular, have to be sought not in any shortcoming of international monetary arrangements, but rather in grave internal defects of these economies themselves. Rigidity of exchange rates, as we well know, requires greater flexibility of prices if balance-of-payments difficulties and the possible need for monetary and fiscal restriction at times of economic stagnation, or a stiffening of exchange controls, are to be avoided. Competition has apparently been imperfect enough in the two reserve currency countries to reduce price flexibility far below the minimum degree necessary for a satisfactory operation of a system of constant exchange rates. "Incomes policy," royal orders for Liverpool's major export industry, and similar devices have proved to be insufficient substitutes.

Fixed *versus* Flexible Exchange Rates: A Question of "Optimum Currency Areas"?

Apart from decisions as to the choice of stabilization instruments under alternative monetary systems, the principle of "effective market classification" is also applicable to the basic choice between systems of fixed and flexible exchange rates. Of all possible policy instruments, the exchange rate normally has the strongest "comparative advantage" as a tool for equilibrating the balance of payments. It would follow that it should be left free to perform this function, liberating other policy instruments for tasks to which they are relatively better suited.

The strength of this argument seems to be materially weakened by the observation that exchange rates are not used for this purpose, with no appreciably disastrous consequences, within unified currency areas. Minor variations of interest rates work just as rapidly and smoothly in this case in keeping regional balances of payments in equilibrium. Why should this most satisfactory state of affairs not be extended to the international plane? This is the *pièce de résistance* of all arguments in favor of fixed exchange rates between national currencies.

The debate over "optimum currency areas," inaugurated a few years ago by Mundell and McKinnon,[14] is usually thought to be intimately related to the issue discussed in this section. The basic question posed in these papers is a very legitimate one: How large should unified currency areas ideally be? The wistfully romantic vision of a single world currency appears to be decidedly less than optimal when taken under closer scrutiny. It would obviously be an even greater deviation from optimality to go to the opposite extreme and let each household have its own currency. Many existing currency areas, usually an outgrowth of historical accident, seem to be too small rather than too large.

There is no inconsistency between this view and the belief that the

14. R. A. Mundell, "A Theory of Optimum Currency Areas," *American Economic Review*, 51 (1961): 657–65; R. I. McKinnon, "Optimum Currency Areas," *American Economic Review*, 53 (1963): 717–25.

pegging of exchange rates between currencies had better be abandoned. Whoever finds this puzzling has fallen victim to a case of mistaken identity. The pegging of exchange rates is not necessarily a closer approach toward currency unification. It may frequently be the exact opposite. Lack of space allows only a brief sketch of the most important aspects of the issue.

To begin with, the constancy of exchange rates is but one attribute of a unified currency area. At least equally important is perfect currency convertibility. It should have become obvious by now that the attempt to preserve a given currency parity is all too often possible only at the expense of more severe restraints on the freedom of international payments. How can it be ascertained that any possible benefits of exchange-rate stability for international commerce always outweigh the disintegrating effects of the trade and payments controls (together with discriminatory devices such as "interest equalization taxes," the tying of aid, etc.) required to maintain that stability? This has never been attempted and would in all probability be impossible, yet the prevailing opinion among most laymen and even some experts seems to be that it is a self-evident proposition.

In our times, currency areas generally coincide with national boundaries and with tariff boundaries. It is extremely difficult to estimate to what extent political unity, absence of restrictions on domestic trade, and a common currency separately contribute toward the greater intensity of interregional as compared to international commerce. I have the impression that the relative importance of currency unification is usually overrated. In any case, the attempt to remove national monetary sovereignty appears somewhat out of place as long as world trade and capital movements are impeded by so many other and presumably much weightier obstacles.

But nobody would deny that currency unification contributes positively, however little, to the intensity of commercial relations. When the same is claimed for the fixing of exchange rates between separate national currencies, and when trade and payments restrictions are applied to preserve an established peg, the official proponents of this system are, in effect, imposing restraints on commercial relations between nations with the intention of promoting the integration of the world economy.

The single-currency analogy can least of all be applied to the system founded at Bretton Woods. It explicitly allows for discontinuous parity changes under stress, an event that is unimaginable between the regions of a single-currency area. But even if governments were to announce that all currency parities are to remain eternally fixed and currencies fully convertible, there would be one difference whose importance is much too little appreciated. Within a currency area, it is not merely *spot* "exchange rates" that are constant over time (without limits of fluctuation, moreover). Since there is complete assurance that claims on debtors in other regions can always be repatriated at the same "exchange rate" of 1:1, no matter how long their maturities may be, all forward "rates of exchange" between regions are in effect fixed at the value 1:1 at all times. It is theoretically imaginable that all governments might assume a binding legal responsibility to guarantee rigidly constant forward rates between their own and all other currencies for any desired maturity, together with a guaranty of unlimited convertibility for any purpose whatsoever. If that happy event ever came about in the real world, the similarity to a unified currency area would indeed be virtually complete. The present state of affairs, or anything we can reasonably hope for in our grandchildren's lifetimes, does not have the remotest resemblance to it.

The equality of all spot and forward rates for an indefinite future, together with the assurance of uninterrupted, unmitigated convertibility, is responsible for the fact that capital moves so swiftly in response to minute changes of interest differentials between the regions of a common currency area. It is this circumstance that makes interest rates such a powerful tool in regional balance-of-payments adjustment. When it is absent and when, in particular, discontinuous alteration of currency parities is permitted, monetary policy becomes a less appropriate, and possibly a dangerously inappropriate instrument for keeping the balance of payments in equilibrium. If it is seriously intended to secure the benefits (together with the burdens) of a single-currency area, there is but one thing that ought to be done: the creation of a single currency.

"Hiccup Rigidity" of Exchange Rates

Acquaintance with the subtle technicalities of forward exchange markets, if nothing else, should convince anyone that discontinuous parity adjustments must be ruled out if a reasonable degree of currency convertibility for capital movements is to be assured. In the Bretton Woods system, such adjustments are, by contrast to the classical gold standard, recognized as a legitimate (though ultimate) tool of policy. The irreparable weakness of this system is that it is entirely impossible to develop a rational set of rules for the appropriate timing and extent of parity changes. The system would become the more unworkable the more precise and the more rational such rules are, for the greater would be the number of people who are enabled to foresee not only the direction, but also the approximate timing of exchange-rate adjustments. There is no chance that it will ever be possible to develop a consistent set of decision or assignment rules for a monetary system that allows for discontinuous jumps of exchange rates unless convertibility is abandoned for capital movements, at the very least. Railroads are capable of overcoming altitude differences of many thousand feet if the path of ascent or descent is reasonably smooth, but trains inevitably derail if one attempts to make them jump discontinuous steps, even though they be no higher than a few inches. Economies and monetary systems are not necessarily better equipped for taking such jumps in their stride.

Conclusions

If economic policy did not have to consider the constraints imposed by practical politics and public prejudices, a few simple guidelines for the assignment of policy tools would emerge.

1) The first and foremost "assignment problem" for macroeconomic policy in any country is whether or not it should have its own currency. The degree of factor mobility between regions is probably the single most important criterion for that decision.[15] A high degree of interregional labor mobility makes it easier to forego the use of monetary policy for employment stabilization within a member region of a common-currency area.

2) A result that is economically equivalent to currency unification would be achieved by the irrevocable pegging of spot and all forward exchange rates for the indefinite future, but this would seem to be an unnecessarily roundabout alternative to the introduction of a single currency and a centralized monetary authority.

3) When a government is unwilling to assume responsibility for the unconditional pegging of the exchange rates for *all* maturities, the pegging of a single one, such as the spot rate, appears not merely unnatural, but is bound to give rise to payments imbalances whenever economic policy deviates even moderately from the narrow path that would be appropriate for a region within a single-currency area. If this stringent requirement is not fulfilled at all times, the use of fiscal policy for internal stability, though technically feasible at least in the short run, will generally conflict with allocative optimality. It would appear that the only legitimate tasks of fiscal policy in an open economy and under any monetary system are the proper allocation of an economy's resources to production of private and collective goods and redistribution of income

15. See R. A. Mundell, "A Theory of Optimum Currency Areas."

and wealth in a socially acceptable manner. Apart from all other considerations, fiscal policy will probably always remain much too inflexible an instrument to be used successfully for the purpose of preserving price or employment stability.

4) The proper recommendation for avoiding market gluts and unemployment appears to be the classical one, price and wage flexibility (and not merely the latter). It is equally apparent that competition is much too imperfect and that wages and prices are consequently too inflexible in most countries to perform the function of employment stabilizers effectively. Insufficient appreciation of the essential role of price flexibility is probably as much responsible for this as the intrinsic difficulties of an active antitrust policy and other measures to strengthen competition.

5) The decision to establish a separate currency having been taken (however wise or unwise that decision may have been), economic disintegration, occasioned by misdirection of trade and capital flows and the possible need for exchange controls and trade restrictions, can only be avoided with certainty if a government resists the temptation to peg exchange rates. It can stand repetition that exchange rates need not therefore be unstable. The degree of stability of flexible rates will depend on the degree of flexibility of monetary policy. Official exchange-market interventions to support private speculation in the interest of avoiding unwarranted short-run oscillations need not be condemned outright, although politically independent central bankers who can be trusted not to use this device in a destabilizing manner—i.e., in a way that opposes a long-run trend—may be in short supply.[16] The greatly enhanced leverage of monetary policy on effective demand in a system of flexible rates makes it a natural and ideal instrument of anticyclical policy.

6) Of all possible monetary systems, the one agreed upon at Bretton Woods probably lends itself least to rational management. To adjust exchange rates by discontinuous steps, and only in the event of a "fundamental disequilibrium," implies that the abrupt changes—by themselves an obviously disintegrating device—must always be preceded by extended periods of maladjustment. There is an unfortunate habit by some to claim the virtues of truly constant exchange rates for this system, by others to claim the advantages of flexible rates for it (occasionally, both are claimed at the same time). Yet the distinguishing

16. More or less by historical accident, central banks usually intervene only in spot exchange markets. In the debate over "international liquidity," few of the participants seem to realize that this elusive variable could, if desired, be increased at any time even by single countries if their central banks chose to intervene in forward rather than spot exchange markets.

feature of the system is probably that it combines the worst disadvantages ever exhibited by both systems during periods of fundamental—and even not so very fundamental—disequilibria: trade is distorted by failure of relative prices on the world markets to adjust smoothly to changing economic conditions, capital flows are distorted, and must frequently be restricted by controls to make the system viable at all, for nobody can have confidence in the continuity of the prevailing exchange-rate structure. International interest differentials lose their role as signals for the appropriate direction of capital flows. Nothing can reveal the essential difference between this system and a common currency area more clearly. Those who have to make this system work must derive their determination to preserve it from the strength of their recurrent conviction that the latest balance-of-payments crisis is going to be the last one.

PORTFOLIO BALANCE AND INTERNATIONAL PAYMENTS ADJUSTMENT

Ronald I. McKinnon

Introduction

Our understanding of the mechanisms by which international payments adjustment may be achieved can be usefully classified into three historical stages. The first stage is usually termed the "elasticities" approach and it is associated with changes in relative prices of domestic and foreign goods. These changes could be brought about by either (1) an exchange-rate adjustment or (2) an inflation or deflation in the level of domestic prices with the exchange rate fixed—as in the case of Hume's famous gold specie flow mechanism. Within such a framework, one could be an elasticity pessimist or an elasticity optimist about the possibilities of affecting trade flows by changing the relative prices of goods that enter trade vis-à-vis those that do not. Unfortunately, econometricians have not been able to overcome their identification problems in order to refute either the pessimists or the optimists.

With the development of the Keynesian analytical framework and associated national income accounting techniques, it became clear that something more is involved in the adjustment problem. A deficit in the balance of trade is associated with an excess of domestic expenditures for (absorption of) commodities over the domestic production of commodities. In order to reduce a trade balance deficit, therefore, it is necessary to reduce domestic absorption relative to domestic production. This was the "absorption" approach to international payments adjustment and the second historical stage in our thinking. It was recognized that both the elasticity and absorption approaches simply emphasize different facets of the same problem. Indeed, the implementation of measures to reduce absorption at the time of a currency depreciation could easily turn an elasticity pessimist into an elasticity optimist.

This paper was written with the generous support of the Ford Foundation, which, however, is not responsible for its contents. It has benefited from the comments of many people associated with the Research Center in Economic Growth at Stanford University—particularly Edward S. Shaw—and from Wallace Oates of Princeton University.

However, both approaches remained disturbingly oblivious to the role of capital movements in the adjustment process and concentrated solely on the adjustment of trade flows in goods and services. Nevertheless, the financial counterpart of a surplus on current account in the balance of payments is the acquisition of financial claims on foreigners.[1] The acquisition of such claims can take place under fixed or floating exchange rates. If there is no offsetting surplus in the government budget, these claims represent a net increase in the stock of financial assets in the portfolios of private individuals which will, in turn, influence their spending behavior. Moreover, if this current-account surplus is used to augment official exchange reserves (which it need not) in maintaining a fixed exchange rate, then the increase in the stock of financial claims takes the form of an increase in the domestic money supply. This is associated with an accounting "surplus" appearing in the balance of payments as a whole.

Even if there is no deficit or surplus on current account, one kind of financial asset can be exchanged for another in the world's capital markets, leaving net asset positions unchanged. When this exchange takes the form of selling long-term bonds for more liquid assets such as money under a fixed exchange rate, again an accounting surplus will appear in the balance of payments with an apparent adjustment problem associated with it. The analytical model developed in this paper emphasizes that facet of the adjustment process associated with both kinds of change in asset positions and hence may be called the "portfolio-balance" approach to international payments adjustment.

In implementing this portfolio-balance approach, there is an interesting parallel that one can draw between (1) government budget deficits and open market operations and (2) trade balance surpluses and external payments flows confined to the capital account. Both affect asset positions in the private sector of the domestic economy in similar ways. For example, a trade balance surplus will cause a net increase in the stock of financial assets in the private sector just as a deficit (on commodity account) in the government budget will. Both increases in net assets may (but need not) take the form of augmenting the domestic money supply held by the private sector. They are both "outside" methods of creating money, to use the terminology of J. G. Gurley and E. S. Shaw.[2]

1. Excluding the possibility that such surpluses are financed by transfer payments abroad.
2. J. G. Gurley and E. S. Shaw, *Money in a Theory of Finance* (Washington D.C.: Brookings Institution, 1960).

Correspondingly, open market operations by the government such as buying bonds in exchange for money have an economic impact which is similar to the purchase of bonds by foreigners for cash from domestic nationals when the exchange rate is fixed. The domestic foreign exchange authorities must convert the proffered foreign money into domestic cash on demand. Both these last two are "inside" methods of creating money, to use again the Gurley-Shaw terminology,[3] since one financial asset is merely exchanged for another, leaving the net financial asset position of the domestic private sector unchanged. Frequent references to inside and outside methods of changing the money supply will be made in the analysis to follow.

The willingness of domestic nationals to trade bonds for money through external transactions, without at the same time being willing to change their net asset position, is essentially the problem of liquidity preference which so disturbs Charles Kindleberger.[4] In the imperfect international capital markets that currently exist, Kindleberger notes, this kind of liquidity preference can lead to apparent balance-of-payments disequilibria which are in some sense spurious. Individuals in the country (western Europe) selling long-term bonds in exchange for more liquid assets (including money) are not interested in reducing their net outside financial-asset position so that there is no tendency to develop a current-account deficit which is the "real" counterpart of the financial capital inflow. Nevertheless, exchange reserves are accumulating, an accounting surplus appears in the balance of payments, and there is an apparent adjustment problem which cannot be ignored.

Describing how adjustment mechanisms operate is, after all, nothing but an exercise in macroeconomic theory for which the idea of portfolio balance is of paramount importance. Therefore, one has to choose an appropriate macroeconomic model or simplifying set of assumptions. Before making explicit assumptions regarding intercountry relationships, what does standard "closed economy" economics have to offer us? The following is an attempt to classify well-known and possibly

3. It should be pointed out that this is the most convenient usage of the "inside-outside" terminology for my purposes but that it does not exactly correspond to the use made of it by Gurley and Shaw. Their inside money creation was only associated with the purchase of private bonds and not the purchase of government bonds held by the private sector. However, either would be an inside method of changing the money supply under my usage.

4. Charles P. Kindleberger, "Balance of Payments Deficits and the International Market for Liquidity," *Essays in International Finance*, no. 46 (Princeton: Princeton University, International Finance Section, 1965).

relevant macroeconomic assumptions about the nature of the economic environment.[5]

> 1) For questions of short-period stability, the Keynesian "fixed price" assumption is appropriate. Commodity prices do not act to clear markets within the interval under consideration, with the possible exception of rates of interest, and the economy is subject to "autonomous" shocks. Nevertheless, changes in the composition of asset portfolios and income levels can still affect expenditure decisions. Comparisons between positions of stationary-state equilibrium constitute the methodology employed.
>
> 2) For a longer time horizon which is not primarily concerned with the problem of growth, the price level becomes an "uninhibited variable" on which the desire to achieve portfolio balance (appropriately specified) has a significant impact. This kind of "neo-classical" environment is that used through much of Patinkin[6] and Gurley-Shaw.[7] It is still essentially static as in (1) in that microeconomic units only react to current prices (or imagine current prices to extend indefinitely into the future).
>
> 3) There is the more modern concept of growth equilibrium associated with a regularly progressive economy where capital is accumulating and relative prices as well as the price level itself may be continuously changing. "Equilibrium" is essentially a state in which ex ante expectations are continuously fulfilled. The time horizon here is longest of all. Portfolio balance in the holding of financial assets is very much associated with real capital accumulation.

The ways in which international adjustment mechanisms operate for each of these three economic environments can be significantly different. In order to capture all the essential aspects of the current debate on the need for continuously increasing international liquidity to permit automatic adjustment processes to function in a growing world economy, a model of growth equilibrium, (3) above, is necessary. Yet, the familiar static Keynesian environment, (1) above, is still of interest in itself and is a necessary "first step" in analyzing the more complex case of growth equilibrium. Only a simple stationary-state model in a Keynesian environment is developed in this paper.

Unfortunately, as is discussed in section I below, "received"

5. I am deeply indebted to Edward S. Shaw for suggesting the usefulness of this classification in dealing with questions of monetary theory. It is similar to that used by J. R. Hicks, *Capital and Growth* (London: Oxford University Press, 1965).

6. Don Patinkin, *Money, Interest and Prices*, 2d ed. (New York: Harper and Row, 1965).

7. Gurley and Shaw, *Money in a Theory of Finance*.

Keynesian theory contains certain logical defects associated with its failure to incorporate correctly portfolio-balance considerations. Since the achievement of portfolio balance is crucial in the adjustment of international payments flows, the basic Keynesian model of a closed economy is reconstructed in section I so that portfolio balance is made explicit. Stationary-state equilibria are explicitly used throughout in examining the response of the economy to autonomous changes in expenditure decisions or changes in monetary policy. It is shown that the ways in which wealth effects enter the demand functions for commodities, bonds, and money are essentially different from those usually assumed.[8] This has important implications for such standard Keynesian concepts as multiplier analysis and shifts in liquidity preference. Inside and outside methods of changing the money supply can then be correctly distinguished.

Section II "opens" the model by introducing foreign trade considerations under the initial simplifying assumption that there are only international commodity transactions and no flows of finance capital. The effects of inside and outside methods of changing the money supply (or equivalent shifts in liquidity preference) are then analyzed for their effects on the balance of payments, exchange-reserve positions, and the level of income. The results are compared to the other limiting case where finance capital is perfectly mobile internationally.[9] One can thus infer what happens when capital is only partially mobile. Most of the analysis is concerned with a fixed exchange-rate system, but the consequences of using a floating exchange rate are also examined.

Section III introduces fiscal policy by a government which is consciously willing to unbalance its own portfolio position through running deficits or surpluses. That is, tax rates and expenditure flows remain fixed even when aggregate income changes so as to alter tax revenues. Once private portfolio balance is considered, it is shown that there is a natural tendency to restore balance in the government's budget if the economy is closed. This tendency is exactly parallel to the tendency to have deficits or surpluses eliminated from the trade balance by changes in the portfolio position of an *open* economy not employing conscious

8. As, for example, those assumed by Don Patinkin in *Money, Interest and Prices*.

9. See Robert A. Mundell, "Capital Mobility and Stabilization Policy under Fixed and Flexible Exchange Rates," *Canadian Journal of Economics and Political Science*, vol. 29 (November, 1963); and R. I. McKinnon and W. E. Oates, "The Implications of International Economic Integration for Monetary, Fiscal and Exchange Rate Policy," *Princeton Studies in International Finance*, no. 16 (Princeton: Princeton University, International Finance Section, 1966).

fiscal policy. However, these natural tendencies are destroyed in an economy which is *both* open *and* employs conscious fiscal policy. That is, a government budgetary deficit and a trade balance deficit become consistent with private portfolio balance. The analysis has implications for multiplier theory, and the use of exchange-rate and tax-rate policy for achieving both internal and external balance.

In section IV, it is shown that monetary policy as conducted through open market operations is not an adequate substitute for either flexible fiscal policy or a flexible exchange rate in maintaining both internal and external balance in a stationary economic environment.

I. A Stationary Keynesian Model of a Closed Economy

The standard Keynesian model stresses the importance of income flows in determining expenditure decisions, and de-emphasizes the importance of balance-sheet considerations. Yet, the famous Hicksian *IS* and *LM* curves relating the equilibrium rate of interest to the equilibrium money income do require portfolio balance of a particular kind. Unfortunately, there are important logical difficulties with this Hicksian analysis which suggest the need to construct a more comprehensive model. The *LM* curve traces out those combinations of interest rates and income levels such that the private sector is just willing to hold the existing fixed stock

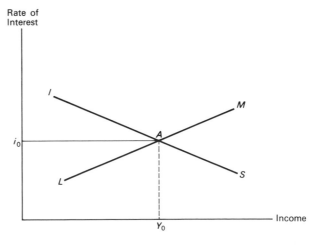

FIGURE 1

of money. Flow equilibrium in the commodity market requires that the *ex ante* desire to spend for investment or consumption be equal to the actual flow of production (real income); or, more familiarly and less accurately, the *ex ante* propensity to invest is equal to the *ex ante* propensity to save. The *IS* curve is the locus of points (interest rate and income combinations) which satisfy this condition of flow equilibrium. The intersection, point *A* in Figure 1, represents a position of both stock and flow equilibrium in money and commodity markets respectively over what is (presumably) a finite and significant time interval. An appeal is made to Walras' Law to assure us that point *A* is also associated with stock equilibrium in the bond market.

Suppose that net investment is positive in Figure 1 at point *A*, as is commonly the case in simple Keynesian models. Then the real capital stock will be increasing and possibly output itself will be increasing. However, the *LM* curve is commonly drawn under the assumption that the money supply is fixed. Can these increments in the capital stock and output be ignored as second-order effects in determining the equilibrium rate of interest? In a recent article, R. A. Mundell convincingly shows that they cannot be ignored.[10]

> ...It is a fallacy to suppose that because flows are infinitesimal in relation to stocks they are of a second order of magnitude with respect to variables incommensurate with the stocks, such as the rate of interest. The rates of change of the capital stock, financial assets, and money supply are dimensionally equivalent to the rate of interest and cannot be disregarded (p. 61).
> ...Positive investment implies a growing capital stock and (presumably) rising output. If the stock of money is constant and output is rising, monetary equilibrium requires that the price level be falling or that the interest rate be rising (p. 62).
> ...An asset-holder would therefore have to weight the importance of a rate of decrease in bond prices equally with the interest rate itself in making portfolio decisions involving choices between money and securities; he would similarly have to take into account the rate of inflation in making portfolio decisions involving the choice between commodities or equities on the one hand, and bonds and money on the other.
> It follows that rates of change in commodity and security prices have a first-order impact on the general equilibrium of the system (p. 62).

10. Robert A. Mundell, "A Fallacy in the Interpretation of Macroeconomic Equilibrium," *Journal of Political Economy*, 73 (February, 1965): 61–67.

Mundell proceeds to correct this logical difficulty by explicitly introducing the rate of growth into the Hicksian analysis since it has the
same dimensions as the rate of interest. For example, the capital stock
and output grow at a constant rate (due to positive net investment) and
if the price level fell at the same proportional rate, monetary equilibrium
could be preserved. The real rate of interest would be above the money
rate of interest by an amount equal to the rate of income growth (the
rate of decline in the price level). Other methods suggested by Mundell
to get out of the logical difficulty are to consider a situation where bond
prices fall continuously, or one where the money supply is in steady-
state expansion at the rate of income growth. (A steady fall in bond
prices is, in general, not consistent with full equilibrium in both money
and bond markets.)

However, all of Mundell's interesting solutions to the purely logical
difficulty in the Hicksian analysis carry the danger of throwing the
Keynesian baby out with the bathwater. That is, attention is shifted
away from questions of short-period income stability and full employment (Model 1 above) to the whole question of growth equilibrium
(Model 3 above). An essential ingredient in Keynesian short-period
analysis—relatively fixed money prices of commodities and labor services—is sacrificed to the more flexible price model of growth equilibrium. Furthermore, once one does move fully to a model of growth
equilibrium, the link between net saving, new money creation, capital
accumulation, and income growth has to be more fully specified. That is,
production technology, the use of inside or outside money-creating
techniques, and asset choices among savers all combine to determine
the equilibrium rate of income growth. It cannot be independently
specified. One cannot any longer accept the *static* Hicksian *IS* and *LM*
curves as given since the level of "equilibrium" income is continuously
changing through time and the idea of equilibrium associated with a
system at rest is no longer relevant. Past investment decisions and future
expectations now determine the equilibrium level of income at any
point in time.

Fortunately, it is possible to remove the logical difficulty so neatly
posed by Mundell and, at the same time, to retain the analytical simplicity of a static Keynesian framework. To use logically consistent
Keynesian equilibrium analysis, one must explicitly use stationary-state
equilibria. That is, at the equilibrium level of income and at the equilibrium rate of interest, with balanced portfolios, it shall be assumed that
there is no *net* investment. The rate of growth is zero in equilibrium, as
is the equilibrium average propensity to save. This is obviously a very

strong assumption and is unlikely to be empirically valid. Yet, it permits us to retain all the key Keynesian concepts such as a positive *marginal* propensity to save, a subset of spending decisions (for commodities) which are "autonomously" determined, rigid commodity prices, and to consider portfolio balance (and hence monetary policy) in a logically unambiguous way within a static framework—something that the old Hicksian framework did not permit. The assumption of stationary expectations can then be reasonably maintained.

Under stationary-state equilibria, there is an apparent conflict between the assumption of a positive marginal propensity to save out of *current* income and the requirement that total net saving is zero *in equilibrium.* Doesn't a rise in the equilibrium level of income, with a positive marginal propensity to save, imply that the equilibrium flow of total saving must increase? Mundell assumed this in introducing his growth schedule into the Hicksian *IS–LM* diagram. His schedule assumes that the rate of saving (and hence the rate of growth) rises with the level of income in or out of equilibrium as one moves to the right along the *IS* schedule.[11]

Fortunately, the dilemma can be easily resolved if one recognizes that "saving" out of current income represents the desire to accumulate real and financial assets. Once the accumulation of these assets reaches a certain desired level vis-à-vis current income and the rate of interest, "saving" out of current income can be assumed to cease. For example, if income in the private sector were to increase once and for all while private asset-holdings remained unchanged, the marginal propensity to save would (initially) be positive as individuals abstained from current consumption to build up their asset-holdings.[12] Saving out of income would then cease as asset-holdings rose vis-à-vis the level of income and equilibrium portfolio balance was achieved. At the new equilibrium income, asset-holding, and interest rate, it is logically possible to assume the absence of net saving. Indeed, static equilibrium in asset-holdings implies the absence of net saving.

Wealth Effects and Equilibrium Conditions

It is necessary to describe the commodities market with both a flow and a stock equation. Consider the flow condition first. It is convenient

11. *Ibid.,* p. 63.
12. This model of stationary Keynesian equilibria was used by McKinnon and Oates in "The Implications of International Economic Integration." However, its full economic implications were not discussed there, particularly its relationship to traditional analysis, the distinction between stock and flow equilibrium in the commodity market, and the way in which wealth effects enter demand functions.

analytically to drop the Keynesian distinction between investment and consumption functions and deal only with an *ex ante* expenditure function for both the household and business sectors. Presumably, consumers can "invest" in durable household goods like business firms invest in working capital. Important components of spending decisions of both firms and households are endogenously determined by the level of income, financial asset-holding, real asset-holding, and the rate of interest. Other components of spending in both sectors can be legitimately considered "exogenous" or "autonomous" with respect to the time horizon being used. The misused concept of exogenously determined net investment in Keynesian economics is neither necessary nor relevant here since net investment is always zero in stationary-state equilibrium.

Let $E(Y, M, B, K, i; \alpha)$ be the *ex ante* expenditure function *per unit of time* for commodities for consumption or for inventory accumulation where Y is actual income (net output flow) per unit of time, M is the stock of money, B is the net stock of *outside* interest-bearing securities *in addition to K*, K is the stock of real assets (consumer goods owned by households, business inventories, goods in process, capital equipment, etc.), i is the rate of interest on B.

People hold stationary expectations regarding Y and i. Since $0 < \partial E/\partial Y < 1$, the Keynesian propensity to save (i.e., not to spend for commodities) is positive. $\partial E/\partial i < 0$ is also assumed.

Money is defined sufficiently narrowly so that the deposit rate is zero and its magnitude is confined to the direct monetary liabilities of the central bank. This would correspond to the conventional definition only if commercial bank deposits had a 100 per cent reserve requirement.

Note that the real capital stock K can be more or less liquid, depending on the state of financial development in the economy. Securities of varying degrees of liquidity can be issued as ownership claims on K without changing the magnitude of K itself. The return on the most liquid of these ownership claims which bear interest would be a rate of interest equal to i. However, as is appropriate for short-period analysis, we shall assume that the financial structure of the economy does not change significantly so that the liquidity of K remains constant throughout the analysis. All internally held private debt—consumption loans, etc.—are assumed to cancel out in private portfolios with no net effect on the expenditure function.

However, the net interest-bearing debt of the government to the private sector definitely does enter the expenditure function as denoted by the argument B. So as to avoid having to worry about changes in the capital value of B associated with interest-rate changes, I shall assume that B is composed of short-term liquid securities. B can be positive or negative. If in the past the government had created money wholly by "inside" techniques, then $B = -M$. In this case, B consists entirely of securities issued by the private sector which are now held by the government. However, if the government had run deficits in the national budget in the past which cumulated to be greater than the existing money supply M, then $B > 0$. Of course any combination of these extreme possibilities may exist. The total net stock of *outside* financial assets (i.e., not including K) is always $B + M$.

What can one say about the effects of the wealth arguments M, B, and K on the aggregate desired flow expenditure for commodities? Notice that within E, as defined here, the "wealth effect" on total expenditures is broken down into three separate arguments: M, B, and K—in contrast to most of the recent work done on consumption functions. One common approach is to work with consumption functions rather than aggregate expenditure functions and to aggregate all wealth effects into a single argument. I shall argue that this approach is useless if it is to be used as a basis for macroeconomic theorizing on the determinants of the aggregate flow demand for commodities and, ultimately, the equilibrium level of income. The fundamental reason is that the partial derivatives with respect to the three wealth variables, i.e., $\partial E/\partial M$, $\partial E/\partial B$, and $\partial E/\partial K$, are not only of different quantitative size but have different signs. That is,

$$\frac{\partial E}{\partial M} > 0, \quad \frac{\partial E}{\partial B} > 0, \quad \text{and} \quad \frac{\partial E}{\partial K} < 0.$$

The above inequalities indicate that an increase in the "outside" stock of either or both financial assets M and B, with Y, K, and i held constant, will *increase* the *ex ante* demand for commodities; whereas an increase in the stock of physical commodities K with Y, B, M, and i held constant, will *reduce* the *ex ante* demand for commodities. An increase in the stock of outside financial assets $B + M$ in the portfolios of the private sector can be viewed as increasing the demand for physical commodities in two ways: (1) There is a direct balance-sheet effect since the stock of physical commodities is now low relative to the stock of financial claims and individuals are induced to alter their balance-sheet positions by purchasing physical commodities. (2) There is a more conventional real wealth effect where individuals increase their current consumption expenditures to make their wealth holdings commensurate with their income levels. Fortunately, it is not necessary to disentangle the two effects either empirically or conceptually in the analysis to follow. Both are contained in the partial derivatives $\partial E/\partial M$ and $\partial E/\partial B$.

What about increases in the stock of outside physical commodities K, such as increases in business or consumer inventories? There are again two effects. Balance-sheet considerations will most certainly lead to an increased demand for financial assets with a correspondingly reduced excess demand for commodities. However, what about the more conventional real wealth effect? Will there not be increased consumption demand for goods because people are wealthier? Here it is necessary to distinguish what people wish to consume from what they want to buy. They may wish to increase their consumption of commodities but it will come from their excess commodity stocks and *not* from new purchases. The real wealth effect associated with K does not induce new spending for commodities. Therefore, because of the balance-sheet effect, there will be a net decline in the demand for commodities given an "outside" increase in K. Hence, $\partial E/\partial K < 0$ in contrast to $\partial E/\partial M > 0$ and $\partial E/\partial B > 0$. *Any expenditure function which aggregates K, M, and B into a single wealth variable loses operational contact with the essential elements of the macro-adjustment process.*

Consider the following set of equilibrium conditions yielding portfolio balance in the private sector of a simple Keynesian economy with rigid commodity prices.

$$E(Y, M, B, K, i; \alpha) - Y = 0 \qquad \text{Commodity market flow condition}$$
(1.1)

$$L(Y, i; \beta) - M = 0 \qquad \text{Money market stock condition}$$
(1.2)

$$R(Y, i; \omega) - B = 0 \qquad \text{Bond market stock condition} \qquad (1.3)$$

$$C(Y, i; \delta) - K = 0 \qquad \text{Commodity market stock condition}$$
(1.4)

The *ex ante* demand functions L, R, and C for holding stocks have no time dimension—unlike E. That is, L, R, and C simply represent target stocks and contain no information regarding the actual speed of adjustment over any discrete time interval. Thus, if Y and i were to be continuously maintained through time, individuals in the private sector would eventually attain the balance-sheet positions described by L, R, and C. In contrast, E is the instantaneous desired rate of expenditures at any point in time and Y is the instantaneous rate of production. Therefore, the commodity market has both a stock and a flow dimension as described by equations (1.1) and (1.4). In equilibrium, the desired rate of expenditures per unit of time must equal new production; *and* desired inventories of commodities in both the household and business sectors must equal actual inventories. In our stationary-state equilibrium with no new net investment, (1.1) and (1.4) *together* imply that desired consumption demand equals desired expenditures equals new production.

Another advantage of the stationary-state analysis, with no continuous creation of new money or outside interest-bearing securities, is that only one equation is required to describe equilibrium in the holding of money and one equation for the holding of outside bonds. New money and outside securities are not being continuously created or consumed, and for purposes of equilibrium analysis, only stock and not flow conditions are required. Baumol provides justification for taking this position.[13] Therefore, we are left with four equations describing the economy: three stock conditions and one flow condition. There are three endogenous variables: Y, i, and K, whose equilibrium values are determined by the stock equations (1.2), (1.3), and (1.4) alone.

Notice how wealth effects have entered the demand functions in the above set of equations. The flow of expenditures per unit of time at any point in time depends on the stocks of money, bonds, and goods held at that same point in time, with each stock having a different effect. But what about the demand functions to hold *stocks* as denoted by L, R, and C respectively? Here, existing stocks of tangible assets (money, bonds, and commodities) do not enter at all, either individually or collectively, as arguments in the stock-demand functions. More precisely, historically determined stocks existing at any point in time are assumed to have only second-order effects on ultimate desired target portfolio positions of the private sector. *The desired level of each stock will depend only on income flow and the rate of interest.* In this stationary-state model, individuals have stationary expectations regarding future income levels and interest rates. That is, they imagine current income and interest rates represent the most probable level of future income and future interest rates. *Since to the individual actual stocks of money, bonds, and commodities existing at any given point in time are not immutable and may be rearranged, these stocks will not enter as arguments in the stock-demand functions L, R, and C respectively.*

13. William J. Baumol, "Stocks, Flows and Monetary Theory," *Quarterly Journal of Economics*, 76 (February, 1962): 46–56.

Consider the same point in a somewhat different way. Under the static assumptions, Y and i together give a measure of permanent income and a discount rate; and hence provide a measure of total real wealth (including human wealth) into the foreseeable future. Thus wealth in this extremely generalized form does enter the stock-demand functions through Y and i. Therefore, existing tangible assets M, B, and K should be dropped from L, R, and C because Y and i already contain them.[14] Any separate effects M, B, and K might have may be considered of a second order of magnitude.

[Most traditional analysis of macroeconomic equilibrum has not distinguished the commodity-flow condition (1.1) from the commodity-stock condition (1.4). This has led to a great deal of confusion regarding the influence of "wealth" effects. For example, Don Patinkin uses a pure Walrasian "stock" model and assumes that *aggregate* tangible wealth enters as a separate argument in the demand for money, the demand for bonds, and the demand for commodities—contrary to what we have just seen.[15] On the other hand, there have been many statistical attempts to measure the demand for commodities considered as a flow in the form of consumption functions. For the household sector, "consumption" has been (inaccurately) defined as expenditures for consumer goods by households per unit of time. Wealth does affect expenditure flows and, again, is usually entered as a single aggregative argument in such functions. But for short-period equilibrium analysis for which the Keynesian idea of a consumption function was designed, we have just seen that one cannot aggregate wealth in this way because each component of real wealth has a qualitatively different effect on the flow of household expenditures. It is vital to distinguish expenditure functions from consumption functions, as the former is the relevant concept for a macroeconomic model. Only when one breaks the commodity market into two equations and comes up with a consistent model of portfolio balance—even one confined to stationary-state equilibria—does the nature of the wealth effect become clear. It affects the stock and flow conditions very differently.]

Being able to drop the wealth arguments M, B, and K from L, R, and C leads to very great analytical simplifications in examining solutions to the above equations. *The equilibrium level of income and the equilibrium rate of interest are now completely determined by equations (1.2) and (1.3) alone.* The equilibrium value of the remaining endogenous variable K may then be obtained immediately from (1.4). Moreover,

14. Edward S. Shaw suggested that the argument be formulated in this manner.
15. Don Patinkin, *Money, Interest and Prices.*

once the three stock equations (1.2), (1.3), and (1.4) are satisfied, one can be confident that the flow equation (1.1) will also be satisfied and the economy will be in a position of stable equilibrium. That is, if holdings of money, bonds, and commodities are fully adjusted to the current level of income and rate of interest, then (under the stationary-state assumption) the desired flow of expenditures for commodities will equal current consumption, which in turn equals current income. To be consistent with the achieved portfolio balance in asset-holding, the private sector's planned rate of expenditures must equal current income flow. [However, one should note that this relationship is not reversible. That is, if the flow equation (1.1) is satisfied, as well as two of the stock equations—say (1.2) and (1.3)—this is not sufficient to imply that the remaining stock equation (1.4) is satisfied or that the economy is in a position of stable equilibrium.]

The Multiplier in a Model of Portfolio Balance

The simplified equilibrium conditions (1.1), (1.2), (1.3), and (1.4) can be used to derive the "multiplier" implications of shifts in any of the demand functions E, L, R, or C as denoted by the parameters α, β, ω, and δ. Generally, these parameter shifts cannot be considered independently of each other, since, for example, a rise in the demand for money or bonds will be associated with a fall in the commodity-expenditure function E and/or the demand for commodities as a stock, C. The standard textbook multiplier analysis is associated with autonomous shifts in the parameter α in the commodity flow expenditure equation. However, such a shift in α has a counterpart shift in β or ω—the desire to hold money or bonds—i.e., $\partial\beta/\partial\alpha < 0$ and/or $\partial\omega/\partial\alpha < 0$. Since we have just shown that Y and i are wholly determined by equations (1.2) and (1.3), then it is enough—indeed it is necessary—to know the shift in β or ω. *It makes a great deal of difference to the final equilibrium position of the economy whether the increased demand for commodities is accompanied by a reduced demand to hold bonds (or, equivalently, an increased desire to issue them) or a reduced demand to hold money.* Generally, one would expect both the demand for money and the demand for bonds to be reduced. However, it will prove convenient analytically to examine each case in isolation.

Suppose an exogenous *decline* in the flow demand for commodities is "financed" by an increase in desired cash-balance holding with no increase in desired bond-holdings. Then, $\partial\beta/\partial\alpha < 0$ and $\partial\omega/\partial\alpha = 0$ with $d\alpha < 0$. One can compute the multiplier impact on Y and i by simply taking total derivatives of (1.2) and (1.3), given an assumed

autonomous shift upwards in β (related to the downward shift in α).
That is,

$$\frac{\partial L}{\partial Y} dY + \frac{\partial L}{\partial i} di + \frac{\partial L}{\partial \beta} d\beta = 0 \tag{1.5}$$

$$\frac{\partial R}{\partial Y} dY + \frac{\partial R}{\partial i} di = 0. \tag{1.6}$$

Solving (1.5) and (1.6) for dY and di, we have

$$dY = \frac{-\dfrac{\partial L}{\partial \beta} \cdot \dfrac{\partial R}{\partial i} \cdot d\beta}{\dfrac{\partial L}{\partial Y} \cdot \dfrac{\partial R}{\partial i} - \dfrac{\partial L}{\partial i} \cdot \dfrac{\partial R}{\partial Y}} < 0 \tag{1.7}$$

$$di = \frac{\dfrac{\partial L}{\partial \beta} \cdot \dfrac{\partial R}{\partial Y} \cdot d\beta}{\dfrac{\partial L}{\partial Y} \cdot \dfrac{\partial R}{\partial i} - \dfrac{\partial L}{\partial i} \cdot \dfrac{\partial R}{\partial Y}} > 0. \tag{1.8}$$

Furthermore, we can plausibly infer the signs of the partial derivatives
which are all positive except for $\partial L/\partial i < 0$. Hence, one can immediately
deduce that $dY < 0$ and $di > 0$ if $d\beta > 0$. That is, equilibrium income
falls and the equilibrium rate of interest rises if the shift is from commodities to money.

If the shift is from commodities to bonds with the demand for money
constant, one can also deduce the signs of dY and di. Suppose $\partial\omega/\partial\alpha < 0$
but $\partial\beta/\partial\alpha = 0$ and $d\alpha < 0$ and $d\omega > 0$. Taking the total derivatives of
(1.2) and (1.3) and solving for dY and di as before, we get

$$dY = \frac{\dfrac{\partial R}{\partial \omega} \cdot \dfrac{\partial L}{\partial i} \cdot d\omega}{\dfrac{\partial L}{\partial Y} \cdot \dfrac{\partial R}{\partial i} - \dfrac{\partial R}{\partial Y} \cdot \dfrac{\partial L}{\partial i}} < 0 \tag{1.9}$$

$$di = \frac{-\dfrac{\partial R}{\partial \omega} \cdot \dfrac{\partial L}{\partial Y} \cdot d\omega}{\dfrac{\partial L}{\partial Y} \cdot \dfrac{\partial R}{\partial i} - \dfrac{\partial R}{\partial Y} \cdot \dfrac{\partial L}{\partial i}} < 0. \tag{1.10}$$

Unlike the first example, an increase in desired outside bond-holdings
leads to a fall in the equilibrium rate of interest. Since in both examples
there was a downward shift in the commodity-expenditure function, the
equilibrium level of income is lowered in both cases.

Can one say for certain in which case the multiplier effect on income
would be the greatest? To make a "fair" comparison, one could specify

that the parameters β and ω in the functions L and R are additive and measure the same functional shifts, i.e., $\partial L/\partial \beta = \partial R/\partial \omega$ and that $d\beta = d\omega$. This is consistent with having the shift in the commodity-expenditure function the same in both cases. The downward shifts in income can be compared by using (1.7) to (1.9) to obtain

$$(dY)_\beta = \frac{-\dfrac{\partial R}{\partial i}}{\dfrac{\partial L}{\partial i}} (dY)_\omega \tag{1.11}$$

where the subscript β refers to a shift in the demand for money and the subscript ω refers to a shift in the demand for outside bond-holdings. $|(dY)_\beta|$ is numerically greater than $|(dY)_\omega|$ if $\partial R/\partial i > -(\partial L/\partial i)$. That is, the multiplier effect of a shift in the demand for money will be greater than the multiplier effect of a shift for bonds if the sensitivity of outside bond-holdings to interest-rate changes is greater than the interest sensitivity of money-holdings. An explanation of this condition is that when the demand for money shifts upwards and expenditures for commodities fall, individuals will also wish to divest themselves of their outside bond-holdings as income falls. Since the actual stock of *outside* bond-holdings is fixed, the rate of interest must rise in order to induce people to hold more bonds. But this rise in the rate of interest also induces individuals to hold less money, as does the fall in income, both of which tend to equilibrate desired and actual cash-balance holdings. If a given interest-rate rise causes individuals to increase their desire for bonds more than they wish to divest money holdings, i.e., $\partial R/\partial i > -(\partial L/\partial i)$, the interest-rate change will have a net additional effect on the commodity market by causing a decline in the demand for commodities. This will make the downward multiplier impact greater than would otherwise be the case, i.e., $|(dY)_\beta| > |(dY)_\omega|$.

Perhaps one way of seeing this intuitively is to note that if $\partial L/\partial i = 0$, then $|(dY)_\omega| = 0$ from (1.9); and correspondingly, if $\partial R/\partial i = 0$, $|(dY)_\beta| = 0$ from (1.7). If desired money-holdings are very interest inelastic, then the multiplier impact of a shift in the desire to hold bonds as denoted by β will be negligible. Correspondingly, if *outside* bond-holdings are very interest inelastic, the multiplier impact associated with a shift in the demand for money will be negligible. If both $\partial L/\partial i = 0$ and $\partial R/\partial i = 0$, one can only have a positive multiplier if there is a simultaneous shift in *both* the demand for bonds and the demand for money in association with a shift in the commodity-expenditure function.

The typical "Keynesian" multiplier implicitly assumes $\partial R/\partial i = -(\partial L/\partial i)$, so one could ignore whether there was a shift to bonds or a shift to money in association with a change in the commodity-expenditure function. However, if a rise in the interest rate simply encouraged people to shift from money to outside bond-holdings, the interest rate would have no *direct* effect on the demand for commodities. But if $\partial R/\partial i > -(\partial L/\partial i)$, a rise in the rate of interest is consistent with a fall in the flow demand for commodities (and also in the target stock-holdings of commodities). If one accepts $\partial R/\partial i > -(\partial L/\partial i)$ as an "empirical" judgment because of its implications for the commodity-expenditure function, then one may conclude that the multiplier associated with a shift in the demand for bonds is smaller.

A simple diagrammatic exposition of some of the above ideas can be obtained by noting again that (1.2) and (1.3) by themselves determine the equilibrium level of income and the equilibrium rate of interest. The excess demand functions for money and bonds each depend on Y and i alone, as depicted by MM and BB in Figure 2. MM is positively sloped

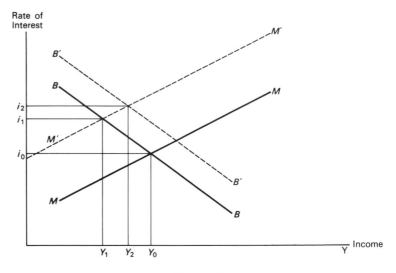

FIGURE 2

since $\partial L/\partial Y > 0$ and $\partial L/\partial i < 0$ so that the interest rate must rise if income rises to preserve equilibrium in the money market. BB is negatively sloped since $\partial R/\partial Y > 0$ and $\partial R/\partial i > 0$, so that the interest rate must fall as income rises in order to preserve equilibrium in the desired stock of outside bond-holdings. Notice that there is no simple way of depicting equilibrium in the commodity market on the same two-dimensional diagram (as the traditional Hicksian *IS* curve attempts to do). In the first place, there are two equations that describe equilibrium in the commodity market; and in the second place, both these commodity-equilibrium equations involve a third endogenous variable *K*—the stock of commodities in existence at any point in time. Therefore, it is not a matter of indifference as to whether one portrays the money and bond markets, or the money and commodity markets, or the bond and commodity markets. Only the money and bond markets can be portrayed in the standard diagram with *Y* and *i* on the two axes. Fortunately, they are enough to illustrate the true equilibrium rate of interest and level of income under stationary-state conditions.

Monetary Policy

Multiplier repercussions associated with increases in β (the demand for money) and a corresponding reduction in the demand for commodities are indicated by the shift from *MM* to *M'M'* so that equilibrium income changes from Y_0 to Y_1. The same shift from *MM* to *M'M'* could portray a reduction in the stock of money *by outside techniques*. Income falls and the interest rate rises in exactly the same fashion. In contrast, a reduction in the stock of money brought about by *inside* techniques— say, the central bank sells bonds for money—necessarily causes a shift in the bond-equilibrium curve to the right as well as a shift in the *MM* curve. This is illustrated in Figure 2 by a shift from *BB* to *B'B'* in conjunction with the shift from *MM* to *M'M'*, yielding equilibrium at (Y_2, i_2). Suppose that the reduction in the stock of money was the same in both cases; then one can say the effect of changing the money stock by outside techniques is more powerful on income since $Y_1 < Y_2$. However, the interest rate rises further when the supply of money is reduced by inside techniques, i.e., $i_2 > i_1$.

In order for a reduction in the supply of money by inside techniques to actually reduce the equilibrium level of income, it is necessary for the *MM* curve to shift farther than the *BB* curve shifts. From our past discussion, one can easily see this is again equivalent to the condition that $\partial R/\partial i > -(\partial L/\partial i)$, which in turn implies that $\partial E/\partial i < 0$. That is, the interest sensitivity of the demand for outside bond-holdings must be greater than the interest sensitivity of the demand for money. If $\partial R/\partial i$ is not much greater than $-(\partial L/\partial i)$, the creation of *inside* money (causing *MM* and *BB* to shift as shown in Figure 2) will have very little depressing effect on the demand for commodities even though the interest rate might rise quite steeply.[16] The increase in the rate of interest simply makes individuals content to hold the increased supply of bonds and the reduced supply of money without any significant spillover to the commodity market. In this (unusual) circumstance, monetary policy carried out by inside techniques will be relatively impotent. *In any case, it has been shown that changes in the stock of money by outside techniques will have a stronger—possibly much stronger—impact on the equilibrium level of income in a stationary "Keynesian" environment.*

II. Adjustment in an Open Economy, Monetary Policy, and Exchange Reserves

The "foreign" sector has two important dimensions. In the commodity market, goods are both sold and purchased abroad. In the financial markets, there can be capital transfers where domestic nationals buy or sell bonds to foreigners and there can be outright transfers of money if there is an international currency such as gold. If gold is a medium of exchange both domestically and internationally, then government authorities need not hold exchange reserves in order to preserve a fixed exchange-rate system. If a domestic currency other than gold circulates, then to preserve a fixed exchange rate and free external convertibility, the governments must hold foreign exchange reserves which they sell and buy freely in the market upon private demand. The economic implications of either of these last two systems are the same—both being fixed exchange-rate systems. I shall assume that the government formally holds exchange reserves to support the international value of a purely domestic currency in order to make the problem of reserve holding explicit.

There are two simplifying limiting assumptions that one can make about the nature of the capital market. Either financial capital is per-

16. To demonstrate this point more rigorously, note that the reduction of the money supply by inside techniques implies $dM = -dB$ where $dB > 0$. From (1.2) and (1.3) we have

$$\frac{\partial L}{\partial Y} dY + \frac{\partial L}{\partial i} di = dM \quad \text{and} \quad \frac{\partial R}{\partial Y} dY + \frac{\partial R}{\partial i} di = dB,$$

so that

$$dY = \frac{dM \frac{\partial R}{\partial i} - dB \frac{\partial L}{\partial i}}{Q} = \frac{dM \left(\frac{\partial R}{\partial i} + \frac{\partial L}{\partial i} \right)}{Q}$$

where

$$Q = \frac{\partial L}{\partial Y} \cdot \frac{\partial R}{\partial i} - \frac{\partial L}{\partial i} \cdot \frac{\partial R}{\partial Y} > 0.$$

fectly mobile so that the interest rate is identical to that prevailing abroad (and hence is parametrically fixed if the country in question is small), or one can adopt the other extreme and suggest that there is no international mobility of capital and all deficiencies in the balance of trade are settled from official foreign exchange reserves. Lack of any external capital mobility is an extreme assumption but it dovetails with the model of a closed economy laid out in section I and will be used here. Since foreign bonds cannot be held under this assumption, the need to introduce another bond market and another interest rate is avoided. Another reason for exploring this particular assumption is that the implications of perfect capital mobility have already been explored in some detail.[17] The conclusions of these earlier works will then be compared to the case where capital is internationally immobile. Throughout the analysis, it will be assumed that the economy in question is small and external repercussions may be ignored.

How does the simple model (1.1), (1.2), (1.3), and (1.4) need to be altered to take foreign commodity trade into account? Notice that the expenditure function E now necessarily includes expenditures for both domestically produced and foreign produced goods. We shall maintain the Keynesian nature of the model by assuming the price level is fixed internally with slack in the economy in the form of underemployed resources. Furthermore, with given external commodity prices, the flow of exports X will be determined by the pegged exchange rate and "autonomous" shocks denoted by k and θ respectively. The flow of imports is determined by the pegged exchange rate and by all the determinants of the level of domestic expenditures. That is, equilibrium in the commodity market can now be written:

$$E(Y, i, M, B, K; \alpha) + X(k, \theta) - I(Y, i, M, B, K; \eta, k) - Y$$
$$= 0 \qquad \text{Commodity Flow} \qquad (2.1)$$

where $I(Y, i, M, B, K; \eta, k)$ is the expenditure function for imports.

However, we now have an additional condition of *flow* equilibrium in the commodity market that must be satisfied in our stationary-state model. Exports must equal imports, otherwise the domestic money supply will be rising or declining. That is, the foreign exchange authorities must provide domestic money in exchange for foreign money to maintain a fixed exchange rate and free convertibility in the presence of imbalance in external trade. A rising or declining money supply is

17. See McKinnon and Oates, "The Implications of International Economic Integration"; and Mundell, "Capital Mobility and Stabilization Policy."

inconsistent with portfolio balance in our stationary-state model; therefore

$$X(k, \theta) - I(Y, i, M, B, K; \eta, k) = 0 \qquad \text{Balance of trade} \quad (2.2)$$

is a condition of equilibrium. (The export function X could also be assumed inversely dependent on the level of domestic absorption expenditures and hence dependent on Y, i, M, B, K if one wished, without changing any essential results.)

The conditions of stock equilibrium must be satisfied in this "open" economy as before.

$$L(Y, i; \beta) - M = 0 \qquad \text{Money Stock} \qquad (2.3)$$

$$R(Y, i; \omega) - B = 0 \qquad \text{Stock of Bonds} \qquad (2.4)$$

$$C(Y, i; \delta) - K = 0 \qquad \text{Commodity Stock} \qquad (2.5)$$

Equations (2.1), (2.2), (2.3), (2.4), and (2.5) now describe a complete economic system. There are five equations but now *four* endogenous variables. Unlike the closed economy model of section I, the money supply M is endogenous (as well as Y, i, and K) in the absence of conscious domestic monetary policy since it can now be influenced by external imbalance. Any trade balance surplus will pump money into the economy, causing portfolio imbalance among domestic nationals who will increase their expenditures for commodities including imports and eventually eradicate the trade balance surplus.

As a simplifying assumption, suppose that imports are always a constant fraction of domestic expenditures in the presence of a fixed exchange rate unless contrary specifications are made.[18] That is, replace (2.2) with

$$X(k, \theta) - mE = 0 \qquad 0 < m < 1 \qquad (2.2')$$

where m is that fraction of domestic expenditures for commodities that goes for imported goods. m will be a function of the exchange rate and is also subject to autonomous "shocks." Now (2.1) and (2.2') together imply $Y = E$. Therefore, combining (2.1) and (2.2') one can write

$$X(k, \theta) - mY = 0. \qquad (2.2^*)$$

(2.2*) can then be combined with (2.3) and (2.4) to describe the equilibrium properties of the system. The endogenous variables Y, i, and M will be determined by these three equations. Notice that Y is now fully

18. One would normally expect that small economies would be more "open" than closed ones. That is, m would be high for small economies.

determined by (2.2*) alone, unlike the model of the closed economy. The money and bond-market equations now simply determine the equilibrium rate of interest and the equilibrium money stock, but do not influence the equilibrium level of income. To see this point, let us trace out the consequences of a change in liquidity preference away from commodities and toward money and see what happens as before. Suppose $d\beta > 0$ and $d\omega = 0$. From (2.2*), (2.3), and (2.4), we have the following:

$$m\,dY + 0 + 0 = 0 \qquad (2.6)$$

$$\frac{\partial L}{\partial Y}\,dY + \frac{\partial L}{\partial i}\,di = dM = -\frac{\partial L}{\partial \beta}\,d\beta \qquad (2.7)$$

$$\frac{\partial R}{\partial Y}\,dY + \frac{\partial R}{\partial i}\,di + 0 = 0. \qquad (2.8)$$

The term $-(\partial L/\partial \beta)\,d\beta$ on the right hand side of (2.7) represents the change in liquidity preference which determines the equilibrium values of di and dM. Solving (2.6), (2.7), and (2.8), we get:

$$dY = 0, \quad dI = 0, \quad \text{and} \quad dM = \frac{\partial L}{\partial \beta}\,d\beta.$$

The equilibrium level of income and the equilibrium rate of interest remain unchanged. However, the money supply does increase by the full amount of the upward shift in liquidity preference. Notice that as long as the government does *not* take any measures to increase the stock of money by outside techniques, the increased supply of money will come from a temporary surplus in the balance of payments. The initial shift in liquidity preference toward money and away from commodities temporarily depresses expenditure for domestic goods and imports, permitting a temporary balance-of-trade surplus. This can only be settled by the movement of international money (bonds are immobile) which is associated with a rise in the domestic money supply and a counterpart increase in foreign exchange reserves. As the money supply increases, income then returns to its original level.

In the closed-economy model of section I, it was noted that a shift in liquidity preference toward money and away from commodities had the same economic impact as a decrease in the supply of money by *outside* techniques. The same is true in the case of an open economy. *An outside decrease in the supply of money by the government will leave the equilibrium income and the equilibrium rate of interest unchanged by inducing a temporary balance-of-payments surplus which restores the money supply to its original position. Foreign exchange reserves of the government increase by the exact amount of money the government had taken out of the economy.*

What are the implications of changing the supply of money by "inside" techniques such as conventional open market operations? Suppose that the government sells bonds to the private sector and reduces the money supply, i.e., $dB > 0$. What effect (if any) will there be on interest rates and foreign exchange reserves in a world of complete capital *immobility*? (Of course, there will still be no change in the equilibrium level of income.) The final equilibrium impact on dM and di can be obtained from equations (2.6), (2.7), and (2.8) by inserting dB on the right-hand side of (2.8) and deleting $-(\partial L/\partial \beta)\, d\beta$ from the right-hand side of (2.7) to obtain:

$$dM = dB\,\frac{\dfrac{\partial L}{\partial i}}{\dfrac{\partial R}{\partial i}} < 0 \qquad (2.9)$$

$$di = \frac{dB}{\dfrac{\partial R}{\partial i}} > 0. \qquad (2.10)$$

From the previous empirical judgment that $\partial R/\partial i > -(\partial L/\partial i)$, we have the $|dM| < |dB|$ from (2.10). That is, the final decrease in the equilibrium money supply is less than the increase in the economy's bond-holdings. Since the initiating open market operation of selling bonds for money decreased the money stock by the *full* amount of the bond issue dB, there must be a temporary balance-of-payments surplus which partly offsets the initial decline in the money supply as full equilibrium is reached. Exchange reserves thus rise but by less than the initial open market reduction in the money supply, in contrast to the case where the money supply was decreased by outside techniques. In summary, one can say that reducing the money supply will increase exchange reserves even when capital is internationally immobile and the equilibrium level of income is fixed. *However, reductions in the supply of money by inside techniques will increase exchange reserves by less than the reduction in the money supply, and will also raise the equilibrium rate of interest.*

One can think of the above results in more intuitive terms. The rise in the rate of interest associated with the reduction in inside money induces people to reduce their real cash-balance holdings. Thus, the balance-of-payments surplus which develops to offset the reduction of inside money only partly restores the initial cash-balance holdings as people now wish to hold smaller cash balances. Thus, the rise in exchange reserves is less than the reduction in the supply of inside money. Notice that if the rise in the rate of interest is steep because the interest sensitivity of bond-holdings is low, i.e., $\partial R/\partial i$ is "small," a reduction in the supply of money by open market sales of bonds will increase exchange reserves very little. If $\partial R/\partial i = -(\partial L/\partial i)$, it would have no effect at all. However, a reduction in the supply of money by a temporary surplus in the government budget can always be counted on to increase exchange reserves by the same amount that the money supply is reduced.

The implications of different degrees of *external* capital mobility for domestic monetary policy can now be assessed by comparing the results of extreme assumptions. The above results were associated with complete external capital immobility, whereas those achieved by Mundell, and McKinnon and Oates assumed perfect capital mobility.[19] Perfect capital mobility implies that the domestic interest rate on bonds is identically equal to that existing in the outside world and, if the country in question is indeed small, this interest rate is completely determined externally and may be considered fixed for analytical purposes. Under this perfect capital mobility, it was found that the equilibrium money stock and the equilibrium stock of bonds are all invariant to domestic monetary policy of *either* the inside or outside variety.[20] Moreover, monetary policy of either type has the *same effect* on the exchange reserve position of the country in question. If the domestic supply of money is reduced by inside techniques, domestic nationals will sell bonds to foreigners causing a capital inflow which restores the stock of money and bonds to their original positions and increases exchange reserves by the amount the money supply was originally reduced. If the stock of money is reduced by outside techniques—e.g., a temporary surplus in the government budget—this induces a corresponding temporary surplus in the balance of trade with which domestic nationals acquire foreign money and turn it over to the foreign exchange authorities to receive domestic money in return. In both the inside and outside cases, foreign exchange reserves rise by the exact amount that the domestic money supply is initially reduced. The rate of interest is fixed externally, which keeps desired cash-balance holdings constant.

Comparing the two extreme cases of mobility and immobility, we see

19. Mundell, "Capital Mobility and Stabilization Policy"; McKinnon and Oates, "The Implications of International Economic Integration."
20. *Ibid.*

that reductions in the stock of *outside* money have the same effect in both cases. Exchange reserves always rise by the amount that the stock of money is reduced as the equilibrium rate of interest is left unchanged. However, in the case of an *inside* reduction in the stock of money, exchange reserves rise less—possibly much less—in the presence of external capital immobility. *Therefore, one can conclude that the effectiveness of inside monetary policy in controlling exchange reserves (which may vary in response to exogenous shocks) is lessened by an increase in external capital immobility. However, the effectiveness of outside monetary policy in influencing exchange reserves is, surprisingly, independent of the degree of external capital mobility.*

With a floating exchange rate, it has been shown that monetary policy regains its ability to control the level of equilibrium income in the case of perfect capital mobility.[21] A decrease in the supply of either inside or outside money was shown to decrease equilibrium income and bond-holdings proportionately. The equilibrium rate of interest was, of course, left unchanged, being determined in the outside world.

What is the impact of changing the money supply when capital is completely immobile *in a floating exchange-rate system*? Now there is no mechanism for offsetting changes in the domestic stock of money to occur via balance-of-payments deficits or surpluses. Moreover, the stock of domestic *outside* bond-holdings is fixed and can be completely determined by the monetary authorities. *Therefore, somewhat surprisingly, it can easily be shown that the purely closed economy model of section I can, for all practical purposes, be used to represent the position of an open economy using floating exchange rates with no external capital mobility.* The equilibrium level of money income and the equilibrium rate of interest must again satisfy the two portfolio-balance conditions that:

$$L(Y, i; \beta) - M = 0 \qquad (2.2'')$$

$$R(Y, i; \omega) - B = 0. \qquad (2.3'')$$

M as well as B is now controllable by the domestic monetary authorities so that Y and i are completely determined by these two equations. Instead of M being endogenous as in the fixed exchange-rate case, the exchange rate k is now endogenously determined. However, k is best thought of as being determined by the equilibrium level of income in such a way as to maintain balance in commodity trade flows. That is, once Y is determined from (2.2) and (2.3) above, k is determined by (2.2''*):

$$X(k; \theta) - m(k) \cdot Y = 0. \qquad (2.2''*)$$

21. *Ibid.*

Both exports X and the share of imports in total expenditures m are functions of k. An increase in the money supply simply raises the equilibrium level of income, inducing an increase in expenditures for imports which is prevented from causing a balance-of-trade deficit by having k rise (the value of the domestic currency depreciates on world markets). The increase in k induces a rise in exports and fall in the share of imports in domestic expenditures so as to maintain external balance. However, what exactly happens to k can be ignored in determining equilibrium income since the parameters of the trade-balance condition (2.2″*) above do not influence equilibrium income as derived from (2.1) and (2.2). Therefore, the effects of changes in liquidity preference or changes in the stocks of money and bonds can be analyzed just as they were in the closed economy model of section I.

For example, the differential effects of inside and outside money creation as portrayed in Figure 2 are exactly the same for an open economy with a floating exchange rate and no external capital mobility. The same is true for the economic impact of fiscal policy, as shall be brought out more clearly in the following section. (Remember that in the case of perfect capital mobility and a floating exchange rate, inside and outside monetary policies are equally powerful in influencing equilibrium income but cannot alter the equilibrium rate of interest.[22]

III. Fiscal Policy and External Balance[23]

Our stationary-state model has not yet explicitly incorporated fiscal policy. To the extent that some levels of government react much like the private sector to changes in revenues (income) by changing expenditures in the same direction, then at this level of abstraction they can be safely integrated into the private sector. Various state and municipal governments could be placed in this category. However, if there are other levels of government which are consciously willing to unbalance their portfolio positions in money and bonds—e.g., maintain expenditures at a constant level even though tax revenues have risen—and these

22. McKinnon and Oates, "The Implications of International Economic Integration."
23. Many of the ideas expressed here for a closed economy may be found in a most interesting article by David J. Ott and Attiat Ott, "Budget Balance and Equilibrium Income," *Journal of Finance*, 20 (March, 1965): 71–77, although the Otts do not have a complete model of portfolio balance. The extension of their ideas to an open economy has been developed by Professor Wallace Oates of Princeton University in writing a comment on the Otts' paper. See Wallace E. Oates, "Budget Balance and Equilibrium Income: A Comment on the Efficacy of Fiscal and Monetary Policy in an Open Economy," *Journal of Finance*, 21, no. 3 (September, 1966): 489–98. The present author has benefited a great deal from correspondence with Oates on the subject.

same units have the power to create or destroy money, then most certainly they cannot be integrated into the private sector. One requires separate equation(s) to describe their behavior. It is this latter type of conscious portfolio-unbalancing governmental activity which shall be called "conscious" fiscal policy.

Suppose that the government fixes expenditure levels for goods and services but sets only the *rate* of taxation as a fraction of income. Then, for any given tax rate, variations in the level of income cause variations in the tax revenues and the size of the deficit or surplus in the government's budget. Suppose further that the government destroys or creates money only when it has budget surpluses or deficits. Then it can easily be shown that the introduction of this kind of fiscal policy into a closed economy leads to a set of equations which are formally very similar to those describing an open economy with a fixed exchange rate and with no external capital mobility. That is, the economy can be described by:

$$E[(1 - t)Y, i, M, B, K; \alpha] + G - Y = 0 \qquad \text{Commodity Flow} \qquad (3.1)$$

$$G - tY = 0 \qquad \text{Balanced Budget} \qquad (3.2)$$

$$L[(1 - t)Y, i; \beta] - M = 0 \qquad \text{Money Stock} \qquad (3.3)$$

$$R[(1 - t)Y, i; \omega] - B = 0 \qquad \text{Bond Stock} \qquad (3.4)$$

$$C[(1 - t)Y, i; \delta] - K = 0 \qquad \text{Commodity Stock.} \qquad (3.5)$$

All the symbols are the same as before except that G is the flow of government expenditures, t is the proportional income tax rate, $(1 - t)Y$ is now private disposable income, and E is now *private* expenditures only, whereas Y remains equal to *total* income.

Equation (3.2) is the balanced-budget constraint emphasized by the Otts, which is justified by the same reasoning that our balance-of-trade constraint (2.2*) was in the previous section. If a surplus exists in the government budget, money is being retired from circulation, causing a contraction in total expenditures, incomes, and tax revenues until tax revenues become equal to the flow of government expenditures. (In an open economy, the same reasoning holds if there is a deficit in the balance of trade.) The balanced-budget constraint recognizes the liquid-asset effects of government deficits or surpluses on the portfolio positions of individuals in the private sector. For an arbitrarily given flow of government expenditures, this is the only way one can make sense of the concept of a full-employment balanced budget determined by an appropriately specified level of taxation, t. It is, for example, necessary to justify the assertions made at the time of the American tax cut in 1964, that income would be sufficiently stimulated to make the government budgetary deficit only temporary. One should keep in mind, however, that the present analysis deals only with stationary-state equilibria and abstracts from the problem of steady growth. In situations of continuous growth, it is quite possible to have continuous deficits or surpluses in the government budget.

Notice that equation (3.2) *by itself* determines the equilibrium level of income. In combination with equations (3.3) and (3.4), the endogenous variables M and i are completely determined. In the open-economy model of section II with no external capital mobility, the trade balance condition (2.2*) determines the equilibrium level of income and (2.3) together with (2.4) determines the equilibrium levels of M and i. Therefore, the analysis of shifts in liquidity preference from commodities to money or the impact of outside versus inside changes in monetary policy are exactly the same as given in section II above. For example, only *inside* changes in the stock of money can affect the equilibrium rate of interest, although such changes cannot affect the equilibrium level of income. A reduction in the supply of inside money through the purchase of bonds by the central bank is accompanied by a *partially* compensating deficit in the government budget which causes the government fiscal authority "to go into debt" by the amount of money issued to cover the deficit. In the open-economy analogy, it would be foreigners who "go into debt" as the foreign exchange authorities acquire foreign exchange reserves when the central bank reduces the supply of inside money.

In the closed-economy model of this section, only changes in the parameters of the balanced-budget constraint (3.2) can affect the equilibrium level of income. If the tax rate is held constant, and the flow of government expenditure is increased, then from (3.2), $dY/dG = 1/t$. That is, the multiplier is simply equal to the reciprocal of the rate of taxation; whereas, if one looks at the open-economy model of section II —where there is no "conscious" fiscal policy—only autonomous shifts in exports (for a given propensity to import) can affect the equilibrium level of income. From (2.2*) we have $dY/dX = 1/m$ in an open economy, so that the multiplier associated with changes in exports is equal to the reciprocal of the propensity to import. In both cases, the multiplier is independent of the conventionally defined marginal propensity "to save." This is so because we have explicitly viewed "saving" as the desire to acquire assets. In a stationary-state equilibrium, where actual asset-holdings equal desired holdings, there is no net saving. In a wealth model, multipliers are derived from pure "balance-sheet" considerations and become relationships between initial and consequential wealth adjustments.

The next step is to consider a more complex economy which is open and within which the government uses "conscious" fiscal policy of the kind suggested above. One might wish to know, for example, if there is still any natural tendency to eliminate deficits or surpluses in the government budget, if G and t are arbitrarily fixed, as in the closed-economy case. Or, is there any natural tendency to eliminate deficits or surpluses in the balance of trade if the exchange rate, k, is fixed? In fact, it is now possible for asset-creating effects of a deficit in the government budget to be offset by a trade-balance deficit which drains outside assets out of the economy in such a way as to be consistent with portfolio balance in the private sector. That is, deficits in the foreign trade balance *and* in the government's budget are consistent with equilibrium when taken together.

The following set of equations describes the conditions for portfolio balance in the private sector:

$$E[(1 - t)Y, i, M, B, K; \alpha]$$
$$+ G_0 + X_0 - I - Y = 0 \qquad \text{Commodity Flow} \qquad (3.6)$$

$$X(k_0) - I = S^f \qquad \begin{array}{l} \text{Foreign Trade} \\ \text{Balance Surplus} \end{array} \qquad (3.7)$$

$$tY - G_0 = S^g \qquad \begin{array}{l} \text{Government Budget} \\ \text{Surplus} \end{array} \qquad (3.8)$$

$$S^f = S^g \qquad \begin{array}{l} \text{Budget-Trade} \\ \text{Constraint} \end{array} \qquad (3.9)$$

$$L[(1 - t)Y, i; \beta] - M = 0 \qquad \begin{array}{l} \text{Money-Stock} \\ \text{Condition} \end{array} \qquad (3.10)$$

$$R[(1 - t)Y, i; \omega] - B = 0 \qquad \begin{array}{l} \text{Bond-Stock} \\ \text{Condition} \end{array} \qquad (3.11)$$

$$C[(1 - t)Y, i; \delta] - K = 0 \qquad \begin{array}{l} \text{Commodity-Stock} \\ \text{Condition} \end{array} \qquad (3.12)$$

S^f is the trade balance surplus. S^g is the surplus in the government budget. In order to have portfolio-balance equilibrium in our stationary-state environment, it is necessary that the *flow* of money being destroyed by a government budget surplus be equal to the flow of money being created by a trade balance surplus—with its counterpart increase in exchange reserves. Therefore, we impose condition (3.9) that $S^f = S^g$ in equilibrium. Although such a condition is consistent with equilibrium asset-holdings in the *private* sector—the main focus of our analysis so far—one must remember that it may not be consistent with the exchange reserve position of the government. A government budgetary deficit and corresponding foreign trade deficit—both of which are flows—will lead to a steady loss of exchange reserves of the same magnitude (in this stationary-state case where capital is internationally immobile). What the analysis suggests is that *there will be no automatic equilibrating force in the private sector to eliminate the foreign trade or budget deficits (surpluses) in an economy which employs "conscious" as opposed to "passive" fiscal policy.*

From the first four equations, one can compute the equilibrium value of Y as a function of X, G, m, and t. Before doing so, however, it is necessary to specify how government expenditures G affect imports I. There are two useful simplifying assumptions one can make: (1) the import content of government expenditures is the same as for private expenditures so that $I = m[E + G]$; or (2) government expenditures have no import content so that $I = mE$. (1) is the more symmetrical assumption to make and is used below to compute the equilibrium value of Y to obtain

$$\frac{X + (1 - m)G}{t + m - mt} = Y. \tag{3.13}$$

The government expenditures multiplier is $(1 - m)/(t + m - mt)$, whereas the export multiplier is somewhat greater, being $1/(t + m - mt)$. If assumption (2) is used so that government expenditures have no direct import content, then both multipliers are equal to $1/(t + m - mt)$. In both cases, this multiplier is substantially less than in a closed economy with "conscious" fiscal policy, where it is simply $1/t$; or in an open economy where fiscal policy is "passive," where it is simply $1/m$. Once Y is determined from (3.13), the equilibrium values of i, M, and K can be determined from equations (3.10), (3.11), and (3.12).

One might be interested to compute what the tax rate t would have to be in order to preserve external balance for any arbitrarily specified level of government expenditures G and exchange rate k (which determines m and X). That is, impose the condition that $S^f = S^g = 0$ and solve the first four equations for t and Y under the assumption (1) above, to get

$$t = \frac{mG}{X} \quad \text{and} \quad Y = \frac{X}{m}. \tag{3.14}$$

Since we have set t so as always to insure balance in the government's budget, this is equivalent to the "passive" fiscal policy assumed in section II; and it is not surprising that the equilibrium level of income only depends on the foreign trade parameters m and X. Notice, however, that t now depends directly on G in order to preserve balance in the government budget. That is, if the government wishes to raise its expenditures, it must raise the rate of taxation proportionately if budget balance is to be preserved—unlike the case of a closed economy. Notice, too, that if there is an autonomous increase in exports, the government must reduce t in order to preserve budget balance and prevent a surplus in the balance of trade from developing.

The positions of the trade balance and the equilibrium level of income are both determined completely by the parameters t, G, X, and m which appear in the first four equations. The rate of interest and the equilibrium money supply can be affected by inside changes in the money supply, but such changes have no effect on equilibrium income or the equilibrium balance-of-payments surplus. Monetary policy of the inside variety can still have a "once-and-for-all" impact on exchange reserves as discussed in section II, although it cannot affect the size of a continuous deficit in the balance of trade underwritten by a government budget deficit. The analysis of this section has assumed capital flows are externally immobile. This assumption will be altered in section IV.

The well-known principle that at least two *effective* policy instruments are needed to achieve two policy goals—such as external balance and a full employment level of income—can now be illustrated. Since monetary policy can affect neither policy goal, we require two other instruments. Let us suppose the authorities can manipulate the exchange rate k and the tax rate t. Both X and m are functions of k where $\partial X/\partial k > 0$ and $\partial m/\partial k < 0$. To achieve full employment income Y^* with external balance, a necessary condition is that k must be set equal to k^* such that $Y^* = X(k^*)/m(k^*)$ and, therefore, exports equal imports at the full employment level of income, from (3.13). This can be done without reference to government expenditures or tax rates. Then again, from (3.12), the appropriate tax rate necessary to achieve both policy goals will be $t = m(k^*)G/X(k^*) = G/Y^*$. Therefore, government tax authorities can simply set the tax rate t at that level which will generate a flow of tax revenues at full employment income which just covers the flow of government expenditures. This can be done independently of the exchange rate set by the foreign exchange authorities. However, both policy variables t and k are now uniquely determined by the specification that both internal and external balance must be achieved.

IV. Differentiated Monetary and Fiscal Policy

Suppose a country decides it is inadvisable to alter the exchange rate or to influence directly trade flows by subsidies and restrictions. This loss of flexibility means that it cannot simultaneously achieve full employment income and maintain external payments balance unless another policy variable can be found to be used in conjunction with fiscal policy. Is it possible for monetary policy to assume the role of an additional effective policy variable if we drop the assumption of external capital immobility? This was the conclusion of Robert Mundell who used a simple Keynesian model of income determination (without introducing portfolio-balance considerations) coupled with the assumption that interest-rate differentials determine the *rate of flow* of capital in or out of the economy.[24] Since Mundell's model apparently deals with stationary-state equilibria (at least growth rates were not made explicit), we shall examine his conclusion using our complete model of portfolio balance in asset-holdings.

Mundell assumes that the impact of monetary policy can be summarized by the effect it has on the rate of interest independently of how the increase in the rate of interest was brought about. An increase in the interest rate both dampens internal demand for commodities (including imports) and improves the balance of payments on capital account. He assumes further that fiscal policy can be measured by the extent of the surplus (which can be negative) in the government budget. He assumes that this surplus has a dampening effect on the demand for commodities (including imports) but has *no* direct effect on external capital flows. To achieve internal full-employment income in his model, there can be many combinations of interest rates and budget surpluses. The locus of such points is set out on line *XX* below. Similarly, to achieve external balance so that deficits in trade are matched by capital inflows, there are many combinations of interest rates and budget surpluses. The locus of these points is set out on line *FF* below. Because capital is externally mobile, the slope of *FF* is greater than *XX*. Monetary policy is used to correct shocks to external equilibrium, whereas fiscal policy is used for internal control. *Q* yields the budget surplus and rate of interest necessary to achieve both internal and external balance.

Let us examine more closely what equilibrium on the *XX* curve implies, thinking for a moment in terms of a closed economy. If the point *P* is associated with a deficit in the government budget, outside assets—money or bonds—are being continuously pumped into the economy, even though the rate of interest and the equilibrium level of income are constant. Clearly this is inconsistent with portfolio balance

24. Robert A. Mundell, "The Appropriate Use of Monetary and Fiscal Policy for Internal and External Stability," International Monetary Fund, *Staff Papers*, 9, no. 1 (March, 1962): 70–79.

in the private sector of the economy. If the government is continuously issuing bonds, an excess supply of bonds will soon develop with an excess demand for commodities and money. The market interest rate will be bid up continuously as new bonds pour into the economy, but this will not completely offset the excess demand for commodities. There is no simple monetary policy one could carry out to insure that the demand for commodities does not increase. Clearly, government budgetary deficits or surpluses are inconsistent with having a stationary equilibrium income and interest rate in a closed economy.

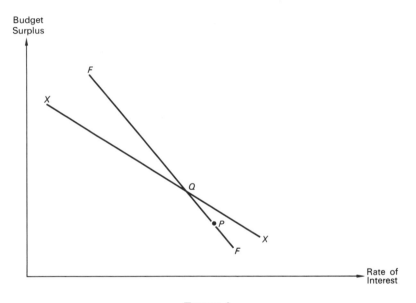

FIGURE 3

But what about an open economy? It was shown in section III that government deficits *can* be consistent with equilibrium in the private sector of the economy if, at the same time, a trade-balance deficit drains off the supply of new financial assets which is being created. In the case of capital immobility, the deficit in the balance of trade would always be equal to the deficit in the balance of payments if the government issues money to cover its budgetary deficit. If it issued bonds, there would be a continuously rising rate of interest to induce people to hold the ever-increasing stock of bonds. No position of stable equilibrium in interest rates *and* income levels would exist.

In the polar case of perfect capital mobility, the government can run a deficit and issue bonds, all of which are purchased by foreigners. This is consistent with portfolio balance in the private sector. The untenability of the assumption of perfect capital mobility is now evident since foreigners are assumed to absorb whatever amount of bonds the government cares to issue. Therefore by lowering the tax rate, t, the government can set any equilibrium level of income it likes with no worry about external imbalance. However, as long as income is stationary, it seems unlikely that foreigners would be willing to purchase ever-increasing amounts of claims on the economy at a fixed rate of interest, although they may be willing to absorb a flow of claims for short periods of time.

It is important, therefore, to formulate some hypotheses regarding capital mobility of an intermediate degree which are consistent with stationary equilibrium income levels and interest rates. To do this, one must posit a certain *stock* of bonds that foreigners are willing to hold at every interest rate rather than be willing to absorb an unlimited flow of bonds at that rate. By raising the domestic rate of interest, one can induce foreigners to hold more domestic bonds, but this is a "once-and-for-all" effort. Therefore, one cannot get a continuous improvement in capital flows by an increase in the domestic rate of interest, as the Mundell model assumes.

In summary, one can say that a deficit in the fiscal authority's budget in a non-growing economy with a fixed exchange rate and no trade controls must eventually lead to a continuous *flow* of exchange reserve losses of the same magnitude. *Monetary policy confined to adjustments in stocks is not an effective substitute for exchange-rate variations to enable the economy to achieve both internal and external balance in a stationary situation over any extended period of time.*

Concluding Comment

The possibilities for and limitations of tailoring monetary and fiscal policy to control both internal and external balance have been outlined for stationary-state equilibria and different degrees of capital mobility. The control of the stock of exchange reserves by monetary policy is quite possible providing that the government is merely responding to shifts in the asset-holding preferences of domestic nationals. For example, a shift in liquidity preference from money to bonds will lead, initially, to a loss in exchange reserves both because of transactions on capital account in international payments flows and possibly because of a temporary deficit in the balance of trade. This decline in the country's exchange reserve position can be avoided if the government uses open market operations to reduce the supply of money.

However, balance-of-payments disequilibria arising out of commodity flow discrepancies cannot be handled by monetary policy. If, for example, the rate of taxation that the government uses is too low relative to the fixed price of foreign exchange, then there will be a tendency for a deficit in the balance of trade to develop to match a persistent deficit in the government's budget. Monetary policy could then do very little to correct either deficit, let alone being able to control the full employment level of income. External *and* internal balance can only be secured if both the exchange rate and rate of taxation are adjustable.

These results have all been developed under the assumption that net saving and capital accumulation are zero in equilibrium. This strong assumption proved valuable in permitting portfolio balance to be introduced into the Keynesian framework in a logically consistent and simple manner—something which seems to have been lacking in standard macroeconomic models. However, there is no doubt that this strong assumption is empirically limiting and a complete analysis of international adjustment mechanisms requires a full model of growth equilibrium within which portfolio balance in asset-holdings is explicitly incorporated. It is then possible to imagine interest-rate differentials causing permanent changes in capital flows. However, the ways in which international capital flows affect growth rates would have to be specified. One can only conjecture that monetary policy of the inside variety may turn out to be a more powerful device for controlling external payments in a growing economy.

COMMENT: "THE ASSIGNMENT PROBLEM"

Richard N. Cooper

As I conceive it, the "assignment problem" involves the association of a *particular* policy instrument with a *particular* policy target and instruction to those who control the policy instrument to achieve a specified value of the target variable. Fundamentally, therefore, the assignment problem arises from a system of decentralized decision-making—one in which several policy-makers are simultaneously and independently attempting to reach their assigned policy targets. Decentralization often does, but need not, involve different institutions, such as a central bank and a ministry of finance; it does involve a division of labor among policy-makers. Centralized and simultaneous determination of the appropriate "policy mix" to achieve a number of interrelated targets would involve no assignment problem.

The assignment problem can be set out more formally in the framework developed by Meade and Tinbergen. We start with certain target variables (y) of economic policy—variables to the values of which we attach direct normative importance. We also have certain instruments (x) of policy—variables over which we have some control, and which in turn influence the values of the target variables. Finally, there is the set of analytical relationships (a_{ij}) between the instruments (x_j) and the targets (y_i). These can be written down in a table or matrix:

TABLE 1

Target Variables	Policy Instruments				
	x_1	x_2	x_3	x_4	$\ldots$
y_1	a_{11}	a_{12}	a_{13}	a_{14}	$\ldots$
y_2	a_{21}	a_{22}	a_{23}	a_{24}	$\ldots$
y_3	a_{31}	a_{32}	a_{33}	a_{34}	$\ldots$
y_4	a_{41}	a_{42}	a_{43}	a_{44}	$\ldots$
$\vdots$	$\vdots$	$\vdots$	$\vdots$	$\vdots$	$\ldots$

Each target y_i is potentially influenced by each of the instruments:

$$y_i = \sum_j a_{ij}x_j, \qquad \text{where } a_{ij} = \frac{\partial y_i}{\partial x_j}.$$

Some of the a_{ij} may of course be zeros. The whole set of relationships can be expressed in concise matrix notation, $y = Ax$, where y is the vector of target variables, x is the vector of instrument variables, and A is the matrix $[a_{ij}]$.

If we specify target values y^* for the target variables and assume there are an equal number of instrument variables, then the appropriate values of the instrument variables are $x = A^{-1}y^*$, and a centralized authority with full information will simply set the instruments at these values to achieve the targets.

With decentralization, however, a process of search or groping toward the targets must take place. The "assignment problem" is to associate with each target an instrument such that when the policymakers respond to deviations from target, their actions lead back to the targets, i.e., the groping will be successful. In formal terms, the system must be stable.[1]

We know from the two-target, two-instrument case examined by Mundell[2] that stability is assured for assignments along the main diagonal when

$$a_{11} > 0, \quad a_{22} > 0, \quad \text{and} \quad a_{11}a_{22} - a_{12}a_{21} > 0.$$

The terms a_{12} and a_{21} indicate the effect of each instrument on the target to which it is *not* assigned. When these "side effects" a_{12} and a_{21} are positive, stability requires $a_{11}/a_{12} > a_{21}/a_{22}$. When these conditions obtain, proper assignment calls for instrument x_1 to be directed toward target y_1, and x_2 to be directed toward y_2. If the inequality were reversed, the assignment should be reversed. This is Mundell's "principle of effective market classification." It will be familiar to international trade theorists in a different guise: each instrument should specialize on that target toward which it has a *comparative advantage*. (An "absolute" advantage is not necessary; a_{21} may exceed a_{22}. Fiscal policy, for

1. Formally, this process of search can be represented as: $\dot{x} = k(y^* - y) = k(y^* - Ax)$, where $\dot{x}$ is the time rate of change in the policy instruments and k is a diagonal matrix representing the speed of adjustment to deviations from targets. This system will be stable if the characteristic roots of kA all have positive real parts.

2. Robert A. Mundell, "The Appropriate Use of Monetary and Fiscal Policy for Internal and External Stability," International Monetary Fund, *Staff Papers*, 9 (March, 1962): 70–79.

example, may have a more powerful influence both on the level of employment and on the balance of payments than does monetary policy, but the latter may still have a comparative advantage in dealing with the balance of payments.)

The stability conditions can be generalized. The requirements for stability are formally analogous to those which Hicks sought for assuring stability of a general market equilibrium. He simplified his problem by neglecting the income effects of price changes, so $a_{ij} = a_{ji}$. The resulting symmetric matrix requires for stability the well-known condition that the determinants of all the principal minors alternate in sign. Here the problem is more complicated since in general $a_{ij} \neq a_{ji}$, but stability conditions can still be specified.[3]

The assignment problem can be regarded as a process of identifying the "own price" of each target variable and of switching rows or columns so that the main diagonal of A dominates the off-diagonal terms in the sense required for stability. I conjecture that stability can always be assured by appropriate switching of rows or columns, except in the special case when A is singular ($a_{11}a_{22} - a_{12}a_{21} = 0$ in the 2×2 case).

This is the assignment problem proper. Even if stability of an unconstrained decentralized system can always be assured by proper assignment, several difficulties might arise. I identify five of them.

First, proper assignment assumes full freedom in assigning instruments to variables. But suppose several different countries are involved. (This can be indicated by partitioning the matrix A into submatrices, with the first diagonal block referring to the targets and instruments of the first country, the second diagonal block referring to a second country, and so on.) Each country can assign only its own instruments. It is at least theoretically possible that stability for the system as a whole would require assignment of one country's instrument to another country's target. So long as nations remain independent in their actions, some targets could not be reached.

This possibility is perhaps improbable, but it is not entirely far-fetched. Monetary policy in the United States, for example, is sometimes said to have a powerful impact on the rate of investment and hence growth *in Canada*. If in addition there were a strong interaction between

3. J. R. Hicks, *Value and Capital*, 2d ed. (Oxford: Clarendon Press, 1946), mathematical appendix. For the general stability conditions for a non-symmetric matrix, see P. A. Samuelson, *Foundations of Economic Analysis* (Cambridge: Harvard University Press, 1947), pp. 431–35. In the case of a symmetric matrix, all the roots are real and this means that the Hicks conditions are sufficient for stability.

U.S. capital flows to Canada and Canadian imports from the United States, it is conceivable that the most important impact of U.S. monetary policy, relative to other instruments (e.g., Canadian commercial policy) would be on Canadian growth, not on the U.S. balance of payments. The same result might be obtained if tighter U.S. monetary policy impeded U.S. exports (since the cost of credit is an important dimension of international competitiveness) sufficiently to offset the gains it generates on the capital account. The specification of targets and instruments must of course be made more precise, but these observations suggest some possible outcomes.

Second, the "comparative advantage" of the instruments may vary with the environment, with the level of the targets, and with the distance the target variables are from the targets. The a_{ij} will not typically be constant, as extensive discussion of the varying effectiveness of monetary and fiscal policies in regimes of fixed and floating exchange rates indicates. With high capital mobility, fiscal policy is said to be relatively ineffective in influencing domestic employment in a regime of floating rates (since the change in net government expenditures will be offset by a change in net exports), while it is effective in a regime of fixed rates. The reverse is true of monetary policy.[4] Or, to revert to a previous example, the influence of interest rates on export competitiveness may sometimes outweigh, and at other times be outweighed by, the influence of interest rates on international capital movements (this possibility assumes, realistically, very imperfect international mobility of capital for export finance).

In short, we have the possibility of a reversal in the relative effectiveness of instruments, analogous to "factor-intensity reversal" in the production of two commodities. Where this is a serious possibility, assignments must be tentative, not once for all, since decentralized decision-making with fixed assignments of instruments to targets may be unstable on some occasions even when it is stable on others.

Third, we should pay attention to the speed of adjustment. Even when stability is assured—proper assignments do not cross national frontiers, and "target reversal" does not take place—a delay in the time taken to reach the targets involves a loss of welfare. The speed of convergence on

4. J. Marcus Fleming, "Domestic Financial Policies under Fixed and under Floating Exchange Rates," International Monetary Fund, Staff Papers, 9 (November, 1962): 369–80. This analysis suggests that in a regime of fixed exchange rates, fiscal policy should be "assigned" to the target of domestic employment, while monetary policy should be assigned to the balance of payments. Sohmen dissents sharply from the latter assignment when exchange rates are fixed but adjustable. The dangers he sees presumably arise from a high international mobility of capital in an adjustable peg system, however, and not from the use of monetary policy to influence capital movements.

targets in a decentralized system will depend on the sign and the size of the off-diagonal elements—the side effects of each instrument on target variables other than the one to which it is assigned. If these side effects are large and of such signs that they work at cross-purposes, the process of convergence on targets will be slow.[5]

It is *two-way* interaction that causes the problem. Zeros above or below the diagonal are helpful. The impact of Mexican developments on the United States is negligible. Mexico, in contrast, is very much concerned with what happens in the United States, but can take it as given; both countries can therefore ignore the feedbacks. With high two-way interaction, however, decentralized decision-making can be costly. Assigning particular instruments to particular target variables, while leading ultimately to the targets, will take a long time. The argument for co-ordinated decision-making becomes more powerful.[6]

Fourth, uncertainty about the analytical relationships linking instruments and targets can also lead to inefficient use of instruments under a decentralized system. Policy-makers and the public will want the target variables to deviate as little as possible from their target values, taking into account the uncertainties. They may, for example, want to minimize some weighted sum of the variances of target variables around their target values. This objective in effect involves the addition of another target to a system that is already (by assumption) exactly determined. The appropriate value for all the instruments will generally be affected by the process of minimizing deviations from targets, and assignment of particular instruments to particular targets will be inefficient; in fact, it can be shown that the extent to which each instrument should be used depends on the variances of the estimates of the a_{ij}. The larger these variances for any j, the less reliance should be placed on the instrument x_j—a common-sense result.[7]

Fifth, the table of coefficients a_{ij} has been depicted here as open-ended, allowing for the addition of further instruments and targets, including those of additional countries. But if the system being described

5. This point is shown more formally and illustrated in my "Economic Policy Adjustment between Interdependent Economies," *Quarterly Journal of Economics* (forthcoming).

6. Kenen's notion of an optimum currency area in this volume can be interpreted in these terms. He indicated that diversity of a region's product mix was of critical importance in determining whether it is an optimal currency area. But he failed to specify how the "region" over which product diversification should be measured is defined, except implicitly as a region with a common monetary and fiscal system. The analysis above suggests that the appropriate jurisdiction of a common monetary and fiscal system should be related to the degree of *two-way* interaction between subregions.

7. See William C. Brainard, "Uncertainty and the Effectiveness of Economic Policy," *American Economic Review*, 57 (May, 1967): 411–25.

is complete, there may be relationships among target variables other than those expressed in the table of coefficients, i.e., the matrix A should be bordered with side conditions. For example, if some of the y's represent the overall payments positions, or the current-account positions of all countries, then under consistent definitions we will have the requirement $\sum y = 0$ for this subset of the y's.[8] This relationship does two things. It imposes a consistency requirement on the targets of policy: $\sum y^* = 0$, for this subset. And it renders one of the instruments superfluous—or makes it available for the pursuit of other unspecified ends —since $m - 1$ instruments are here sufficient to assure the attainment of m consistent targets. Mundell has called this superfluity of instruments "the redundancy problem" and elsewhere in this volume shows how it can be linked, through the nature of the payments system, to determination of the level of world prices.

I will close by interpreting some of Sohmen's remarks in light of this framework. He asserts that "all important difficulties in the assignment of policy variables to different targets can thus be attributed to insufficient price flexibility in the real world." It is not clear what is meant by this. On the interpretation I have given to the question, "assignment problem" difficulties always arise when (1) there is a multiplicity of objectives; (2) a decentralized system of policy-making is used; and (3) two-way interactions among instrument and target variables are high. While he has not specified fully the system he has in mind, Sohmen's discussion seems to imply that he would deny the importance of the last source of difficulties, the existence of high two-way interactions, when price flexibility is high. I hope it does not do too much injustice to his remarks to write down his system as follows:

TABLE 2

TARGETS	INSTRUMENTS			
	Government Expenditures $(+)$	Exchange Rate $(-)$	Open Market Purchases	Price and Wage Level $(-)$
Public goods	+	0	0	0
Balance of payments	0	+	0	0
Net foreign investment	−	+	+	0
Domestic employment	+	+	+	+

Signs were chosen to increase the value of the assigned target; proper assignments are along the main diagonal.

8. We ignore the asymmetry created by additions to monetary gold.

Here the main diagonal represents the proper assignment, and all entries above the diagonal are zero, so those interaction effects are assumed negligible. An increase in government expenditures worsens the trade balance (net foreign investment), but open market operations do not affect the level of public goods provided; once the desired level of the latter is achieved, monetary policy can be used to achieve the desired level of net foreign investment without further iterations.

This table does not conform in construction with the matrix $[a_{ij}]$. The exchange rate and the price level are assumed to vary freely, and hence are not, strictly speaking, policy instruments. Several of the zeros arise because the exchange rate is allowed to adjust freely to changes in the other policy variables. Open market sales cannot improve the payments position, for example, because the resulting capital inflow drives up the exchange rate and worsens the trade balance by a corresponding amount. Similarly, a fall in the price level is compensated by an appreciation of the exchange rate. Having decided that the "own price" of the balance of payments is clearly the exchange rate, that that of domestic employment is the domestic wage and price level, and that these variables should move freely to accommodate other changes. Sohmen's policy model reduces to:

TABLE 3

TARGETS	INSTRUMENTS	
	Government Expenditures	Open Market Purchases
Public goods	+	0
Net foreign investment	−	+

This system is always stable under decentralization, and everything else takes care of itself—although control over open market operations (which determines net capital outflow, not the overall balance-of-payments position) perhaps belongs in the hands of a foreign assistance agency rather than the central bank! It assumes foreign trade price elasticities are high, exchange speculation is stabilizing, and internal price and wage adjustments can smoothly and efficiently preserve full employment of domestic factors of production. In adopting this particular set of assignments, Sohmen takes a clear position on factual issues that have been the object of extensive theoretical and empirical debate over the last three decades—and which are still debatable.

COMMENT: "THE ASSIGNMENT PROBLEM"

Pascal Salin

I agree with a number of the main points made in Professor Sohmen's paper about, for instance, the role of international liquidity, the opposition to discontinuous parity adjustments and to the Bretton Woods arrangements, and the importance of price flexibility in economic analysis. Other points seem more questionable, however.

On the whole, my comments will be related to the following problem: Does Professor Sohmen think that there is a single equilibrium point (in a multidimensional analysis of macroeconomic policy), or are there several equilibrium points? And what kind of equilibrium (or equilibria)?

It is clear that Professor Sohmen believes that there is a single equilibrium point (in a world of perfect flexibility, he says, involuntary unemployment would be ruled out). I also agree with the currently accepted view that underemployment is nothing but a disequilibrium situation—provided we look at it in a multimarket framework—as Patinkin, for instance, has shown most clearly. The only problem is whether the disequilibrium can be cleared at once or not. Taking this view, there is a unique equilibrium position in the labor as well as in other markets. All this is very simple; but we should not fail to consider the immediate implications of this view, namely, that the only meaning of economic policy is to strengthen and accelerate the processes which would lead anyhow to market equilibrium (or sometimes to replace artificially one process by another faster process). In this context, it is by no means sufficient to state that the role of economic policy would be minimal in a world of perfect price flexibility. For, in the case of incorrect expectations price flexibility is not all that matters; lags are introduced into the adjustment process, and economic policy would retain a significant function, namely, to reduce these lags.

Now, you may ask why I begin with such very general comments but herewith is the explanation, in the form of some consequences related to Professor Sohmen's paper:

The first implication is that, if economic policy is nothing but a way to accelerate adjustment processes, its welfare effects are extremely

243

difficult to estimate. For instance, Professor Sohmen argues that international monetary arrangements and domestic policies are of interest only insofar as they reduce the gap between the present state of the economy and an optimal state in real terms. *But it is by no means self-evident that faster adjustment to equilibrium implies increased welfare.* Let us take an example. Assume that two policy mixes are available to us, one of which allows general equilibrium to be reached more quickly but at the expense of more unemployment during the adjustment period. At the same time, assume that welfare is much more closely related to the level of employment than to, say, the level of the balance-of-payments deficit. Therefore, the problem of economic policy (in the context of the assignment problem) is best expressed without direct reference to any kind of welfare concept. We are much more aware of what we are doing if we only take the speed of adjustment as a given target of economic policy without welfare implications. This is only a minor point.

The discussion of the combination of monetary and fiscal policies is a much more important point. My first comment in this context bears simultaneously on Professor Sohmen's paper and on the articles of Professor Mundell which he quotes. According to the opinion expressed by both authors, monetary policy would have little effect on income under fixed exchange rates, while fiscal policy would be ineffective under flexible exchange rates, if international mobility of capital is assumed. The reason why fiscal policy is considered to be ineffective under flexible rates is that, in the latter case, the additional public debt required to finance the increase in government expenditure would be entirely absorbed by the rest of the world. As a consequence, under flexible exchange rates, a revaluation of the exchange rate would induce a trade deficit just sufficient to cancel out the effect of the government's deficit on the domestic market for goods and services.

Developing Professor Mundell's argument, Professor Sohmen has rightly pointed out that a terms-of-trade effect should be taken into account as well. I would suggest that we must go even farther.

The bare assumption of international capital mobility does not imply, of course, that the response of the *ex ante* balance of payments to changes in the rate of exchange is immediate. If the reactions of the balance of payments are slow, it is quite possible that during the early part of the period the rate of exchange will rise beyond its long-run equilibrium level. Then the effects of changes in the rate can be said to be perverse in the short run. Speculation (anticipating the later adjustment) can fill the gap in the foreign account. In such situations, there will be no immediate change in real absorption due to the trade balance, and the effects of fiscal policy *will* be positive during the relevant adjustment period. Note that the arguments imply that we speak in terms of adjustment speeds, not in terms of the final level of aggregate demand.

I wonder why Professor Sohmen suggests, in this context, that changes in fiscal policy are necessarily matched by changes in the supply of interest-bearing government debt. For, as we all know, the increase in government expenditures can be financed, for instance, by an increase in the money supply instead of an issue of new interest-bearing debt. In this case it is quite possible that the supply of newly created money will be more than sufficient to satisfy the increase in the transactions demand for money brought about by the impact of an expansionary fiscal policy; the resulting excess supply of money will then be eliminated by an increased[1] demand for idle balances induced by *a fall in the interest rate.*[1] In addition, if the authorities do increase the public debt, it is possible that the increment will be absorbed by the home market, not the external market, if, for example, there is at the same time an excess internal supply of money and an excess internal supply of commodities greater than the excess supply of money. It is also possible to assume that the private sector is more sensitive to changes in the rate of interest than to changes in the price level, so that the additional issue of government securities can be absorbed by the internal market. This may be the case, in particular, if individuals anticipate rising prices, which imply an increase in the real rate of return on securities.

To sum up, the effects of a fiscal policy measure supplemented by a well-defined financing technique such as the issuing of government securities cannot be evaluated unless we have sufficient knowledge of equilibrium conditions for the private sector's portfolio on the one hand, and for the government's portfolio on the other hand.

The opinion that money creation under fixed exchange rates leads to capital export relies on the assumption that at least some part of the newly created excess supply of money will be allocated to an increased demand for securities and will therefore induce a decrease in the rate of interest. But, in fact, since we are in a disequilibrium situation, it is possible that the existing stock of securities is already too high, or just sufficient, so that the new money could be allocated to the repletion of cash balances or to an increased demand for commodities. In such cases, neither changes in the rate of interest nor changes in international

1. On this point see, for instance, T. Puu, *The Effects of Monetary and Fiscal Policy* (Uppsala: Almqvist & Wiksell, 1965), and R. A. Musgrave, *The Theory of Public Finance* (New York: McGraw-Hill, 1959), chapter 22.

capital flows need appear. Monetary policy will, therefore, be effective even under fixed exchange rates.

I would suggest that a more convenient method to design or mix economic policies is to combine the instruments in such a way as to maximize the adjustment speeds (this view is more in line with Professor Mundell's 1960 paper[2] than with Professor Sohmen's and the other papers of Professor Mundell which he quotes). But the following remarks are also needed: (1) Fiscal policy must be conceived in a very narrow way. (2) The response of all (macroeconomic) markets should be taken into account. (3) The relevant equilibrium concept is a long-run one, i.e., equilibrium implies that existing stocks of all assets equal desired stocks for all economic units including the State.

To illustrate, let us return to Professor Sohmen's example (p. 189). Assume a positive excess demand on the commodity market together with a positive surplus in the balance of payments (and fixed exchange rates). The *ex ante* balance-of-payments surplus can conceal either of two cases: a surplus in the trade balance with a (smaller) deficit or a surplus in the balance of autonomous capital; or, a deficit in the trade balance with a larger surplus in the capital balance.

In the latter case, we actually have an instance of positive excess demand at home and simultaneously a trade deficit. But not in the former. The first case can be explained in the following way: the price ratio between home and foreign prices is such that national residents want to exchange money (or securities, etc.) against domestic commodities rather than against imported commodities. A restrictive fiscal policy cannot help to solve this kind of problem when it appears, for instance, as a consequence of a disturbance in desired money holdings by national residents. Cheap money will not solve the problem of external balance if we have an initial deficit in the capital balance, since it would only increase the capital deficit and deplete the existing stock of international reserves. In this respect, fiscal policy must take into account the level of the various assets desired and held in portfolios, in particular the desired stock of foreign currencies.

Moreover, the policy mix to be chosen is related not only to the overall balance of payments but also to its structure, because if we want a stock equilibrium in reserves, for instance in a stationary economy, we must get equilibrium in the balance of trade.

2. R. A. Mundell, "The Monetary Dynamics of International Adjustment under Fixed and Flexible Exchange Rates," *Quarterly Journal of Economics*, 74 (May, 1960): 227–57.

COMMENT: "PORTFOLIO BALANCE AND INTERNATIONAL PAYMENTS ADJUSTMENT"

Anne O. Krueger

In his opening remarks, our chairman stated that the purpose of this conference is to bring our scientific apparatus to bear on the unresolved problems of the international monetary system. There can be no doubt that McKinnon's paper does precisely that. His contribution is really twofold: (1) the revision of the standard general equilibrium model, used in earlier analyses of the assignment problem, to incorporate portfolio-balance considerations explicitly; and (2) the application of the revised model to the analysis of the appropriateness of various policy instruments in achieving external and internal balance.

There is so much in McKinnon's paper that is provocative that a coherent discussion of it is difficult. In reading it, one has to suppress the urge to sit down with pencil and paper and work out variants and extensions of the model. That, however, would provide material for a separate paper. The twofold aspect of McKinnon's paper implies that there are two distinct lines of discussion: the structure of the underlying model, and its application to problems of external and internal imbalance. Ronald Jones will address himself to the former question, and I shall consider the applicability of the model to analysis of payments disequilibria.

McKinnon recognizes that his contribution is only a first step. He envisages future extensions in which the price level, assumed constant in his model, will become a variable, and, further still, in which growth equilibrium models are developed.

My remarks bear largely on the limitations of the model as it now stands. This should in no way be taken as a criticism of McKinnon since he recognizes them and since his contribution is the stimulus to the questions I shall raise. These questions rather indicate the tremendous originality of the paper and the amount of work remaining before portfolio-balance considerations are integrated into analysis of the adjustment mechanism in a way satisfactory to most of us.

I will comment first on the applicability of the general equilibrium approach to short-run balance-of-payments considerations. Next, I would like to consider the usefulness of the model (and its possible

247

extensions) for the assignment problem. Lastly, the usefulness of the portfolio-balance model in general to international monetary phenomena will be considered.

There is a fundamental question as to whether comparison of two full general equilibria is the appropriate methodology for analyzing the adjustment of external and internal imbalance. Equilibrium in McKinnon's system is defined as a state in which all individuals hold their desired stocks of all assets, and there is zero excess demand in the commodity market. Since desired assets are equal to asset-holdings for all individuals, the average net propensity to save is zero. Hence, for all equilibria, $S = I = 0$. Now, as an identity $I - S \equiv X - M$. The only conceivable type of "external imbalance" at equilibrium is in the capital account, and even that is ruled out for the private sector since at equilibrium desired holdings of each asset equal actual stocks. In this system, then, the only type of external imbalance possible is that generated by government operations, since the private sector is always in external balance, by assumption. It may be that in the real world only government operations geared at changing the income level do lead to external imbalance, but external imbalance on trade account in the private sector cannot be analyzed in terms of the model.

The problem of using a full general equilibrium model to analyze the assignment problem is illustrated in McKinnon's verbal description of his results. For instance, consider his analysis of the effects of an upward shift in liquidity preference with fixed exchange rates and capital mobility. In this case he argues there is a *temporary* depression in expenditures on domestic goods and imports, generating a *temporary* trade surplus, paid for by international money associated with an increase in domestic money. This analysis is probably correct. But *at equilibrium* (the only situation with which his model can deal) there is no surplus. Analysis of the dynamics of adjustment would probably generate McKinnon's verbal result, but the model does not. Other instances might be cited.

It may well be asked, more fundamentally, whether all external and internal imbalances, properly viewed, are not the result of disequilibrium. The one "equilibrium imbalance" McKinnon finds is when a government's deficit is offset by a payments balance deficit—surely not tenable in the long run. If external and internal imbalance can only exist in disequilibrium, the dynamic adjustment mechanism may well be the appropriate focus of investigation. It may be that static stability and the correspondence principle are all that need be invoked.

While the comparison-of-equilibria method of analysis could conceivably handle a shift in preferences among assets, it is doubtful whether a shift in the desired income-wealth ratio, or an increase in permanent income with a consequent desire for more assets can be handled within this framework. The rate of adjustment to the desired asset position would be the critical variable in determining saving. In this case, the time path of adjustment is probably the appropriate focus of inquiry. It is difficult to see how the McKinnon model, even extended to handle neo-classical growth equilibrium, can handle the question in a framework satisfactory for analysis of external and internal imbalance.

As the model presently stands, it is manifestly short-run in nature, as McKinnon recognizes. He explicitly points this out in introducing his model. That in itself is sufficient to indicate that the comparative statics approach within a general equilibrium framework is inadequate to handle the problem of adjustment to new desired wealth levels associated with income changes.

Along the same line, it has long since been recognized that adjustment in the financial markets is probably more rapid than adjustments in the commodity market. Use of McKinnon's model with varying rates of adjustment in the different markets might yield some important insights into the nature of external and internal imbalances and alternative adjustment mechanisms. But this again is outside the comparative statics general equilibrium framework.

Let me now turn to the usefulness of McKinnon's model in providing additional insight into the assignment problem. To date, all discussions of the problem have been explicitly short-run in nature. The standard assignments of monetary policy for external imbalance and fiscal policy for internal imbalance must be so, for, with a constant trade deficit, it is manifestly impossible for a country to attract more and more short-term capital without incurring an ever-increasing volume of interest obligations. No one is prepared to say that, period after period, the rest of the world will keep supplying a constant flow of capital to a deficit country while its ability to repay is unchanged. Indeed, even if the rest of the world could continue to supply fresh capital, the deficit would increase simply because of interest payments.

McKinnon's model, as it now stands, remains short-run. The price level is fixed, assets valuation is independent of the interest rate, income does not vary with changes in the community's stock of outside or foreign assets. McKinnon's ambition to extend the model to cover growth situations may enable him to handle these problems as well as many others. What, for example, is the effect on income of government open market operations? Surely interest-earnings on bonds must be considered. The wealth-income link does not exist in McKinnon's model, and yet is surely important for analysis of portfolio considerations.

To the extent that McKinnon generates different substantive results than those of the standard assignments, they stem from the assumed difference in absolute magnitude between $\partial B/\partial i$ and $\partial M/\partial i$, i.e., between the interest sensitivity of bond- and money-holdings. This difference in turn generates a differential effect on the system between changes in inside money and changes in outside money. It will remain to the econometricians to prove whether there is a significant difference. This armchair empiricist is somewhat skeptical and remains to be convinced.

These limitations of the general equilibrium approach should not be interpreted to detract from McKinnon's contribution. Rather, portfolio-balance considerations are worthy of considerable exploration, and may be a promising tool to deal with questions other than the assignment problem. One such question that comes to mind is the "liquidity problem."

It is frequently assumed that the "liquidity problem" could not exist under flexible exchange rates. If "liquidity" is defined as official holdings of reserves, this is true. But, if the demand for international liquidity is defined as private plus official demand, the results could be quite different. With no official intervention under flexible rates, individuals' portfolio considerations might induce them to wish to hold more foreign currency than under fixed rates. Speculators' demand for stocks of various foreign currencies would increase. Their additional demand plus private individuals' increased demand under flexible rates might be greater than official demand under fixed rates.

Portfolio considerations might also be used to estimate demand for official holdings of reserves. Most discussions of official demand for reserves seem to treat the demand either as irrational, necessary for transactions purposes, or alternatively as a method of buying time to make adjustments to shifts in a country's international payments position. A portfolio approach might suggest that governments perform an insurance function for the private sector in holding reserves of foreign currencies.

In summary, McKinnon has performed a great service in raising portfolio-balance considerations in the analysis of international payments problems. While the model in its present form cannot be relied upon to resolve many problems of the international monetary system, it offers a new approach and one worth further development.

COMMENT: "PORTFOLIO BALANCE AND INTERNATIONAL PAYMENTS ADJUSTMENT"

Ronald W. Jones

I shall restrict my remarks to the paper presented by Professor McKinnon. In particular I wish to concentrate upon the structure of his model instead of the various results he obtains that are of interest to trade theory.

His model is interesting and deceptively simple. Three types of assets are involved: money, bonds, and real assets. The crucial relationship is the demand equation for each type of asset. In his own words, "The desired level of each stock will depend on income flow and the rate of interest." In equilibrium the desired level for each stock is equated to the actual existing level of that stock. Invoking Walras' law, McKinnon concentrates only on the two equilibrium-stock conditions involving money and bonds.

In a closed model (no trade), these two conditions suffice to determine equilibrium levels of income and the rate of interest once the stock of money and bonds is given. The situation is slightly more complicated in an open model. Consider just the case in which the exchange rate is fixed and international capital is immobile (i.e., domestic bonds are not acquired by foreigners, and vice versa). Suppose the demand for imports is proportional to the level of income, and that the level of exports is given (since the exchange rate is fixed). For a full equilibrium (with portfolio balance), argues McKinnon, the *trade* account must be in balance or else the money supply would be changing. This determines the equilibrium level of income, and the bond equation determines the rate of interest that must prevail at this equilibrium level of income in order to clear the bond market. Of course the demand for money is also determined. If this does not equal the initial domestic stock of money, temporary balance-of-trade deficits or surpluses will have produced the required change in the money supply.

This is all quite simple and neat. Before discussing the crucial behavioral stock-demand relationship underlying the results, I wish to comment upon several other aspects of his model.

In order to analyze a stationary economy and not get involved with phenomena associated with growth, McKinnon wants net savings and

251

investment zero in the equilibrium position. But he wishes to retain "all the key Keynesian concepts such as a positive *marginal* propensity to save." This could be achieved by positing the usual kind of Keynesian savings function and have other relationships (e.g., zero net-investment functions) such that equilibrium takes place where the positively sloping savings schedule crosses the income axis. More leeway could be provided in an open economy, where savings or dis-savings at home would be matched by dis-savings or savings abroad of an equivalent amount. McKinnon chooses a different procedure. The level of income is not the prime determinant of savings. Rather, the existence of savings is an indication of an imbalance between *desired* holdings of wealth in various forms and *actual* levels. That is, savings reflect a *dis*equilibrium state of affairs, and return to the zero level once the desired target wealth level is achieved. However, McKinnon's analysis then leaves open a question of considerable importance for "dynamic" analysis: What determines the rate at which people wish to save, i.e., to make up the difference between desired and actual asset-holdings?

On the expenditure side McKinnon groups together *ex ante* consumption and investment in inventory accumulation in his E-function. (In equilibrium, by assumption, net investment is zero so that E is equal to consumption. And consumption, in turn, equals income.) He makes a point of arguing that the components of wealth, M (money), B (bonds), and K (real assets), must appear separately as arguments in the expenditure function. For example, an increase in M would presumably cause E to rise while an increase in K, by temporarily yielding a position where more goods are held than desired, would cause a reduction in E. However, I think that to leave the argument at this stage unduly complicates matters. What is at issue is the distinction between *total* demand and *excess* demand. In the standard theory of demand and exchange (e.g., as in Walras), total demand for any commodity depends upon prices and the *value* of the commodity endowment. The *composition* of that endowment enters as an argument only in excess-demand functions. But it appears in a simple fashion—by subtraction of the initial holdings from total demand. I would argue that the same kind of thing can be done in McKinnon's model, thus consolidating some of the arguments in the expenditure function.

In introducing his paper, McKinnon claims that, "for questions of short-period stability, the Keynesian 'fixed price' model is appropriate." It seems somewhat curious to me that this "short-period" model is one in which income levels adjust to asset positions. The comparative statics results obtained in McKinnon's paper all relate to positions of full equilibrium where desired and actual asset-holding are in balance and savings have been wiped out. For example, despite the early discussion of the expenditure function, it never has a role to play in the comparative statics results. The point is that considerable time might be required to reach such equilibrium states.

Quite aside from the question of timing is the question of the specification of the asset-demand equations that are basic to his model. Whereas, in the expenditure function, McKinnon argues for the inclusion of all the individual asset stocks as arguments, in the asset-demand equations he goes to the opposite extreme and argues that none should appear. The demand for each type of asset depends only upon the rate of interest and the level of income. This allows for an extremely simple development of the model, and I think it is a position that can be supported. However, I would argue that an alternative line of development might reveal more clearly the basic nature of the model. To see that such an alternative might be useful, just consider two situations in which the rate of interest and the level of income are comparable but the initial asset-holdings are not. For example, let the stock of M in the second situation be much larger than in the first. According to the McKinnon formulation the "demand" for each type of asset would appear to be the same in the two situations whereas it might seem more plausible to argue that the "demand" for each type of asset would be greater in the second situation.

As an alternative consider introducing actual wealth, W (equal to $M + B + K$), into the demand equation for each type of asset. This admittedly destroys the simple form of his relationships and, in a closed model, makes it impossible to use just the demand equation for money and bonds to solve for equilibrium Y and i if the supply of money and bonds is given. An additional variable, W (or K, if B and M are given), is introduced. But I would also suggest a new relationship, which, I believe, serves to capture the spirit of McKinnon's model. Let desired wealth depend upon the level of income and the rate of interest, and, in equilibrium, be equal to actual wealth. The basic equilibrium stock conditions could be written as:

$$M^*(i, Y, W) = M \tag{1}$$
$$B^*(i, Y, W) = B \tag{2}$$
$$K^*(i, Y, W) = K \tag{3}$$
$$\tilde{W}(i, Y) = W \tag{4}$$
$$W = M + B + K. \tag{5}$$

The first three equations involve "demands" for the three types of assets. The forms of the demand functions are constrained by the requirement that M^*, B^*, and K^* always add to existing wealth, W. That is, Walras' law applies to the stock demand-supply equations so that, say, given the first two equations, the third is redundant. For any existing aggregate wealth level, the demand functions specify how the *composition* of that wealth is affected by the interest rate and the level of income.

The fourth equation suggests that for any interest rate and income level (where expectations are that they will continue, as in McKinnon), there is associated a desired level of wealth ($\tilde{W}$). That is, the question of the desired *level* of aggregate wealth is separated from the question of the desired *composition* of any *given* level of wealth. Full equilibrium is attained when all equations are satisfied. For comparing states of full equilibrium it would be easier to work with the set of three equations (1), (2), and (4) to solve for i, Y, and W given M and B as parameters. Equation (5) could be used to determine K, and equation (3) is redundant.

I would argue that it is interesting to distinguish between full equilibrium and a state of "partial" equilibrium in which the "composition" equations, (1)–(3), are satisfied but the "level" equation, (4), is not. That is, it may take considerable time for the community to accumulate sufficiently to bring actual wealth, W, up to the level of desired wealth, $\tilde{W}$, whereas income levels and the rate of interest may be close to clearing existing asset markets. If so, an explicit adjustment relationship of the form (6) could be substituted for (4),

$$\frac{dW}{dt} = f[\tilde{W}(i, Y) - W],\tag{6}$$

and the path to full equilibrium, in which target wealth levels are reached and savings wiped out, could be explored. It seems reasonable to require $f(x)$ to have the same sign as x, and more detailed specification of the function involves saying something about the rate at which the community wishes to save to achieve targets. Of course the "composition" equations, (1–3), as well as (4), may not be satisfied. In this case adjustment equations, much like (6), need to be added. In particular, it may be more reasonable to suppose rapid adjustment in the rate of interest than in the level of income.

For states of full equilibrium this system reduces to McKinnon's two equations in money and bonds as functions only of i and Y—by substituting $\tilde{W}$ for W in (1) and (2). For example, consider the effect on the demand for money of an increase in the level of income at a constant rate of interest. From his equation (1.2) this is $\partial L/\partial Y$. From (1) and (4) above this is expressed by

$$\frac{\partial M^*}{\partial Y} + \frac{\partial M^*}{\partial W} \cdot \frac{\partial \tilde{W}}{\partial Y}.$$

The first term is presumably positive, expressing, say, an increased demand for money for transactions purposes if Y rises and the interest rate and actual wealth remain constant. But as Y rises the desired wealth level presumably also rises, as given by $\partial \tilde{W}/\partial Y$. This, in turn, would normally lead to an increased demand for all forms of wealth, including money, at a constant rate of interest *if* actual wealth rises (via savings out of income for some period of time) to the new level of desired wealth, as shown by (4). These are the factors that are buried in McKinnon's $\partial L/\partial Y$ term. For states of "partial" equilibrium, the term $\partial \tilde{W}/\partial Y$ would have to be modified by $dW/d\tilde{W}$ as determined by (6) in order to specify, for any particular passage of time (in which i remains constant) how the demand for money has been affected by the increase in Y.

A final word about Walras' law is in order. Whereas the demand functions for assets that I have introduced in (1–3) are constructed such that $M^* + B^* + K^*$ equals W (equals $M + B + K$), the same is *not* generally true of McKinnon's $L(i, Y) + R(i, Y) + C(i, Y)$. This latter sum is what I have called $\tilde{W}$, and unless (4) is satisfied this does not equal $M + B + K$. Is the discrepancy between aggregate target asset, $L + R + C$, and actual $M + B + K$ always equal to the difference between income and expenditure? This is what McKinnon suggests in his remarks on Walras' law. And yet this need not be the case. The difference between $(L + R + C)$ and $(M + B + K)$ reflects the *total* future accumulation planned by the economy (assuming i and Y, and expectations as to the constancy of i and Y, remain unchanged). If individuals do not plan to hit targets in one period, this difference will not equal income minus consumption for that period, much less McKinnon's income minus expenditures (which include intended investment). But there *is* a relationship among his demand-supply relationships for money, (1.2), and for bonds, (1.3), and the discrepancy between Y and E. If McKinnon's demand for money, L, is in balance with the stock of money, and if his demand for bonds, R, equals the supply, B, then income, Y, must equal expenditure, E. For the latter represents consumption plus planned accumulation *in the form of real capital assets*. Since Y always equals consumption plus savings, and by assumption all savings are directed toward the accumulation of real capital assets (money and bond markets being cleared), Y must equal E.[1]

Whatever form the model takes, two important questions need more discussion than is given here: (1) What is the nature of the relationship between target asset levels (individually or aggregated) on the one hand and income levels and the rate of interest on the other? and (2) What determines the rate at which accumulation to hit targets takes place?

1. I am indebted to my colleague, Hugh Rose, for this latter point. Note, however, that if money and bond markets are not cleared—McKinnon's (1.2) and (1.3) not satisfied—there is no necessity for the excess or shortfall to be matched exactly by $Y - E$, for more than one period may be required to hit targets.

SUMMARY OF DISCUSSION

I

Professor McKinnon emphasized five points in replying to the comments by Professors Krueger and Jones. First, there is the question of why foreign securities and foreign money do not appear in McKinnon's open economy equilibrium conditions. The answer here is simplicity. For this question does not arise in the two extreme cases of perfect capital mobility and complete capital immobility. Under perfect capital mobility, foreign and domestic securities do not have to be differentiated; under capital immobility, a wealth-owner has the option of holding domestic securities only. If it is possible, and McKinnon thinks it is, to infer from these two extreme cases what would happen under partial capital mobility, the added complications of having to introduce a foreign security and interest rate into the model may not be warranted.

Second, McKinnon would agree that his mathematics are confined to writing down equilibrium conditions whereas dynamic aspects of the adjustment process are only described verbally in his paper. Thus, although his equilibrium conditions always specify equilibrium in the balance of trade, it is clear that, in the process of getting to an equilibrium, the balance of trade may become positive or negative. In particular, an exogenous rise in exports would entail an initial balance-of-trade surplus. The surplus, in turn, means that domestic nationals are accumulating financial assets and a dynamic adjustment process is set off which bids-up the demand for commodities and imports until trade-balance equilibrium is restored. Although McKinnon agrees that he has simply written down the final equilibrium conditions and not the dynamic adjustment processes, the latter seem to be visible, or easy, enough to understand once they are suggested.

Third, McKinnon would not argue that governments could forever run an unbalanced portfolio position. Nevertheless, it is useful to distinguish between a sector which does strictly maintain portfolio balance, the private sector (or in some cases state or local governments), and a

257

sector which does, at least to some extent, use "*conscious* fiscal policy," that is, does not worry about portfolio balance in its own position. Of course, conscious fiscal policy has an effect on foreign exchange reserves, and this puts a severe limit to the extent to which governments can ignore the problem of portfolio balance.

Fourth, there is an issue which seems to disturb both Professors Jones and Krueger; and that is the time horizon which is operative in McKinnon's model. Economists have been conditioned to think of asset choices as involving a long-run time horizon. This view is often incorrect. Doubling everybody's money balances tomorrow will certainly have an immediate and substantial effect on spending decisions. It is precisely because changes in certain kinds of asset-holdings, inventories, consumer durables, and so on, have immediate and substantial effects on people's spending decisions that McKinnon would not be ready to rely upon traditional analysis. In spite of the difficulties of specifying speeds of adjustment exactly, McKinnon would not consider his model as a very long-run one and would not grant that one can ignore the effects of asset accumulation over the short run.

The fifth and last point concerns an issue raised by Ronald Jones: Is McKinnon justified in leaving out assets as arguments, even in aggregated form, of the stock demand functions for assets—in contrast to the flow condition of the model where the level of assets is very important? McKinnon would argue that his procedure is a legitimate one, particularly in the framework of a stationary-state model. For, if people really take their current level of income as fixed, do not expect the interest rate to change in the future, and are free to adjust their stocks of individual assets as they please, existing stocks will not determine their eventual desired stock-holdings. This seems to be a logically consistent position though it should not be taken as an empirical judgment about the world. On the other hand, when considering flow conditions and intended rates of expenditure over a given interval of time, it is indeed correct to state that stocks must enter, and enter in a disaggregated form, as in McKinnon's model. It is possible but not likely that this asymmetry of the model in its treatment of stock and flow conditions would disappear in the context of a full model of growth equilibrium. Such a model would require stock and flow conditions for both the bond and money market as well as for the commodity market. Each of these conditions would have wealth in disaggregated form as an argument. The rate at which one tries to get rid of money balances at any point of time would depend on one's existing money stock, bond stock, and commodity stock. However, even in such a growth model and certainly in a stationary-state model, the target level of stock holdings vis-à-vis income flows could still be independent of existing stocks.

Professor Sohmen expressed broad agreement with Professor Cooper's characterization of the assignment problem and of his position. In addition, Sohmen would emphasize again the importance of considering the balance of trade as a policy target in addition to the balance of payments in particular with respect to the welfare implications of monetary systems. Turning to Salin's comments, Sohmen argued that the conclusions on whether fiscal and/or monetary policy are ineffective in certain systems depend of course on the assumptions used. If one uses the assumptions of Mundell's models with respect to capital mobility and the smallness of the country under consideration, the interest rate is exogenously given; then it follows necessarily that fiscal policy is ineffective under flexible exchange rates and effective under a fixed exchange-rate system. Obviously such assumptions are unrealistic and different results follow when they are loosened.[1] For instance, by relaxing the assumption that the interest rate is exogenously determined, monetary policy can be made to affect the level of income even under fixed exchange rates. In that case the assignment problem is not quite as clear-cut.

Sohmen then turned to the problem of whether a country should adopt fixed or flexible exchange rates. In Salin's work[2] and in the Mundell article on which it is based,[3] this choice depends on the degree of capital mobility. Take Mundell's diagrammatic analysis; changes in interest rates are plotted against changes in the terms of trade (the latter being due either to changes in the exchange rate or in domestic price levels under fixed exchange rates). Then there is one locus of points associating values of the terms of trade with interest rates along which there is full employment and another one along which there is balance-of-payments equilibrium. The economy is in over-all equilibrium at the intersection of these two curves. Mundell considers the directness of approach to equilibrium under alternative exchange-rate regimes and concludes, for example, that, when capital movements respond very readily to interest-rate changes, a system of fixed exchange rates is

---

1. See Egon Sohmen, "Fiscal and Monetary Policies under Alternative Exchange-Rate Systems," *Quarterly Journal of Economics*, 81 (1967): 515–23.

2. Pascal Salin, "La Controverse des Changes Flexibles et le Problème de l'Equilibre Simultané Interne et Externe," *Economia Internazionale*, 18, nos. 3, 4 (August and November, 1965).

3. Robert A. Mundell, "The Monetary Dynamics of International Adjustment under Fixed and Flexible Exchange Rates," *The Quarterly Journal of Economics*, 74, no. 2 (May, 1960): 227–57.

preferable because it leads to equilibrium more directly (without oscillations). On the other hand, if capital mobility is weak, flexible exchange rates would be more appropriate. Sohmen would object to this line of analysis on the grounds that it is not so much the directness or cyclicity of the approach to equilibrium that is important, but the speed of response of the system. In some cases, one may have cycles for a week or two and then get reasonably close to equilibrium; in others, there may be a direct approach to equilibrium but it may take fifteen years of unemployment to get there. Changing the terms of trade under fixed exchange rates is a very laborious process since it requires adjustment of the whole domestic price level; on the other hand, the required change in the terms of trade under flexible exchange rates may come about in a few hours. Therefore, the speed with which various instrument variables can be changed is an important criterion in judging the relative efficiency of alternative monetary systems.

Finally, Sohmen disagreed with Mundell's conclusion (in "The Monetary Dynamics...") that a cyclical approach to equilibrium is possible under flexible exchange rates even if capital is perfectly mobile, implying a horizontal foreign-balance curve. For, under flexible exchange rates, the speed of response of the foreign exchange market is almost infinite and cycles would be ruled out. As a general proposition, Sohmen would think that under flexible exchange rates and in the absence of government intervention there would be an almost direct approach to equilibrium along the foreign-balance curve.

II

Professor Krueger opened the discussion from the floor by taking issue with Sohmen's view that there may be a contradiction between the policy recommendations resulting from an analysis of the "assignment problem" and the desire to have developed countries engaging in capital exports. Sohmen seems to argue that if monetary policy is used to correct a balance-of-payments deficit, say, in the United States, a net capital import will ensue. This does not follow from the assignment-problem analysis. One could, for instance, well imagine the United States as a large net capital exporter; as a consequence the United States may well have a deficit "below the line" in spite of its large trade surplus. If the United States could not or did not want to finance this deficit with gold, they could increase the inflow of short-term capital and yet be left with a net outflow of capital—though a smaller one.

Professor Sohmen agreed that one might want to distinguish between the flow of long- and short-term capital and that one may be compensated by the other without any change in the trade balance. What Sohmen had in mind, however, was that, if the assignment analysis calls for an expansionary *fiscal* policy, the balance of trade will tend to deteriorate. For instance, had the United States really adopted a mix of expansionary fiscal policy and tightening monetary policy a few years ago in order to maintain internal and external balance, the outcome would probably have been a substantial deterioration of the trade balance and not just a compensation of short-term and long-term flows within the capital account. The most advanced country in the world should not, in Sohmen's view, have substantial trade deficits nor, for that matter, aim at substantial reductions in the usual level of trade surpluses for any length of time.

The discussion focused, next, on Sohmen's assertion that, under flexible exchange rates, the approach toward equilibrium would be direct, or at least extremely rapid. *M. Salin* questioned the view that under flexible exchange rates the approach to equilibrium would take place along a *given* foreign balance line. For it is necessary to distinguish between short-run and long-run equilibria, and between *ex ante* and *ex post* magnitudes. It is true that one may always be on the foreign-balance curve which is a short-run curve. In the long run, however, this curve rises (or falls) and, though there may always be equilibrium along it at any point of time, this is only *ex post* equilibrium. Yet, from the point of view of cycles or speed of approach to equilibrium, it is how fast actual equilibrium approaches long-run or *ex ante* equilibrium which is significant. This means that the return of balance-of-payments equilibrium may take a very long time even under flexible exchange rates.

Professor Sohmen disagreed. Balance-of-*payments* equilibrium under flexible exchange rates is achieved almost instantaneously, though balance-of-*trade* equilibrium may indeed take a long time to achieve. In fact, in the mathematical system that underlies Mundell's diagrammatic analysis, you do not get any oscillations at all if you assume the speed of response in the foreign exchange market to be infinite. Therefore, with flexible exchange rates, whatever the disturbance to the system, it is possible to achieve interest rate changes and any necessary change in the terms of trade immediately because the exchange market reacts instantaneously.

Professor Mundell pointed out that Sohmen's argument laid bare an important problem. For, if one assumes simultaneously perfect capital mobility, *and* flexible exchange rates, *and* an infinite speed of adjustment in the foreign exchange market, the system can never be out of equilibrium. The economic meaning of a system which can never be out of equilibrium is not clear at all. Of course the balance of payments defined by the change in official exchange reserves must always be in equilibrium in a flexible exchange-rate system in which there are no official exchange reserves. In that sense Sohmen's argument is correct; but the discussion so far makes it clear that it is vital to make a distinction between the different time periods which are involved. This point was raised by Salin and comes up very clearly in the discussion of McKinnon's paper. In the short run under flexible exchange rates, the hour-to-hour, or minute-to-minute, fluctuations in the exchange rate can only result in disequilibrium in people's portfolios. Then there is another time period in which prices in commodity and bond markets are adjusted. In Mundell's view, the discussion between Salin and Sohmen makes it clear that the analytical models used so far are too simple to achieve a refined analysis of these dynamic problems. The particular ingredients of the bond and the money markets (the portfolio market if you wish) should be put into the model explicitly.

Professor Sohmen asked whether, in view of this, Mundell would still adhere to the policy conclusions he drew in his 1960 article. *Professor Haberler*, as chairman of the session, thought that it was time for Mundell to say a few words since he, after all, had started all these hares which participants had been chasing around in circles.

Professor Mundell stated that he seemed to have created a lot of trouble by using, in his early papers, a definition of monetary policy that he no longer liked or accepted. He used the traditional Keynesian concept of monetary policy as involving the interest rate. In working through some of the dynamic problems of adjustment, he made the assumption that bank-rate adjustment was the instrument of monetary policy and stated that the money supply had to be adjusted to make that rate effective in the market. While at the International Monetary Fund, he worked on the problem of whether monetary and fiscal policy should be used for internal or external balance, a problem currently discussed at the Fund. That was the origin of the crossing scissors device and of the monetary-fiscal policy mix. That, however, left many people unconvinced.

In order to make the point very clear, Mundell then made the stronger assumption of perfect capital mobility. As a result, instead of saying that interest-rate policy has to be used for external rather than internal policy, it became possible to say that under fixed exchange rates interest rate or monetary policy had no effect whatsoever on internal balance in the domestic economy. However, Marcus Fleming at that time had written an important paper on the internal-external balance problem; in that paper, he uses a change in the money supply as his definition of a change in monetary policy. And he came up with the Keynesian conclusion that an expansionary fiscal policy may improve external balance if capital is sufficiently mobile. This ambiguity in Fleming's conclusion led Fleming to wonder if defining monetary policy as interest-rate policy *à la* early Mundell might not be preferable. To Mundell neither definition was acceptable; interest-rate policy did not mean much in a world of capital mobility; nor could the central bank control the stock of money under capital mobility. Under perfect capital mobility, it became necessary to define monetary policy as changes in the portfolio of the central bank since a country cannot fix the interest rate nor determine the money supply exogenously. An open market operation is monetary policy and whether that changes the money supply depends on the balance of payments. If the central bank conducts an open market purchase and that leads to an equivalent loss of reserves there is no change in the money stock. In other words, the money supply becomes endogenously determined by the interest rate.

The main point, according to Mundell, is that looking at monetary policy as open market policy under perfect capital mobility leads to quite different conclusions than looking at it as interest-rate policy under capital immobility. This suggested to Mundell that there was something wrong with the basic Keynesian framework on which the analysis, under either capital-mobility assumption, was based. For capital mobility should not make that much difference to the choice of monetary or fiscal policy.

There are at least three defects in the basic Keynesian framework. The first concerns the fact that the effect of investment cannot be considered of the "second order of smalls." That point was discussed by McKinnon in his paper; he also uncovered the second defect, one which relates to the *IS* curve. The Hicksian interpretation of the Keynesian system is incorrect. For equilibrium in the commodity market is not determined by the intersection of the saving and investment schedule but by the demand for and supply of the stock of commodities. The investment schedule in the Keynesian system, Mundell stated, determines the demand for and supply of the stock of commodities and is itself a full general equilibrium curve. Therefore, equilibrium in a Keynesian-type model is not given by the intersection of an *IS* and an *LM* curve, but of an *LM* curve and the investment schedule itself. This determines the level of income. The amount of savings or the consumption function do not enter directly at all. The proportion of income saved determines the rate of growth of the system, not the level of income. A third defect in the Keynesian system concerns the interdependence of the curves used in traditional analysis since any excess supply of money *ipso facto* affects the excess demand for goods and therefore the position of the *IS* schedule. There are thus, according to Mundell, many defects in the basic Keynesian models he used to reach his conclusions, and Sohmen may well question the validity of policy conclusions derived from faulty models. In fact, however, it turns out that these models, under perfect capital mobility, yield classical conclusions and are more or less immune to the defects that originally existed in the Keynesian model. For instance, a doubling of the money supply under flexible exchange rates and perfect capital mobility doubles money income. This is a perfectly classical conclusion derived from a purely Keynesian model and is identical to the conclusion which can be derived from the model used by Hume, or models devised by Robert Triffin and J. J. Polak.

Thinking of this problem in the more general terms of the assignment problem, or the principle of effective market classification, yields a very natural conclusion. Under flexible exchange rates the exchange rate—the price of a currency—will be determined by the excess demand or supply of that currency in world markets. The excess demand and supply of money does not determine the interest rate. In the world market, it is bundles of currencies which are traded against each other; and the exchange rate equates the demand and supply of these currencies. Under fixed exchange rates, on the other hand, it is possible to apply the Leontief-Hicks principle of composite commodities; the supply of money has to be adjusted in order to keep one currency convertible into another at a fixed rate. Again, the principle of market classification can be applied and leads to the question: What, under fixed exchange rates, is most effective in changing an excess supply of money? The answer is simply the money supply itself.

As a consequence, Mundell would now extend the validity of his results beyond the case of perfect capital mobility. Whether there is capital mobility or not, as long as exchange rates are fixed, the proper role of the monetary authority is to adjust the money supply until people want to hold the stock of money that is compatible with equilibrium in the given exchange rate. That is, the conclusion that monetary policy has to be used for external balance under fixed exchange rates is independent of the question of capital mobility.

To illustrate, United States experience makes it clear that it does not matter what individual selective controls are imposed except insofar as these controls alter the excess supply of money. If people do not want to hold the additional quantity of money that is supplied by increases in the domestic assets of the banking system, reserves will flow out and the money stock will adjust. The policy conclusions, if not the analysis that led to them, stand reinforced. Obviously the concept of portfolio balance is important to the analysis of the assignment problem. Ultimately it is portfolio balance, including the central bank's portfolio, which determines the speed of adjustment in the system. And this is why McKinnon's paper really does bear on the question of speeds of adjustment even if it does not bear the "speed of adjustment" title which Mundell originally suggested.

At this point, *Professor Haberler* brought the session to a close. As he put it, the hares that were being chased around in the session managed to breed during the chase—which bears the promise of many future hunts.

PART 5

THE SEIGNIORAGE PROBLEM AND
INTERNATIONAL LIQUIDITY

THE DISTRIBUTION OF SEIGNIORAGE FROM INTERNATIONAL LIQUIDITY CREATION

Herbert G. Grubel

While Webster's dictionary defines seigniorage as the difference between the circulation value of a coin and the cost of bullion and the minting, for the purposes of this paper I generalize the meaning of the term seigniorage and redefine it as the net value of resources accruing to the issuer of money.

All world monetary reform plans which envisage the creation of fiat money through some supranational agency have to face the problem of how to distribute the seigniorage to which their operations give rise. In this paper I discuss some theoretical and practical issues surrounding the nature of seigniorage, which enable me to classify existing plans for monetary reform on the basis of some criteria to be developed. The paper closes with the description of a scheme for distributing newly created reserves which incorporates some insights gained by the preceding analysis.

In order to focus exclusively on the problem of seigniorage I assume that a supranational bank has been formed which issues liabilities, acceptable to all countries in the settlement of debts, that agreements on the rate of growth in liabilities, on the role of gold, and on other critical points have been reached. At the appropriate place in the analysis I shall introduce assumptions about the operations of the bank, whenever they have a bearing on the problem of seigniorage.

I

Seigniorage arises because of two special characteristics of money. First, money serves as a store of liquid wealth and as a medium for making efficient transactions in the course of everyday business. Economic units acquire these services of money by surrendering assets in the same way

This paper was written while I held a summer appointment at the University of Chicago with the Rockefeller Foundation research project in international economics which was directed by Harry G. Johnson. The analysis has benefited from comments made by participants at the Chicago Conference on International Monetary Problems, Harry G. Johnson, Max Corden, and especially Wilson Schmidt. I also acknowledge the helpful comments Arthur Freedman and Hans Stoll made on an earlier version of the paper.

they purchase the services of houses, common stocks, and life insurance contracts. Money, once added to portfolios in this fashion, is maintained as a rather constant fraction of wealth, circulates in only slowly changing payments cycles, and the issuers of money never have to return the resources they obtained in the initial exchange. Whenever wealth and income are growing, the public constantly adds to its money holdings and to the resources held by the money-issuers.

Second, money is what society wants it to be: precious metals, stones, coins, paper currency, demand deposits, savings accounts, negotiable paper, etc. Any of these instruments can serve the purposes of money as a medium of exchange and store of wealth if the proper social and economic institutions and conventions exist.

However, the amount of seigniorage arising from the issue of each of these kinds of money varies and depends on the cost of producing the money and the services or interest payments attached to it. Ultimately, as will be seen shortly, the size of seigniorage depends on the monopoly position of the money-issuing institution.

Under conditions of perfect competition and free entry, as one would expect to prevail in the production of commodity money, such as gold, seashells, or cows, the mining, collecting or production of money requires resources which in equilibrium are worth as much as they bring in the market place, permitting only normal returns and no seigniorage to the entrepreneur.

Even in the classical case of seigniorage—the minting of coin from precious metals—the profits a sovereign could obtain through this activity were strictly limited. Silver and gold bullion were an effective substitute for minted coins and limited the sovereign's monopoly power over the provision of a circulating medium and store of wealth. Thus, when a sovereign would try to issue coin with a metal-value content too far below its face value, the market would accept it only at a discounted value. Forcing the acceptance of that kind of money in settlement of private or government debt would yield a net revenue to the sovereign, but it would be more appropriate to call this a tax rather than seigniorage. In the long run, the difference between the metal value of coins and their face value could only be equal to the value of the convenience provided by having bullion of guaranteed weight and fineness available for transactions.

The low cost of production of paper money and checking-account services appears to present the greatest opportunity for someone to earn large seigniorage. However, here too, the existence of competition and free entry permits only normal profits to be earned in the long run. The goldsmiths are considered to have been the first issuers of paper currency in the form of deposit receipts for gold, which began to be acceptable for the settlement of debts in place of the gold itself. The legendary first goldsmith who noticed that he needed to keep only a fraction of the gold deposited with him to meet occasional demands for withdrawal obtained seigniorage in the amount of the deposits he was free to use for his own purposes. Such a lucrative business soon attracted competitors who, in order to obtain deposits of their own, began to offer inducements to the owners of gold, such as interest payments on deposits. By the normal process of competitive responses, these interest payments would ultimately become so high that the business of storing gold and issuing paper money could bring only normal returns.

In modern, institutionalized fractional-reserve banking, competition and free entry also tend to eliminate seigniorage through the provision of services and interest payments to depositors. Even in the United States, where entry is not free and interest payments on demand deposits are illegal, seigniorage gets eliminated or at least reduced substantially, by the competitive offering of services and by the development of substitutes for demand deposits, such as savings accounts, which do yield interest.

In the long run, seigniorage persists only when competition is imperfect, either through collusion or, as is most frequent, as a result of legal or constitutional arrangements. The outstanding example of the latter is, of course, the widespread constitutional monopoly of central governments over the issue of coins and paper money. The essential features of this money are the absence of very close substitutes, the non-bearing of interest, its non-convertibility, and the very low cost of production.

Central governments normally have responsibility for regulating the money supply, including the demand deposits created by the private banking system. This regulation is carried out through the medium of legal reserves, often called high-powered money. Since these required reserves also bear no interest, are non-convertible, and cost very little to bring into existence, they represent another source of seigniorage to central governments.

These points can be made somewhat more precisely by consideration of the following simplified balance sheet of an issuer of money.

Money-Issuing Institution

A		L	
Cash assets	CA	Deposits	D
Investments	I		
TOTAL ASSETS	TA	TOTAL LIABILITIES	TL

The amount of seigniorage (S) is equal to the permanent stream of income flowing from investments (I) at the market rate of return (r), minus the permanent stream of interest payments to the holder of deposits (D) at the rate (i), minus the permanent stream of real resource expenditures required to service the money obligations issued (C), all discounted at the appropriate market rates of interest. Letting subscripts refer to the relevant time periods, we have:

$$S = \frac{I_1 r_1 - D_1 i_1 - C_1}{1 + r_1} + \frac{I_2 r_2 - D_2 i_2 - C_2}{(1 + r_2)^2} + \cdots$$
$$+ \frac{I_n r_n - D_n i_n - C_n}{(1 + r_n)^n}. \tag{1}$$

Under perfect competition in the production of commodity moneys the Ir and Di elements are zero and the issuance of money involves no change in balance-sheet positions. For the first goldsmith i was zero and if his real costs, $C_1, \ldots, C_n$, were small, seigniorage came to approximately the present value of the stream of interest payments. Perfect competition and free entry tend to raise the interest payments on deposits (i) to such a level as to reduce S to zero. It is interesting to note that while U.S. banking laws prohibit the payment of interest on deposits, thus seemingly giving the banks large seigniorage, the legal requirement that banks keep a certain proportion of their assets as non-interest-bearing deposits with the central bank reduces the quantity of seigniorage. It should also be pointed out that the cost of producing and servicing money obligations takes many forms. The cash reserves which have to be maintained by most money-issuing institutions require protection, the building of safes, hiring of guards, etc. Checking accounts need to be serviced, paper money has to be replaced as it wears out and protected against counterfeiters, and so on.

It follows from this analysis of the nature of seigniorage that the amount of resources accruing to a world central bank through the issuance of international reserves depends on the degree of monopoly awarded to the institution by international agreement. The coexistence of other internationally acceptable money instruments reduces seigniorage. It also follows that if the world central bank has to pay interest to the holders of the money it has created, it will have seigniorage only to the extent to which the market rate of interest earned on its investments exceeds its operating costs and interest payments.

II

Before turning to a consideration of the alternative ways in which money-issuing institutions can distribute the seigniorage accruing to them, it may be worthwhile to try to estimate what quantities of resources are involved in such a distribution.

Assuming that the cost of producing and servicing the non-interest-bearing money issued by the U.S. federal government is zero, the cumulative total of seigniorage at the end of 1965 would have amounted to $60.9 billion.[1] In the year 1965 alone seigniorage of the federal government would have been valued at $3.3 billion. As a proportion of income, the stock of seigniorage money in existence at the end of 1965 represented approximately 10 per cent of the $570 billion of income produced in the preceding twelve months. Thus, if the high-powered money to income ratio remains constant in the future, the U.S. federal government would get seigniorage equal to a little over one-tenth of increases in real income.

As can be seen from equation (1) above, whenever $r > i$, assuming C is zero, there exists some seigniorage. The federal government issues some forms of liabilities, which are often referred to as "near-money" and which bear interest below the long-term interest rate or marginal productivity of capital. At the end of 1965 there were $67 billion of short-term Treasury bills outstanding, on which an average annual interest of approximately 4 per cent was paid. Under the assumption that there were no costs associated with servicing the "near money" and that the long-term rate of return on capital was equal to 6 per cent, seigniorage due to the stock of outstanding Treasury bills was valued at $22.2 billion.

A world central bank creating additions to international reserves on which it pays no interest and which cost nothing to produce or service would gain command over sizable resources also. Assuming that the total world reserves of $70.2 billion[2] at the end of 1965 grew at 3 per cent annually and exclusively in the form of created fiat money, the seigniorage would be $2.1 billion in 1966. In the year 2000 the addition would be $5.9 billion. Assuming 3.5 and 4.0 per cent growth rates, the seigniorage in the year 2000 would be $8.2 billion and $11.1 billion respectively.

For the world as a whole, income statistics are not reliable. However, if we assume that U.S. income is one-quarter or alternatively one-tenth of non-communist world income, then seigniorage would be 1/30 or 1/100 of increases in world income respectively, again assuming that

1. U.S. currency in circulation outside the Treasury and Federal Reserve banks plus member bank reserves with the federal reserve banks. Source: *Federal Reserve Bulletin*, vol. 52, no. 8, August, 1966, p. 1190.
2. The composition of the reserves was $41.9 billion gold, $5.4 billion reserve positions in the Fund, and $22.9 billion foreign exchange. Source: *International Financial Statistics*, vol. 9, no. 6, June, 1966.

international reserves increase proportionally with income. It may be more reasonable, however, to express world seigniorage as a proportion of world trade, which amounted to $173 billion in 1965.[3] The $70 billion reserves represent 40.5 per cent of world commerce. If reserves grow at the same rate as does trade, then seigniorage will be equal to 40.5 per cent of increases in trade. If reserves grow at half the rate at which international commerce expands, seigniorage will be equal to 20.3 per cent of the expansion.

From the earlier discussion of the nature of seigniorage it follows that these estimates of the size of resources accruing to the world central bank have to be revised downward to the extent that the bank's monopoly is imperfect and other payments media, such as gold and national currencies, continue to circulate. Thus, if increases in reserves were half-gold and half-fiat money, then seigniorage would fall from an equivalent of 20.3 per cent of increases in world trade (as computed above under one of the assumptions) to 10.1 per cent of such increases. Unless the degree of the bank's monopoly changes through time, however, the fraction remains constant. As argued above, payment of interest on the reserves created by the bank and costs of operation reduce the quantity of seigniorage.

III

The substitution of fiat for commodity money provides society with at least two important advantages. First, the growth in commodity money in the past has often been erratic, rising with new discoveries and changes in technology, and slowing down with the appearance of diminishing returns. These varying rates of growth tended to cause price instabilities, business cycles, and uneven growth rates. Fiat money, on the other hand, permits an orderly growth of money stocks and the use of monetary policy in efforts to combat business cycles. Second, fiat money frees resources which otherwise would have been devoted to the production of commodity money.

I believe that the strongest arguments in favor of establishing an international money-creating institution rest on the first advantage and only to a lesser degree on the second. The arguments for the use of conscious monetary policy for growth and stability, however, are well known and need not be discussed any further here. Instead, I turn to a brief analysis of the quantity of social savings arising from the substitution of fiat for commodity money.

3. That is, world trade excluding trade of the Sino-Soviet area, Indonesia, and Cuba; see *ibid.*

Consideration of the resources actually spent on the production of gold, the international commodity money *par excellence*, permits us to make an estimate of the savings that would have been realized if fiat money had been used in the past. Unfortunately, however, such an estimate has to be rather rough for two reasons. First, the production of gold is likely to have involved an element of rent so that the market value of gold exaggerates the true opportunity cost of the resources that went into its production. Second, the provision of fiat money itself requires resources, for which no reliable cost estimates are available.

However, assuming that the rent of gold producers in the past has been zero and that it would cost nothing to produce fiat money, then the value of the present stock of monetary gold, $42 billion, represents the maximum social savings that could have been obtained from the fiat-for-commodity money substitution. Any more precise statements will have to await further research.

The analysis of the social savings that would have been available in the past can easily be applied to derive estimates of gains that will accrue if fiat money is substituted for gold in the future. Between the end of 1958 and 1965 the world stock of monetary gold rose from $39 to $43 billion, which amounts to approximately a 1.3 per cent compound rate of increase. Projecting this growth rate into the future suggests the opportunity for a maximum saving of $1 billion of resources in the year 2000. While this figure overstates the social saving due to neglect of the rent element and cost of alternatives, the entire estimate is an understatement since it considers only official gold-holdings. Over the past seven years gold production has been nearly twice as large as the addition to monetary gold-holdings. If the official support of gold prices were abandoned, private speculative demand for gold would probably become very small and in the year 2000 the resources saved by not mining gold would most likely be well above $2 billion.

IV

Analytically, there are three basic ways in which an international institution can distribute the seigniorage it obtains through the creation of fiat money. The first method, which I propose to call the free market solution, requires that the bank pay interest on its deposit liabilities. The rate of interest is to be such that the income from the bank's investments is just used up by the cost of operating the bank (including the formation of contingency reserves) and the payments to deposit-holders. This condition has been analyzed more formally in connection with equation (1) above.

The advantage of this solution is that the international bank acts merely as a neutral financial intermediary. On the average, the holders of money get back the resources they surrendered in acquiring it, partly in the form of a stream of interest payments and partly in the form of the convenience provided by the international acceptability of the asset.

The second basic method of distributing seigniorage I shall call the central government solution since it is employed almost universally by national governments. These authorities use the resources accruing to them from the issuance of money to acquire public goods. Rational governments should set the level and pattern of their expenditures as dictated by criteria of efficiency and equity and then set tax rates such that the revenue raised, plus seigniorage, will cover the expenditure. In principle a world central bank can similarly spend the resources it acquires on world public goods, or redistribute world income. However, it faces the major obstacle of not being part of a genuine world government regularly taxing the public and spending on world-wide public goods.

The third method of distribution might be called the demand-type solution. In economic analysis this method is often referred to as "money coming as manna from heaven" or "dropping money from an airplane." It is used analytically to achieve increases in the money supply with neutral effects on resource allocation. A somewhat more precise formulation of the method is that in some way or another the long-run average balances of all money-holders are increased by the percentage by which the over-all money supply is to be increased. One can think of several logical, though not necessarily practical, ways of increasing money-holders' balances by a stated percentage: a legal re-stamping of the face value of currency or the mailing of currency after proof of average balances held. The essential feature of such schemes is that everyone should benefit from seigniorage in proportion to the average long-run demand for money. The use of the scheme assures that there will be no interpersonal transfer of resources between people as a result of the money creation per se.

As studies of the demand for money suggest, distributing seigniorage proportionally to long-run average money-holdings is neutral only under the assumption of a rather specific demand function for money. In principle, newly printed money could also be distributed proportionately to wealth—human and physical—to income, perhaps adjusted for type of occupation, or on the basis of a formula combining various elements of these criteria. It is no easy matter, of course, to devise such a formula and there may not even exist one which could do justice to the diversity of human tastes and goals. This fact, in combination with the existence of public goods as means for distributing seigniorage, explains why national governments have not in the past resorted to such methods of issuing new money. For the world monetary system, however, the formulation of distribution criteria with a neutral effect on resource transfers may be an efficient solution to the problem raised by the non-existence of a government with world-wide taxation authority.

V

We are now in the position to examine the working of the most prominent plans for a new world monetary order from the point of view of how they deal with the phenomenon of seigniorage.

A regime of perfectly flexible exchange rates eliminates the demand for international reserves, and consequently the seigniorage problem does not exist. The gold standard as advocated by Rueff and Heilperin [4] as well as the Hart-Tinbergen-Kaldor [5] plan for a commodity-reserve currency involve commodity money par excellence and therefore do not give rise to seigniorage either. The resource cost of these plans, especially the storage and spoilage of perishables under the Hart-Tinbergen-Kaldor plan, represents their most serious drawback. [6]

The gold exchange standard and any system using national moneys as reserves give all of the seigniorage to the countries issuing these currencies. This fact has been pointed out by Triffin in his first diagnosis of the gold exchange standard system, and it provides an economic rationale for the often-voiced demands that dollars and sterling be supplemented by other currencies in their role as international reserve vehicles.

It would be misleading, however, to consider that the $20 billion of outstanding dollar obligations to foreign official institutions in 1965 represent the full value of seigniorage accruing to the United States. Elsewhere I have analyzed [7] in great detail and prepared some

4. Most of the plans for monetary reform have been reprinted in H. Grubel, ed., *World Monetary Reform: Plans and Issues* (Stanford: Stanford University Press, 1963). References are to chapters in this book. Rueff: chap. 18; Heilperin: chap. 19.

5. A. G. Hart, N. Kaldor, and J. Tinbergen, *The Case for an International Reserve Currency*, UN Conference on Trade and Development, background document, E/conf. 46/P/7, Geneva, 1964.

6. See H. Grubel, "The Case against an International Commodity Reserve Currency," *Oxford Economic Papers*, vol. 17, no. 1, March, 1965.

7. H. Grubel, "The Benefits and Cost of Being the World's Banker," *National Banking Review*, vol. 2, no. 2, December, 1964.

computations showing that the U.S. interest payments on dollars held by foreigners, the need to hold more gold than a non-key-currency country and the administrative costs of providing world banking services reduce the value of the seigniorage considerably below the gross one cited above. I have argued furthermore that if the key-currency role of the dollar and responsibility for the world monetary system limit the range of economic tools available to combat U.S. cyclical and structural employment and trade imbalances in an efficient manner, then losses attributable to this limitation may by far outweigh any gains from seigniorage.

The Stamp plan[8] is an example of the central government solution. It envisages the use of the seigniorage to redistribute world income by giving the newly created world currency to the underdeveloped countries. In the first version of the plan the distribution would occur at the initiative of a world investment agency, while in the second version each country would decide by itself how much aid to give to what underdeveloped country. The size of the seigniorage is equal to the full increase in world liquidity under plan 1, since under it the holders of the investment bank's deposits receive no interest. In plan 2 Stamp suggests payment of some interest on deposits and seigniorage is reduced.

The Triffin plan is an example of the market-type solution and solves the seigniorage distribution problem through the payment of interest to deposit-holders.[9] As long as the earnings on the Triffin bank's assets are fully used up in the operation of the bank and in the distribution of interest among the holders of the international currency, there is basically no net transfer of resources among countries attributable to creation of the currency. This is true even if for some reason the bank decided to acquire all its assets through the purchase of securities in just one country, which through the financing of its deficits with the bank's currency obtained real resources from other countries. The decisive point is that the securities held by the bank require interest payments, which discounted at the market rate of interest are just equal in value to the loan itself. The nations running the trade surplus and lending to the other country similarly receive a stream of future income, which in the absence of any costs of operating the bank, would be equal to the present value of the resources transferred. The lending country's rights to future income may be worth slightly less because of the cost of operating the bank, but as a compensation for this, these rights are highly liquid. Any country which feels that it has sufficient liquid assets can, of course,

8. See M. Stamp, in Grubel, *World Monetary Reform*, chap. 3.
9. See R. Triffin, in *ibid.*, p. 39.

always stop accumulating them through appropriate balance-of-payments policies. To the extent that interest rates charged on "loans" by the Triffin and Stamp banks fail to reflect the marginal productivity of capital in the creditor countries, there will be an element of subsidy accruing to the initial recipient of the loan.

The Keynes plan [10] and other proposals to increase liquidity through the expansion of quotas essentially wish to distribute seigniorage in proportion to the individual countries' contribution to the long-run demand for reserves and therefore fall in the category of demand-type solutions. The details of the distribution formula were left open by Keynes and are settled by the Bretton Woods agreements on the size of quotas in the IMF plan. Keynes' proposals carry the added feature of requiring "creditors," that is countries accumulating bancor and lending resources to the rest of the world, to pay an interest charge of 1 per cent per annum. These interest payments make no sense from the standpoint of efficiency or equity, and they were designed to put pressures on surplus countries to adjust their payments balances. In practice they were to be used to pay the cost of operating the Keynes bank.

The multiple currency proposals of Bernstein, Lutz, Posthuma, and Roosa [11] all envisage distributing the seigniorage to the major industrial countries, essentially in proportion to their long-run demand for reserves. The details of arriving at distribution formulae are left to negotiations. It is clear that the institutionalization of such plans would result in an ultimate seigniorage-type transfer of resources from the less developed to the industrialized countries whenever the former add to their holdings of reserves.

None of the multiple currency proposals except that by Roosa envisage payment of interest on deposits of national currencies with the bank or to the holders of the new reserve asset. Roosa thinks that the bank should be paid interest, perhaps 3 per cent during conditions such as prevailed in 1965, on national currency deposits turned into internationally acceptable assets. These interest payments are considered as being a fee for making the domestic asset more liquid.[12] From the above analysis it follows, however, that such fees make no sense from the point of view of efficiency and they create an undue problem of setting the exact rate and distributing the revenue.

10. See J. Keynes, in *ibid.*, chap. 2.
11. See E. Bernstein, F. Lutz in *ibid.*, chaps. 9 and 12 respectively; R. V. Roosa, *Monetary Reform for the World Economy* (New York: Harper and Row, for the Council on Foreign Relations, 1965).
12. Roosa, *Monetary Reform.*

VI

The insights gained from the preceding analysis and my understanding of the problems of world monetary reform lead me to recommend the following system of distributing newly created reserve assets, which I think would not only be desirable but also practical.

First, instead of using national currencies as deposits with the world central bank, international reserves should be increased simply by making a bookkeeping entry. This procedure recognizes explicitly the monopoly nature of the bank and the nature of money in the economy. Little is accomplished by building an institution which caters to the lack of sophistication of the few bankers who still have not grasped the point that a bank is not a "cloakroom" as Professor Machlup has put it,[13] and does not have to hand back whatever it receives in deposit. The world's money will be what mankind makes it through a set of legal treaties, and there is no rational need for rights to convert this money into national currencies, gold, seashells, or anything else.

Second, whatever the planned rate of increase in the world's total reserve assets, they should be distributed to all national governments on the basis of a formula which reflects as closely as possible the countries' long-run demands for reserves. It will not be easy to reach agreement on such a formula, but once its key role in any reform scheme is recognized and the necessary resources are devoted to its formulation, success will ultimately be reached. Since this method distributes seigniorage without intercountry resource transfers, interest should not be paid on the part of reserve-holdings given to each country by the bank in the past. Because no payments are due, the bank has to make no investments, which in my view is a great advantage. The management of a world central bank portfolio would not only require substantial resources, it would also give the bank's managers an undesirable degree of power, since their investment decisions will have great influence on national capital markets, interest rates, and balances of payments.

The recommended distribution of seigniorage also rejects the view that the bank's activities should be linked to any world income redistribution schemes. Not only is such a package more difficult to reach agreement on, but the current world needs for liquidity and for income redistribution may well have considerably different expected lives. In the long run, income redistribution objectives may disappear, but the demand for liquidity is much more certain to remain. Given the dif-

13. F. Machlup, "The Cloakroom Rule of International Reserves," *Quarterly Journal of Economics*, vol. 79, no. 3, August, 1965.

ficulties encountered in changing human institutions, it would not be wise to plan an arrangement today which with great certainty will have to be changed in the not so distant future.

Third, countries should be free to use their reserves without limit and prior negotiations. However, whenever their holdings fall short of the cumulative total of reserves allotted to them by the bank, they will pay interest at a rate reflecting the productivity of capital in the world. The bank will redistribute the interest receipts to the countries which are in surplus.

This provision recognizes explicitly the fact that when a country runs a deficit it affects the welfare of others in the long run because it obtains real resources. The privilege to borrow is very valuable and its usefulness in meeting whatever difficulties a country faces is in no sense reduced by the contractual obligation to pay a market price for the privilege to use resources produced by others.

It should be pointed out that if interest payments are restricted to this purpose and the quantity of resource transfer is guaranteed in real terms through some price-index clause, the exact distribution of newly created assets becomes much less of a problem. If a certain country receives more assets than it truly needs in the long run, the rest of the world will not be obliged to transfer free net resources to that country when it uses its "excess" assets to finance imports, because the country will pay and the rest of the world will receive interest payments reflecting the opportunity cost of these funds.[14]

VII

Summarizing briefly, the analysis has shown that in a free market economy there exists no problem of seigniorage because the supply of money is a market activity like any other and entrepreneurs earn only normal returns. This proposition is most obvious in the case of commodity moneys, but it was also seen to apply to the minting of bullion and the issuance of paper currency. In the last case provision of services and payment of interest to the holders of the liquid assets tend to eliminate excess profits from the business of issuing these assets.

Only when institutions are able to obtain a monopoly in the production of money, which allows them to keep out of the market effective

14. This principle underlies the proposal by F. Modigliani and P. Kenen that countries be in fact free to choose their own rate of increase in international reserves, as long as they aim to hold cumulative amounts of reserves acquired in this fashion and pay interest on any shortages. See their "A Suggestion for Solving the International Liquidity Problem," *Banca Nazionale del Lavoro Quarterly Review*, no. 76, March, 1966.

substitutes and to prevent the payment of interest to holders of the money, will there be seigniorage in the long run.

Some plans for world monetary reform avoid the problem of how to distribute seigniorage by providing for flexible exchange rates or commodity money. The remaining plans envisage distribution of seigniorage in one of three ways. First, the market solution, where a world central bank invests in assets at the market rate of interest and in turn pays interest to the holders of the reserve assets. Second, the central government solution, where the resources are used to provide world public goods or to redistribute world income. And third, the demand solution, where each country receives seigniorage in proportion to the amount its long-run demand for reserves adds to the creation of the seigniorage.

If I had to cast a ballot for one of the solutions to the problem of seigniorage from a world central bank, I would vote for flexible exchange rates. Among the second-best solutions, I would prefer the demand solution for reasons presented above.

INTERNATIONAL MONETARY REFORM
AND THE DEVELOPING COUNTRIES:
A MAINLY THEORETICAL PAPER

W. M. Corden

I

From the point of view of the developing countries the main proposals for international monetary reform through the creation of additional liquidity fall under three headings. First, there are those proposals or practices, such as the Collective Reserve Unit Scheme and various "swap" arrangements, which actually exclude the developing (and some other) countries, the extra liquidity being initially distributed to a limited group of industrial countries. Secondly, there are those proposals which discriminate neither for nor against particular countries, but which would distribute the extra liquidity on some uniform principle, such as the size of IMF quotas or perhaps on the basis of balance-of-payments deficits incurred. These schemes may be regarded as neutral in their attitude to developing countries. Thirdly, there are those schemes which actually favor the developing countries by tying liquidity creation to development finance.

The interests of the developing countries seem to be plain. The first is that the advanced countries increase their own liquidity by some device or other so as to avoid a competitive scramble for reserves, world deflation, and hence an adverse movement in the prices of the developing countries' exports. The other interest of the developing countries is that out of the three types of scheme listed above the choice be the third in preference to the second or the second in preference to the first.

I do not intend in this paper to present a general review of these issues nor—heaven forbid!—a new scheme for international monetary reform to favor the developing countries. Nor do I intend to present evidence or statistical calculations for what is also rather obvious, namely, the need of the developing countries for both liquidity and development finance. A general review of the issues, a new scheme for linking liquidity creation with development finance, and evidence that the developing countries have need for liquidity and are concerned not only with

I am indebted to H. W. Arndt for helpful comments.

finance for development but also with building up their reserves, are presented in a report prepared by a group of experts appointed by UNCTAD.[1] This report sets out most of the issues affecting developing countries admirably and arrives at quite reasonable conclusions. I do not intend to duplicate this report here. Rather, I shall pursue certain of these issues rigorously—at a more theoretical level—not so much in search of new conclusions but rather in search of the precise assumptions implicit in existing conclusions. Since I have no new scheme to propose, no new facts to present, and no real disagreement with generally accepted conclusions, the value of what follows can only be in putting more precisely what is usually left to be implicit or regarded as obvious.

I am interested in three questions in this paper. The first is this: Is it really inevitable that the developing countries gain when the advanced countries create extra liquidity among themselves even though none of this extra liquidity goes to the developing countries? Precisely what mechanism do we assume? Is there not at least a possibility that the developing countries would lose if an exclusive scheme, such as the Collective Reserve Unit proposal, were adopted? In more general terms, how are outsiders affected when a group of countries get together and (in effect) provide each other with liquidity? This question is discussed in section II of this paper.

The next question is concerned with the logic of excluding some countries from international liquidity-creating arrangements. Why might an exclusive scheme, such as the Collective Reserve Unit proposal, be preferred to a universal scheme, such as one based on the size of IMF quotas? Why might Germany, say, think she would benefit from joining with Sweden or Switzerland in a mutual liquidity-creating arrangement, but not with Brazil? This is really the negative form of a positive question: What are the gains and losses to different countries from the mutual creation of extra liquidity? This is a fundamental question which underlies the issue of which countries will or should be excluded from the inner circle. It is not only a question here of whether the outsider loses from being excluded, but also whether the members of the scheme themselves lose through his exclusion. It should be mentioned here that to say that the outsider loses by being excluded is not to say that he loses by comparison with the situation where there is no liquidity-creating scheme at all. That question will be discussed in section II. It is rather to say that he would have been better off if he had

1. United Nations Conference on Trade and Development (UNCTAD), *International Monetary Issues and the Developing Countries* (New York: United Nations, 1965).

been included. This question of the gains and losses to different countries from mutual liquidity creation is discussed in section III.

These two questions would be of particular interest if international monetary reform took the form of our first type of scheme, namely one which actually excludes some or all of the developing countries, the extra liquidity being distributed to a limited group such as the Group of Ten. At the time I thought about this paper this seemed a very likely outcome of international negotiations. After the 1966 annual meeting of the board of governors of the International Monetary Fund it appears much less likely. Opinion has swung strongly toward our second type, the scheme which is as far as possible non-discriminatory between countries and which is operated not through an organization with limited membership but through the International Monetary Fund. But universality is not yet certain; it is also relevant that some countries, such as France—not to speak of communist countries—may voluntarily exclude themselves. Thus the questions are still of interest, though frankly of less immediate interest in mid-1966 than in 1965 or early 1966.

The discussion in section III leads to the more general issue of what we mean by the burden of balance-of-payments adjustment. This issue is considered in section IV. While it is certainly an important matter that calls for rigorous analysis it is only peripherally related to the main subject of this paper, namely the bearing of international monetary reform on developing countries. So section IV is a rather lengthy footnote.

Finally, in section V, I look briefly at the logic of the proposals to link liquidity creation with development finance.

II

Let us imagine a three-country world. Two of the countries enter into some kind of mutual arrangement to grant each other a given amount of liquidity. The third country is the outsider. The question is whether this third country will gain or lose from the arrangement. Call the two liquidity-creating countries *A* and *B* and let them represent the advanced countries. The third country, *C*, represents the developing countries. *C* is assumed to maintain continuous balance-of-payments equilibrium by appropriate exchange-rate adjustment. The question then really is how *C*'s terms of trade are affected by the arrangement. Assume further that in the absence of the extra liquidity both *A* and *B* try to run balance-of-payments surpluses so as to increase their reserves, but both fail. The mutual liquidity arrangement avoids this competitive scramble for reserves. Our problem then is to determine how such a scramble affects C's terms of trade. Finally, assume that the method of attempted balance-of-payments improvement which A and B use is that of deflation of expenditure. Exchange rates, tariffs, and export subsidies are held constant, and there are no quantitative import restrictions.

The analysis for this case is simple. Deflations in A and B intended to improve their balances of payments would reduce the demand for C's exports. It is assumed that the deflations would create unemployment and underutilization of capacity in A and B (which are, it must be remembered, the industrial countries) but would not significantly lower their factor prices. On the other hand the prices of C's exports are assumed to be more flexible so that in the first instance not only C's balance of payments but also its terms of trade deteriorate. C would then devalue appropriately to eliminate its balance-of-payments deficit, accompanying this with some deflation of its own to maintain internal balance. This worsens its terms of trade further. The net result is thus for C's terms of trade to deteriorate. The essential feature is that there has been a reduction in world expenditure (taking place in $A + B$) which reduces demand for the goods of $(A + B)$ and of C. In $(A + B)$ this causes unemployment and in C it lowers relative prices directly and through the exchange rate. Thus all suffer, $(A + B)$ through unemployment and C through worse terms of trade.

This seems to me a realistic story, and is the one which people usually have in mind when they say that international monetary reform is needed for the sake of the terms of trade of the developing countries. In the absence of extra liquidity, a competitive scramble for reserves, at least in mild form over a longer period, seems very likely. At present it also seems likely that deflation, or at least a significant "restraint" in fiscal and monetary policy, would be the main policy instrument in the advanced countries.

The story would be no different if an alternative or additional policy instrument in the advanced countries were restriction of imports either quantitatively or through tariffs. Provided the restriction did not discriminate in favor of the developing countries, again the demand for their exports would fall and their terms of trade would deteriorate. It is true that if they retaliated with import restrictions, instead of using the exchange rate to maintain balance-of-payments equilibrium, their terms of trade might not deteriorate. But their real incomes would still decline. And in any case it seems more sensible to assume that they are applying the optimum tariff (or import restrictions) initially and continually.

Neither would the story be different if one element in the balance-of-payments-improving policies of the advanced countries were reductions in foreign aid and investment. Again, initially the balance of payments of *C* would worsen. Finally, one could allow for effects on rates of growth. Deflation in the advanced countries is likely to reduce their rates of growth both through restriction on the supply of funds for investment and through discouraging the inducement to invest. This is likely to worsen the terms of trade of the developing countries further or to deprive them of an improvement which would otherwise have taken place (unless indeed the foregone growth of the advanced countries is heavily biased toward replacing imports from developing countries).

Is it possible to obtain a significantly different story? It is indeed possible, though I make no pretence of suggesting that the alternative stories are more realistic than the one I have just outlined. But it seems worth considering the alternatives to satisfy oneself about the main possibilities. In our story so far we have made two assumptions, namely (1) that the instruments of balance-of-payments policy in *A* and *B* would be expenditure adjustment either alone or combined with import restrictions; and (2) that in the absence of the additional liquidity there would be a competitive scramble for reserves by *A* and *B*, though their balance-of-payments situations would not actually be changing. Let us now remove assumption (1), in subsection (*i*), then remove assumption (2) in subsection (*ii*), and finally remove both together in (*iii*).

i

One possibility is that the main instruments of balance-of-payments policy are exchange rate devaluations. The scramble for reserves would then consist of competitive devaluation. In the first instance this would worsen *C*'s balance of payments, but we then assume that *C* devalues so as to restore or maintain equilibrium. The situation would be unstable, but there is no reason to suppose that *C*'s terms of trade would be affected one way or the other. *C* would lose only if there were an inconvenience in continually changing exchange rates relative to gold, or if there were some rigidity which prevented it from devaluing, so that an alternative device would have to be used, such as import restrictions, which reduced the gains from trade.[2] Another possibility—but even less

2. This must be qualified for the consequences of a real balance effect. Competitive devaluations will raise the price of gold in terms of currencies and hence raise the real value of countries' gold balances. We have then a form of general liquidity creation. The main effect would be eventually to bring the devaluations to a halt. Insofar as *C* wished to keep constant the real value of its gold reserves it would permit itself a balance-of-payments deficit for a period, thus involving improved terms of trade for it.

probable—is that A and B, in the absence of the extra liquidity, engage in competitive subsidization of their exports. This would actually improve C's terms of trade, unless C were so unwise as to attempt to restore its balance of payments by subsidizing its exports in return.

ii

Now remove the assumption that in the absence of the extra liquidity there would be a competitive scramble for reserves by A and B. Instead, assume that of the two advanced countries, B is the deficit-prone one. In the absence of the extra liquidity B would have to eliminate a deficit by some kind of adjustment. The extra liquidity makes it possible for B either to see out a temporary deficit and so avoid adjustment altogether or to postpone adjustment. We must then consider how the adjustment by B would affect C. If it affected C adversely then we can say that the extra liquidity, by avoiding or postponing adjustment, has benefited C. But we shall see that there is at least a theoretical possibility—though hardly a realistic one—that the result comes out the other way, with C actually losing from the extra liquidity. I assume now that expenditure adjustment is the only instrument of policy.

In the absence of the extra liquidity B has to reduce expenditure. Assuming internal balance initially in A and B, this creates excess unemployment in B and A. While B could do nothing about this, A could increase its expenditure sufficiently to restore internal balance within A. The reduced expenditure in B reduces the demand for C's goods and the increased expenditure in A increases demand for C's goods. Clearly the outcome depends on the relative marginal propensities to import from C. If the marginal propensity to import from C were much higher in A than in B there would be a net rise in demand for C's goods. Granting a very plausible assumption, the net result of this mechanism would be deflationary—that is, the fall in B's expenditure would be greater than the rise in A's. The assumption required is that B's marginal propensity to import from A is less than the marginal propensity of A to spend on its own goods. Suppose that the former is 20 per cent and the latter 50 per cent. If B's expenditure falls by \$100, B's demand for A's goods falls by \$20. So A has to increase expenditure by only \$40 to take up the slack of demand for its own goods. If the marginal propensity to import from C is 10 per cent in both countries, the demand for C's goods falls by \$6. Thus there is some presumption that the effect of the balance-of-payments adjustment would be adverse for C; it would be avoided only if the marginal propensity to import from C

(or to give foreign aid to *C*) were sufficiently higher in *A* than in *B*. In other words, granting expenditure variations as the method of adjustment, there is some presumption that the provision of extra liquidity would benefit *C*.

The practical question which this analysis raises is whether there is any reason to believe that the prospective deficit countries are or are not the countries with relatively high propensities to import from the developing countries or to provide foreign aid or investment. Aside from the reserve currency countries, I can see no obvious answer to this question—no presumption in fact to expect particular advanced countries rather than others to be the prospective deficit countries. The reserve currency countries are a special case. The United States is "foreign-aid prone" (at present!) and the United Kingdom has a high propensity to import from developing countries; and at the moment it is arguable that they are both deficit-prone. Would extra liquidity enable them to sustain their deficits (and thus benefit the developing countries)? On the one hand—and this is probably the main consideration—extra liquidity provided to these countries would strengthen their reserve positions and thus avoid, or at least postpone, liquidity crises and adjustment. On the other hand, extra liquidity provided to other countries makes these less dependent on the liquidity which is fed to them through reserve currency deficits. Greater pressure may be put on the United States and the United Kingdom to eliminate their deficits, perhaps by refusing to provide emergency liquidity through "swap" arrangements and the like. If this is the reaction, the developing countries could conceivably lose from arrangements which create more (permanent) liquidity all round, especially if the share of the extra liquidity going to the United States and United Kingdom is not high.

iii

There remains the case where the instruments of policy are devaluation or export subsidies and where, in the absence of extra liquidity, *B* has to eliminate a balance-of-payments deficit. To limit the taxonomy a little, I shall assume devaluation and not export subsidies. *A* and *B* can now be assumed to adjust expenditure so as to maintain internal balance. In the absence of extra liquidity *B* devalues and reduces expenditure while *A* increases expenditure. The effects of the two expenditure changes can be analyzed as before. *B*'s demand for *C*'s goods falls and *A*'s demand rises. But this time there is no net deflationary effect. If, for example, the marginal propensity to import from *C* were higher in *B* than in *A* the demand for *C*'s goods on this account would fall. Similarly, if the marginal propensity to give foreign aid to C differed between A and B the two expenditure adjustments would alter the amount of aid received by C. (This is particularly relevant if expenditure adjustment is carried out by fiscal rather than monetary policy.) In addition there is the effect of B's devaluation to consider. This further reduces B's imports and pulls in the same direction as the effects of the expenditure change. But in addition B's exports will increase; the prices of its exports will fall. If C tended to import the type of goods B exports its terms of trade would tend to improve. On the other hand, as we have seen, if C tended to export the type of goods B imports (so that the marginal propensity to import goods from C in B is high) B's terms of trade would tend to worsen. Whether on balance C's terms of trade improve or worsen depends then on the pattern of its trade on the export and import side.

III

The members of a group of advanced countries, such as the Group of Ten, may come to a mutual arrangement to provide each other with some liquidity. The question then arises: Should extra members be admitted to the group and indeed do any outsiders wish to join the group? Should Austria join the group? Greece? Australia? Mexico? Where should the line be drawn? Presumably the existing members of the group all expect to gain from the arrangement among themselves. If they prefer to keep, say, Mexico out of the scheme, then they must assume that even though Mexico might gain from joining, they would lose marginally from Mexico's membership. This is the question of who will be included in the privileged circle, and in particular whether the developing countries will or should be included. We could put the problem more formally. A and B form the inner group and C is the outsider. C will make an application to join only if its inclusion is expected to yield a gain to itself, and (assuming rational national selfishness) its application will be accepted only if its inclusion is expected to yield a gain to $(A + B)$. The "optimum" or "politically feasible" liquidity area will, in principle, be defined in this way. The issue really is whether bringing in the developing countries is just a form of foreign aid. If their participation were not of mutual benefit, but only of benefit to them, it would indeed be just another form of aid. There may of course be good reasons for advocating this type of aid, but at least one should be clear about what is being advocated.

One approach to the problem is to assume that extra liquidity benefits deficit countries by enabling them to "absorb" more goods and services than they would otherwise be able to do (to live longer beyond their means) and that this benefit is at the expense of surplus countries who must correspondingly "disabsorb." In that case if C is expected to be a frequent or perennial deficit country—that is, if it is expected either to get into temporary deficits not followed by equivalent temporary surpluses later or to get into a long-term deficit requiring a fundamental adjustment which it would only postpone if provided with liquidity— then C will not be admitted. With this approach, restoring external balance would be a "cost" to the deficit country and a "gain" to the surplus country since the former would command less and the latter more real resources. With this simple reasoning it is always in the surplus country's interest to eliminate the imbalance, but it cannot succeed in doing so if the deficit country does not co-operate, for the latter can always prevent adjustment by failing to disabsorb appropriately. It takes two in a two-country world (and at least two in a multicountry world) to get rid of an imbalance. The deficit country can be made to agree only if it runs out of reserves.

One might conclude from this simple approach that if C is expected to get into deficits rather than surpluses it will not be admitted, while if it were expected to get into surpluses rather than deficits it would not want to join. But expectations might differ. Both C and $(A + B)$ might think they have more chance of getting into deficit than into surplus and so both would see a gain from C joining. More important, countries may have high risk-aversion and thus attach heavier welfare weights to losses than to rises in absorption. Therefore, if a country considers there is a small chance that it will get into deficit and a large chance that it will get into surplus it may still see a gain in joining a liquidity-creating scheme.

The practical question which this approach raises is whether developing countries are more likely to be deficit than surplus countries. Is there an "inevitable deficit" behavior pattern for developing countries? It seems to be frequently implied that this is so, and perhaps is true of important ones among them, such as India and Indonesia. On the other hand it clearly does not apply to Thailand and Malaysia. And what is inevitable? Whether surpluses for developing countries in general, sustained over any length of time, can be expected is difficult to say. Will there be another Korean-style raw materials boom? Will the developing countries acquire governments as financially cautious as previous colonial administrations in many countries? Why single out developing countries? Times change. Within recent memory France appeared to be a persistent deficit country. And what is to distinguish Indonesia from the United Kingdom—both now apparently reformed in intentions but until recently sharing a devotion to prestige projects and excessive military expenditures as part-causes of somewhat persistent deficits. The UNCTAD report cited earlier provides evidence that many developing countries have in fact taken opportunities to build up their reserves in recent years.

The approach outlined here implies that the gain from extra liquidity accrues solely to the deficit country or at least to all those countries which consider they have some chance of getting into deficit. But this is too simple and must be qualified. A certain type of gain from extra liquidity may accrue *both* to surplus and to deficit countries. Certain costs of balance-of-payments adjustment are transitional costs and are borne both by the surplus and the deficit country. Extra liquidity can avert these costs insofar as it makes adjustments to *temporary* deficits unnecessary. These gains do not accrue when liquidity is used to postpone fundamental adjustments. I shall assume now that adjustment consists not only of appropriate expenditure variation to maintain internal balance, but also of the use of "switching devices" such as exchange-rate alteration. The restoration of external equilibrium requires the surplus country to transfer resources from traded goods (exportables and importables) to non-traded goods, and the deficit country to transfer resources from non-traded to traded goods. This transfer of resources may involve a real, though no doubt once-for-all cost. Furthermore, in the deficit country producers' surpluses will rise in tradeable goods industries and fall in non-tradeables (with the opposite movement in the surplus country). This redistribution of income will involve a loss in social welfare if in terms of the social welfare function losses in producers' surpluses are more heavily weighted than gains.

These costs of transition must be borne by both countries irrespective of which takes the initiative of eliminating the imbalance. For example, if the developing countries as a whole have to eliminate a deficit relative to the advanced countries as a whole, the developing countries must transfer resources from, say, services into import-replacing manufacturing and from crops for the home market to crops for export, while the advanced countries must transfer resources out of export industries which specialize in supplying developing countries (e.g., capital-goods industries) and out of industries which compete with imports from developing countries (e.g., textiles). The advanced countries may prefer to give the developing countries extra liquidity rather than suffer so painful an adjustment.

IV

I have introduced so far two elements in what might be called the "burden" of balance-of-payments adjustment—a burden which is avoided or postponed through the creation of extra liquidity. The first is the burden of *disabsorption*—of having to reduce real expenditure—which must be borne by the deficit country.[3] The second is the transitional cost which may be borne by both deficit and surplus countries. But in the literature one finds a third concept of burden of adjustment, one which helps to explain why a country such as Germany has made so little attempt to eliminate its surplus.[4] Has this third concept no place in our analysis? First I shall spell it out rather carefully as I have not seen a rigorous statement of it elsewhere.

For simple exposition I shall assume that this is the only type of burden; in practice all three types of burden may be relevant. I also assume a world of only two countries (countries *S* and *D*—the surplus and the deficit country). This third concept depends on the following two crucial assumptions:

1) The two countries are interested only in achieving that level of aggregate demand for their own goods and services which enables them to attain what each considers its optimum combination of rate of change of prices and rate of unemployment. Each country has a "Phillips curve" or transformation curve between price change and unemployment, and its social welfare function determines the optimum point on this transformation curve. This optimum position I shall henceforth call *internal balance*.

2) The only policy instruments permitted are changes in aggregate expenditure in each country. Instruments which switch expenditure as

---

3. I accept the criticism which was made to me at the conference by Professor Machlup and earlier by Professor Arndt that this is a rather odd use of the term "burden." It might be better to say that the surplus country bears a burden and the deficit country receives an unearned bonus as long as no adjustment is taking place. The act of adjustment which compels the deficit country to live within its means ends the surplus country's burden and the deficit country's bonus. But the fundamental economic point remains that eliminating a deficit requires the deficit country to reduce its absorption—to lose its bonus—and this will certainly feel like a burden to its people and government. It might also be added that the size of this "burden" depends not only on the size of the deficit to be eliminated and the utility of the foregone absorption but also on the efficiency with which the adjustment takes place. The more the adjustment avoids unemployment or underutilization of capacity and the less it distorts the trade structure the more efficient it is.

4. T. Scitovsky, *Requirements of an International Reserve System*, Essay in International Finance no. 49 (Princeton: Princeton University, International Finance Section, 1965).

between home and foreign goods, such as exchange-rate alterations or quantitative import restrictions, are ruled out. Thus a country can eliminate a deficit only by reducing expenditure, including expenditure on its own goods, and can eliminate a surplus only by increasing expenditure.

The simple model which results is set out with more precise assumptions and with a diagram in Appendix 1. The level of demand for one country's goods depends not only on its own level of expenditure but also on the expenditure of the other country. Suppose country *S* is initially in internal balance and wishes to stay there; then, if expenditure by country *D* increases, this requires a reduction of expenditure by country *S*. For the extra demand in *D* for *S*'s goods will have an inflationary effect in *S* which *S* can only avoid by reducing its own expenditure on its own goods.

With this concept of the cost of adjustment the social welfare is assumed to depend in each country on the level of demand *for* its own goods and services (or, alternatively, on the level of production). By contrast, with the first concept used earlier, the social welfare depended in each country on the level of demand or absorption *by* each country for goods and services produced either at home or abroad.

Thus, this time, there is a burden from balance-of-payments adjustment which consists of the burden of having too much inflation or too much unemployment, or in other words the burden of having to depart from the optimum point on the Phillips curve. It is really the cost of foregoing switching devices, such as alteration of the exchange rate, since with the use of such devices it would always be possible to stay at the optimum point. This burden can be divided up between the deficit and the surplus country in various proportions. When liquidity is very limited and there is no pressure on surplus countries to eliminate their surpluses the burden is wholly borne by the deficit countries.[5]

If each country varies its own level of expenditure so as to attain internal balance an equilibrium pair of expenditures in the two countries will result.[6] But it would be pure coincidence if this resulted in external balance. Thus the sustaining of internal balance for both countries requires unlimited liquidity for the deficit country. If the deficit country wishes to eliminate the imbalance it must reduce expenditure. The surplus country will respond by increasing its expenditure,

5. *Ibid.*
6. This statement assumes that the model is stable, the condition for stability being that the sum of the marginal propensities to import in the two countries is less than unity. This is explained in Appendix 1.

but if this increase is appropriate to maintain it in internal balance it will not keep the deficit country in its internal balance. (All this comes out clearly in the diagram.) Thus the deficit country must depart from internal balance, this being the cost of adjustment to it. The surplus country, which remains in internal balance, incurs neither gain nor loss. Alternatively, the surplus country may be forced to eliminate its surplus, while there is no pressure on the deficit country through shortage of liquidity to eliminate the deficit. The surplus country would then have to increase expenditure. The deficit country would reduce expenditure so as to maintain its internal balance. The result would be for external balance to be restored by means of the surplus country departing from its internal balance while the deficit country stayed in internal balance. This time the cost of adjustment is wholly borne by the surplus country. Finally, if pressure were exerted both on the deficit and the surplus country both would depart from internal balance and the burden of balance-of-payments adjustment would be shared.

In considering the relevance of this discussion to the developing countries it should be borne in mind that they have not generally forsworn the use of switching devices such as exchange rate devaluation or quantitative import restrictions. Furthermore, most of them are probably less afraid of inflation than the advanced countries and are quite ready to use inflation to eliminate a surplus. In the case of the less industrialized among them it is probably also true that a reduction in effective demand is less likely to cause unemployment because of greater downward flexibility of factor incomes; insofar as inadequate demand does lead to unemployment it is less noticed because it merges with the more permanent structural type of unemployment (or underemployment), and tends to be literally *disguised*. (In other words, the Phillips curve is steep and the position on the curve is not an important element in the social welfare function.) For these reasons the discussion of this section is probably not very relevant to developing countries and this section should be regarded as no more than a lengthy footnote.

V

In section III, I considered the case where "two advanced countries, *A* and *B*, come to a mutual arrangement to provide each other with some liquidity," but I did not specify the technicalities of the scheme. Of course there are many forms such schemes can take, as the proliferation of plans and the taxonomy of the Ossola Report remind us.[7] In the type

7. R. Ossola *et al.*, *Report of the Study Group on the Creation of Reserve Assets* (Washington, D.C.: U.S. Government Printing Office, 1965).

of scheme I have had in mind so far, the participating countries receive liquidity—that is, certificates of some kind which we can call Collective Reserve Units—without having to give up actual resources at the time. Countries may buy these units with their own currencies, and the body creating the units, say the IMF, then keeps these currencies as backing for the units. Only in the event of liquidation of the scheme would the currencies be used and so in real terms the units paid for. In a sense new international money will have been created which is distributed to countries without cost. (Alternatively, we could say that countries have to create new domestic money in order to buy the new international money.) Each country gains from the units it receives insofar as there is a possibility that it may run into deficit, while it loses from the units distributed to other countries insofar as they may run into deficit with it. Now if it gains from the units it receives it will (or should) be prepared to pay something for them. Indeed if the new money were real gold it would pay for them, the payment being the price of gold. In receiving costless certificates countries appear to be getting something for nothing (at least until liquidation of the scheme). Why not charge them something for it and give the profits to the poor? In other words, why not make them *buy* the new units just as they are normally prepared to buy gold? The units could first be given to poor countries who, if they prefer liquidity, would hold them and otherwise would sell them to the rich countries. The rich countries would be no worse off than if new gold had been discovered and then sold to them, while the poor countries would be the beneficiaries of what is the equivalent of a new gold discovery. There is indeed a new discovery, a form of technical progress in international financial management, the discovery that a gold-substitute can be produced without having to dig it out of the ground. Why not pass the fruits of this technical progress on to poor countries? Why not? Or why?

As this issue has been put exceptionally clearly by Professor Machlup I shall quote extensively from his article:

> The discovery that international money can be produced with cheap ink and paper, and need not be produced with hard work applied to metal dug out of the ground, affords a large saving. Should the holders of this cheap international money be the sole beneficiaries of the reduction in cost? If they are prepared to acquire additional gold reserves by surrendering real resources, one should think that they can pay the same price for a perfect substitute, for the deposits in the international reserve institution. The first spenders of the new deposits will be the beneficiaries of the technological

progress in the production of international money, and these first spenders may "just as well" be the developing nations.[8]

On the other hand, Professor Machlup asks:

> If a group of industrial countries, used to holding "tokens" for their financial settlements, want to increase their stocks of tokens because they want more to hold and more to hand back and forth among one another in settling temporary payments balances, why should they not be permitted to create such tokens for themselves without having to surrender real resources to poor countries?

This appears to be the real issue in plans which link international monetary reform with aid to developing countries, though it is not put so explicitly in the papers or reports which advocate these schemes, such as the UNCTAD report[9] to which I referred earlier. The best-known of these plans is the Stamp Plan.[10] The UNCTAD report has advanced a slight variant of this, and the Hart-Kaldor-Tinbergen commodity reserve scheme might also be put under this general heading.[11] As I have not seen the comparison made elsewhere, I have briefly compared these three schemes in Appendix 2. But the whole exercise, I must confess, is rather academic. The Hart-Kaldor-Tinbergen scheme is really of such awe-inspiring complexity that it is hardly surprising that neither the Ossola nor the UNCTAD committee gave it further consideration. The other schemes are of course perfectly feasible, but it appears that they are not favored by those people whose opinions matter in the countries that matter. The Ossola committee did not speak officially for governments or central banks, but nevertheless the following remark from its report seems rather conclusive: "Most members believe that the provision of capital to developing countries is a problem quite distinct from the creation of reserves and should be achieved by other techniques."[12]

To return to the real issue in these plans, the way Professor Machlup has put the matter does not appear to me to be quite the whole story. It

8. F. Machlup, "The Cloakroom Rule of International Reserves: Reserve Creation and Resources Transfer," *Quarterly Journal of Economics*, 79 (August, 1965): 353.

9. UNCTAD, *International Monetary Issues*.

10. M. Stamp, "The Stamp Plan—1962 Version," *Moorgate and Wall Street*, Autumn, 1962, reprinted in H. G. Grubel, ed., *World Monetary Reform* (Stanford: Stanford University Press, 1964), pp. 80–89.

11. A. G. Hart, N. Kaldor, and J. Tinbergen, "The Case for an International Commodity Reserve Currency," memorandum submitted to UNCTAD published in *Trade and Development*, Conference Proceedings and Documents (New York: United Nations, 1965).

12. Ossola *et al.*, *Report of the Study Group*, p. 69.

must be remembered that some countries may lose from a general international distribution of liquidity. They would lose also if there were a large discovery of new gold which was then bought by various other countries and later used by these countries to sustain deficits. We might say that the national gain from a receipt of gold or other international money is in these cases greater than the international gain. The potential losing countries are those which will run surpluses that, because of the extra liquidity, the deficit countries will make no effort to eliminate. If the surpluses are not eliminated, the surplus countries lose in terms of real absorption, while if they do take steps to eliminate them by expenditure increases they lose in terms of departure from internal balance. Clearly they would be better off if the deficit countries eliminated the deficits by departing from *their* internal balance. It follows that if extra liquidity in the form of units of some kind were sold to countries with the profits going to developing countries we do not just cream off the profits from technical progress and give them to the poor, leaving the rich as well off as before. Rather there is some redistribution from some of the rich countries to the poor. Nevertheless, it seems to me that, broadly speaking, Professor Machlup has put the issue correctly. There would probably be a substantial *world* gain from extra liquidity. Few, if any, countries could be regarded as certain losers. The argument for a link between liquidity creation and development finance is put indirectly and unconvincingly in the UNCTAD report.[13] So I shall conclude by quoting Professor Machlup's much better statement of the argument:

> . . .a very plausible argument can be made, on political as well as economic grounds, for combining development aid and reserve creation in one package deal. It may be politically difficult to obtain the appropriations for foreign aid that the governments may deem desirable; they may find it easier to get legislative approval for a plan establishing an international reserve institution whose investments will include securities of development-finance organisations. In political questions one cannot always insist on logical neatness and semantic clarity. The economic case for the package deal must rest largely on tradition: historically, international reserves have always been earned through the surrender of real resources and, to industrial countries, the cost of reserves under a plan of distributing new reserves first to less developed countries is not any higher than the cost of reserves under the gold standard.[14]

13. UNCTAD, *International Monetary Issues*, pp. 28–31.
14. Machlup, "The Cloakroom Rule of International Reserves," p. 353.

Appendix 1

The Burden of Balance-of-Payments Adjustment: A Diagrammatic Statement

Assume a world of two countries (S and D) with a constant exchange rate, tariffs, etc., the only instruments of balance-of-payments adjustment being variations in the level of expenditure (E_s and E_d). Initially prices in both countries are held constant. Let S's imports from D be M_s and D's imports from S be M_d. Let the demand for S's goods be H_s and for D's goods, H_d. Then

$$H_s = M_d + (E_s - M_s) \qquad (1)$$

$$H_d = M_s + (E_d - M_d). \qquad (2)$$

In Figure 1 expenditure by S (E_s) is shown along the horizontal axis and expenditure by D (E_d) along the vertical axis. The line SS' shows the

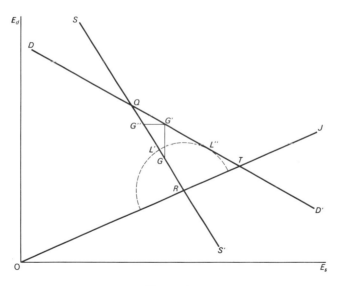

FIGURE 1

various combinations of E_s and E_d which achieve that given level of demand for S's goods (H_s) which S regards as optimum, this being *internal balance*. A greater level of demand would lead to more employment but also to a greater rate of change in prices; lower demand would involve more unemployment and more price stability. (The price changes must be assumed to operate only in the next period since in the current period prices are assumed constant.) Similarly DD' shows the various combinations of E_s and E_d which achieve the given H_d that is regarded as optimum by D. At the point of intersection Q both countries are in internal balance.

Assume the marginal propensities to import (m_s, m_d) are constant in each country and equal to the respective average propensity, so that

$$m_d = \frac{M_d}{E_d} \tag{3}$$

$$m_s = \frac{M_s}{E_s}. \tag{4}$$

From (1), (3), and (4)

$$E_d = -\frac{(1 - m_s)}{m_d} E_s + \frac{H_s}{m_d}. \tag{1.1}$$

From (2), (3), and (4)

$$E_d = -\frac{m_s}{(1 - m_d)} E_s + \frac{H_d}{(1 - m_d)}. \tag{2.1}$$

(1.1) is the equation for the line SS' and (2.1) for the line DD'. From (1.1) the slope of SS' is $-(1 - m_s)/m_d$ and from (2.1) the slope of DD' is $-m_s/(1 - m_d)$. The case represented in Figure 1 is one where SS' is steeper than DD', i.e., where

$$-\frac{(1 - m_s)}{m_d} < -\frac{m_s}{(1 - m_d)} \tag{5}$$

and from (5)

$$m_s + m_d < 1. \tag{5.1}$$

In other words, if the sum of the marginal propensities to import is less than unity SS' will be steeper than DD' in Figure 1.

It can be shown that this case represented in the diagram (sum of the marginal propensities to import less than unity) is the condition for stability of the model. Suppose that the initial combination of E_s and E_d happens to be the one which yields the point G on the diagram. S is then in internal balance but the demand for D's goods is below internal balance. So E_d is increased, taking the system to G'. Now S is above its internal balance and E_s is reduced, taking the system to G''. We can see that the system moves toward Q. Alternatively, if we had started at G', so that D was in internal balance, a change would have been initiated by S, bringing the system to G'', and so on. The system will move toward Q from any point on the diagram. This stability condition will henceforth be assumed.[15]

Next, introduce the balance of payments. The line OJ shows the various combinations of E_s and E_d which achieve balance-of-payments equilibrium, i.e., that constant level of net surplus or deficit compatible with autonomous capital movements. The slope of OJ is m_s/m_d. Points above OJ yield balance-of-payments deficit for D and points below OJ yield surplus for D (deficit for S). In the case represented in Figure 1 the pursuit of internal balance by both countries would yield a deficit for D.

Now let D run out of liquidity and be compelled to aim its expenditure policy at balance-of-payments equilibrium. It will therefore reduce E_d, aiming for OJ. At the same time S will adjust E_s so as to remain on SS'. Thus the system will move along SS' and settle at R, the point of intersection of SS' with OJ. At this point D has achieved its objective of balance-of-payments equilibrium and S has achieved its objective of staying in internal balance. But of course D is now below internal balance and has more unemployment than it wants. Alternatively we might conceive of a situation where D has unlimited liquidity but S is, for one reason or another, forced to take steps to eliminate its balance-of-payments surplus. S must then aim for OJ while D can vary E_d so as to stay on DD'. The equilibrium will then be the point T where DD' intersects OJ. At this point S is above internal balance and has more inflation than it wants. Another possibility is that there is some pressure on both to restore payments equilibrium. In that case the final equilibrium may be between R and T. D will have rather more unemployment and S rather more inflation than indicated by their optima. In other words, the adjustment burden is shared. At R the burden is wholly borne by D and at T wholly by S, the burden being defined in terms of departure from internal balance.

We might ask what motive S could have for wishing to reduce or eliminate its surplus. Provided it stays on SS', does it matter to it whether or not D eliminates its deficit? A motive can be introduced if an element other than the internal balance concept is introduced into

15. This can be put in terms of the assignment problem discussed at the conference. We have two targets (SS' and DD') and two instruments (E_s and E_d). If the system is to be stable and the sum of the marginal propensities to import is less than unity, instrument E_s must be assigned to target SS' and instrument E_d to target DD'. This is of course the natural assignment. But if the sum of the marginal propensities were greater than unity this assignment would lead to instability. Stability would require S's expenditure policy (E_s) to be aimed at D's internal balance (DD') and D's expenditure policy (E_d) at S's internal balance (SS').

S's social welfare function. The greater its surplus the more real resources it gives away. Assume that this is regarded as a social loss. If the surplus could be reduced without altering the level of demand for S's goods there would be a rise in social welfare, while social welfare would stay constant if a given departure from internal balance were associated with an appropriate reduction in the surplus. The optimum point is at R where the surplus is eliminated and internal balance is maintained. One can conceive of an indifference-curve map showing positions of equal welfare to S. One such indifference curve (the dotted curve) is shown in Figure 1. A movement along the curve from L (on OJ between R and T) represents at first an increasing surplus combined with reduced excess demand in S until L' is reached. At L' the surplus is at its maximum for this curve but the economy is in internal balance. Beyond that the surplus falls off but the economy goes into increasing unemployment. This indifference curve is the one which happens to be tangential to DD' and therefore represents the highest level of social welfare S can reach given that D follows a policy of staying on DD'. Thus equilibrium in this case will be at the tangency point L'' (a point that could coincide with T). It is the best that S can do given that D has so much liquidity it need not take any steps to eliminate its deficit.

Finally it must be noted that the prices of S may be changing relative to the prices of D; so far it has been assumed that such a change takes place only "in the next period." Suppose equilibrium is at Q; this may represent (but need not) a greater rate of change of prices for D than for S. Defining E_s and E_d in money terms, SS' and DD' then move upwards, but DD' moves up faster. If price elasticities of demand for imports happened to be unity the slopes of SS', DD', and OJ would not change since import propensities would not change. In this particular case Q will move leftwards and the money value of the deficit will increase. With prices of D rising faster than in S, if the import demand elasticities were greater than unity, m_s would fall and m_d would rise. So OJ would flatten and the slopes of DD' and SS' might change. The flattening of OJ indicates that the money value of the deficit represented by a given point Q would have increased.

Appendix 2

Schemes Linking Liquidity Creation with Development Finance

Two main schemes have been proposed which link liquidity creation directly with development finance. The first is the Stamp Plan.[16] This is

16. Stamp, "The Stamp Plan."

quite straightforward and provides for the creation of credit certificates by the IMF which are then lent to the IDA which in turn passes the certificates on to developing countries. These countries then use the certificates to buy imports, so that advanced countries obtain certificates (in fact, buy liquidity) through exporting. Countries which are members of the IMF agree to receive the certificates from central banks or monetary authorities in settlement of international obligations up to a defined limit equal to their quotas. If a country finds that another member will not honor a certificate tendered to it or if the other country has its full quota the Fund would redeem the certificates, if necessary in gold. A country which suffers from overfull employment and does not want to accept additional export orders can notify the IDA that it does not want the proceeds of loans to be spent within its economy; in this case it need not accept certificates directly from their first owners, though it must still honor certificates tendered to it by other countries up to the limit of the quota. The certificates would of course have a constant value in gold.

The UNCTAD report scheme is a slight variant of this.[17] The certificates (or fund units, as they are called in this case) are in the first instance distributed to members of the IMF generally on the basis of some such criterion as the size of IMF quotas; thus they are not distributed initially only to developing countries. In return, each country provides the Fund with an equivalent amount of its own currency. The Fund then passes part or all of those currencies received which are the currencies of developed countries on to the IBRD or IDA which in turn pass them on to the developing countries. The developing countries use the currencies to pay for imports.

> The share of each of the developed countries in the transfer of real resources will depend on its willingness and ability to obtain export orders as a result of Bank loans. Those whose share in the orders is larger than their share in the original liquidity creation (among the developed countries taken as a group) will have to bear a higher share in real terms in the transfer of resources. But to the extent that they share more in the orders (and consequently in the transfer of real resources) they will gain reserves at the expense of those who fail to match their share in the original liquidity creation by correspondingly obtaining orders against Bank loans.[18]

On first sight this scheme seems a little puzzling. Who gets the liquidity? The countries which receive the fund units—that is, all

17. UNCTAD, *International Monetary Issues*, pp. 23–28.
18. *Ibid.*, p. 27.

members of the IMF—or the developing countries which receive the currencies of other countries? The matter is best explained with an example. Suppose that a non-reserve currency country, such as France, receives $100 million worth of fund units and provides the IMF, and thus indirectly the developing countries, with $100 million worth of francs. The developing countries want to use these francs to buy, say, Swedish goods. Since the franc is convertible into gold, dollars, or fund units, the developing countries convert the francs into, say, gold and fund units and these are then paid to Sweden in payment for Swedish exports. In this example France loses all the liquidity she gained initially; the liquidity has in fact been given to the developing countries and bought by Sweden. Alternatively the developing countries might have kept some or all of the liquidity and simply converted the francs into gold or fund units to hold. If the developing countries bought some of their extra imports from France, say $20 million worth, France would lose only $80 million of the fund units, gold, etc., and the net gain in liquidity to France would be $20 million. France would in fact have bought some liquidity through extra exports.

Thus the UNCTAD report scheme differs from the Stamp scheme only insofar as there is a time lag between the issue of fund units to IMF members generally and the conversion of the currencies received by developing countries. In the Stamp scheme no extra liquidity reaches the advanced countries until the developing countries spend some of their extra resources; in the UNCTAD report scheme the extra liquidity goes to the advanced countries directly, and is subsequently redistributed among them and to developing countries.

The Hart-Kaldor-Tinbergen commodity reserve currency scheme might also be regarded as a scheme which would create a gold substitute to be bought mainly from developing countries.[19] The gold substitute would be a bundle of commodities which would be backing for new international money. The commodities would be mainly but not wholly supplied by developing countries. The new "gold" this time would not (from an international point of view) be costless since resources would have to be used to produce the commodities. The commodity producers would gain through higher prices, in fact through rises in producers' surpluses. In addition the scheme embodies a price stabilization element, so that there would be some net gain to producers and consumers from greater stability.

19. Hart, Kaldor, and Tinbergen, "The Case for an International Commodity Reserve Currency."

COMMENT: "THE DISTRIBUTION OF SEIGNIORAGE FROM INTERNATIONAL LIQUIDITY CREATION"

Wilson E. Schmidt

In the version of his paper presented at the conference, Professor Grubel equated the amount of seigniorage with the social gain, in freeing resources to produce other goods and services, which would result from the substitution of fiat money for commodity money. The seigniorage problem is one of finding a mechanism for distributing that social gain. In his earlier view, the cause of the problem lay in the absence of a world government which could employ the seigniorage to provide public goods—the typical national solution. Professor Grubel has rightly rejected these views in revising his paper. As he argued before in the conference version, seigniorage can be wiped out if the world central bank makes no profits. Paying interest on the money created achieves this result. Yet the social gain remains. Thus, seigniorage is something other than the social gain, namely the profit to the issuer of money. Furthermore, there is a mechanism to distribute the benefits of freeing resources from the production of commodity money. It consists of a decline in the world price level as the resources are alternatively employed to produce additional goods and services plus a deterioration in the terms of trade of the commodity-money producers. Finally, the cause of the problem, as originally conceived, lies not in the absence of a world government but in the unwillingness of the monetary authorities to allow the world price level to decline for reasons which need not be discussed.

What problems remain in the revised version? Professor Grubel's concept of neutrality is still very restricted. He seeks to avoid real transfers of resources as a result of the creation of money. His proposal to distribute fiat money according to the long-run demand for money, however, takes no account of the terms-of-trade effects of substituting fiat money for commodity money. As noted above, the terms of trade of commodity-money producers will deteriorate and the benefits and costs of this will be distributed according to the pattern of trade, not according to the demand for money. Thus, neutrality cannot be achieved by distributing reserves proportionately to the demand for money. Grubel presumably includes the commodity-money producers

305

among the recipients of fiat money when he allocates it in proportion to the demand for reserves; it is difficult to see why he excludes them with respect to the terms-of-trade effects. They should be wholly in his peer group or wholly out of it.

It is difficult to see why Grubel is so concerned about obtaining the right demand function for reserves for allocating the fiat money when the solution lies not in a function but in a simple rule which he himself perceives. Leaving aside the terms-of-trade effects mentioned above, net resource transfers will be avoided if the fiat money is loaned at the world market-rate of interest. The country which receives the fiat money in payment for its surplus will be compensated for the loss of real resources.

Elsewhere Grubel has opposed the use of interest rates, believing them to play only a mythological role.[1] His current position seems more accurate given his assumption of a single world capital market. If that assumption is dropped, some interesting results are obtained which question whether interest rates should be charged and extend our knowledge of the advantages of fiat money.

Grubel notes that the use of fiat money provides a social gain by releasing resources from the production of gold. While this is relevant for additions to the stock of international liquidity, it cannot support the use of fiat money in place of the existing gold because the use of existing gold does not absorb any real resources. As it is possible to reconstruct the international monetary system with or without the existing stock of gold, the analysis of international monetary reform is incomplete. Is there a social gain in demonetizing the *existing* stock?

When a country exports gold or fiat money, it enjoys more real resources than it otherwise would while the country accepting those assets has fewer real resources than it otherwise would. The fiat money may be created by credit which carries interest, and a repayment date can be scheduled. Or it can be created though a permanent grant. In contrast, interest is typically not paid on gold and the maturity of the transfer is indeterminate since the recipient of the gold can regain the foregone resources whenever it (and other countries) pursue policies designed to shift it back to the original owner. A gold movement is the equivalent of a zero-interest callable loan.

Elsewhere it has been shown that zero-interest loans are inefficient techniques for transferring real resources among countries on the assumptions that yields on capital differ among countries and capital is

1. Herbert G. Grubel, "The Cloakroom Rule of International Reserves: Comment," *Quarterly Journal of Economics*, 80 (August, 1966): 485–87.

immobile.[2] Suppose country D wishes to export $1.00 of gold in exchange for an equivalent amount of real resources. Suppose that the monetary authorities of country D know that two years from now they will have to pursue policies to cause the return of the gold and the relinquishment of the equivalent amount of real resources. Country D thus enjoys $1.00 of real resources for two years. If the yield on capital in D were 5 per cent (which becomes the discount rate if we assume no mobility of capital among nations), the present value of the benefits of the two-year, interest-free loan of $1.00 is 9.3¢. If the yield on capital in the surplus country (S) which will receive the gold is 4 per cent, S will lose 4¢ per annum for two years. Since the yield on capital in D is higher than in S, it would be possible to find a larger, two-year loan with an interest rate in excess of 4 per cent (but below 5 per cent) which will give D the same present value of benefits, i.e., 9.3¢, while S actually gains. Thus, the initial real transfer of resources from S should be increased—financed by a loan with a positive interest rate—and the shipment of gold should be avoided.

If the yield on capital in S were in excess of 5 per cent, there would be no loan which would benefit S while giving D the same present value of benefits. In that event, the transfer of real resources should be decreased and the smaller surplus covered with a grant. For example, if the yield on capital in S is 6 per cent, the loss of $1.00 of real resources for two years costs S 11¢ in terms of present value. Since D would be just as happy with a lump sum grant of 9.3¢ because it has the same present value of benefits as the gold shipment, S might as well reject the gold and provide a lump sum grant of 9.3¢ to D; it has a lower present cost to S, namely 9.3¢.

The inferences to be drawn are: (1) in addition to the cost to society of producing gold, the use of the existing stock of gold imposes a real cost because it is an inefficient method of transferring real resources; (2) in some instances it is preferable to create fiat money through credits with interest rates and repayment dates and in other instances through grants, depending on the relative yields on capital of the surplus and deficit countries; and (3) the plans for international monetary reform which provide grants to the less developed countries should be reexamined in the light of this argument.

2. Wilson E. Schmidt, "The Economics of Charity," *The Journal of Political Economy*, 72 (August, 1964): 387–95.

COMMENT: "INTERNATIONAL MONETARY REFORM AND THE DEVELOPING COUNTRIES"

Larry A. Sjaastad

Two rather different strands run through Mr. Corden's mainly theoretical paper on the stake of the developing countries in world monetary reform. Corden is principally concerned with the probable reaction of the developed countries to the international liquidity shortage. In some parts of his paper, he analyzes the probable effect on the less developed countries of an intensification of the competition for reserves. In these parts, he quite clearly views the question in the traditional stock demand-supply context. Yet in other parts, Corden takes a different view, in that his emphasis is upon flow relationships. It seems to me that the relevance of these two relationships for world monetary reform is decidedly different, and much of my comment is addressed to this difference.

Let me use part I to refer to those paragraphs in Corden's paper that deal with stock relations, and part II in reference to the flow-relation paragraphs. In part I, the major concern is with the possibility that, in their scramble for a given stock of reserves, the developed nations will pursue a deflationary path damaging to the less developed countries because of the consequent decline in the demand for their exports. I suppose we agree here that the competitive deflation might well lead to falling rates of growth and possibly even to falling levels of output. This in turn will reduce the demand for the less developed countries' exports, presumably turning the terms of trade against them. If the less developed countries were pursuing an optimal tariff policy prior to this event, no counterattack on their part could lead them to their original position.

It seems to me that this situation is quite analogous to a shift in the demand for money within a country; unless an increased demand is met by an increased supply, the deflationary activities of the many economic units involved will drag down the level of prices or the level of output, and our experience points to some of each. Certainly the less developed countries are not likely to be helped by such an event, and the obvious way to avoid such a disaster is either a move to reduce the demand for reserves (perhaps via flexible exchange rates, a measure lacking support at this conference) or a move to augment the supply in some low-cost manner. My guess is that the less developed countries have but the slightest interest in *how* this problem is resolved, just that it is resolved in some way consistent with sustained growth. My argument here is that the less developed countries do not constitute a significant portion of the total demand for reserves; that they are not likely to share in any seigniorage income from the creation of new liquidity; and that their reserves typically earn interest in the form of deposits of a major reserve currency in one of the world's financial centers, an arrangement not likely to be changed by world monetary reform.

Part II of Corden's paper analyzes a quite different animal. Here he is concerned with how persistent balance-of-payments disequilibria are resolved, disequilibria that stem *not* from a desire to enlarge holdings of reserves, but rather from chronic excesses of imports over exports. This problem, it seems to me, has little to do with world monetary reform, as it can in no way be attributed to a shortage of "international" money, and presumably will continue to exist after the liquidity squeeze has abated. Nevertheless, by an intermingling of these two separate issues, Corden inadvertently exaggerates the stake of the less developed countries in world monetary reform, as any foreseeable reform (short of flexible exchange rates) cannot be imagined to solve, in the long run, Mr. Wilson's overvalued pound sterling or Argentina's inflation.

Another issue that Mr. Corden treats is the manner in which an enlarged supply of international money might be realized. Here he examines various proposals leading to a once and for all transfer of import capacity to the less developed countries. Again, a separation of the issues is necessary. That the less developed countries have a stake in world monetary reform is clear enough; whether or not that reform carries with it a foreign-aid bonus has little to do with the functioning of the international monetary system and even less relevance for a theoretical discussion of the need for and consequences of that reform.

It seems to me that there is one important aspect of world monetary reform that receives inadequate emphasis in Corden's paper. Corden describes at length the possible negative effects for the less developed countries of competitive deflation and/or devaluation by the more developed countries. That this page out of Keynes is a dramatic one cannot be denied, but its relevance is doubtful. I say this because I think that the more plausible answer to the question of what will happen if the existing reliance on major reserve currencies and fixed exchange rates is continued is that world trade rather than world income will suffer. Corden worries about the possibility that liquidity-induced deflations in the more developed countries will deal a serious blow to the less developed countries. I think that it is self-evident that such a course of action hurts the more developed countries rather than the less developed countries and hence ought to be rather more a concern for those worrying about the former. I think that the real threat is that rather than embarking on a dramatic course of deflation in their quest for reserves, the more developed countries are going to create a myriad of relatively invisible obstacles to imports and capital outflows such as is the harvest from the "new economists" in the United States. This, I think, is a real fear in Latin America, for example. The other fear, it seems to me, is that mercantilistic practices with respect to exports of the more developed countries will be further established which, together with the rather high rates of effective protection in these countries, will preclude the further development of those viable industrialized sectors in the less developed countries. There is, particularly in Latin America, a growing awareness of the high costs of import substitution and an increasing confidence in trade as a major source of growth. The existing trend among the more developed countries toward import control—either as individual nations or as members of a common market—poses a major threat to these aspirations. World monetary reform, while far from a panacea, can serve a limited role in relaxing some of the growing constraints to trade with the developing countries. I submit that these real, as opposed to monetary, effects of reform are the factors of major consequence.

SUMMARY OF DISCUSSION

I

The seigniorage problem, the topic of Professor Grubel's paper, pro-voked a good deal of discussion, both with respect to the meaning of the term "seigniorage" and its application to the international monetary system. Some of the problems that came up have been clarified in the revised versions of Professor Grubel's and Professor Johnson's con-tributions and in Professor Schmidt's comment. The summary of the discussion of the seigniorage problem which follows, however, bears witness to the problems of definition which lurk under a seemingly straightforward concept.

Professor Johnson opened the discussion by emphasizing the necessity of distinguishing between the social saving from the use of paper money and seigniorage. In some cases, seigniorage is an appropriation of the social saving involved in the substitution of paper for commodity money. Take the two extreme cases: one where the world bank creates money which bears no interest and has the privilege of investing what it receives from its depositors in interest-bearing assets; the other where the world has to use commodity money. In the first case, the world bank appropriates the seigniorage; in the second, resources have to be in-vested in the creation of commodity money and a social loss equal to the interest foregone on the funds which could have been invested arises. The social gain to be had from the substitution of paper for commodity money, then, arises simply from the possibility of holding, against monetary liabilities, assets which bear interest and presumably corre-spond to those desired by the economy. In this example, the central or the world bank appropriates the seigniorage. On the other hand, if the bank pays enough interest on its liabilities to exhaust the return it earns on its assets, there is no seigniorage. The social saving, however, re-mains. In fact, it increases in the sense that the payments of interest to depositors makes the latter willing to hold a larger ratio of money to income. Since the cost of money creation is zero by assumption, social welfare increases. Johnson stated that it is important to distinguish

313

between two elements in the cost of money creation: real costs and transfers. Take a bank. Operating costs, book keeping costs, and so on, are real social-resource costs; the payment of interest is not a social cost but a transfer. The social saving from the paper for commodity-money substitution is equal to the difference between the costs of operating the bank and the rate of return on assets and this is equal, under competitive assumptions, to the transfer to depositors. Note, however, that the levy of seigniorage reduces the social gain by decreasing the rate paid to depositors and hence the money-to-income ratio.

Professor Cooper pursued this point. Even under a commodity-money system, seigniorage is not zero. It is not zero in the sense that pure rents are enjoyed by the producers of the commodities that serve as money. This stems from the generally correct proposition that rents, like seigniorage, derive from some restriction of supply. The great debates over monetary metals in the nineteenth century involved disputes over the distribution of the pure rents arising from the monetization of commodities. The same problems arise in a multicommodity standard. To summarize, both the question of the real social costs of generating money and that of income transfers among individuals arise even under a commodity standard. The creation of fiat money puts into the hands of governments the rents that are otherwise enjoyed by the producers of monetary metals. As *Professor Johnson* remarked, the existence of pure rents accruing to producers of the commodity money implies an upward–sloping supply curve of commodity money. The same phenomenon would occur in a credit money system, of course, if the supply curve of banking services was upward sloping. There would then be seigniorage in the sense that banks earn rents even though, at the margin, the cost of production of banking services is equal to their value.

Professor Niehans made three points. First, he felt that what Johnson called seigniorage and what Johnson called an inflation tax are both of the same general nature. For both seigniorage and the inflation tax depend on the monopoly position of the issuer of money. If the rate of return on assets (net of operating costs and "normal" profits) and the rate of interest on deposits are equal, both seigniorage and the inflation tax vanish.

Second, Niehans argued that four elements of the "seigniorage problem" should be distinguished. The first is technological progress in the production of money which releases real resources; an example would be the transition from gold to paper money. The second element is a transfer from the private to the government sector of the economy; this is seigniorage proper and should not be confused with the first element above. Third, the levy of seigniorage may involve distributional effects within the private sector; therefore the burden on holders of money may not be equal to the seigniorage gained by the monetary authority. The fourth element of the problem concerns the misallocation of real resources which occurs when the economic system is in monetary disequilibrium. Whether the creation or lack of creation of money produces inflation or deflation, misallocation of resources results and the losses have to be assessed.

Third, Niehans addressed himself to the international implications of the seigniorage problem which, he would agree, lie at the heart of recent and heated debates over the distribution of the gains from international reserve asset creation. There seem to be two solutions to the distribution of seigniorage: a market solution and a non-market solution. While Niehans would opt for a market solution, he sees Grubel's as a non-market solution. The problem with a solution based on the demand for reserves is that the demand cannot be specified without a specification of the costs of reserves. If the additional reserves are handed out at zero cost the demand for reserves may well turn out to be infinite in the long run. There is another option, besides distributing seigniorage on the basis of a demand concept or formula, and that is to create a market organism to distribute the gains from seigniorage. If the international institutions paid interest on deposits and earned interest on assets the seigniorage would be distributed. This amounts to saying that the international money-producing industry should be treated as a publicly-regulated industry subject to certain rules designed to make it behave roughly as if it had no monopoly power.

Professor Mundell agreed that under a competitive banking system seigniorage goes to zero in the sense that the interest paid on money and the return on real or financial assets can only differ because of the real cost of producing banking services, or because of reserve ratios required to keep the issued money convertible into other moneys. In Grubel's formula, competition would reduce the numerator to zero; so much is quite clear. However, Mundell stated, the link between that question and that of reserves is a complete red herring. Inflationary finance could cause distortions and a welfare loss if money is paid from a world central bank to national central banks in such a way that the latter do not identify this receipt of money with a return on existing money-holdings. But introducing money into the system and giving it to national central banks in proportion to the amount they already hold is, in fact, equivalent to paying interest on existing assets and will be identified as such.

There is no welfare cost to inflation when the newly issued money causing the inflation is paid as interest on existing balances. To take an extreme case, suppose the world central bank paid 50 per cent interest on its IOUs. If the real growth rate of the world is 3 per cent and a naive quantity theory can be applied, this would cause an inflation rate of 50 per cent minus 3 per cent, or 47 per cent. But this 47 per cent inflation has been compensated for by the fact that the new money that has come into the system accrues as interest on the world central bank's IOUs. In that sense, this issue of money is completely neutral and implies no pure welfare cost. The nature of the demand for reserves on the part of the world community makes no difference whatsoever.

Professor McKinnon returned to Niehans' suggestion that one should opt for a market-type solution. If one used the market to expand the money supply and the banking system was perfectly competitive (zero profits) and free to issue as many deposits as it wanted, the price level would be indeterminate. Since there are social gains associated with the determination of the price level a pure market solution of this type would not be desirable. One way out would be to consider the issue in terms of an optimization problem with a stable price-level constraint. Since the bank has a choice of the amount of interest it pays to depositors, one can consider the problem as that of setting an interest rate on deposits which will, in some sense, optimize S in Grubel's formula. Of course, the problem is complicated by the fact that the choice of a deposit rate will also affect the amount of loans the bank can extend and hence the return on assets on the one hand and the money-income ratio on the other.

At this point of the discussion, *Professor Machlup* stated that too many things seemed to come under the heading of seigniorage. This abundance of usages, according to Machlup, threatened to confuse different concepts: the social gain and its distribution, cost and rents, and seigniorage in its strict sense. It is misleading to use the word seigniorage in lieu of these other things. First, the social gain that has been referred to above goes back to Adam Smith; that is, if money which costs nothing to produce is substituted for commodity money, there is a social gain. Second, there is the issue of how this social gain is distributed. There is no necessary connection between the question of seigniorage and the social gain. There could be seigniorage without there being a social gain, and there could be a social gain without there being seigniorage. Seigniorage is a profit which the issuer of the money makes through some sort of institutional cut or monopoly power. Third, there is the question of rents. It can easily be shown that rents can accrue to the producers of commodity money. Suppose, for instance, that the price of gold is doubled. Machlup asked: Is it not quite clear that in that case there is a social cost and a rent? And that this rent is something that suddenly accrues to the producer of gold? It would only confuse matters to call this rent seigniorage. Fourth and finally, though seigniorage may be zero in the sense that the present value of a competitive bank's assets is equal to the present value of its liabilities, significant short-run effects may result. Money creation creates a drain on present resources, and this draft of resources should be a matter for concern even though the issuer of money pays interest and the present value of the right to issue money may be zero.

It belonged to *Professor Grubel* to close the discussion of the seigniorage problem. He pointed out that if the newly created international reserve asset is handed out in proportion to countries' long-run demand for reserves no interest should be paid by the issuing authority on these assets. However, whenever a country uses these assets to finance a deficit it should pay for the fact that it is borrowing resources from the rest of the world, and should do so at a rate which reflects the opportunity cost of the funds. Similarly, a country which accumulates reserve assets should be compensated for the fact that it lends resources.

Turning to Machlup's comments, Grubel stated that he would agree except for the last point. In a competitive banking system, the right to issue money does not enable a "representative" banker to make more than a normal rate of return. Supposedly, the rate of return on the funds deposited with the bank would be the same whether they are used internally or externally. On the other hand, Grubel agrees that one should distinguish seigniorage from the social saving that accrues to society from the substitution of fiat money for commodity money though the two are often related. The real problems lie not so much with the definition of and distinction between transfer, social costs, rents, distortions, and so on, as with the measurement of seigniorage when all these other elements enter the picture. Finally, one must, as Wilson Schmidt noted, distinguish between the existence of seigniorage and the seigniorage problem. The latter concerns the distribution of seigniorage, which often is equivalent to the distribution of the social savings from the substitution of fiat for commodity money, and is resolved automatically by the market itself under a so-called free market solution.

II

Four main points were made in the discussion of Professor Corden's paper. The first concerned the distribution of the gains from international liquidity creation; the second, the nature of the burden of adjustment; the third, the growth-promoting effects of additional liquidity; the fourth, the (lack of) importance of the currencies contributed to the liquidity-creating institution.

Professor Balassa referred to the first three of these points in his formal comment on Kafka's paper. (As has been noted, Kafka and Corden read their papers at the same session because of scheduling problems. The reader is referred to Part III of this volume for Balassa's complete comments. Only the briefest summary of his remarks on Corden's paper is included below for convenience.)

According to Balassa, Corden's paper can be interpreted in terms of the seigniorage problem. The distribution of new reserve assets determines in part who will gain and who will lose. It is not evident, however, that surplus countries always lose since they may use the newly distributed liquidity to buy additional commodities.

Second, an additional loss in world income may result from a deficiency in international liquidity. This loss stems from the departure from an efficient structure of world trade associated with restrictive and competitive balance-of-payments measures.

Finally, Balassa stated, additional liquidity may enable developing countries to avoid disruptions in their long-term plans and the attendant costs in terms of investment and growth rates.

Professor Grubel also emphasized the effect of liquidity on growth rates, but this time on the growth rates of developed countries. An increase in international liquidity could prevent developed countries from raising trade barriers and restricting expansion for balance-of-payments purposes. Thus liquidity creation could favor expansionary policies on the part of developed countries and hence higher saving and growth rates. The developing countries would again benefit in the process.

Professor Machlup discussed and clarified the concept of cost or burden of adjustment. Machlup pointed out that Corden had outlined three types of costs of adjustment: first, to use Corden's terminology, the disabsorption drain; second, the transitional costs of adjustment; and third, deviations from the optimum point on a country's Phillips curve, or what Machlup would rather call too much inflation or too much unemployment. Machlup would not call the first of these, the disabsorption drain, a cost of adjustment at all. Rather, it is the objective of adjustment. If a country has been spending too much and wants to adjust, it has to stop spending that much; this will of course be unpleasant for the country but should not be called a burden of adjustment.

Machlup himself proposed a different classification of the real costs of adjustment, also into three groups. First, there is the cost of transferring resources because adjustment implies a reallocation of resources and to transfer resources is usually costly. There are losses of invested capital and there is the cost to labor of working in new places and new occupations. Second, there may be a special cost of encouraging or compelling this transfer of resources, for example, the cost of government intervention. Third, there may be a cost of reduced efficiency of resources in the new occupations to which they have been transferred. The first two of these costs are transitional. The third may well be permanent, but it may in some cases be negative, that is, a gain rather than a loss in efficiency.

Machlup then asked where Corden's deviation from the optimum point on a country's Phillips curve would fit in the classification above. In Machlup's view, it is a cost of bringing about the transfer of resources needed for adjustment. Inflation in one country is one way of bringing about a reallocation of resources through changes in the terms of trade, in the relative prices and costs of various goods. Unemployment is another way of bringing about such a reallocation of resources, albeit a very inefficient one. In other words, departures from optimal points on the Phillips curve are really part of the more or less transitional costs of engineering the transfer of resources implied in the process of readjustment. Finally, there is the question of whether it is true that, as has been recently argued, this cost is relatively greater for developing than for developed countries. In a recent Princeton study,[1] Benjamin J. Cohen argues that this cost of engineering the transfer of resources and of actually transferring them is typically much larger in less developed countries than it is in advanced countries.

Sir Roy Harrod addressed himself to one important factor which helps to explain the proposed exclusion of the less developed countries from liquidity-expanding schemes. Sir Roy would prefer a more universal scheme which would also include the less privileged nations. Stating this preference, however, is not enough. One must also try to understand *why* the less developed countries are discriminated against, for example, in the schemes considered by the Group of Ten, and whether such discrimination is based on a valid rationale.

One reason for such discrimination is based on the argument that developing countries cannot afford to lock up "real" resources in

---

1. Benjamin J. Cohen, *Adjustment Costs and the Distribution of New Reserves*, Princeton Studies in International Finance, no. 18 (Princeton: Princeton University, 1966).

reserves. Another basis for discrimination is the intellectually more respectable argument—at least on the surface—that developing countries have to be excluded because they are unable to contribute worthwhile currencies to a liquidity scheme while members of the Group of Ten can. This argument does not make sense to Sir Roy. For, from an examination of various schemes designed to increase international liquidity, it is clear that the currencies contributed would play no part whatever, except in the event of dissolution of the scheme or the withdrawal of a particular country from it.

It would therefore seem to Sir Roy that, if this argument is the sole ground for discriminating against the less developed countries, the latter could guarantee the convertibility of whatever initial contribution they make to the new scheme. Should they fail to honor this guaranty, on the withdrawal of a member the international liquidity-creating institution could have recourse to a quite effective sanction, i.e. by not supplying the defaulting country with any more reserve units.

Professor Kafka voiced complete agreement with Sir Roy's view as to the lack of importance of the currencies contributed. Furthermore, even in the event of dissolution of the scheme, no great problems would arise since repayments could be scheduled over a number of years. For instance, in the event of dissolution of the International Monetary Fund, debts do not have to be paid off immediately but over a period of five years.

Dr. Corden replied briefly to the points made in the discussion from the floor. Corden wished especially to emphasize the distinction between permanent and transitional costs of adjustment. Suppose that, at a given point of time, a country is in deficit and that it now wishes to take steps to restore external balance. It may do this by deflating, and incurring unemployment as a result, or by imposing import restrictions. Both the costs of unemployment and of import restrictions are permanent and not transitional. For, unless circumstances change exogenously, import restrictions or unemployment have to be maintained permanently in order to preserve external balance. Transitional costs are only those which occur while resources are moved from one point or occupation to another.

From this it follows that the cost of adjustment suggested by Balassa, that is, the departure from an efficient trade structure, is permanent in nature if import restrictions rather than exchange-rate changes are used to restore equilibrium. Similarly, Corden would agree with Machlup that unemployment is a cost of adjustment, but to Corden it is a permanent one (unless prices can change by enough to restore external balance without unemployment). In fact, the unemployment created by a general policy of deflation can be considered to be the cost of foregoing proper switching devices.

Finally, Corden voiced agreement with Sir Roy's argument as to worthwhile currencies, namely, that the currencies contributed do not really matter. The rationale which leads "practical men" and bankers to pay attention to currencies contributed is not clear. The logic of their position, according to Corden, can perhaps be interpreted as follows: By a worthwhile currency these men mean the currency of a country which is not always likely to be in deficit. They may be thinking in terms of deficit-prone and surplus-prone countries. Then, underdeveloped countries do not have worthwhile currencies because they are deficit-prone.

As *Professor Machlup* pointed out, and Corden agreed, the fallacy of that argument is readily apparent when one considers the case of the dollar or of sterling.

APPENDIX: A NOTE ON SEIGNIORAGE AND THE SOCIAL SAVING FROM SUBSTITUTING CREDIT FOR COMMODITY MONEY

Harry G. Johnson

The original meaning of seigniorage, the difference between the circulating value of a coin and the cost of the bullion and minting, involves a once for all gain to the issuer on the issue of money. Owing to the durability of the precious metals, especially gold, one can reasonably assume that this gain is realized only once per unit of money in existence, though, presumably, worn, clipped, or sweated coins would come back eventually for melting down and reissue. If one wished to take account of that, one would regard the money supply as yielding a flow of seigniorage $(v - c)_1, (v - c)_2, \ldots, (v - c)_\infty$, which could in turn be summed into a capital value of the right to issue money:

$$\sum_{t=0}^{\infty} \frac{v - c}{(1 + i)^t} = (v - c) \frac{1 + i}{i}$$

where v is circulating value, c cost, and i the interest rate ruling over the period between recoinages. This expression differs from the usual formula for the capitalized value of an income flow because the first yield accrues immediately.

Seigniorage can be levied, presumably, because the public is prepared to pay a premium for the convenience of having coins of uniform size and certified as to weight and fineness of metal, greater than the cost of minting precious metal into such coins, and because the state can impose a monopoly of minting and thereby extract the difference. By taxing the conversion of metal into coins the state discourages the use of coins in payment as contrasted with the barter of precious metal for goods, and thereby imposes a welfare loss on the community. On the other hand, to the extent that the circulating value of coins is above their real resource cost, the levy of seigniorage reduces the real resources required to be invested in creating any given money supply, and so gives rise to a social saving. A full analysis of the welfare effects of seigniorage in a commodity-money system, however, would require an analysis of its effects on the supply of precious metals, which does not seem worthwhile pursuing here, if only because any social saving is likely to be negligible.

Now consider the replacement of a commodity money—the issue of which is assumed for simplicity not to be subject to seigniorage—by a purely paper money, assumed to be non-interest-bearing, and to cost nothing to print. The replacement frees the resources embodied in the stock of commodity money for other more productive uses and yields a social saving equal to the value of these resources. This social saving accrues to the monetary authority, which is able (by assumption) to persuade (or force) the public to surrender the commodity in exchange for paper. The monetary authority can then invest the resources formerly embodied in the money stock in productive assets. The "seigniorage" resulting from the operation can be thought of either as a capital sum— the real value of the money supply—or as a flow of income to the monetary authority equal to the real value of the money supply multiplied by the average rate of return on whatever assets the paper money (more accurately, the resources released by the substitution of paper for commodity money) has been invested in. (These may be government debt, in the case of a central bank, or public goods of some sort, if the government is assumed to appropriate the seigniorage.)

Now, retaining the assumption that money is non-interest-bearing and costless to issue, assume that the economy is growing and that additional money is issued at a rate sufficient to keep the price level stable. The issue of this money entails a social saving *by comparison with what would occur under a commodity-money system*, where real resources would have to be devoted to producing the additional money. If for simplicity the commodity-money system is assumed to be able to produce the monetary metal at constant cost, the social saving referred to is equal to the real value of the additional money issued. If, more realistically, the monetary metal is assumed to be a depletable resource, the marginal real cost of extraction of which rises as more is extracted, the price level in the commodity-money system would have to fall over time, so that some part of the increase in the money supply would be provided costlessly through appreciation of the existing stock, and the social saving from the issue of additional money instead of the production of additional commodity money would be less than the real value of the increase in the paper money stock. In the extreme case of inability to produce additional commodity money, the additional real balances demanded as a result of economic growth would be provided by a fall in the price level, at zero social cost. This result would also occur in a paper-money system in which the money supply was held constant. (Obviously there is no difference between a paper- and a commodity-money system if the money supply [in nominal terms] is constant.) But social welfare will be higher in a paper-money system with a fixed money supply than in one in which the money supply is expanded to keep the price level constant, because in the former system the falling trend of prices provides a yield to the holders of real balances and encourages a greater use of money, which greater use increases welfare at no social cost. (This proposition is subject to the qualification that if prices fall at a percentage rate greater than the rate of return on real assets, the public will want to hold money rather than real assets and the system is likely to break down.)

The issue of additional paper money at a rate sufficient to keep the price level constant yields seigniorage to the monetary authority equal to the real value of the quantity of money multiplied by its rate of growth. It follows from the previous paragraph that this seigniorage will be equal to the social saving implicit in the use of credit money rather than commodity money, if the marginal real cost of production of the monetary commodity is constant, and otherwise will exceed that social saving, which may be zero. Furthermore, by comparison with a paper-money system in which the quantity of money is fixed (and subject to the qualification mentioned at the end of the previous paragraph), the levying of seigniorage by a monetary policy of maintaining stable prices involves a social loss, resulting from the restriction of the use of money as a consequence of its zero yield. In other words, the maintenance of a stable price level imposes an "inflation tax" on holders of money, by comparison with a policy of keeping the money supply constant and allowing prices to fall over time (subject again to the aforementioned qualification).

Putting together the two concepts of seigniorage as the gain from the replacement of commodity by paper money, neither of which bears interest, and the gain to the monetary authority from issuing the additional paper money required to keep the price level stable while growth goes on, total seigniorage at any point of time is the sum of (1) the real growth of the money supply and (2) the yield on the investment of the resources freed by the past substitution of the existing paper money supply for commodity money. That is, seigniorage received by the monetary authority and available for distribution is $(i + g)M$, where i is the interest rate available on assets and g is the growth rate of demand for money at a stable price level, both defined for an appropriate time unit, and M is the existing money supply (indifferently measurable in nominal or real terms).

Now suppose that there are real costs incurred in maintaining the stock of money. In the case of currency, the notes have a production cost which includes the cost of the fine paper and intricate printing necessary to forestall forgery and the cost of maintaining security; in addition the notes wear out and have to be replaced. In the case of deposit money there are bookkeeping costs. Let these costs be at the rate c per unit of money per period of the previous analysis. Then the seigniorage on the existing stock of money becomes $(i - c)M$. As for the seigniorage on the issue of new money, such issue involves assuming the obligation of the cost stream c, the present value of which will be c/i. Hence the net seigniorage of this kind will be, not gM, but $[(1 - c)/i]gM$. The formula for total seigniorage is therefore

$$\left[(i - c) + \frac{(i - c)}{i}g\right]M = (i - c)\frac{(i + g)}{i}M = \frac{(i - c)}{i}(i + g)M.$$

This formula also represents the social gain from the substitution of paper money for commodity money when the paper money is expanded so as to maintain a stable price level and when in the commodity-money system the real cost of production of the commodity money is constant so that the price level would be stable in that system also.

The foregoing formula applies at a moment of time and adds together an income flow from the existing money stock and a capital gain for the monetary authority accruing from the expansion of the stock; it therefore assumes implicitly that the capital gain on past increases of the money supply has been invested by the monetary authority at the ruling rate of interest. The flow of income from seigniorage available to the monetary authority for current utilization may be one or the other of these two elements of income, but cannot be the sum of the two. That is, by always investing the capital gain the monetary authority can secure an income stream $(i - c)M_t$, where M_t is the stock of money at time t; alternatively, by always consuming the capital gain the monetary authority can secure an income stream $(i - c)M_0 + \{[(i - c)/i]gM_t\}$, where M_0 is the money stock existent at the time the policy of consuming capital gains commenced and will be zero if that policy has always been followed.

In the preceding formulas, c has been defined as a real cost stream associated with the operation of a unit of the money supply. Alternatively, c may be conceived as an interest charge paid to the holders of money to induce them to hold it. Such a charge represents, not a social cost, but a transfer of seigniorage (and of social benefit from a paper money as compared with a constant-cost commodity-money system) from the monetary authority to the holders of money. If the provision of money were competitive, as for example it would be in an unregulated deposit-banking system, *c* would be equal to *i* and there would be no seigniorage, no income flow for the monetary authorities either from earnings on the stock of money or from capital gains. Such a system would obviously require some means of limiting the rate of increase of the money supply to what would be consistent with a stable price level; alternatively, the monetary authority might deliberately forgo seigniorage and pay interest on money equal to what it earned on the assets backing the money supply. The payment of interest on money would eliminate the social loss due to the restriction of the use of money by the extraction of seigniorage.

This analysis has some obvious implications for current discussion of the problem of international monetary reform and the analysis of reform proposals. To elucidate these, it is convenient to assume that credit money is costless to operate, and that in the alternative commodity-money system the real cost of production of the monetary commodity is constant.

In the first place, a number of proposals for the reform of the international monetary system, such as the first Stamp Plan and the report of the UNCTAD expert group, have seized on the notion of a flow of social saving implicit in the expansion of international credit reserves rather than gold reserves and argued that this saving should be placed at the disposal of the less developed countries. This means in effect retaining a commodity-money system, so far as new credit reserve-holdings by the developed countries are concerned. (The Hart-Kaldor-Tinbergen proposal goes further, seeking to establish a full commodity reserve money system at the international level and in so doing to eliminate the social saving accruing to the world from the use of credit rather than commodity reserves, in order to achieve the extremely doubtful benefits of stable nominal—not real—prices of primary products.) The fact that there is a social saving implicit in the use of credit rather than commodity money, however, does not—contrary to the tenor of some of the arguments employed—mean that allocation of this social saving to the less developed countries would entail no real sacrifice by or loss to the developed countries that accumulate additional reserves. This would be true if the only choice available in international monetary reform lay between a commodity-reserve system and a credit-reserve system in which the social saving had to be distributed to the less developed countries; but in fact the choice lies among credit-reserve systems with differing distributional consequences. Furthermore, it is possible to define a credit-reserve system that would be distributionally neutral: distributional neutrality requires merely that each country that contributes to the social saving by holding additional reserves receives back the amount of its contribution in the form of command over the real resources saved. Such a distributionally neutral system for expanding international liquidity could be established by means of a composite reserve unit scheme in which countries' participations corresponded to their shares in the expansion of the demand for reserves.

In the second place, the foregoing analysis indicates that, if the distributional question about alternative liquidity schemes is formulated in terms of the levying and distribution of seigniorage—which assumes that no interest is paid on holdings of credit reserves (or, more generally, interest is paid at a rate below the rate of returns on the assets held against such reserves)—the distribution problem may arise in either or both of two forms. That is, the scheme could pay no interest on its liabilities (credit reserves held by the various countries) and charge a commercial rate of interest on its loans, thereby collecting seigniorage in the form of an annual income which would have to be distributed according to some agreed principle. At the other extreme, it could realize the seigniorage as a flow of capital gains from the expansion of holdings of non-interest-bearing international reserves, distributing these as cash grants according to some agreed distribution principle. As a middle course it could charge interest on its loans at a rate below the rate of return on, or alternative opportunity cost of, the real investments financed by those loans, receiving seigniorage partly as an explicit income flow to be distributed by an income-allocation rule and partly as an implicit flow of capital gains distributed by a loan-allocation rule. To the extent that it paid interest on holdings of international reserves, part of the seigniorage potentially collectable would be redistributed automatically according to the distribution of ownership of the international reserves that constitute its liabilities. Finally in this connection, it should be noted that to the extent that seigniorage is realized as an income flow not subject to a distribution rule, the distribution problem is left to determination by the management of the scheme—which may, of course, appropriate it to itself in the form of operating outlays (salaries, opulent office facilities) or spend it on the provision of public goods (such as research on international monetary problems).

In the third place, an important conclusion of the foregoing analysis is that any international liquidity plan that invokes the explicit or implicit collection and redistribution of seigniorage is necessarily inefficient and involves a social waste, inasmuch as seigniorage is derived from paying a rate of interest on reserve liabilities less than the alternative opportunity cost of holding them, and thereby restricts the holding of reserves and the realization of the full potential social saving from the use of credit money. An optimal system would pay a rate of return on reserve money equal to the rate of return available on investments made on commercial terms. Such a system would involve foregoing seigniorage, and the associated power to redistribute the social saving implicit in the expansion of reserve holdings; instead, this saving would be distributed automatically to the countries that held the additional money. (A distributionally neutral scheme for allocating seigniorage in proportion to additional credit reserves held would achieve the same result if countries rationally took account of the seigniorage earned on their reserve-holdings.)

The foregoing analysis rests on the theoretical abstraction of assuming a single world rate of return on real investment. In the real world of imperfect international mobility of capital, the rate of return on real investment and correspondingly the alternative opportunity cost of holding reserves vary internationally. If nevertheless it is required of a liquidity plan that it pay a uniform rate of interest on its liabilities and charge a uniform rate of interest on its loans, there will necessarily be implicit seigniorage in the form of a capital gain to borrowing countries whose rate of return on real investment exceeds the plan's lending rate, and most probably also explicit seigniorage in the form of income accruing from a difference between the plan's deposit and lending rates; and therefore there will necessarily be a problem of determining the distribution of the seigniorage. If no explicit rules are laid down, the problem will be solved by the discretionary control of the management of the plan over the rationing of loans and the disposition of the plan's operating income. The alternative of adjusting deposit and loan rates to the circumstances of individual countries, suggested by the criteria of distributional neutrality and optimal supply of reserves, would obviously encounter difficulties when reserves were used to finance deficits and surpluses. This is a problem that others might be interested in pursuing.

PART 6

THE PROBLEM OF WORLD STABILITY

INSTITUTIONAL CONSTRAINTS AND THE INTERNATIONAL MONETARY SYSTEM

A. C. L. Day

The purpose of this paper is to investigate the relationships between the working of the international monetary system and the institutional constraints which limit the degrees of freedom within which the system can operate. These constraints are primarily political in origin and include the outcome of political processes which lead the political and monetary authorities to attempt to achieve aims such as a high degree of employment or stability of exchange rates.

There is, of course, a great deal of room for discussion, along normative lines, of the virtues and vices of these various policy aims. But at least equally useful is a discussion, along positivist lines, of evidence about the way in which the interworking of the economic system and the political system leads to particular outcomes. There is room, in other words, for an analysis in terms of a science of political economy, which sets up hypotheses about the workings of both the economic and political systems and then attempts to test them against the evidence. Traditionally, political economy has been regarded as something of an art, and perhaps it will inevitably remain predominantly such for some time to come. But there is a largely unexploited field of investigation, which economists are well qualified to enter more actively, which does not involve trying to devise ideal politico-economic systems, but which investigates the interaction of these two major parts of the whole social system. This paper attempts to be a preliminary essay in the science of political economy, designed to set up a few hypotheses—rather than a traditional discourse, which leans toward trying to construct some kind of compromise between an ideal and a workable international monetary system. The task of trying to test any hypotheses is by no means an easy one because relatively little quantitative information is available about the preferences and the decisions of voters and politicians. But at least I hope that the attempt is worthwhile, and I might add that there could be no more appropriate place to start to approach a positivist science of political economy than in the University of Chicago, where the economics department has provided such an effective lead in the positivist approach to economics.

The analytical framework for looking at what can usefully be called the "degrees-of-freedom problem" is now familar—the classic sources being the early postwar work of Meade and Tinbergen. It is, however, worth summarizing it, at the first stage, in the context of a very simple international economic system with two countries with no growth whose relationships consist solely in trading goods, with no international capital movements except for movements of gold (the international means of payment) which is all held by the monetary authorities. The world supply of gold is fixed, and for the moment it will be assumed that the monetary authorities in each country follow the very unsophisticated rule that they wish to achieve a situation where net changes in their gold stock are zero—i.e., a balance-of-payments equilibrium. It is clear that they have to pay some attention to the gold stock, because at least it is impossible to allow a situation to come about where the gold stock is zero. But this is a very unsophisticated assumption, because it ignores all questions about the authorities' views on an optimum positive level of currency reserves; that is a matter which will be considered later.

Let it also be supposed that the government of each country has a view on the appropriate level of domestic activity—which can reasonably be called "full employment" for short. In practice, this amounts to some compromise between accepting too much unemployment and too much inflation. Since this compromise is politically determined, there is no necessary reason to assume that it will be a stationary position; it may vary, for example, with the stage of the electoral cycle and with recent historical experience—as undoubtedly has happened in Britain. A fuller understanding of the politico-economic system would demand a detailed discussion of the factors determining governmental decisions about the unemployment-inflation trade-off. Although it is counter to a substantial body of evidence, it can be supposed for the sake of our initial analytic model that the desired point is clearly specified and is stable.

The position of one of the two countries in our world is now conveniently represented on a diagram whose vertical coordinates measure net gold gain or loss (per unit period of time) and whose horizontal coordinates measure (un)employment, the percentage of capacity output or the speed of inflation, as is convenient. (We can take it that the horizontal scale measured in terms of one of these three can appropriately be transformed—not of course necessarily linearly—into a scale measured in either of the other two [see Fig. 1].)

There is some point, conveniently measured where the axes of the diagrams cross, which is the situation desired by the political authorities

—i.e., "full employment" and zero gold loss (or gain). The familiar
Meade-Tinbergen argument shows that, in order to satisfy these two
constraints, it is in general necessary to have two degrees of freedom—
e.g., domestic fiscal policy plus exchange-rate adjustments. The normal

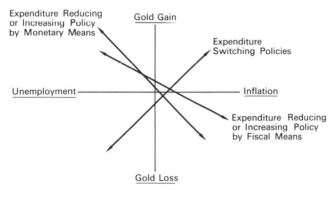

FIGURE 1

analysis emphasizes the advantages of combining an expenditure-
switching policy (e.g., import controls or exchange-rate changes) with
an expenditure-increasing or reducing policy (e.g., changing the budget
surplus). On the diagram, expenditure-switching policies are represented
by a movement in some northeasterly or southwesterly direction, while
expenditure reducing and expenditure increasing policies involve north-
westerly and southeasterly movements respectively. Clearly, there is a
useful sense in which it is more "efficient" to make up the necessary
parallelogram of forces which leads to the desired center point by combining elements of two movements which are roughly at right angles to
one another. In principle, it is possible to make up the parallelogram
from any pair of lines which are not parallel to one another—for
example, some domestic tax cuts which have a relatively big impact on
imports and other tax reductions which have a smaller proportional
effect on imports. Or it might be that contractionary monetary measures
might have a relatively bigger impact on the balance of payments than
expansionary fiscal measures of a magnitude just sufficient to leave the
domestic level of activity unchanged. It is not hard to conceive of circumstances in which such a combination of instruments might be used.
All the same, it is reasonable to suppose that such a combination would
be "inefficient" in that it involves large changes to achieve moderate-
sized results, in that it might be difficult to judge its impact accurately in

face of our lack of precise knowledge of the relevant parameters, and that serious dynamic problems might well arise if (for example) the two largely counteracting forces operated with significantly different time-responses.

This kind of analysis can be generalized, for a single country, to take account of three or more desired policies by introduction of additional dimensions.

The more significant development, for present purposes, is to take account of the other country. The central point here is simply that (ignoring all the discrepancies and inconsistencies of statistics in the real world, which sometimes make it appear as though practically every country has a payments deficit) the gold loss of one country equals the gold gain of the other. In terms of the diagram, the vertical coordinates of one country on its diagram are necessarily identical in magnitude with (and opposite in sign to) the vertical coordinates of the other country on its diagram. Moreover, any policy action taken by the government of a country with an open economy almost invariably involves a vertical component (i.e., a change in its payments position) as well as a horizontal component (a change in unemployment, etc.). And almost invariably, any disturbance to the position of a country involving a vertical component also involves a horizontal component. So whenever one country takes policy measures, say to adjust its domestic position toward the desired situation, it almost invariably disturbs the position of the other country—and by no means necessarily in the direction of the latter's chosen domestic equilibrium.

The source of freedom in face of this situation which is obvious (to economists at least) is exchange-rate flexibility of some kind or another. It is important that this is not the only possible source of freedom. The previous analysis leads to the conclusion that so long as a country has two policy instruments available which are not precisely "parallel" in their action, it can restore its dual-natured desired position in face of any change imposed by the actions of the other country (or, of course, any exogenous change in the parameters of the system). But exchange-rate changes have certain outstanding features. For one thing, they are expenditure-switching—i.e., NE–SW movements. There is indeed another very important policy instrument of this kind, namely changes in the intensity of import controls. But even if one leaves aside all the standard welfare arguments, there is a most important limitation to the use of this instrument which does not apply to exchange-rate adjustments. It is that there are limits beyond which the instrument cannot be used. One limit—where controls are so intense as to prevent any foreign transactions—is a solution in the sense that it makes the problem of achieving zero gold loss a non-problem. More practically, it can reasonably be assumed that no government would wish to tighten import controls more and more, beyond some point or other—perhaps a convenient way of expressing this is to say that at some point tightening of controls becomes a non-linear instrument. At the other extreme, non-linearity is obvious: import controls cannot be reduced below zero. On the other hand, exchange-rate adjustment can, in principle at least, be used indefinitely in either direction: neither $1¢ = £1$ nor $\$100 = £1$ is inconceivable.

It is probably reasonable to suppose that the use of some conceivable pairs of instruments—other than those containing changes in the intensity of controls as one of the two instruments—might also be constrained within limits set by this kind of non-linearity. For example, a government finding itself at full employment but with a modest gold loss might wish to combine contractionary monetary measures and expansionary fiscal measures as outlined above. But quite conceivably, one or the other of these instruments might have to be pushed so far as to reach into a zone where it does not "bite" any more. So if there are these non-linearities in the effectiveness of instruments, we have reinforcing arguments in favor of combinations of instruments working (as it were) more or less at right angles to one another.

This kind of consideration is particularly important in view of the possibility (for which there does appear to be some empirical justification) that the rate of inflation associated with "full employment" (as determined by political processes) may not be the same in each country in the system. If the desired rate of inflation is substantially higher in one country than the other, one can expect (in the absence of "perverse" elasticities) that there will be a trend toward increasing payments deficit in the country which is more tolerant of inflation. Within limits this could be met by (for example) changes in controls or the fiscal-monetary policy mix. But sooner or later, there is a good chance that the limits may be reached. Moreover, additional complications may arise for dynamic reasons which are for the most part excluded from this analysis. For example, one country may be more effective than the other in achieving the desired "full employment" position in face of disturbances; in view of asymmetry of price-level changes in relation to the level of activity around full employment, the country whose stabilization policy is less effective can be expected, on average, to have a relatively fast rate of inflation compared with its desired rate. Again, additional complications are introduced by allowing for economic growth in terms of the differential effects between countries of growth on the balance of payments.

Nevertheless, it may well be that, within quite broad limits, the dual aims in each country of achieving payments equilibrium and "full employment" can be achieved by policy mixes which do not include exchange-rate adjustment (or, for that matter, changes in the intensity of import controls). Suppose, for example, that use is made of a mix of fiscal and monetary policies, and assume that their effects are "non-parallel" as described above. The standard Meade-Tinbergen type of analysis applies: there are three independent policy objectives (two "full employments" and one payments equilibrium between the two countries). But in contrast with the exchange-rate-flexibility solution, there is now a "spare" policy instrument—there are four available instruments, namely fiscal and monetary policy in each of the countries, whereas there can be only one exchange rate between the two countries.

One implication of this is that one country could set one of its two domestic instruments arbitrarily (e.g., a balanced budget). It is plausible that this greater freedom is one of the reasons why countries choose to use domestic policies rather than exchange-rate policies in order to try to achieve the dual aims of "full employment" and payments equilibrium: in quite a genuine sense, governments can feel more free to control their own affairs if they rely purely on domestic instruments. This seems the more plausible in view of the fact that our comparative static model is highly formalized; in practice, one is concerned with a dynamic adjustment process and the greater freedom which can sometimes be enjoyed by one country and sometimes by the other, in the four domestic instruments case—rather than with the two domestic instruments plus exchange rate case. Generalizing for the moment to an n-country world, the same general principle applies—there is still just one "spare" instrument. (No additional degree of freedom is added: in an n-country system there are $2n$ instruments and $2n - 1$ objectives— i.e., n "full employments" and $n - 1$ balanced payments, since balance for $n - 1$ automatically implies balance for the nth country.)

This suggests that the relative advantage of the two domestic instruments case becomes less, the larger the number of countries. But for many practical purposes, the effective number of countries is quite small; a large part of the international adjustment problem between the advanced industrial countries which can expect to achieve the dual aims hypothesized above concerns a handful of major countries, such as the United States, Germany, France, Britain, Italy, Canada, and Japan. Our n is larger than 2, but not so much larger.

The obvious reluctance of most major countries to use exchange-rate adjustment as a normal policy instrument can be approached in another way, in terms of the degrees of freedom analysis. Returning to the simple case where $n = 2$, then there is only one exchange rate. In principle, this can be determined in several different ways, depending upon political decisions.

> 1) The political decision can be made in *both* countries to leave the rate entirely to competitive market forces. This solution has its intellectual attractions. There is, however, remarkably little evidence that it would be acceptable politically in a world where almost all governments take an active role in economic management. Generalizing to an n-country world (even where the effective n is, say, 6 or so) the likelihood of acceptance of this ground rule by all countries for long periods of time seems very small.
>
> 2) One country (in a two-country world) may determine the rate and the other accept the decision purely passively. Again, such an outcome seems highly implausible in a world of managed economies.
>
> 3) The decision about the rate (again limiting ourselves to a two-country world for the moment) may be the result of agreement or bargaining between the two countries. This kind of case is worthy of further consideration.

In the first place one can consider some kind of formal political agreement—a treaty or a joint committee, or collaboration between exchange accounts. Clearly, such agreements will not necessarily be at all easy to reach. Conditions could easily arise where there would be no agreement about the direction of movement of the rate. If countries A and B were at the position described in Figure 2, A would fairly clearly like an exchange depreciation which would take it toward payments equilibrium and "full employment"; country B might dislike an exchange appreciation, which would take it further away from "full employment", and would prefer to rely mainly on domestic expansionary policies. It is true that if there were full collaboration on all aspects of economic policy, A would forgo its depreciation on the understanding that B would expand domestically, with the multiplier consequences of putting A nearer to payments equilibrium and full employment. But that is to hypothesize much more than agreement about exchange-rate policy. Moreover, if one were to follow the track of full political agreement on all economic policies in some federal or confederal political institution, the possibilities of conflict of interest between different "countries" still arises—as is shown by national experiences between regions.

One of the easiest agreements to reach is to leave things unchanged—and in view of the many conflicts of interest in attempting to reach agreement on exchange-rate policy which can be conceived and can be observed in the real world, the forces leading to an agreement to leave things where they are seem to be very powerful (as seen in the workings of the tripartite agreement of the late thirties and the IMF since the war). Exchange-rate adjustment by agreement can easily mean no adjustment at all.

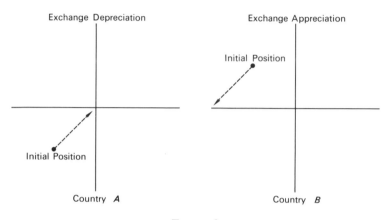

FIGURE 2

An alternative possibility arises where both countries take an active role in deciding the exchange rate, but do not enter any explicit agreement and instead carry out implicit bargaining. Here, the analysis of oligopoly theory and the theory of games can perhaps be usefully applied. As a first step one might suggest the relevance of the kinky oligopoly demand curve, where a decision-making unit chooses to hold a price stable for long periods of time, because it calculates that it may lose by a change made in either direction.

All of this is no more than a sketch of possible lines for investigation. But at least it suggests that there may be good rational reasons why countries prefer a fixed-rate system to a flexible-rate system, and why adjustments in a system such as today's (which is formally an adjustable-peg system) are in fact so rare.

Up to this point, the argument has assumed a very naive policy with regard to gold reserves—namely, that the desired position is one of zero net change in the reserves. A rather more sophisticated and realistic analysis would be one which assumes that countries are also concerned with a desired *level* of reserves (and of course it is not difficult to hypothesize still more sophisticated desired situations, such as a desired rate of change of reserves in the process of adjustment to a desired level of reserves).

Analysis in terms of a desired level of reserves involves close parallels with the analysis of modern monetary theory in terms of real balance effects and the like. In many ways, the international economy approximates quite closely the models of the kind of analysis where there is a simple claim (paper money or gold), desired holdings of which are a function of the value of income and expenditure.

Two lines of attack could be followed in order to obtain empirically some kind of information about the desired level of reserves of individual countries. One has been followed by Kenen and Yudin.[1] It is to use a cross-section analysis to estimate the reserves which each country would hold if it conformed to "average" behavior. But this approach has its limitations (as Kenen and Yudin allow). It cannot ascertain whether the governments of individual countries do wish to conform to average behavior in relation to variables such as past experience of payments instability. And it cannot be used to detect an "absolute" excess or deficiency of reserves.

The other possible approach would be to try to relate the decisions and actions of individual governments to their reserve positions, on the basis of the assumption that a country which takes steps to increase its reserves regards the current level as inadequate in relation to its other policy decisions (e.g., for fixed rates, absence of import controls, and "full employment"). Clearly this kind of positivist analysis would not be easy. Firstly, one cannot necessarily accept that the avowed reason given by politicians for policy decisions is the real reason for the decision. Second, most policy decisions are taken for a variety of reasons—politicians know that their actions generally have diagonal effects on our diagrams rather than purely horizontal or vertical ones. Third, there is no reason to suppose that complex institutions such as the governments of countries make decisions which are necessarily consistent with one another—and the situation is made the more complex when the relevant policy decisions are largely made by quasi-autonomous central banks.

Nevertheless, the approach would be worth trying. Certainly, a general knowledge of the economic policy decisions of the major countries today suggests that almost none of them regards its own

1. Peter B. Kenen and Elinor B. Yudin, "The Demand for International Reserves", *Review of Economics and Statistics*, 47 (August, 1965): 242–500.

reserves as excessive, since none of them appears deliberately to be following policies designed to reduce the level of reserves. On the other hand, it is easy to identify countries where the actions and decisions of the government and monetary authorities indicate that they regard the level of reserves as inadequate. To say the least, the evidence is suggestive.

The problems which all this leaves us with are, however, still hard to answer—and here I can only pose them. In the standard analysis of the theory of economic policy, the aims of governments are taken as exogenous data. But in any science of political economy, one needs to try to understand the interrelationships between economic performance and policy aims. It is, for example, quite plausible that the desired level of "full employment" is a function of the level of reserves: a country with high reserves (and a given socio-political situation) may decide to choose "fuller" employment and a faster rate of inflation, because its reserves are relatively large, so that it is "safe" internationally to accept faster inflation. Or again, a country whose reserves are rising might take such a view, through normal political and administrative processes. The hypotheses would be worth testing, that such relationships are one of the factors which have contributed to the postwar trade cycle; it certainly would not be surprising if it were demonstrated that Britain's postwar trade cycle is to a significant extent a "planning cycle" of this kind.

It is clear that the difficulties in identifying significant factors determining the decisions of governments (and central banks) are immense. In many ways, they are similar to those now being tackled by microeconomists trying to understand the factors determining the decisions of large firms. In each case a great deal of work is necessary before reasonably convincing answers can be given. Fortunately, the aim of this conference is merely to tackle unresolved issues pertaining to international monetary reform—and not necessarily to solve them.

THE CRISIS PROBLEM

Robert A. Mundell

Meaning of Crisis

"Crisis" implies a disequilibrium, and therefore a change, so severe that it threatens to undermine the stability of parameters hitherto regarded as constants. In economics the threatened parameters are usually institutional structures or fixed points within a structure. In our context the institutional structure is the present international monetary "system," and crisis implies a threat to the maintenance of a fixed point within the system.

Is the gold exchange standard a "system"? A system is an aggregation of diverse entities united by regular interaction according to a form of control. The gold exchange standard can be identified as a system if we can perceive the order in the interaction of its components and outline the form of control. We shall argue first that a system of control can be identified in the gold exchange standard and that it therefore qualifies as a system.

"Collapse" is the breakdown of order, the subversion of an institutional parameter, and crisis is impending collapse. Collapse can come about either because certain boundary conditions are reached, or because the control mechanism is such that the equilibrium of the system is an unstable one. We shall refer to the first threat as a "structural crisis" and the second as a "control crisis," and attempt an explicit formulation of both concepts in the context of the gold exchange standard.

The "crisis problem" is the problem of preventing a threat of collapse from materializing, and thus the problem of preserving the institutional structure. Its purpose is conservative in substance and therefore excludes solutions based on flexible exchange rates, the gold standard, a dollar standard, or a supranational central bank, all of which alter institutional equations in the present system. That does not mean these panaceas are undesirable, but only that they lie outside the mandate of the crisis problem.

Rules of the System

To identify the order—the rules of the game—in the gold exchange standard, and explore its consequences, we have to know the rules under which it is operated. The rules constitute a combination of laws, commitments, conventions, and gentlemen's agreements by which the inner country (the United States) pegs its currency (the dollar) to gold and the outer countries (Europe) peg their currencies to the dollar, either directly, or indirectly through a secondary reserve currency like the pound sterling or the franc. This means that the United States acts as *residual* buyer or seller of gold, whereas Europe acts as a *residual* buyer or seller of dollars. The United States has to take up (supply) any excess supply of (demand for) gold offered to it, and Europe has to take up (supply) any excess of dollars offered (demanded) on exchange markets.

The boundary conditions of the system are given by the U.S. stock of gold and Europe's stock of dollars; the United States and Europe, respectively, cannot supply gold or dollars they lack. But there is an asymmetry in these conditions, because, as long as gold and dollars can be exchanged at the United States Treasury, Europe has access to additional dollars in exchange for gold. The total reserves (dollars and gold) of Europe therefore constitute its boundary condition, whereas the gold reserve of the United States represents its constraint.

Control of the system rests on U.S. monetary policy on the one hand, and Europe's gold-dollar portfolio on the other. When the United States expands the dollar supply it puts upward pressure on world incomes and prices—directly, because of interest rate effects and spending changes in the United States, and indirectly because of increases in European reserves. Similarly, when the United States contracts the dollar supply, it puts downward pressure on world prices.

Europe's gold-dollar portfolio is the other control variable. When Europe converts dollars into gold it weakens the U.S. reserve position and stimulates or compels a monetary contraction[1] and when it converts gold into dollars it strengthens the reserve position and permits or compels a monetary expansion. Europe's gold-purchase policy thus influences U.S. monetary policy, while the latter "determines" world prices and incomes. When U.S. monetary policy is forcing inflation on the rest of the world, Europe can stimulate or compel a contraction by

1. I shall speak throughout of "expansion" and "contraction" and rising and falling prices rather than increases or decreases in the rate of expansion or contraction of money and prices, but the reader should have no difficulty in making his own translation into a growing economy.

gold purchases; and when U.S. monetary policy is deflationary, Europe can entice an expansion by gold sales.

We may thus express the control mechanism of the system as follows: The United States expands or contracts its monetary policy according to whether its gold position is excessive or deficient, and Europe buys or sells gold from the United States according to whether U.S. policy is causing inflation or deflation. The gold exchange standard therefore constitutes a "system" and it is with its implications that we must now be concerned.

Operation of the System

The system can be formulated in precise mathematical terms. The purpose of doing so, of course, is not to lend an impression of spurious precision to central bank behavior.[2] The purpose is rather to be explicit about the possibilities inherent in the mechanism, and to see what help the formulation is in uncovering possibilities easily missed by unaided intuition.[3]

Figure 1 plots Europe's gold holdings (G) on the abscissa and U.S. dollar liabilities (D) on the ordinate. Given the stock of gold in the world as a whole, the line $R_1 R_2$ plots the relation between Europe's gold holdings (and therefore U.S. gold holdings as the residual) and U.S. dollar liabilities, which preserves the U.S. gold-reserve ratio at its desired level. Thus if Europe holds OR_1 of gold, none is left over for the United States and dollar liabilities must be zero, whereas if Europe holds no gold (so that the United States holds it all), U.S. dollar liabilities are OR_2. (Given one dollar's worth of gold as the unit in which gold is measured, the slope of $R_1 R_2$, with a negative sign, is the reciprocal of the U.S. reserve ratio, which is assumed to be less than 1.[4])

The line $P_1 P_2$ plots the relation between Europe's gold holdings and U.S. dollar liabilities that preserves a given money supply (composed of dollars and gold) in the world as a whole, and therefore (supposing no lags) a given level of prices or incomes. Thus a dollar supply of OP_2 would be exactly sufficient to maintain a given level of prices so Europe's gold holdings would have to be zero to preserve that price level; and,

2. I know of no central banker who would like to think that his actions can be expressed in a system of differential equations.

3. Mathematical formulation of the system, however, and formal proofs about its behavior, are reserved for the Appendix.

4. *D* may be taken to represent the aggregate supply of nongold money in the world as a whole, rather than simply the foreign central bank holdings of dollars, since we are not concerned here with exchange margins, imperfect substitutability of one currency for the other, or more than one currency area. The gold stock, equal to OR_1, can readily be adjusted to take into account private gold hoarding.

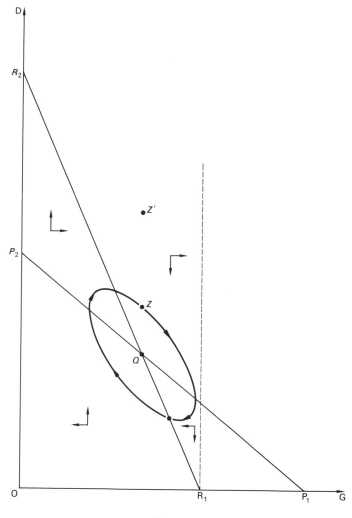

FIGURE 1

similarly, if the dollar supply were nil, gold holdings in Europe would have to be OP_1. The slope of P_1P_2 (with negative sign) is the reciprocal of the dollar price of gold, which, as already noted, is taken to be unity.

The two lines represent targets of policy. When the U.S. reserve ratio is below (above) the desired ratio, which is the case whenever D is above (below) R_1R_2, U.S. authorities will reduce (increase) D; and when the world money supply is above (below) that which preserves the price level implied by P_1P_2, which is the case whenever G is right (left) of P_1P_2, Europe will purchase (sell) gold to encourage restraint or expansion in the U.S. We thus get "direction forces" at each point in the diagram indicated, in each quadrant, by arrows.

Control Crisis

It may be seen at once that the system may be stable or unstable, depending on the intensity of the forces acting on the control variables. Let α be the rate of dollar expansion in the United States expressed as a proportion of excess gold reserves; let β be the rate of gold purchases in Europe expressed as a proportion of the excess of the world money supply over its equilibrium level; and let μ be the gold-dollar equilibrium reserve ratio in the United States. Then, assuming α, β, and μ are constant, the system is stable or unstable according to whether

$$\frac{\alpha}{\beta} \gtreqless \frac{1}{\mu}.$$

(In the borderline case, the system, from an initial point in the graph such as Z, would oscillate hopelessly [and elliptically] around the equilibrium Q.) Thus if $\mu = 25$ per cent, U.S. monetary contraction must be more than four times European gold purchases; if this were not the case the world money supply would increase (decrease) when the price level was too high (low) and the dollar supply overexpanded (underexpanded).

The system might break down even in the event that it is otherwise stable. Boundary constraints are given by the axes and by a vertical line from R_1. Hitting the latter boundary would imply a suspension of gold payments in the United States—structural collapse—or a cessation of the rules of the game. Thus it is entirely possible that, given a sufficiently large disequilibrium such as that indicated by the point Z', the system could break down because it hits the barrier where the U.S. runs out of gold.

There are means of easing the situation, thus reducing the risk of crisis. A higher U.S. reserve ratio, a reduction in the European β variable, or an increase in the U.S. α variable would diminish the risks of instability, as would an increase in μ. An increase in the price of gold would move the gold barrier from R_1 to the right, flattening both R_1R_2 and P_1P_2.

Reversal of Control

The easier way is to reverse the control variables. A strongly stable system, in the sense that it will always reach the equilibrium price level and gold supply, can be created if the United States governs its monetary policy by the need for a stable price level in the world, and Europe's gold purchase policy is determined by the need to preserve a given gold ratio in the United States. Specifically, if the United States contracts the dollar supply whenever world prices are above equilibrium, and expands the dollar supply whenever they are below equilibrium, and if Europe buys gold when the United States has an excessive reserve, and sells it whenever U.S. reserves are deficient, equilibrating forces are assured. The policy mix in the diagram would be reversed and the arrows would point toward equilibrium.

The theoretical explanation is the usual one—the *principle of effective market classification*. European gold policy has a comparative advantage in affecting the U.S. gold stock, and U.S. monetary policy has a comparative advantage in determining the level of world prices.

Conclusions

The present system has crisis-laden features if it is run in such a way that Europe tries to protect itself against U.S. inflation by reducing the U.S. gold reserve, and the United States tries to protect itself against gold losses or gains by tight or expansive monetary policies. On the other hand, the gold exchange standard has strong built-in stabilizers if it is run so that the United States tries to protect Europe (and itself) against inflation or depression, and Europe tries to protect the United States against excesses or shortfalls of gold. The optimal policy is a good-neighbor policy, the epitome of central bank cooperation.

In practice this means that the United States would have to concern itself, under the gold exchange standard, with global stability, whereas Europe would have to concern itself with the U.S. reserve position, using its own gold to empty into (take out of) the London market when hoarding increases (diminishes). To this end an enlargement of the London gold pool might be helpful.[5] That approach—tame as it is—would be my solution to the crisis problem.

Appendix: Alternative Dynamic Mechanisms

Let $\bar{G}$ be the world gold stock and G the stock held in Europe, so that $\bar{G} - G$ is the stock held in the United States; then excess gold reserves in the United States are $\bar{G} - G - \mu D$, where D denotes dollar liabilities and μ the fractional reserve ratio. Let M be the world stock of money consistent with the equilibrium price level, so that $G + D - M$ is the

5. The pool would be excessive if it drew an undesired amount out of public hoards; the important rule is to keep a "balance of uncertainty" in play.

amount of money in excess of its equilibrium quantity. Then what choices of the parameters α, β, γ, and δ will make the following dynamic system stable?

$$\dot{D} = \alpha[\bar{G} - G - \mu D] - \gamma[G + D - M]$$
$$\dot{G} = \delta[\bar{G} - G - \mu D] + \beta[G + D - M].$$

Suppose first that $\gamma = \delta = 0$. Then, redefining D and G as discrepancies from their equilibrium values, the characteristic equation is

$$\lambda^2 + (\mu\alpha - \beta)\lambda + \alpha\beta(1 - \mu) = 0$$

and the characteristic roots will have negative real parts, assuming $\mu < 1$, only if

$$\mu\alpha - \beta > 0$$

as noted in the text. On the other hand, if $\alpha = \beta = 0$, the characteristic equation is

$$\lambda^2 + (\gamma + \delta)\lambda + \gamma\delta(1 - \mu) = 0$$

which must be stable. In fact, since the discriminant

$$(\gamma - \delta)^2 + 4\gamma\delta\mu > 0$$

a cyclical solution is impossible.

COMMENT: THE PROBLEM OF WORLD
STABILITY

Marina v. N. Whitman

Being of a somewhat cowardly disposition, I shall confine these comments to those aspects of Day's paper dealing directly with the question
originally assigned to him, "the redundancy problem." The larger
questions he raises concerning the determinants of political decision-
making on matters of economic policy are equally stimulating and
perhaps more urgent, but they present too vast a field to plow in a
limited time.

In considering the redundancy problem, Day contrasts a world of
fluctuating exchange rates, in which the number of policy targets is
exactly equal to the number of available instruments (the $2n - 1$ goals
are n full-employment positions and $n - 1$ balance-of-payments equilibria), with the fixed exchange rate world in which monetary and fiscal
policy are used by each country to achieve internal and external balance
simultaneously. In the latter case, he argues, there are $2n$ instruments
available to achieve the same $2n - 1$ goals, leaving one "spare" instrument available to be used for other purposes by the "nth" country,
which is relieved of the necessity of achieving external balance.

I would suggest that the whole emphasis on redundancy is somewhat
misplaced or at least incomplete. To see why, let us consider four possible situations with differing implications for the relationship between
targets and available instruments:

1) Assume a world of $n - 1$ flexible exchange rates and, let us say,
n fiscal policies used to achieve internal balance. So far, the system is
just determined; there is no redundancy and, incidentally, no problem
of reserves. But if we now introduce another instrument, monetary
policy, and assume that countries are not concerned either with the
composition of their payments balances or with their reserve levels, the
world will have $n - 1$ additional instruments available. Why $n - 1$?
Because if we follow Mundell in assuming that, in a world of considerable international capital mobility, monetary policy is better directed
toward external than toward internal goals, it is interest rate *differentials*
between countries rather than interest-rate levels which are relevant.
More specifically, there are only $n - 1$ interest-rate differentials

351

consistent with the maintenance of equilibrium. That is, in the absence of a universal agreement among countries not to use monetary policy for the purpose of altering these differentials, such manipulation would react back on exchange rates through their effects on balance-of-payments positions and would lead to disturbing, and possibly unstable, cyclical movements around equilibrium. To avoid such disturbances, the $n - 1$ interest-rate differentials would have to be set equal to agreed fixed values, but these values would not all have to be zero. Such differentials might be used, for example, to stimulate international flows of capital from capital-rich to capital-poor countries.

2) Now consider a world of fixed exchange rates (with the further assumption that other forms of expenditure-switching policies are avoided, for any of the reasons Day suggests) and n balance-of-payments targets all equal to zero, implying constant reserve targets for all countries. Now the question of the "redundant" instrument and its allocation is closely tied to the nature of international reserves. Under the sort of "pure dollar standard," with gold essentially demonetized, envisioned by Despres,[1] for example, it appears that the "nth" country is the United States, freed from concern with its external payments position by the fact that its liabilities are fully acceptable as others' reserves, and that it therefore has no need for reserves of its own. Its position would be essentially that of a country able to produce unlimited amounts of gold at zero cost in a gold standard world. But, in reality, this nth country still has two responsibilities which constrain its two available policy instruments: (a) to keep the purchasing power of the dollar stable and (b) to avoid using monetary policy in a way which would interfere with the reserve targets of other countries. So again, we have no redundancy, but rather n fiscal policies directed toward internal stability and $n - 1$ monetary policies (interest-rate differentials), all pegged to the position maintained by the United States. The system is just determined and stable, but in giving up flexible exchange rates the world has lost the use of monetary policy for other goals, such as the achievement of a desirable pattern of international capital movements.

3) This situation differs from the previous one only in that the balance-of-payments targets of the $n - 1$ countries comprising "the rest of the world" are no longer assumed to be zero, but rather positive,

1. Emile Despres, "Proposal Re Change in U.S. Gold Policies: A Proposal for Strengthening the Dollar," in *Guidelines for International Monetary Reform*, Hearings, Subcommittee on International Exchange and Payments of the Joint Economic Committee, 89th Cong., 1st sess., 1965, pt. 2: suppl.

implying a desire for continuously increasing reserve levels. The situation will remain stable as long as the implications of the pure dollar standard are universally accepted; as long, that is, as all countries including the United States itself are indifferent to that country's own balance-of-payments and reserve positions. There will then be $2n - 1$ available instruments, as before, along with n internal stability goals but only $n - 1$ balance-of-payments (reserve) targets.

4) Finally, let us take a giant step toward reality by modifying the assumption of situation (3) that the world is indifferent to the reserve position of the United States. Specifically, consider a "mixed reserve" standard, under which the willingness of the rest of the world to hold dollars as reserves is dependent upon the balance-of-payments and reserve position of the United States. Now we are in trouble; we have the same number of instruments and internal goals as before, but there are now n balance-of-payments targets (desired reserve positions) and the system is one instrument short. To look at the problem another way: if countries' external-balance targets are fundamentally inconsistent—as is the case when the rest of the world aims at running surpluses in order to increase their reserves, but at the same time any increase in the deficit of the United States is universally regarded as a situation of "imbalance"—then the achievement of their external balance targets by $n - 1$ countries necessarily implies that the nth country will fail to achieve its target. This is, in fact, the sort of situation implied by the competitive increases in interest rates which have occurred in many of the major countries over the past five years. We have moved from the problem of redundancy to that of deficiency. Clearly some additional instrument or outside solution is required, and the stage is set for the crisis problem.

In moving on to Mundell's succinct formulation of "the crisis problem," I should like to ask first a preliminary question of definition. Is the "gold exchange standard" normally defined in terms of who "pegs to" what, exemplified by a situation in which European currencies are pegged to the dollar and the dollar is in turn pegged to gold, or in terms of the types of reserves held by various nations? The definition I have generally encountered has been cast in terms of the latter, defining the gold exchange standard as a world-wide system wherein some countries hold as reserves the currencies of certain other countries, which themselves hold reserves in the form of gold. Mundell's definition, on the other hand, seems to be formulated in terms of the "peg." It might be worth investigating whether the alternative definitions have identical implications for the functioning of the world monetary system; I suspect that they may not.

To move on to substantive matters, I find myself with two fundamental questions regarding the elegantly simple model presented by Mundell. The first is whether one can really generalize the "imported inflation" hypothesis which is regarded by many as the motive force underlying the behavior of France's president in matters of international financial policy. Is it reasonable to equate de Gaulle with France, France with Europe, and Europe with the "rest of the world"? More specifically, why should Europe use such an indirect approach to internal stability as pressure on United States monetary policy through purchases or sales of gold? What prevents the nations of Europe from taking a more direct approach to internal stability, as, for example, the use of fiscal policy, particularly since the use of fiscal policy for internal balance by the United States is implicit in Mundell's model? Or, if it is not, we are faced with a puzzling asymmetry in the model: internal stability is cited as an explicit goal of the European nations, but not of the United States.

This indirectness postulated by Mundell seems especially fraught with difficulties in view of the complicated and unexplored relationship which exists between Mundell's concept of "world internal stability" (that is, some trade-off point between full-employment and price stability for the world as a whole), and the "internal stability" goals of individual nations. For example, if different countries have different Phillips curves, or different social welfare functions which will lead them to different optimum points on the same Phillips curve, the resulting inconsistency in goals will represent an aspect of the crisis problem which cannot be readily solved by Mundell's suggested application of the principle of effective market classification. Mundell, in his "The Redundancy Problem and International Standards," defines the difficulty somewhat differently, but goes no further toward solving it, when he puts it in terms of the problem of choosing appropriate country weights for a world price index[2]. These complications suggest strongly that the achievement of internal stability should be primarily a goal of national policies, rather than one of formalized international cooperation.

To pursue the matter somewhat further, let us ask which is the more accurate description of the existing international monetary system,

2. Robert A. Mundell, "Appendix: The Redundancy Problem and the World Price Level," part 6 of this work.

whether we call it a gold exchange standard, the Bretton Woods system, or something else: that offered here by Mundell, or the one first suggested by Triffin[3] and formalized by Kenen[4] some years ago? The Triffin-Kenen model is based on the assumption that the rest of the world's marginal propensity to hold dollars (as an alternative to gold) is governed by its confidence in the dollar, which in turn depends primarily on the current reserve position of the United States. The implication of this system is that there will be a world monetary crisis whenever the composition of new reserves, consisting of available gold production plus increased dollar liabilities, differs from the desired composition. That is, crisis will be inevitable if the desired rate of total reserve increase and the desired composition of reserve assets on the part of the rest of the world together lead to a continuous deterioration of the United States reserve position. The cure for such a situation must lie either in the direction of Despres' world, where the willingness to hold dollars does not depend on the United States reserve position, or in the creation of a world central bank, such as Triffin's suggested XIMF, which is somehow able to make its own liabilities immune to the conflict between quantity and quality, or confidence, which faces the dollar as a reserve currency.

Mundell's description of the international monetary system is very different from Triffin's, and his anticrisis prescription sounds very different from either of those just mentioned. But is it? He argues for a system of perfect central bank cooperation, in which the United States uses its monetary policy to stabilize the world price level (via the external spillover effects of inflationary or deflationary pressure on its own economy, which Mundell assumes to be a dominant influence on European levels of economic activity) and Europe adjusts its purchases and sales of gold so as to maintain the desired ratio of United States reserves to dollar liabilities. But this implies that the United States need have no concern for its own reserve position, since Europe is assumed to be willing to adjust its reserve composition to suit United States needs, without any feedback on the European desired reserve-asset composition from the degree of "support" required for the United States reserve ratio. In essence, we are brought back to a weak form of

3. Robert Triffin, "The Return to Convertibility" and "Tomorrow's Convertibility," Banca Nazionale del Lavoro, *Quarterly Review*, vol. 12 (March and June, 1959).
4. Peter B. Kenen, "International Liquidity and the Balance of Payments of a Reserve-Currency Country," *Quarterly Journal of Economics*, 42 (November, 1960): 572–86.

the Despres solution; gold is not explicitly demonetized, but if Europeans are assumed to be willing to allow their gold-dollar holdings to shift passively in response to the requirements of the reserve currency country's own reserve ratio, the implications for the functioning of the world monetary system are essentially the same.

COMMENT: THE PROBLEM OF WORLD STABILITY

Jürg Niehans

I shall first comment on Day's interesting paper paying particular attention to the nature, significance, and various aspects of the so-called redundancy problem. This will be followed by some remarks on Mundell's rationalization of what he calls the "crisis problem."

As Day's paper was circulated, its title seemed to indicate that it was intended to be about institutional aspects of the international adjustment mechanism. I thus expected—naturally, I think—a discussion of, say, voting rights in some international organizations, legal requirements for a change in the price of gold, or the relations between treasuries and central banks. This expectation seemed to be confirmed by the research program outlined in the first few pages of the paper. What followed, however, was about entirely different—and highly analytical—problems. In the jargon of today, these problems are starting to be put under the heading of "the redundancy problem." Day does not explain in general terms what the redundancy problem is, but from the contents of his paper it is clear enough that he means the whole complex of interesting and largely unsolved problems arising from the fact that the number of policy instruments may exceed the number of targets. It may at first appear that this is an esoteric case, the typical economic problem being that of scarcity, with respect to policy instruments no less than with respect to resources. This impression is misleading, however. In fact, the number of policy variables can usually be made arbitrarily large just by using a finer classification. We are, to give an example, entirely free at least in principle, either to classify tariff policy as a single instrument or to call each tariff rate a separate instrument. The same could, of course, be said about the targets. Seen in this light, the general case is one of an arbitrary relationship between the number of targets and the number of instruments depending on our system of classification. In any given case, we thus seem to have an even chance to be faced with what is now called the redundancy problem.

The redundancy problem is obviously a close neighbor of the assignment problem. Both have to do with the efficient use of policy instruments based on what can appropriately be called their "comparative

357

advantages." But there is also an essential difference between the two groups of problems. In the assignment problem it is assumed that only one instrument is used for each target. We are thus invited to solve the problem of the efficient pairing-off of instruments and targets from the point of view of decentralized decision-making. The redundancy problem, on the other hand, has to do with the efficient selection of instruments in a process of centralized decision-making, taking into account the simultaneous effects of each instrument on all targets.

Going through Day's paper, the redundancy problem seems to include quite a number of interesting subproblems. Some of them can be discussed in terms of a single country. There is, first, the fundamental question—not explicitly posed in the paper—of what we mean by the "efficiency" of some policy. Day's discussion and diagram seem to suggest that he is thinking in terms of the shortest possible route along the policy vectors from the initial point to the target point. A more explicit treatment of this problem would probably have to be in terms of speeds of adjustment along different adjustment paths and of the welfare costs connected with deviations from the target. It may then turn out that what on Day's diagram is the shortest route is not always the most efficient one.

There is, second, the problem whether in the case of redundancy it is always most efficient to select just as many instruments as there are targets or whether it may perhaps be preferable to use more instruments than we have targets. If efficiency is indeed measured by the distance we travel on Day's diagram, it is clear that the optimal route always includes a number of policy instruments just equal to the number of targets. On a two-dimensional graph, for instance, it would be disadvantageous to use more than two instruments.

If we have a general proposition about the number of instruments to be used, we still have to consider their efficient selection. Day puts forward the proposition that, in terms of his diagram, the two policy vectors should come as close as possible to working "at right angles," i.e., that the selected instruments should in some sense be "as different as possible." I confess that the reasoning behind this proposition is not clear to me. If efficiency has to do with minimizing the route along the policy vectors from the origin to the target, Day's rule would often lead to an inefficient selection. If efficiency is defined in some other—and perhaps better—way, it is still hard to see why the optimal policy vectors should be close to being at right angles.

Other problems have to do with the many-country case. Assuming proper accounting practices, if the balance of payments of one country is in equilibrium, the balance of payments of the other country cannot help but be in equilibrium, too. If each country, taken in isolation, has just as many instruments as it has targets and if the targets include balance-of-payments equilibrium, then all countries together have one instrument to spare. As a consequence, we seem to have the problem of what could or should be done with the spare instrument. This is the original meaning of the redundancy problem, nicely stated in Mundell's short note. It seems to me that the significance of this subproblem is smaller than it is sometimes assumed. The problem would exist, it is true, if countries were happy whenever their international accounts were in equilibrium, no matter what the absolute level of their real reserves. However, this seems to be a rather unlikely state of affairs—fortunately, the monetary theorist is tempted to say—because it would make the international price level indeterminate. If the level of real reserves is considered too, there is no spare instrument left. For a given amount of nominal reserves, say gold, the remaining instrument will have to be used to bring international prices to that level which makes actual reserves in real terms (i.e., the purchasing power of nominal reserves) equal to desired reserves. Mundell shows elegantly how under different monetary standards the redundancy disappears as soon as the absolute level of real reserves is given its proper place. It disappears in exactly the same way as in general equilibrium theory the indeterminacy of the absolute price level disappears as soon as the demand for real cash balances is introduced. Only in general equilibrium theory we do not usually worry about "redundancy" in the first place.

If the demand for real reserves is given proper attention, it may, of course, still be true that the number of policy instruments exceeds the number of targets, internationally as well as nationally. From a purely cosmopolitan point of view, the choice of an optimal combination of instruments could presumably be based on the same criterion as in the one-country case. In the more realistic case in which countries are not willing to subordinate their national welfare to cosmopolitan criteria, there is, however, the additional problem of the distribution of adjustment costs among the countries concerned. This is the problem of the "sharing of the burden." In the present context it must suffice to point out that if there is no redundancy of instruments this problem does not arise. The sharing of the burden is then simply determined by what each country has to do to permit everybody to reach all targets. Whenever we discuss the sharing of the burden of international adjustment, we are thus, explicitly or implicitly, in the middle of the redundancy problem. In summary, while the redundancy problem as originally formulated does perhaps not seem to be of far-reaching significance, the redundancy of policy instruments in relation to targets, if interpreted in the wider sense of Day's paper, includes a considerable number of problems which are both important and analytically interesting.

Mundell's paper on what he calls the "crisis problem" is, as far as I know, the first attempt to formalize the working of the gold exchange standard in terms of a theoretical model. Considering how much is being written on the gold exchange standard without an explicit theoretical framework, this fact alone makes it an important contribution. In addition, it testifies to the remarkable amount of mileage one can get out of the principle of effective market classification. As a description of the actual working of the gold exchange standard and in proposing a practical solution to its difficulties the paper does not seem to be quite as successful. This applies to various elements of the analysis.

With respect to targets, we may note that the actual U.S. target is not just a certain ratio of gold to dollar liabilities. The absolute level of gold reserves seems to be important, too, and, in addition to balance-of-payments considerations, prices, incomes, and employment also seem to play a role. On the European side, on the other hand, the target is not just a certain level of total reserves; the gold/dollar ratio and to a certain extent even the U.S. reserve position are also important. As a consequence, the actual target lines may have a different shape and this may in turn affect the stability of the system.

A second consideration has to do with the behavior of the partners if the system is out of equilibrium. If the U.S. feel their dollar liabilities are too high, they are not necessarily restricted just to reduce D, and in many cases they will also try to increase U.S. gold reserves, i.e., reduce European gold-holdings (if they make efforts to correct the deficit at all). Their arrow, instead of being vertical, would then go downward and to the left. Similarly, European countries suffering from inflation, instead of just buying gold, may try to reduce their surplus or buy gold against dollars. In the latter case their arrow would point southeast. In terms of the mathematical appendix this means that all of the parameters α, β, γ, δ will generally be non-zero at the same time.

There is, third, the problem of the reasons for collapse. One possibility is an unstable combination of behavior parameters. Mundell's particular assumptions give the impression that, under present conditions, instability is a rather likely case. If, however, the behavior assumptions are modified in the way suggested above, the chances for stability are considerably improved. If Mundell erred at all, he certainly erred in the direction of stability pessimism. A second possible cause of breakdown is the reaching of boundary conditions. Mundell identifies these boundaries with the axes and the zero-line for the U.S. gold stock. It is not clear, however, how the axes can be boundary constraints if at the same time the target lines intersect the axes, thus indicating that the two parties may be quite happy even on the axes. A similar consideration applies to the U.S. zero-gold line in relation to the U.S. target line. Two further sources of trouble, not explicitly mentioned by Mundell, could perhaps be identified in this context. The first is what we are now used to calling the problem of confidence. In terms of the model, the problem of confidence seems to consist in the fact that countries adopt increasingly destabilizing behavior patterns. The temptation to do so will generally increase with the distance of the system from the equilibrium point. There may thus be a region of stability in the neighborhood of equilibrium surrounded by an area of instability. "Crisis" could then be defined as a position just on the stability border. Finally, it does not seem inconceivable that the target lines do not intersect in the way Mundell assumes but that the slope of the $P_1 P_2$ line is greater (in absolute value) than that of the $R_1 R_2$ line; this would obviously reverse many of the stability problems.

The last and, from a practical point of view, the most important point has to do with policy conclusions. What Mundell calls the "reversal of control," while probably contributing to stability, seems to be a rather artificial construction. It would imply that the U.S. should forget all about its balance-of-payments and domestic business conditions, while European countries should concentrate on keeping the U.S. happy with her reserve position. I cannot help feeling that this sounds somewhat like saying that peace on earth would be secured if mice went after cats. Apart from obvious political considerations, the basic problem is that Mundell urges us to consider the problem as one of decentralized decision-making where each partner controls only one variable (thus pushing either vertically or horizontally). This may be an undue limitation and it may in fact be more fruitful to consider the more general case where each partner simultaneously influences both instrument variables, thus pushing in a diagonal direction. I suggest that this not only corresponds more closely to the present state of affairs, thus making it more stable than Mundell indicates, but also is a better formalization of the urgent problem of developing a strategy of monetary cooperation. Even in such a wider perspective it remains true, however, that it is of prime importance for the stability of the monetary system that the U.S. pay attention to the evolution of world prices and that European countries take into consideration the U.S. balance-of-payments position. To have made this essential point in a forceful way is a major contribution of Mundell's paper.

SUMMARY OF DISCUSSION

It will be convenient to divide the summary of the discussion into four parts. The first summarizes interventions which questioned the relevance of the papers' approach to the problem of world stability (Cortney), or the relevance of some of the theoretical solutions (Sir Roy Harrod). The second summarizes shorter interventions dealing with the target-instrument issue and the potential sources of crises. The third outlines the authors' reactions to the discussion. The fourth is an expanded version of a comment by Eugene Birnbaum.

The time left for discussion during this session, which preceded the closing remarks of Professor Johnson, was quite limited. This explains why some of the ideas that came up are not fully developed but are merely suggestions.

I

Mr. Philip Cortney began by stating that he was not quite sure what one should call today's monetary system. It is a strange system based on a double standard reminiscent, in some ways, of the bimetallic silver-gold system. And it is fraught with the same dangers of instability; one standard, gold, being likely to drive out the other. It is also a system which does not correspond to the assumptions incorporated in Mundell's crisis paper.

In particular, Mundell's division of the world into two blocks with well-defined policy aims seemed misleading to Cortney. Take, for instance, the United States balance-of-payments deficit. Mundell's argument seems to imply that the present mechanism of control works as follows: when the United States loses gold it reduces the supply of dollars. This is not the way U.S. deficits are controlled; to the extent that they are, it is by means of administrative measures and exchange controls. Between 1952 and 1964, the United States lost more than 10 billion dollars worth of gold which the federal reserve system replaced by some 20 billion or more of government bonds. Monetary expansion, far from being reduced, was increased over that period.

363

In general, Cortney felt that discussion of the problem of international reform missed the real and relevant problem. Examples of this inability to tackle the real issues abound. For example, few people after World War II were willing to recognize the incompatibility of the multiple aims of international monetary reform, aims such as currency convertibility, price stability, full employment, free multilateral international trade, and fixed exchange rates. Or take the discussions of international monetary reform which, for such a long time, neglected the adjustment problem. The duty of academicians, Cortney stated, is to make statesmen understand the realities of the situation rather than to dodge the real issues.

Cortney then asked what the real issues in the liquidity problem are. Cortney argued that there is no such thing as a direct connection between the international liquidity problem and the level of world trade. Trade is financed by commercial banks and not by gold. The real problem of international liquidity is a *gold* liquidity problem. This is the only real liquidity problem everybody talks about without wanting to put the dot on the *i*. Many solutions to the gold liquidity problem have been proposed: a rise in the price of gold, a decrease in the price of gold, or even a demonetization of gold. And yet, only one solution is consistent with the maintenance of a free world and the avoidance of administrative and exchange controls, namely, an increase in the price of gold.

The real problem is one of inadequate gold liquidity, and such a problem is most likely to occur after major wars. This is the main lesson to be learned from a paper by Cortney which was circulated at the conference.[1] In normal times a link exists between the stock of monetary gold reserves and global monetary circulation. With a fixed price of gold, the system remains in equilibrium. Big wars disturb this equilibrium by causing an inflation of money and prices. To quote Mr. Cortney's paper:

> If and when this equilibrium is disturbed by a big war and the concomitant inflation of money and prices, and if we thereafter reinstate the link—however loose—between the gold monetary reserves and the monetary circulation (like in 1925 and in 1946), it is essential to set the price of gold at the right value in order to obtain an adequate global monetary gold stock and an adequate annual increase in the quantity of gold produced.
>
> After the money and price inflation accompanying a big war, any monetary system based on gold (as for example

1. Philip Cortney, "The Price of Gold after Big Wars," paper circulated for discussion at the Chicago Conference on International Monetary Problems.

the I.M.F. system instituted in 1946) contains the seeds of collapse unless a new price of gold has been correctly decided upon.[2]

The present monetary system has avoided collapse so far, in spite of an incorrect price of gold, for a variety of reasons: the initially huge gold stock of the United States; United States postwar aid programs; the chronic United States balance-of-payments deficits which provided the rest of the world with dollar monetary reserves, but at the cost of undermining confidence in the dollar; new gold discoveries and Russian gold sales; finally in the past three years, exchange controls and the potentially unstable resolve of governments not to "upset the apple-cart."

The urgency of finding a solution to the gold liquidity problem, however, is great. Cortney's solution would be an increase in the price of gold. Such an increase would not be inflationary since it presupposes first that governments put an end to past inflationary practices. It is designed to put an end to inflation without precipitating the world into a deflation. The latter is the real danger of a collapse of the present system. Therefore, Cortney's "plan" would be, first, to restore international monetary order, that is, eliminate inflation; second, to re-establish a mechanism for balance-of-payments adjustment; and, third, to increase the price of gold in order to put the monetary system, the huge credit structure which has been built since the beginning of World War II, on a sounder gold basis. There is no other basis for the monetary system.

Sir Roy Harrod addressed himself to the question of targets and instruments by asking whether flexible exchange rates were really available as an instrument. This is of course quite a relevant question, since, for instance, the number of targets quite often exceeds that of instruments. But the question is: Are flexible rates possible or is it necessary to devise substitutes such as income policies?

Economists tend to dismiss too easily the contention of commercial or central bankers, that flexible rates are to be ruled out, as prejudice, a preconceived notion, or as a result of these bankers' impression that flexible rates would interfere with their power position. Yet it may be true that flexible rates are unworkable. True, absolutely floating rates with no intervention whatsoever are *possible*. Sir Roy, however, is convinced that such complete freedom for fluctuations would involve an intolerable amount of oscillation.

2. *Ibid.*, p. 11.

The large degree of oscillation associated with such completely freely fluctuating exchange rates would not stem from destabilizing speculation. The large movements of short-term capital which occur in today's world are not so much speculative as precautionary. People do not speculate when they move capital in response to expectations of exchange-rate changes; for the most part they are covering commitments and hedging assets. Speculation is secondary. The probability of large oscillations in exchange rates, in a system where authorities do not intervene at all, stems from the large size and lumpiness of disturbances to the market. For instance, the purchase of the British Ford Company by the United States Ford Company meant a massive sale, 400 million dollars, quite a large amount in relation to the size of the United States deficit. Similarly, oil payments, both on current and capital account, are extremely lumpy. Suppose such a purely temporary, but large and discrete, disturbance occurs and affects the dollar unfavorably. Then, in the absence of official intervention, the dollar is likely to fall until it is so low that people start buying it out of purely precautionary motives. In other words, oscillations in foreign exchange rates are likely to exceed by far the adjustments in rates required to maintain equilibrium over the longer run.

Monetary authorities are likely to find such a situation intolerable and to enter the market to cushion such large fluctuations. The problem now becomes: Is a system of fluctuating rates *with* some intervention possible? In Sir Roy's view it is doubtful. True, such a system could work if only a few currencies fluctuated, as it did in the 1930's when sterling alone was floating. However, a system where several *important* currencies float, with some official interventions, would be difficult to work. Important currencies are those in which international transactions are invoiced and settled and there are at the very least twelve of them.

The reason why such a system would probably not work is that a dozen central bankers would have to make a decision every day as to the level at which they should intervene against a dozen other currencies. And these dozen people would most likely differ in their estimates of what the situation is and what interventions are required. As one central banker put it, such a situation would not last; the central bankers would ring each other up and say: "For heaven's sake, let us agree among ourselves on what our rates are going to be and let them stay there."

The trouble with a system of exchange rates subject to official intervention is that it incorporates the defects of fixed rates under the guise of flexible exchange rates. One way to get some exchange rate flexibility is the adjustable peg system. The latter, however, is likely to generate very large and perverse capital movements. This would mean that reserves are just as, or more, necessary under the adjustable peg than under a perfectly fixed rate system.

Dr. Marsh suggested a way out of Sir Roy's problem. Sir Roy had argued that, in order to have a workable floating-rate system, central banks should be prevented from interfering with exchange rates. Several economists have proposed a supranational central bank to help solve the world's monetary problems. Marsh suggested that the role of the IMF or the supranational central bank should be precisely to keep central banks from interfering with exchange rates. The supranational bank could carry out this function with the help of a very simple criterion, namely, that countries' exchange reserves should stay constant plus or minus a small amount required for carrying out minor smoothing operations, on both sides of the market.

Moreover, Canada's experience with floating rates was a successful one. Changes in the Canadian exchange rate were kept within a small range in spite of very limited intervention by the Bank of Canada. This would suggest to Marsh that, perhaps, a flexible rate system works even better in practice than it does in theory.

Sir Roy Harrod stated that he agreed, insofar as he would not deny for a moment that flexible rates could work very well for one or two countries. What he would argue, however, is that a similar degree of flexibility among all major currencies may not be feasible.

Professor Machlup stated that Sir Roy's argument is based on the assumption that every major country would worry about what other countries' exchange rates were. This is not necessarily the case. Some countries would not bother at all. For instance, the United States might have no interest in what other countries do about their exchange rates vis-à-vis the dollar. Some countries might decide to intervene in the foreign-exchange markets while others would stay out of the game and let the markets determine the exchange rates. (Because of time limitations this particular argument was continued outside the conference room and out of reach of the rapporteur's ears.)

II

Dr. Walter Salant, turning to the redundancy problem and the related assignment problem, emphasized four points. First, when it is recognized that balances of payments are asymmetrically defined in actual statistical practice, the redundancy problem disappears in the sense that the sum of all balances of payments is not zero. Second, even though the system may be in equilibrium in an *ex post* sense when, neglecting the asymmetry problem, each balance of payments is equal to zero, it may not be in equilibrium in an *ex ante* sense. That is, countries are not only concerned with the change in their reserves but also with the level of their reserves. As a result, the goals of each country with respect to desired reserve levels may be incompatible.

Third, turning to the assignment problem, Salant noted that the use of the word decentralization in that context might be misleading. It does not seem that the question of assignment of instruments to targets has anything to do with decentralization, at least in the usual institutional sense of the term. Fourth, how does one decide whether two particular actions constitute the same or different instruments? Salant suggested that, from an analytical point of view, two policy actions represent different instruments if their relative effect on several targets is different; otherwise, they are the same instrument. Two different elements of fiscal policy may constitute two different instruments. For example, a change in corporate taxation may affect the balance of payments relative to the level of employment in a different way than a change in personal taxation would. On the other hand, suppose a particular change in fiscal policy has the same relative effect on various targets as a particular change in monetary policy; then these two actions are the same instrument for analytical purposes, even though, for conversational purposes, one may be called monetary policy and the other fiscal policy.

On the question of targets and instruments, *Professor Sohmen* pointed out that his and most treatments of the assignment problem involve an *exact pairing* of instruments and targets. One is not limited to having one instrument assigned to one single target; in practice, several instruments are normally used simultaneously for each target. It would conceptually be possible to incorporate in formal models a weighted average of different targets as the decision variable and the exact mix of instruments could then depend on several indicators at the same time. With such a procedure, the problem of instability is less important than with an exact pairing of one target per instrument.

Mr. Swoboda commented on Niehans' and Salant's suggestion that instruments could be classified according to the way in which they affect target variables. Such a procedure is useful but subject to the qualification that the way in which instruments affect targets depends on the environment or circumstances. For instance, "monetary policy" will or will not affect internal balance depending on the size of the country and the degree of capital mobility. Moreover, instruments should be defined in as operational or elementary a way as possible, in terms of a specific policy action rather than in terms of some effect of that action. For instance, defining monetary policy as interest-rate policy leads to the conclusion that it can be used as an instrument to affect internal balance. Yet for a small country under perfect capital mobility this conclusion is incorrect. The reason is that monetary policy has been defined in terms of one of its usual (but not necessary) consequences rather than in terms of the action actually taken by the monetary authority, for instance, an open market operation.

Dr. Corden made two comments on the question of targets and instruments. First, Niehans mentioned the question of burden-sharing, a topic which had also been Corden's concern in his paper. This may suggest that, if one interprets the burden of balance-of-payments adjustment as that of failure to attain a target, costs of adjustment arise because there are not enough instruments to reach each target. Some countries will deviate more from their targets than others, and these deviations can be interpreted as the burden of adjustment. These remarks suggest an integration of the theory of burden-sharing with "targets-and-instruments theory."

Second, Corden wondered whether it would not be worthwhile to relate the targets-and-instruments theory to orthodox theories of welfare economics. This would mean thinking of a target, not simply as a point in some feasible set or on some particular indifference curve, but as the reaching of the highest possible point on an indifference map.

Returning to the redundancy problem narrowly defined, *Professor McKinnon* commented on Niehans' introduction of desired reserve-holdings. Niehans had argued that when desired reserve-holdings in real terms are introduced, the nth instrument is used up in determining that price level which equates desired and actual reserve-holdings expressed in real terms. In one sense, it is correct to say that only one extra degree of freedom is used up in the process. In another sense, however, specifying desired reserve levels for each of n countries implies the loss of n degrees of freedom and the problem becomes greatly complicated.

Professor Niehans pointed out that the reason why only one degree of freedom is lost in his analysis is that he only considers the final equilibrium position. McKinnon's suggestion as to the importance of individual countries' target stocks of reserves would be extremely important in the analysis of the dynamic transition to the final equilibrium position. It is quite right that one would need additional elements, probably differential equations, to determine the characteristics of the transition period.

As to the crisis problem, *Professor Mundell* wished to refute one misinterpretation of the source of crises in the present international monetary system. It has been argued recently that short-term capital movements are disequilibrating in the current international context of adjustment under fixed exchange rates. According to this argument, reliance on interest-rate policies may lead to capital movements, especially of the short-run kind, whose motivation bears no relation to differences in the productivity of capital or to profitability.

One of the examples cited to illustrate this thesis is the Italian crisis of 1963–64, the subject of de Cecco's paper. The fact that capital flowed out of Italy—at a time when Italy had a crisis and needed the money—and flowed into Germany—at a time when Germany had an excess of reserves and did not want the money—is taken as evidence of the destabilizing character of short-term capital movements in the present system. Mundell would argue emphatically that that particular episode is no reflection whatsoever of the disequilibrating nature of short-term capital flows. Rather, as de Cecco's paper shows, it is a reflection of a completely erroneous application of tools to targets, in particular of monetary policy.

Mr. Swoboda argued that a misunderstanding of the nature of capital movements could lead to a wrong assignment of targets to instruments which in turn could lead to a crisis. This can be expressed in the context of a comparative statics model within which crisis means the non-existence of an equilibrium position as a consequence of certain systematic policy measures.

Take a Keynesian-type model of a world composed of two countries, Europe and the United States, and assume perfect capital mobility. It can be shown that, if the United States sterilizes net reserve flows, European monetary policy has no effect whatsoever on the interest rate or the level of income, whatever the size of Europe relative to the United States. Now suppose that some inflationary pressure develops in Europe and that European central banks try to check it by selling securities in the open market. The only result is an improvement in Europe's balance of payments and a worsening in the United States balance of payments. The reason, of course, is capital flows. To call these perverse serves only to hide the real problem, the abdication of fiscal policy as an instrument of control over income levels—a fiscal crisis—and to invite exchange controls. Capital flows here are only perverse in the sense that countries are following the wrong policy mix.

III

Professor Day replied very briefly to some of the arguments evoked by his paper. First, Day would agree with Sir Roy that the difficulty of obtaining true flexibility in a world of several major centers is a very important problem. It is precisely the kind of problem Day had in mind in the first part of his paper, namely, the interrelationship between the economic system and political processes. Second, Day expressed full agreement with Mrs. Whitman's, Mr. Niehans' and Mr. Salant's analysis of the relevance of desired levels of reserves in the analysis of the redundancy problem. Moreover, as a practical possibility, Mrs. Whitman's analysis of the possibility of a shortage of instruments is very relevant.

Professor Mundell began by stressing once more the importance of understanding correctly the roots of the Italian crisis of 1963–64. The fundamental mistake was the misguided reaction of monetary authorities to the incipient crisis of 1963. Italy had a deficit and suffered inflationary pressures at the same time. A tight monetary policy was needed in order to acquire the reserves needed to finance the deficit. Instead of achieving monetary tightness by open market operations and/or higher reserve requirements, the Italian authorities, as de Cecco has pointed out, achieved tightness by cutting the commercial banks' access to the Euro-dollar market. This, however, deprived them of the reserves they needed, turned the incipient balance-of-payments deficit into an actual one, and caused the capital outflow to Germany. These capital flows, again, were not destabilizing per se but resulted from an incorrect monetary policy. The moral is simply that if you have a system of fixed exchange rates you have to run it properly.

The same conclusion applies to the management of the gold standard as a whole and this is the topic of Mundell's crisis paper. If agreement cannot be reached on international monetary reform we have to make do with the system we have and must run it properly. The only point Mundell would like to add to the discussants' remarks on his paper is that United States economists perhaps do not pay enough attention to the importance of United States monetary policy in determining the world price level. Mundell's paper is concerned not only with the United States balance of payments but also with aggregate dollar-holdings including private American holdings. Even if the direct effect of United States monetary policy is on the United States price level this already affects the world price level since United States production represents at least one-third of production in the Western world.

The next question, which bears an intimate relation to the last point mentioned by Mundell, is the redundancy problem. Rather than being a problem, redundancy simply states that there is an excess of one instrument and the discussion has made the function of the instrument perfectly clear. The function is to insure world stability. In Mrs. Whitman's discussion there are $n - 1$ interest-rate differentials. The function of the last instrument is then to set the world level of interest rates. If there are $n - 1$ price ratios, the function of the last instrument is to determine the world level of prices, that is, in quantity theory terms, the absolute level of prices.

In one sense the determination of the absolute world level of prices is the topic with which Cortney deals. Mundell argued that Cortney's point could be put in terms of a general equilibrium model. Suppose we have three goods in the model, money and two commodities. Originally, gold constitutes a given fraction of the money stock. Suppose now that a war occurs and that prices and the stock of money are doubled. The only difference between the pre- and postwar situation is a doubling of the absolute level of prices *and* the fact that the additional money which has been issued is supported by credit—paper money—and not by gold —"hard money." A naive rendering of Cortney's theory is that "what goes up must come down."

The theoretical basis of Cortney's argument is an application of the Pigou effect to the international monetary system. As Harry Johnson once put it, gold has the advantage of being nobody's liability. Cortney would say, according to Mundell, that gold has the advantage that nobody can print it. The point here is that the world price level is now determined by a stock of paper money, which is somebody's liability, with only a narrow gold base to support it. What Cortney seems to be arguing is that the stabilizing influence of the Pigou effect on the world price level can operate only on this gold base.

The possibility of a crisis resides in the possible breakdown of the credit component of the monetary system. Then the system has to return to its prewar level and deflation ensues. Mundell would disagree completely with any proposal to increase the price of gold. Yet one point remains: it is necessary to find the proper relation between the "hard money" and the credit component of the international monetary system. And it is also true that there is a potential threat of collapse to a system where international money is based on gold, the dollar, and sterling. The conversion of the credit or paper component into hard money or gold can destroy part of the international money supply. A massive conversion of dollars into gold by Europeans would destroy international reserves, hence collapse the international money supply, and bring on a panic.

To sum up, Mundell would argue that, in the present system, the world price level is largely determined by United States monetary policy.

To make the system viable it must be operated according to certain rules. The United States will have to pay attention to the world price level. In 1965 and 1966, United States monetary policy was too easy and world prices increased excessively. The problem now is to restrain monetary expansion and stabilize the world price level without bringing on a world recession in the process.

IV

In the course of the discussion of the "seigniorage problem" (Session V) *Mr. Birnbaum* pointed out that issues discussed under the name "seigniorage" were often raised by politicians who were, in fact, primarily concerned with control of the system. This of course is the key problem in Mundell's analysis of the crisis problem: Who *does* and *should* control what variable in order to make the system stable? Lack of time prevented Mr. Birnbaum from developing his ideas further during the world stability session, but he promised to expand on his argument in writing later. The following is a summary of his argument:

Any system of international monetary order requires various tacit or formal understandings concerning standards of appropriate behavior. According to Professor Mundell's paper on the crisis problem, the two principal conditions for stability of the existing international gold exchange standard are that the United States concern itself with global stability in determining policies that affect the rate of foreign receipts of U.S. currency, while the other countries in the system determine the composition of their official reserve assets, as between gold and dollars, after taking account of the adequacy of the U.S. gold reserve position. The stability requirement that outside countries accept an obligation to hold dollars (when they might otherwise have preferred gold) constitutes a partial surrender of national sovereignty to the reserve currency country. In return, the reserve center must offer a *quid pro quo* that is generally regarded as adequate; otherwise, the stability of the system may be threatened.

The structure of any international monetary system implies certain losses and gains of sovereign power among countries and international institutions that may prove to be important in determining whether certain major economic and political policy goals tend to be checked or facilitated. An awareness of the international monetary power structure is perhaps of particular importance in order that government policy-makers can more fully discern the effectiveness of measures that would modify or reform the system. Even technical "improvements" of the international monetary system may involve significant shifts in the international power structure; these shifts could lessen, rather than enhance the ability of the system to accommodate the attainment of major economic and political policy goals.

The failure up to now to achieve more rapid progress toward an agreement on international monetary reform is a natural outcome of existing major policy differences between national governments. For nearly fifteen years following World War II, the other major countries were willing to delegate power to the U.S. as an expression of trust in U.S. policies and confidence in its continued economic strength. The fact that major industrial countries, such as France, are no longer willing to accumulate official dollar reserve balances, constitutes a withdrawal of the power that had previously been conferred upon the United States. As a result, the U.S. has adopted policies of retrenchment with respect to those programs and activities that may lead to foreign official accumulations of liquid dollar balances.

There has been a similar retraction of sovereign power conferred previously by countries to the International Monetary Fund at Bretton Woods. As originally embodied in the IMF articles of agreement, member countries were, in effect, assured in advance of virtually automatic balance-of-payments financing through access to Fund resources in the currency of their choice, in the amount of 25 per cent of their quota per annum, for three to four years, subject to the conditions that (a) the member was to be in good standing with the Fund; and (b) the member was to have a balance-of-payments need consistent with the purposes of the Fund.

The power of deciding whether the conditions governing the appropriate use of Fund resources had been satisfied by an applicant country was vested with the Fund's board of executive directors to be determined by a majority of the voting power. As the size of each Fund member's vote is weighted by the size of its quota, the United States, having the largest quota, exercised more influence than any other country in the shaping of general Fund policy and practices. However, the Fund system is one of proportional representation, with no single country holding a majority of voting power. Thus, the fact that the U.S. position always seemed to dominate in the Fund resulted not from the U.S. voting power alone, but rather from the fact that the U.S. position was generally aligned with the view of the overwhelming majority of other member countries: it was a merger of policies of the vast majority of the Fund membership that dominated in the Fund.[3]

3. It should be noted that the size of the U.S. vote has accorded it a potential veto over those selected issues that require a four-fifths majority of the total Fund

Since the late 1950's, however, several of the major European countries have increasingly manifested dissatisfaction with various actions
associated with this alignment of power. For example, the Europeans
have objected to an alleged misuse of the IMF as a "foreign aid agency
of the United States."

On July 20, 1962, the executive directors formally approved a change
of policy concerning the currency composition of drawings from the
Fund which marked a profound change in the power structure of the
IMF. According to the new policy, members wishing to draw resources
from the Fund were no longer to specify the particular currency they
wished to draw, subject only to executive Board confirmation that the
drawing would represent an appropriate use of Fund resources. Instead,
a new arrangement was announced, whereby the IMF managing
director would consult "informally" in advance with each potential
creditor country for the purpose of obtaining its special consent as to the
use and amount of its currency to be utilized in the drawing. In effect, a
second voting procedure was introduced under which a member could
effectively veto the potential use of its currency in Fund transactions.
Since the new procedure was introduced at a time when European currencies had become more useful, it made possible a significant shift of
power within the Fund toward Europe, and away from the traditional
majority alignment of the Fund membership. The new policy thereby
reduced the international "sovereignty" of the Fund, and with it the
effective power of the United States to influence Fund policies and
practices.

In October 1962, the Fund, faced with near exhaustion of its useable
loanable funds—at least if large drawings by the United States and the
United Kingdom might have to be satisfied—agreed to the establishment of the so-called general arrangements to borrow; however, the
new arrangement accorded further recognition to this shift of power.
The major industrial countries formed the Group of Ten—empowered
to determine when and if any one of the member-countries of the Group

---

voting power, e.g., amendment of the articles, increase of member-country quotas,
increase in number of executive board members, etc. As the Fund has continued
to acquire new members and the quotas of other countries have increased more
rapidly than that of the United States, the U.S. voting power has continued to
decline. At this juncture it exceeds 20 per cent of the total vote by only a small
margin. By comparison, the accumulated voting power of EEC member countries
now stands so close to 20 per cent as to assure this bloc of a similar veto power for
all practical purposes. It might be also noted that Fund executive board votes have
traditionally been unanimous (although the formality of an actual vote is usually
dispensed with).

should have access to an additional supplementary fund of six billion dollars for balance-of-payments financing. By denying the right of other Fund member-countries to participate in the Group, or to have direct access to this additional international liquidity, the effect of the arrangement was to increase the power of those (European) participants of the Fund whose views did not merge with the traditional international consensus.

The ultimate in the postwar shift away from the delegation of power to an international consensus for determining the conditions under which countries may have access to substantial amounts of international liquidity is probably represented by the complicated proliferation over the last half-decade of central bank swap arrangements and so-called "Roosa bonds." These arrangements provide for the provision, *or denial*, of balance-of-payments financing on an *ad hoc*, bilateral, country-by-country basis, rather than through the intermediary of a permanent international establishment.

The United States may have been forced by circumstances to resort to the creation of such stop-gap arrangements. However, by comparison to the "grand design" at Bretton Woods, it should be recognized that the international monetary order that has emerged provides less assurance of the continued availability of a large source of balance-of-payments financing. Instead, the potential availability of international liquidity has become increasingly sensitive and vulnerable to *ad hoc* national political considerations.

It is clear that continued policy disunity among major countries works at cross-purposes to the successful negotiation of significant international monetary reform. In view of the expanding world need for international liquidity, an outright failure of such efforts, or only minor success, would ultimately leave but two fundamental choices for the United States: further retrenchment with respect to its basic policies of freedom of international trade, capital movements, massive support for mutual defense establishments and the economic development of less developed countries, etc.—as the price for prolonging the present international monetary arrangements—or, instead, allowing the remaining U.S. gold-holdings to decline to the point where preservation of the existing close link between the dollar and gold becomes no longer tenable.

Severing the present close link between the dollar and gold would tend to place the world on a dollar standard; this would not necessarily imply fluctuating exchange rates. On the contrary, so long as the U.S. economy remained productive and sound, its abundance of goods and services would continue to remain internationally price-competitive at current exchange rates. Accordingly, foreign holdings of dollars would continue to be needed, and the present fixed exchange-rate system with respect to national currencies, as embodied in the IMF articles of agreement, could be retained as the keystone of the international monetary system—subject, of course, to occasional adjustments of the peg—as envisaged at Bretton Woods.

It should also be recognized that severing the present link between the dollar and gold would not remove effective constraints upon U.S. policies and programs. The fact is, of course, that we live in an interdependent world; the United States and its policies would continue to be subject to the close scrutiny of other nations, and there would continue to be a necessity to adhere to recognized standards of appropriate national behavior. However, the constraints of such a new international monetary order would have been made more consistent with the attainment of major economic, rather than political, policy goals, on both the national and international level. This seems a desirable goal for the further evolvement of the international monetary system.

APPENDIX: THE REDUNDANCY PROBLEM AND THE WORLD PRICE LEVEL

Robert A. Mundell

I

The combined balance-of-payments surpluses of the surplus countries exactly matches the balance-of-payments deficits of all the deficit countries, since the global balance (when asymmetrical treatment of gold or other reserve assets is avoided) is zero. This means that if each country has a distinct instrument to control its balance of payments there is an additional degree of freedom. Only $n - 1$ independent balance-of-payments instruments are needed in an n-country world because equilibrium in the balances of $n - 1$ countries implies equilibrium in the balance of the nth country. The *redundancy problem* is the problem of deciding how to utilize the extra degree of freedom.

II

Let B_i be the balance of payments of the ith country, p_i its control variable, and

$$\frac{dp_i}{dt} = \alpha_i B_i \qquad (i = 1, \ldots, n) \tag{1}$$

the adjustment equation linking variations in the control variable to the target. Then if

$$\sum_{i=1}^{n} B_i = 0 \tag{2}$$

it follows that

$$\sum_{i=1}^{n} \frac{1}{\alpha_i} \frac{dp_i}{dt} = 0 \tag{3}$$

whence, upon integration,

$$\sum_{i=1}^{n} \frac{1}{\alpha_i} p_i = \text{constant}, \tag{4}$$

assuming the "speeds of adaptation," the α_i's, to be constant. Thus interdependence of the targets, as implied by (2), implies interdependence among the instruments; if some control variables are rising, others must be falling, a necessary consequence of the fact, given the adjustment equation (1), that if some countries have deficits others must have surpluses.

III

If all countries "use" price levels to correct the balance of payments, (4) implies that an "index of price levels in the world as a whole is constant," the weights in the index being the reciprocals of the speeds of adaptation. Under a gold standard system, for example, (4) can be identified with an international version of the quantity theory of money.

To see this we need to find an interpretation of the constant of integration in (4) and the speeds of adjustment in (1) and (4). Thus, suppose we consider a gold specie standard in which the balance of payments is identically equal to the change in gold reserves. Then

$$\frac{dG_i}{dt} = B_i \qquad (i = 1, \ldots, n) \tag{5}$$

where G_i is the gold stock of the ith country. From (1) and (5) we get

$$\sum_{i=1}^{n} \frac{dG_i}{dt} = \sum_{i=1}^{n} \frac{1}{\alpha_i} \frac{dp_i}{dt} \tag{6}$$

whence

$$\bar{G} = \sum_{i=1}^{n} \frac{1}{\alpha_i} p_i \tag{7}$$

where $\bar{G} = \sum G_i$ is the world's gold stock. G must be a constant if (2) and (5) are to be consistent, so that (7) fixes the relation between the world's stock of gold and a world index of prices.

But what are the weights in the world price index? From a version of the quantity theory of money, applicable to each country, we have

$$G_i V_i = p_i O_i, \tag{8}$$

where O_i is output in the ith country, taken as given, and V_i is income velocity. If this holds at every moment of time we get

$$\frac{dG_i}{dt} = \frac{1}{V_i} O_i \frac{dp_i}{dt} \tag{9}$$

assuming income velocity is constant. Taking account of (5), then,

$$\frac{dp_i}{dt} = V_i \frac{B_i}{O_i}. \tag{10}$$

More usefully (for some purposes), the *proportionate* change in the national price level is

$$\frac{1}{p_i} \frac{dp_i}{dt} = V_i B_i^* \tag{11}$$

where B_i^* is the balance of payments expressed as a fraction of national income and the speed of adaptation in (1) turns out to be the ratio of income velocity to output. This equation shows that price-level adjustments under the gold specie standard are governed by the balance of payments expressed as a proportion of national income, so that relatively small percentage adjustments occur in big countries compared to small countries unless income velocities are markedly different.

Solving for the world price-level index by substituting $\alpha_i = V_i/O_i$ in (7) gives

$$\bar{G} = \sum_{i=1}^{n} \frac{1}{V_i} p_i O_i \tag{12}$$

or

$$\bar{G}V = \sum_{i=1}^{n} p_i O_i \tag{13}$$

in the special case where income velocity (or its reciprocal, the ratio of money to income) is the same in all countries. In a fractional reserve banking system where gold reserves are linked to money supplies according to the equation $G_i = \mu_i M_i$, where M_i includes bank money, the equation corresponding to (11) would be

$$\frac{1}{p_i} \frac{dp_i}{dt} = \frac{V_i}{\mu_i} B_i^*$$

where μ_i is the fractional reserve ratio, while that corresponding to (12) would be

$$\bar{G} = \sum_{i=1} \frac{\mu_i}{V_i} p_i O_i.$$

We may therefore conclude that the simple gold standard "solution" to the redundancy problem results in the stabilization of world income if all income velocity and reserve ratios are identical. Differences in income velocities or fractional reserve ratios can, however, produce "distortions," since countries with low ratios of international reserves to national income will have relatively high speeds of adaptation and relatively low weights in the world price index.

IV

The solution is the same, in principle, under a world currency standard, but it differs somewhat under a standard in which a national currency is used as international reserves by other countries. The reserve ratio in the reserve currency country is unity, while that in other countries is less than unity, which means that a greater "share" of the burden of adjustment will be shifted to the other countries. If, for example, the U.S. income represented one third of world income, and the ratio of dollar reserves to national money supplies were 5 per cent in each country outside the United States, the U.S. "weight" in the world price index would be 10 times as large as that in the rest of the world, despite the fact that U.S. production was only one half as large. The reserve center authorities could, however, stabilize domestic prices entirely by sterilizing the domestic monetary effects of deficits and surpluses and shifting the entire burden of adjustment onto the rest of the world.

A still different system results, however, in a bi-reserve system in which gold and (say) dollars are used as international money. If the United States maintains a reserve ratio of gold behind monetary liabilities, control of the system is shifted once again to, and shared between, the other countries who can determine, by their gold-dollar policies, the level of world prices and the U.S. "share" in the distribution of adjustment.

In each of these cases the redundancy problem is "solved" in a different way, and has different implications for world stability. Thus, in the final analysis, the redundancy problem, conceived of as the problem of using the free variable, reduces to an international standards "problem," that of determining an index of world prices and the weights to be accorded in that index to each country.

APPENDIX: THE ITALIAN PAYMENTS CRISIS OF 1963–64

Marcello de Cecco

Between 1962 and 1964 the rapid growth of the Italian economy, which had proceeded undisturbed for almost ten years, was suddenly interrupted. A balance-of-payments crisis began to develop in 1962, became violent in 1963, and was more than solved in 1964. It is the purpose of this note to inquire into the proximate causes of that crisis and to analyze the conduct of the Italian authorities in coping with it.

The main causes of the crisis were a very large increase in imports (much larger than the increase in exports) in 1962 and 1963, and a reversal in the direction of capital movements, an outflow of private capital from Italy replacing the inflows of previous years. (See Table 1.)

The acceleration of imports was due to several reasons. Around 1961, virtual full employment had been reached in several sections of the labor market. In the preceding years, a wage pause had been enforced

TABLE 1
THE ITALIAN BALANCE OF PAYMENTS
(In Millions of U.S. Dollars)

Current Account	1960	1961	1962	1963	1964	1965
Visible trade	−893	−1086	−1423	−2495	−1487	−474
Shipping	249	281	299	119	332	361
Tourism	530	647	723	748	826	1061
Emigrants' remittances	305	417	508	522	551	674
Income from investments	−11	−51	−90	−113	−98	−88
Other services	62	107	43	131	83	62
Errors and omissions	−16	22	117	−27	69	−38
TOTAL	320	315	181	−933	277	1559
Government transactions	74	46	67	43	58	69
TOTAL	394	362	249	−889	335	1628

Capital Account						
Investments	378	620	−189	−338	427	−96

| GRAND TOTAL | 772 | 982 | 60 | −1227 | 762 | 1532 |

SOURCE—Istituto per il Commercio Estero (ICE), *Movimento Valutario* (Rome, 1961, 1962, 1963, 1964, 1965, 1966). Imports are CIF.

by the Italian labor unions and a backlog of wage claims had formed. The impact of this backlog was felt in 1962–63. Moreover, excess demand in some sections of the labor market induced considerable wage drift. At the same time, civil servants and employees of the numerous governmental and semigovernmental agencies obtained large salary increases. Pensions were also raised.

All these redistributive movements brought about a large increase in demand for consumer goods of all kinds. This created brisk expectations on the part of business, so that the demand for investment goods kept increasing rapidly.

On the supply side, national resources were not sufficient to accommodate these large increases in demand. Agricultural production had been in crisis for several years; Italian industrial development had deprived it of its best labor resources. Moreover, it was plagued by disappointing harvests. Meat production, which had been declining since 1960, was about 30 per cent less in 1963 than in 1962. Equally grave declines were registered in the production of wheat, rice, butter, and a host of other important staples of the Italian average diet, which was, because of economic development, shifting toward richer foods. The production of consumer durables, also affected by the redistributive movements we have just mentioned, had a much better chance of coping with the increased demand since productive capacity was expanding rapidly. It was impossible, however, for an increase in the demand for automobiles of about 50 per cent, as took place in 1962–63, for example, to be met by national production.

These were the main determinants of the large increase in imports of consumption goods. Brisk business ahead and full capacity production in the investment sector also caused imports of investment goods to increase, although not by as much as those of consumption goods. (See Tables 2 and 3.) Had Italian difficulties been limited to these points, the payments crisis would have been quite manageable. A package of moderate and selective credit restrictions and fiscal measures could have restored balance without much difficulty.

An intricate financial situation, however, had developed in Italy at the same time, as the result of the interaction of numerous political and economic factors. In 1960 the Italian stock market had fallen, after ten years of almost unchecked advance. It had picked up, but fell again in the middle of 1962. This time the decline became self-reinforcing and steep. The main causes of the slump were the expected nationalization of electricity, the terms of which were unknown, and the expected introduction of a tax on stock dividends. As utilities shares had, tradi-

TABLE 2
IMPORTS CIF
(In Billions of Current Lire—Seasonally Adjusted
Quarterly Figures)

	QUARTERS			
	I	II	III	IV
1960	681	741	760	769
1961	789	811	818	844
1962	888	916	962	1,024
1963	1,082	1,153	1,226	1,280
1964	1,253	1,162	1,049	1,053

PERCENTAGE CHANGE OVER PRECEDING QUARTER

1960	. . .	8.7	2.7	1.2
1961	2.6	2.8	0.8	3.2
1962	5.2	3.2	5.0	6.4
1963	5.8	6.6	6.3	4.4
1964	−2.1	−7.3	−9.7	0.3

SOURCE—Istituto Nazionale per lo Studio della Congiuntura, *Quaderno Analitico n.22—Commercio con l'Estero* (Rome, 1965).

tionally, attracted the bulk of middle-class savings, uncertainty about their future induced their owners, little versed in the art of "playing the market," to leave the market altogether. Fear of the announced tax, which would have made the identity of share-owners known to the authorities, reinforced the trend. A large part of the funds that left the stock market went to inflate the real estate market; another part was exchanged for liquid assets and began to be illegally transferred abroad.

TABLE 3
COMPOSITION OF IMPORTS
(In Billions of Current Lire)

	Consumer Durables	Consumer Non-Durables	Total Consumer	Building Materials	Industrial Transport Equipment	Plant & Equipment	Total Investment	Fuels & Lubricants	Other Auxiliary	Total Auxiliary	Grand Total
1960	207	1047	1255	147	123	786	1057	408	231	640	2953
1961	250	1054	1305	167	127	972	1267	436	254	691	3264
1962	333	1150	1484	197	153	1182	1533	497	276	774	3791
1963	492	1554	2046	226	164	1403	1794	569	629	901	4743
1964	432	1547	1979	214	145	1205	1564	331	345	974	4519

SOURCE—Istituto Centrale di Statistica, *Annuario Statistico Italiano* (Rome, 1965).

Italian entrepreneurs began to hedge against all possible risks on their lire-denominated investments by transferring funds abroad and substituting bank credit as operating capital for their firms.

The amount of Italian banknotes, deposited on "capital account" with Italian banks by "non-residents," swelled from $700 million in 1962 to $1500 million in 1963. (See Table 4.) Foreign private investments in Italy, which had been $378 million in 1960 and $620 million in 1961, went to − $189 million in 1962 and − $338 million in 1963. (See Table 1.)

TABLE 4
OUTFLOW OF ITALIAN BANKNOTES
(In millions of U.S. Dollars)

	1960	1961	1962	1963	1964
January	14	22	65	115	98
February	11	26	80	150	73
March	18	29	107	259	91
April	15	48	66	245	58
May	15	39	76	171	...
June	9	35	60	75	...
July	3	12	34	57	...
August	1	2	16	21	...
September	20	28	56	90	...
October	30	36	80	144	...
November	31	29	72	96	...
December	16	21	54	45	...
YEAR	185	329	765	1470	...

SOURCE—Banca d'Italia, *Relazione 1963* (Rome, 1964).

Capital exports took all the well-known forms: underinvoicing of exports and overinvoicing of imports; purchases of emigrants' remittances and of receipts from tourism before they reached Italy; and, most important of all, physical abduction of Italian banknotes abroad.

In 1961 and 1962, the governor of the Italian Central Bank asked repeatedly for fiscal measures to reduce the pressure of demand on the economy and the balance of payments. He expressed the hope that, could those measures be applied promptly, there might be no need to sacrifice the rate of growth of investments. He also made clear that monetary restraint would be delayed and dampened by the necessity to supply the financial market, impoverished by the escape of capital toward supposedly safer forms of investment, with enough liquidity to absorb the large quantity of debentures that several governmental agencies were preparing to issue to finance the nationalization of electricity and many other pluriennal expenditure plans.

The finance minister, Mr. Trabucchi, began to take some measures to restrict demand. Meanwhile, it was decided to offset the payments deficit by allowing the Italian commercial banks to borrow short-term funds abroad, mainly on the Euro-dollar market. As a result, the country's official reserves did not feel the strain of the payments deficit, but kept increasing, albeit at a reduced rate.

In the summer of 1963 a cabinet crisis developed. In the vacuum of power that followed, the Central Bank was left alone to cope with the payments crisis. It had only monetary policy to rely upon, as all hopes of a package of fiscal and budgetary measures had to be abandoned because of the cabinet crisis.

The credit squeeze began in September, a most appropriate month for it as the resumption of full-scale production, after the traditional August slowdown, created pressing needs for operating capital. In order to effect the squeeze, the authorities chose to restrict the foreign indebtedness of the commercial banks. The latter were requested not to increase their foreign liabilities beyond the level reached in August, 1963, and, if possible, to reduce them.

The credit squeeze was tough and effective. The money supply (including time deposits), which had been increasing at a (continuously compounded) rate of 4–5 per cent per quarter in 1962 and the first half of 1963, increased by 2.21 per cent in the fourth quarter of 1963 and by 1.16 per cent in the first quarter of 1964. The balance of payments, by April, 1964, had firmly gone back to surplus. Imports, which had been rising at an average 5.7 per cent per quarter in 1963, decreased by 2.1 per cent in the first quarter of 1964. Exports, which had been increasing in 1963 at an average 2.4 per cent per quarter, rose by 3.7 per cent in the first quarter of 1964. (See Tables 1, 2, 4.)

The method chosen by the authorities to effect the credit squeeze, however, bore some important consequences. By asking the banks to stop the inflow of short-term capital that had, up to September, 1963, served to offset the payments deficit, the authorities suddenly made the deficit public. Between September, 1963, and March, 1964, official reserves fell by $458 million. A much publicized gold sale of $200 million took place in the first quarter of 1964.

The sudden revelation of the Italian deficit was quite a trauma for international financial opinion, which had remained remarkably unaware of the crisis. As a result, the "gnomes" began to operate: while the lira remained at a premium vis-à-vis the dollar in the spot market, a wider and wider discount began to open against it in the forward market, beginning in September, 1963. The existence of a large margin between spot and forward lire between September, 1963, and March, 1964, with the spot rate remaining at a premium, might be taken as evidence that the Italian authorities were holding the spot rate, while they let the forward rate go. This policy was consistent with their internal monetary policy as the large margin between the two rates would discourage arbitrageurs from investing in the Italian market with forward cover. But it was, at the same time, likely to induce pure speculation in the forward market. This in fact took place in violent form and, in 1964, the authorities had to intervene in the forward market, pledging large funds to offset sales of forward lire. International assistance had to be secured, in addition to these moves, to shore up the lira, and the new Italian government had to replace the just lifted credit restrictions with very severe fiscal and budgetary measures.

It is not unreasonable, therefore, to believe that the method chosen to effect the credit squeeze contributed a new facet to the Italian crisis and helped it to escalate into a currency crisis when the basic payments problem was already being solved, whereas an increase in legal reserve requirements might have borne the same effects on the economy but might have caused less violent repercussions in the foreign exchange market. The price the country had to pay in terms of GNP, employment, and investment to come out of this crisis became very high—as a look at Table 5 will reveal—for deflation had to be carried on well into

TABLE 5
PRODUCTION OF INVESTMENT GOODS AND CONSUMPTION GOODS—INDICES
(Base 1953)

	INVESTMENT GOODS					CONSUMPTION GOODS				
	1961	1962	1963	1964	1965	1961	1962	1963	1964	1965
January	195	224	238	249	225	163	188	201	216	193
February	202	228	228	247	235	167	185	195	214	194
March	202	221	236	237	228	167	186	200	215	195
April	204	224	242	229	240	168	188	207	216	201
May	206	226	243	227	244	170	190	207	208	208
June	208	212	250	222	224	173	186	209	203	213
July	214	227	243	225	247	176	191	209	211	215
August	212	229	245	203	247	175	191	212	192	211
September	217	228	252	226	252	175	190	217	202	213
October	217	224	252	226	252	179	192	218	200	206
November	217	236	245	223	256	185	196	215	202	215
December	223	239	244	228	252	184	200	212	199	212
ANNUAL AVERAGE	210	226	247	229	244	174	190	209	207	206

SOURCE—Istituto Nazionale per lo Studio della Congiuntura, *La Congiuntura Italiana* (Rome, April, 1966).

1965, while it might have lasted only six months and hurt the economy much less.

The lesson to be derived from the Italian experience is straightforward: under convertibility conditions, the incorrect choice of policy variables to bring about the reabsorption of a payments deficit can cause consequences only vaguely connected with the basic payments situation. Once a currency crisis has developed, there exists a standard procedure, formed in the last few years, to deal with it. International assistance against speculative attacks on the currency concerned is one part of this procedure; the other part is deflation, to be brought about in the country whose currency is in crisis, speedily and deeply enough to induce the dramatic improvement in the balance of payments that will convince the "gnomes" to desist from their practices.

This procedure, once initiated, goes on irretrievably. The package of deflationary measures has to be applied, even if the basic balance of payments of the country concerned has already been restored by a previous dose of deflation and a reiteration of the same treatment would therefore be exactly the opposite of what might be called for.

Once international assistance has been provided, the country in crisis loses much of its freedom to choose the policy that it considers appropriate for its own economy. International assistance, in fact, is usually a granting of short-term loans from other countries, which gives the creditors powerful leverage to influence the debtor's own economic policy.

PART 7

CLOSING COMMENT

THE "PROBLEMS" APPROACH TO
INTERNATIONAL MONETARY REFORM

Harry G. Johnson

When Robert Mundell and I conceived the idea of holding this conference, we had two major considerations in mind.

First, having attended the Bellagio conferences and other discussions of international monetary reform, we felt that there was a need for a conference that would stand back from current policy issues and problems and attempt to bring to bear upon the problem of international monetary reform the kind of theoretical and analytical techniques that academic economists command but practical policy-makers generally do not. Conferences concerned with current problems of international monetary reform tend to involve themselves in discussion of detailed issues aroused by particular current events or reform schemes; and such conferences can go on forever in this way, because in between conferences history generates new particulars and fresh information or perspective on past experience. Our aim, by contrast, was to dig more deeply into fundamental theoretical issues respecting the international monetary system itself. In this connection, we conceive of economists as having two sorts of functions: as production instruments for turning out consumers' goods in the form of applications of existing knowledge to current problems, and as production instruments for turning out producers' goods in the form of better knowledge and analytical formulations and approaches for application to current problems. We planned this conference to concentrate on serving the second function, and to focus on the improvement of our intellectual machine tools.

The second, and related, consideration was that we felt that the generation of economists that customarily is invited to conferences on international monetary reform is a rather senior one, and that somewhere between that generation and the students in graduate school is a generation that is seasoned and well-trained enough to tackle the problem of international monetary reform in a fruitful way but so far has been left to the rather unrewarding role of explaining to its students and colleagues why the analysis and solutions propounded by its seniors are not really adequate. We therefore planned this conference to be a conference, not exactly of the middle-aged—because no one is ever that

393

old in our profession until he has become a grand old man—but of the intellectually mature young, whom we thought would combine an interest in and capacity for pure theory with the ability to apply it to the problems of the international monetary system.

There was obviously a certain a priori complementarity between these two ideas, of a conference on the theoretical aspects of the international monetary system, to be composed primarily of younger economists. But the experience of the conference's sessions has revealed two unexpected problems in holding a conference on problems.

The first problem has been that not everyone has seen the problem in the way we conceived it: a few of our participants have rebelled against the whole conception of isolating the theoretical problems for examination, and have instead insisted on tackling the whole range of problems from the standpoint of arriving at a practical program of international monetary reform. Their contributions to the discussion have carried the strong implication that the isolation of theoretical problems and the treatment of them by elaborate analytical techniques is too remote from the concerns of the practical policy-making economist to be useful, or, in some cases, even tolerable. One cannot deny people the right to express this opinion if they hold it, and it has certainly been expressed forcefully at various points in our proceedings; but I do not think that the urge to start discussion from the current policy problem has fostered deeper understanding of the theoretical issues, and in some cases it has served to obscure them. The problem has been that, contrary to the assumed complementarity of the two objectives of the conference mentioned earlier, it is just not true that youth is a guaranty of intellectual purity and political innocence. However, from a broader point of view, this is probably just as well, since some of our participants have been deeply involved, in spite of their relative youth, in hard problems of practical policy-making and negotiation; and their insistence on the magnitude of the gap between pure theory and practical policy-making may contribute to the development of a more broadly based theoretical framework.

The second problem has been that someone had to specify the theoretical issues to be discussed; and it is by now no secret that the problems were defined to follow very closely the work of Robert A. Mundell, our convener. I do not believe that that procedure was at all unfair; on the contrary, I believe we all agree that Mundell's contributions to the pure theory of this subject have significantly changed our ways of approaching it, and that he has pioneered important new lines of analysis that have enabled us to bring the tools of theory to bear far more effectively than heretofore. In particular, he has set a new high standard of rigor for the application of general equilibrium and dynamic stability analysis, and has been extremely original in demonstrating how to formulate problems so that the answers provided by these techniques fall elegantly and precisely into place.

Mundell's predominance in the drawing up of the program has, however, in practice raised two problems encountered in the actual proceedings of the conference.

First, the program did not in fact stick rigorously to a rational assignment of separable theoretical problems. In particular, the session on regional arrangements among less developed countries was perhaps wrongly conceived and almost certainly wrongly placed in the program. Not only does the subject slice into the international monetary system from a geographical or country-type point of view rather than a theoretical problem point of view, but so far as something can be done with it on the theoretical level it really belongs for discussion with the optimal currency area problem. This particular program arrangement was forced on us by Kafka's inability to attend the first day of the conference, but the subject of the interest of the less developed countries in international monetary reform also cuts across the lines of theoretical problem specification, with unsatisfactory results.

Second, it has become clear in the discussion that the problems Mundell's work has defined are of greatly varying degrees of usefulness or durable theoretical interest. Perhaps a recognition of which problems and approaches are worth sustained further work and which are not will be the most lasting contribution of this conference to the evolution of the field.

Specifically, it seems to me that the optimum currency area problem has proved to be something of a dead-end problem. The concept had considerable transitional importance, in challenging the nationalistic assumptions on which the traditional arguments over fixed versus floating exchange rates had been based and raising the issue of the appropriate domain for a currency. But once one probes into that question, the simplicity and charm of the concept are seen to derive from its balancing of two opposing considerations—the geographical immobility of labor and rigidity of wages, which suggests minimizing the currency area to maximize the ease of monetary adjustment, and the requirements for maintaining the "moneyness" of money, which suggests maximizing the currency area. Once other determinants of the ease of adjustment are introduced into the analysis, and particularly once capital movements are introduced and the domain of capital mobility is assumed to be larger than the domain of labor mobility, the problem becomes too complex for its statement to be very illuminating. Thus, while Peter Kenen's paper extended the original Mundell analysis in a fruitful way along one possible dimension of greater realism, it seems to me unlikely that any further major theoretical breakthroughs can be made within the confines of the optimum currency area concept—though of course it will probably be useful for theorists to work out exercises of the kind Kenen has done, and it may be that someone will turn up a new and illuminating approach to the problem that our discussions failed to reveal.

In the same way, it seems to me that the concept of the seigniorage problem raises too many difficult theoretical issues, once it is inspected, to repay the organization of analysis of those issues around that particular concept. In a quite different way, the redundancy problem seems of limited theoretical interest—not because it raises theoretical complexities when probed into, but because it defines neatly and once for all a political problem inherent in the present system. The problem arises from the fact that in an n-country world only $n - 1$ countries have to assign a policy instrument to the maintenance of balance-of-payments equilibrium; this leaves one degree of freedom, and the question is, which country is to be allowed to enjoy it? Finally, the crisis problem as Mundell has formulated it seems to be a particular instance of the more general assignment problem.

I have dwelt at length on the problems of organizing and arranging the program for this conference, because conferences are a fixture of contemporary professional life, someone has to organize them, and it is possible in this activity as in others to learn from experience. Let me conclude with a brief evaluation of the positive results of the conference.

In my judgment, the most useful and productive session of the conference was the one on the adjustment problem, and this despite the fact that neither author of the papers discussed abided strictly by his contract. I think it was the high point of the conference for two sorts of reasons.

First, as Richard Cooper's comment made brilliantly clear, many of the problems that theorists have recently been working on can be fitted readily into the framework of the Tinbergen-Meade analysis of targets and instruments of policy; and that analysis suggests many directions for useful further work. The assignment problem is only one of these problems. That problem stems from the decentralization of decision-making in the actual conduct of economic policy, and there seems no reason to confine analysis to the assumption that each instrument must

be assigned only one target to pursue; on the contrary, it would seem
fruitful to devote attention to the question of devising optimal rules for
co-ordinating instruments, or relating the use of each instrument to a
combination of targets, so as to maximize the effectiveness of policy and
the stability of the policy-governed system. The mathematical problem
here is obvious enough; the real difficulty would be to make the solution
operational in the real world.

The redundancy problem appears as soon as the analysis is extended
from an open economy to a closed world system; but it is only one of
the problems, and not the most important, that appears when one considers the world system. One of the major problems that has not been
discussed in the conference is the possibility, of great importance in the
real world, that the international objectives of the various nations may
not be consistent with one another. Marina Whitman has pointed out
that countries may not want a balanced balance of payments; the surpluses (or more rarely deficits) they want may not be consistent. Of equal
practical importance, countries have objectives not merely with respect
to the over-all balance, or the flow of international reserves, but also
with respect to the composition of their balances of payments. The
Canadian government, for example, wishes to reduce the inflow of
foreign capital, and seeks to accomplish this by balance-of-payments
policy rather than by the mix of budgetary and monetary policy. Many
Europeans apparently take the view that, as a developed region, Europe
should be a net exporter of capital to the rest of the world. Thus far,
international monetary theorists have tended to take the easy way out,
of assuming that balance-of-payments objectives are confined to over-
all balance and are thus necessarily mutually consistent.

This is one reason why practical policy-making economists can claim
some justification for rebelling against abstract model-building as an
approach to understanding international monetary problems. Another
is that the theory has assumed that countries in fact have the capacity to
use the policy instruments assumed to be available in setting up the
theory. In fact, for various reasons countries may lack the technical
ability to use one or more of the major instruments: the central bank
may lack the capacity to control interest rates, or the government may
lack the constitutional power to use fiscal policy for stabilization purposes. (This is quite apart from the problem of political limitations on
the willingness of governments to use their policy instruments to pursue
their stated policy objectives.)

These observations suggest that in this field theorists have been con-
centrating on first-best analytical problems, and that a great deal of

interesting work remains to be done on second-best problems. We (and particularly Mundell) have gotten a great deal of mileage out of fairly simple general equilibrium systems and their dynamic properties; the results have shed important light on the nature of some important problems, if only by enabling their essence to be reduced to a question of the direction in which the arrows of motion point on a simple equilibrium diagram of the kind that has regularly appeared on our blackboard during the conference. But we have not done much about the difficult and messy problems that arise when, as is often the case in the real world, the general equilibrium system is inconsistent or incomplete.

The second reason why the adjustment-problem session was a high point stems from McKinnon's attempt to introduce more sophisticated monetary theory, based on the concepts of portfolio management and wealth-income relationships, into the analysis of adjustment. It is a familiar fact that historically international trade theory has largely drawn its analytical tools from general economic theory, and has frequently tended to lag behind general theory in its intellectual development and sophistication. The only major exception has been the theory of the second-best, where international trade theory has made a contribution of far-reaching importance to general economic theory. This generalization is especially valid for international monetary theory. Though no one can deny the importance of Hume's analysis of the price-specie flow mechanism to the development of monetary theory in general, it is fair to say that even in to modern times the classical analysis of international monetary adjustment has generally proceeded by analyzing the impact of adjustment on the separate national economies involved as if they were isolated from world trade, except for the effect of international disequilibrium on domestic money supplies, and has consequently achieved only a very imperfect analysis of the international monetary system as a system of which national economies are integral parts. More recently, international monetary economists have built models of international adjustment and policy problems which have employed as building blocks quite naive Keynesian models of the national economy, in which consumption has been made a simple function of income and investment a simple function of interest rates—or with scarcely more sophistication total expenditure a function of both—and in which no attention has been paid to recent developments in the theories of consumption and investment which have stressed the function of saving and investment as a means of adjusting actual to desired stocks of wealth. It is high time for international monetary theorists to take account of these developments and to integrate them into international monetary theory. It is true that the applicability of these developments at present is rather remote, since to make them manageable one is obliged—like McKinnon—to focus on long-run static equilibrium situations (stationary states), whereas the relevant questions for those interested in policy concern monetary disturbances arising among countries in the process of moving toward long-run static equilibrium wealth-income relationships. But the ability to cope with such problems is, I believe, a secondary problem of developing the appropriate mathematical tools for handling the shorter-run problems within the longer-run capital-theory framework; that framework is both more fundamental economically, and more elegant intellectually, than the Keynesian apparatus of purely flow relationships on the real side of the analysis, and it is a matter mainly of time and effort to develop its implications for short-run disequilibrium situations. Thus, while McKinnon's paper may have seemed to many members of the conference to have required much more intellectual effort than its fruit would justify, I would not be surprised if in ten years' time most of us will be talking McKinnon's language as a matter of course.

In conclusion, I would like to suggest that theoretical analysis of the problems of the international monetary system has been dominated and excessively restricted by concern with the mechanics of analysis, and that the time has come for introducing some elements of welfare economics into the study of international monetary problems. For example, how should the welfare costs and benefits of disequilibrium be specified, so as to permit analysis of the welfare implications of varying the speed of adjustment of policy instruments; to deviations of actual from target levels of the indicators of policy objectives? Or to permit the development of rules for sharing the burden of adjustment between deficit and surplus countries? What can be said in theory about the welfare aspects of financing a deficit by borrowing, or suppressing it by controls, instead of eliminating it by deflation as rapidly as required by the limitation of the reserves available? These are problems of great concern to practical policy-makers, with respect to which rigorous economic theory should be capable of contributing much more than it has done so far.

INDEX

INDEX